D1205722

MAKING THE GRADE

Grades 5–6

By the Staff of Score@Kaplan

Foreword by Alan Tripp

Simon & Schuster

This series is dedicated to our Score@Kaplan parents and children—thank you for making these books possible.

Published by
Kaplan Educational Centers and Simon & Schuster
1230 Avenue of the Americas
New York, NY 10020

Special thanks to: Jennifer Shore, Peter Dublin, Susan Christie Woodward, Alex Pirie, Tony Palermino, Barbara Brook Simons, Jean C. Lawler, Gail Derecho, Ingrid Stabb, Joseph Pigato, Elizabeth Phythian, Julia Spiker, Glynnis Roberts, Michelle Green, Anthony Haro, Tony Farrell, Dawn Netherton, Eric Lewis, Jennifer Brandon, Chip Miller, Mila Hayward, Laura Kupperman, John Supp, Heather Farnham, Kelly Schram, Thong "Tony" La, Beth Zeilinger, David Walsh, Renee Whitney, Robert Drake, Judy Galbraith, and Carol Sullivan.

Head Coach and General Manager, Score@Kaplan: Alan Tripp
President, Score@Kaplan: Robert L. Waldron
Executive Editor and Series Creator: Jay Johnson
Series Content and Development: Intentional Educations
Educational Content Editor: Julie Landsman
Assessment Pull-Out Section Authors: Preeti Shah and Dr. Paul Glovinsky
Resources Section: Amy Sgarro and Doreen Beauregard
Production Editors: Richard Christiano, Julie Schmidt, and Maude Spekes
Layout Design and Desktop Production: Krista Pfeiffer
Creative Director: Phil Schein
Illustrations: Lorie Park and the Wild Goose Company
Production Coordinator: Gerard Capistrano
Managing Editor: Kiernan McGuire
Cover Photography: Michael Britto and Kingmond Young

Library of Congress Cataloging-in-Publication Data
Making the grade: learning adventures for your family/by the staff of Score@Kaplan
p. cm.
Contents: [1] Grades 3–4 — [2] Grades 5–6 — [3] Grades 7–8.
ISBN 0-684-83693-9 (v. 1).— ISBN 0-684-83694-7 (v. 2). — ISBN 0-684-83695-5 (v. 3)
1. Education, Elementary—Parent participation—United States.
2. Home and school—United States. 3. Education, Elementary—
Activity programs—United States. I. Kaplan
Educational Centers (New York, N.Y.)
LB1048.5.M34 1997
372.1'04—DC21 97-3407
CIP

Manufactured in the United States of America
Published Simultaneously in Canada

March 1997

7 6 5 4 3 2 1

ISBN: 0-684-83694-7

CONTENTS

Foreword

Good grades can be encouraging and satisfying, and we at Score@Kaplan are always pleased when the kids that attend our educational centers do well on their report cards. Even so, we want so much more for our children than straight As. Many of us were honors students ourselves, so we know that "making the grade" is only the beginning. What we really want for our kids are good grades and everything that good grades are supposed to represent.

- We want our kids to master the key communication systems that make civilization possible: language (spoken and written), math, and music.
- We want them to build their critical thinking skills so that they can understand, appreciate, and improve their world.
- We want them to continually increase their knowledge, and to value learning as the key to a happy, successful life.
- We want them to always do their best, to persist when challenged, to be a force for good, and to help others whenever they can.

We know these are ambitious goals, but our children deserve no less. Our mission at Score@Kaplan is to create great opportunities for learning and development for kids across the country. We've already helped thousands of children through programs in our centers, and we're eager to reach thousands more with this series of books designed for parents of first through eighth graders.

Simple Principles

We owe the remarkable success of Score@Kaplan Educational Centers to a few simple principles, and we would like to highlight these points as you consider working with this book to create great Learning Adventures for your child.

- We expect every child to succeed.

- We make it possible for every child to succeed.

- We reinforce each instance of success, no matter how small.

Such simple principles are easily understood, but understanding them is simply not enough. The purpose of this book is to help you put the above principles into practice in order to support and enhance the academic development of your child. As a parent facing ever growing demands at work and at home, you need useful, practical answers now. We'd like to share what we've learned in our work with thousands of children across the country. We'd like to show you how to put these principles to work.

Assessing Your Child

Just as a good physician performs a thorough diagnosis before prescribing treatment, we recommend starting with a thorough assessment of your child's academic status. At Score@Kaplan, we have learned that excellent grades don't always indicate academic excellence. As standards have eroded, more and more children get As and Bs in school. We often come across "straight-A students" whose actual skills lag behind national standards by a full grade level or more. And if your child's grades are poor, you will probably find it useful to improve your understanding of exactly what that means.

One helpful approach in assessing your child's skills is to ask yourself the following questions, especially as they relate to what you were capable of at your child's age:

1. How much is my child reading? At what level of difficulty?

2. Has my child mastered appropriate language arts skills, such as spelling, grammar, and syntax?

3. Does my child have the ability to express appropriately complex thoughts when speaking or writing?

4. Does my child demonstrate adequate mastery of all age-appropriate math skills, such as mastery of addition and subtraction facts, multiplication tables, division rules, etc.?

These questions are a good starting place and may give you new insights into your child's academic situation and how things have changed since you were a child. At the same time, the subjective assessment guidelines included in this book will help you to understand how your child is grasping school material, homework, and key concepts in language arts, math, and science. You will probably be surprised by the results, no matter what grades your child is earning at school!

What's Going On at School?

Teaching is a noble profession, and we have made the acquaintance of many fine teachers in the communities where our educational centers are located. Unfortunately, we have found a tremendous amount of disarray in those same teachers' school districts. No one seems to agree on what parents and students should expect of schools, and we are a long way from reaching a national consensus. In the meantime, many districts are striving to be all things to all people. Until we refocus our public and private institutions on excellence in learning, we can expect uneven results and knowledge gaps for children at every ability level, no matter how "good" the school district.

Parents will always need to monitor the situation at school and take responsibility for their children's learning. Even if your children attend the best school in the country—public or private—you should find out what your child should be learning at each grade level and match that against what your child actually learns. If knowledge gaps develop, you can work with your child's teacher to see that they are filled. Because class sizes are mostly too large and teachers are mostly overworked, parents need to take responsibility for this challenge. With the appropriate tools, you can catch and correct learning gaps before they become a problem.

Encouraging Your Child to Learn at Home

There is so much you can do to enrich your child's opportunities for learning at home. This book is full of fun Learning Adventure activities you can do with your child that will help to build an understanding of key concepts in language arts, math, and science. Judging by our experience at Score@Kaplan, the more kids understand, the more they enjoy learning. Each small experience of success reinforces confidence, brick by brick. As you help your child learn, please bear in mind the following observations drawn from experiences in our centers:

- Positive reinforcement is the key. Try to maintain a ratio of at least five positive remarks to every negative one. If you're not sure how you're doing, keep a tally for a day or two. The patterns you see may not be as positive as you would expect.

- All praise must be genuine. This is easy when children are doing well, but even when they are having difficulties you need to find something to honestly praise. For example: "That was a good try," "You got this part of it right," or "I'm proud of you for doing your best, even though it was hard."

- When a child gets stuck, giving the answer is usually not the most effective way to help. Try asking open-ended questions or rephrasing the problem, such as: "Maybe there's another way to do that," "I wonder what made you think of doing it that way," or "What would happen if you changed...?" (Questions that begin with "Why" should be avoided, since they will probably make your child feel defensive.)

- Remember to be patient and supportive. Children need to learn that hard work pays off.

For Parents of Unusually Bright Children

In the case of unusually bright children, you may need to seek out the kind of academic challenges they may not be getting in school. Gifted children are at risk of assuming that all learning is easy and boring. We often find that such children become extremely upset when faced with a challenge they cannot immediately conquer. When children face a difficult problem, they run the risk of making mistakes or being wrong, a prospect that can be quite scary for kids who depend on being right all of the time.

Consequently, a bright student can actually feel more threatened by a challenge than a weaker student would. We believe that it is healthier for children to come face to face with such challenges at an early age, because they can be taught that making mistakes is okay, that nobody is expected to be perfect all the time, and that hard work and perseverance are more important attributes than the ability to guess an answer right away.

We come across far too many children who have done very well in math through prealgebra, only to fail miserably as they begin algebra itself. Typically, such children rushed through their "boring" and "easy" math homework during the early years. As a result, they did not actually master the material. They also may not have learned patience and perseverance. The solution requires a complete review of math basics, followed by intensive encouragement to overcome angry outbursts and bad attitudes (these usually indicate significant fear of failure). We often are successful in getting such students back on track, but problems like this can be avoided entirely when they are addressed early on.

Parents Are Key

In many ways, especially as regards motivation, parents are not so very different from their children. At Score@Kaplan, we often come across parents who need some encouragement. We are happy to offer it. In our experience, we have found that parents are uniquely suited to helping their children learn. Our simple principles apply to parents too, and you'll find lots of support in this book:

- We expect every parent to succeed.
- We help make it possible for every parent to succeed.
- We reinforce the success of each parent-child team.

We are doing our best to open new Score@Kaplan centers across the country. Since we may not have arrived in your neighborhood yet, we invite you to look to the encouraging anecdotes, home learning resources, and useful hints throughout this book. We hope to share our discoveries with you and encourage your efforts to accelerate your children's learning.

There's More to Life than Academic Excellence

Most parents recognize that academic excellence is just one of many things they would like to ensure for their children. At Score@Kaplan, we are committed to developing the whole child, and that is another key component of "making the grade." We emphasize:

- Academic skills and critical thinking
- Positive reinforcement to build confidence and a love of learning
- Extensive experience with setting and achieving goals
- Great role-model relationships with positive, admirable adults

Score@Kaplan instructors are known as "coaches," and for good reason. Great coaches instruct, lead, motivate, and serve as role models. Most importantly, they share responsibility for the performance of each team member. Likewise, our coaches guide, inspire, and cheer on the children under their care and take ownership in the outcome. If there is one thing we at Score@Kaplan have learned about children, it is that they rarely get too much positive attention from people who care about them. And every time we pay attention to a child, we get so much more than we give.

Alan Tripp
Head Coach and General Manager
Score@Kaplan

How Do You Foster Your Child's Interest in Learning?

In preparing this series, we surveyed scores of parents on this key question:

- Try to make the learning fun
- Incorporate learning into play with children
- Have children "teach" parents
- Make learning tasks interesting to children
- Incorporate children's imagination into the learning
- Set up regular times for homework
- Help children with their homework, but don't "do it" for them
- Let children know a parent's expectations and goals for learning; offer appropriate rewards
- Set a good learning example for children (regular reading habits, etc.)
- Parents should listen closely to their children, and should teach and practice active listening
- Always answer or respond to children's questions
- Allow children to make mistakes
- Be patient and consistent with children
- Spend time with children
- Don't push children to learn
- Explore learning options outside the classroom for more challenge or for remediation
- Allow children to learn by doing
- Surround children with educational materials and tools for learning
- Immerse children in appropriate learning environments, like libraries
- Offer children constant praise for their efforts
- Keep a positive, encouraging attitude with children; avoid anger and scolding
- Make each child in your family feel they are special; tell them this ALL THE TIME
- Offer firm guidance and set limits when it comes to learning
- Get involved with activities and events in the classroom and in the school
- Vary approaches to different children; what works for one child may not work for another
- Make sure children are learning the basic concepts in math, science, language arts, etc.
- Be aware of children's progress in school, as well as their shortcomings
- Express an interest in children's activities and schoolwork
- Limit TV viewing time at home and foster good viewing habits
- Work on enlarging children's vocabulary
- Emphasize learning accomplishments, no matter how small
- Accept where your child is at, and praise their efforts
- Seek help and advice from trusted sources (e.g. classroom teacher, your parents, other parents) if you're stymied by problems concerning your child's education

How to Use This Book

You want to do all you can to foster and support your child's successful progress through school—those important years in which learning and growing should reward the effort and enthusiasm your child invests.

The nature and amount of effort and enthusiasm children bring to their school work directly affect each child's educational rewards. But your child's effort and enthusiasm also depends significantly on the effort and enthusiasm you provide at home. You already knew that or you would not have purchased this book. What you want to know is how to best use this book to help fulfill your goal of promoting your child's enjoyment of learning and success at school.

The core of this book lies in Section III, where the Learning Adventure activities that you can do with your child show you ways to take advantage of time you spend together learning and developing valuable skills. The two sections that precede those activities provide a context that you will find valuable in observing and thinking about your child as he experiences his school years.

The Big Picture

Because being a parent sometimes feels like being entangled in an infinite web of questions, we focus *Making the Grade* around some very basic questions that all parents ponder as they worry about how best to contribute to their children's education.

Get Your Bearings—the Opening Sections

Section I—What Should My Child Be Able to Do?—focuses on your growing child, how he develops, how he learns, how schools look at his progress, and how a parent can fit into his educational world. Section II—What's Being Covered in School?—gives you a look at what schools are likely to be expecting your child to learn by the completion of his present grade.

We have kept these opening sections as brief as possible; their purpose is to give you useful background and guidance for what you do with the Learning Adventure activities. We recommend that you read Section I in order to easily and quickly gain a useful perspective on factors that affect your child's learning and school experience. We expect you'll read this section initially and return to browse through it from time to time later on as you enjoy watching and participating in your child's learning.

We expect that you'll use Section II primarily for reference, to look up information about school expectations in specific areas of learning for your child at the appropriate grade level, and to review for yourself, as needed, specific school content that you may not have thought about for many years! To provide for convenient, quick access, we present each of the three content areas—language arts (which includes reading), math, and science—separately. Each content area provides an outline of expectations for 5th grade and then for 6th grade, followed by a sort of bird's-eye view of the content covered during those two years of schooling—descriptions or explanations of the concepts and skills listed in the two grade outlines.

If your child is presently in grade five, you can simply skip the grade six outline and save reading it for next year. If she is in grade six, there's no reason to read the grade five outline unless you're interested in seeing what she probably should have learned in the previous year. We expect parents to use Section II of the book in widely different ways. You may find reading through the content a fascinating trip down memory lane where you might discover new learnings that were not offered during your school years. Or you may simply dip into the content sections only when you feel a need to brush up on something. Maybe it's a spelling or punctuation rule (how to use apostrophes to show possession in plural nouns) or the meaning of a concept (like erosion), or both (the concept of perimeter and how it is calculated).

Know Your Way Around

Sprinkled throughout the book are sidebars and short features containing tips, advice, strategies, stories, and the latest research to help you make your child's 5th and 6th grade years true Learning Adventures. Look for these icons to help you know who is giving you information and why:

Whenever you see the "house" icon, expect "learning at home" advice from our Score@Kaplan coaches, teachers, and parents from around the United States.

The "blackboard strategy" icon offers thoughtful, sometimes inspiring tips and approaches for parents on learning and parenting.

Parents and students have a lot to juggle every day! Our "juggler" icon signals practical "try this at home" tips and activities.

If it has anything to do with the Internet, computers, software programs, or learning technology, you'll find it under our "computer" icon.

The "book" icon yields learning-related excerpts from recommended books and authors, as well as reading and other bookish matters.

Finally, the Score@Kaplan logo signals insights from Score's coaches and stories from our national educational centers, intended to give you everyday insights you can use at home with your children.

The Heart of the Book—Learning Adventure Activities

The bulk of the book consists of learning activities and hundreds of "What's More" activity ideas geared specifically to the 5th and 6th grade curricula and tailored for learning enjoyment at home. These are activities designed for parents to do with their children.

Time—Your Most Precious Resource Money, property, and the best connections in the world cannot come closer to the value of time you spend with your child. We are convinced that the best way for parents to promote their children's educational success is for them to spend time with their children; the more time spent, the better the payoff! Our activities are offered as ways to help you focus that time on enjoyable learning.

Perhaps most often the time may involve your helping to get the Learning Adventure activity started and then taking a back seat, checking in, remaining interested, supportive, and inquisitive about what your child is learning. Several activities feature games you play together, where your involvement continues actively throughout the activity. Many activities can expand to include other family members or friends. You may be surprised by how many of the activities suggest valuable ways to use "down time" together, ways to take advantage of time you normally don't even realize you have available—driving time, waiting time, meal prep time, clean-up time.... You'll soon discover all kinds of time just awaiting your educational use. And most of these activities offer attractive alternatives to TV-viewing time.

In short, the core of this book contains ways parents and children can enjoy doing things together that contribute to school success. At the same time, they contribute to building a foundation of memories that secure your youngster's confidence in himself and in the parental support that encourages him to reach forward and learn more.

How to Use the Activities You can use these Learning Adventures in any of a variety of ways—the rule is suit yourself, or more to the point, suit your child. There is no required order. (You can even jump into an activity from the next grade, or last grade, if it seems appealing to and appropriate for your child.) Select activities to build further upon strengths and interests you observe your child to have. Also select activities to assist your child where he may be having trouble or to augment work being done at school. Of course, you should also select activities simply because they appeal to you—they look like something you and your child can enjoy together.

Don't worry if you and your child do activities that "she doesn't really need" or that you've done before. Enjoyable repetition provides practice that reinforces and consolidates your child's learning. One of our authors recalls with special pleasure the endless games of Twenty Questions played with her family at Sunday supper and on almost any long car ride.

To provide an organizational structure and accommodate parents who wish to select activities according to subject area and grade, the activities are grouped accordingly. Thus, you can pick out a science activity related to any particular core area of the grade five curriculum. The "At a Glance" section of each activity will tell you which core area or areas the activity addresses, the main skills it promotes, the materials needed to carry it out, and approximately how much time it will take. The rest of the activity provides step-by-step instructions to help you do the activity. Of course, you can augment and adjust the steps as best suits you, your child, and your home environment. Each activity concludes with three or more suggestions of further activity ideas—the "What's More" sidebars—that you and your child can pursue.

Link Up with Learning As you can see, choosing and carrying out activities should be linked to keeping in touch with what your child is doing at school and how she feels about it. Nothing beats talking with your child; in addition, use the strategies discussed in the essay in Section I called "How Are Children Evaluated?" and in the Section IV questions under "The Parent-School Partnership," as well as the materials in our "The Home Learning Quizzes" Section to help you assess what your child knows and can do, along with charting her progress and your own home learning knowledge and awareness.

More Support—Questions and Resources

The last section responds to the concerns most parents have and indicates where you can obtain further resources for promoting your child's educational development and pleasure.

We expect you'll browse among the questions out of curiosity, as well as consult them when particular questions or issues become important in your child's school life. We hope the resource listings will lead you to specific materials to contribute to activities you choose to do with your child, and give you avenues for enlarging your own learning.

Last, but Essential—The Home Learning Quizzes

Our book concludes with what we view as an invaluable tool for you and your child—your assessment materials. By using the strategies for learning about your child (and—surprise—probably a bit about yourself while you're at it), you will maximize the benefit (and pleasure) you and your child will experience.

Parents' Pages The Parents' Home Learning Quiz (pages 1–8 of the pull-out) enables you to teach yourself more and more about your child, how he learns, and what he is learning. As your child's learning coach, taking this quiz and reading the introductory material enables you to periodically assess your own knowledge and awareness of your child's progress, and discover more about how to maximize your child's education. You'll also be able to assess your own style of interaction with your child. Enjoy these new insights!

Your Child's Pages The Kid's Home Learning Quizzes (pages 9–16 of the pull-out)are meant to be fun "How much do I Know?" questions taken right out of the grades five and six curriculum in language arts, math and science.

Much like the popular *BrainQuest*™ series, these are sometimes easy, sometimes challenging at-grade-level questions for your child to tackle. Approach the quizzes like a game of trivia or one of the Learning Adventure activities: "See how many of these you can get right..." Then congratulate your child on each right answer! There's no grading or scoring, just the good feeling of being able to have your child point out to you how much he knows.

While not a scientific tool to measure your child's grade-level abilities, the tougher problems and wrong answers will give you and your child good indications of where more learning needs to take place. (Or they may cover skills your child hasn't been taught yet in school.) Use outside resources and appropriate Learning Adventure activities from Section III to help practice and reinforce the skills. See if your child can answer the quiz questions correctly after having more practice with the skills. And so the learning fun and quizzing continues....

Communicate with Score@Kaplan

And last but not least, we want to hear from you. We consider the parents who use our books to be invaluable resources. We want to hear your assessment of activities, your ideas, your success stories, and the questions that you want us to address in the future.

The "About Kaplan" pages at the back of the book give you a variety of ways to contact Kaplan and our Score@Kaplan centers. Write, call, or E-mail us with your feedback and experiences. If you're online, subscribe to *Score! Edge,* our free electronic newsletter for parents and for students. Receive great home-learning advice, tips and contests, and plug into new language arts, math, and science activities. Subscribe to *Score! Edge* at www.score.kaplan.com or at www.netscape.com. Turn the *Making the Grade* experience into a lifetime of enjoyable learning for your family.

What Should My Child Be Able to Do?

How Do Children Develop?

Children develop sporadically, surprisingly, rapidly, unexpectedly . . . . You can add just about any adverb you want, or any ten, and still not have the complete picture. Parenting can sometimes feel a lot like coping with cooking. Just as you've got the onions browning nicely, the rice boils over; while you're cleaning up that mess and cutting up the broccoli, the onions start to burn. It's just that children never stay the same. Their lives, their bodies, and their abilities are in continuous change. Sometimes the changes are steady and easily measured, and sometimes they are sudden and surprising. When it's not exhausting, it's exhilarating to be around children. In those moments when we surface for a breath above the sea of soccer, socks, and successes, we can appreciate what a privilege it is to witness the young human being in our care growing toward adulthood.

FEEL REAL GOOD

Sometimes just a pat on the back is motivation enough for my child in learning. Sometimes I pay a dollar for each good grade he receives. But I'd like my child to feel good about his grades with or without the dollar. It's important for him to internalize the motivation we can help give so that he feels good about himself and his accomplishments.

And as we fret about our own children, it is reassuring to remember that children throughout the world (along with their parents) are moving through the same developmental stages and have been doing so for countless generations.

Anxiety-Free Thinking About Your Child

We all have our worries about our children; are they too tall, too short, not enough of this, too much of that? Society, schools, grandparents and in-laws, and our own internal monitors all seem to be waiting to judge our children's performance (and ours as well). We've put some topics into this section to help you think about your child as the wonderful and unique person that she is, and to put to rest some of the anxiety you may feel.

WHAT YOUR CHILD CAN DO

The worst thing in the world is when a parent says in front of a child, "He can't do this," and the kid is standing there and hearing this negativity. One boy had a lot of basic skills he needed to work on. He and I started to work together to build his confidence. He was so determined to master spelling that he tackled it over and over again—it was almost too much. But after his mom said he couldn't do spelling, I pulled her aside and talked to her about Score@Kaplan's belief in "relentless positivity." I told her he can master spelling, he can do it if you believe in him, and you can coach him at home. Eventually, this boy's mother would cry at the end of every session because she was so amazed at what her child could do.

THEY FEEL LOVED

Acceptance seems to matter most for children's overall adjustment and sense of self-worth: because they feel loved, they feel lovable.
—from *Beyond the Classroom,* Laurence Steinberg, Ph.D. (Simon & Schuster, 1996)

There's no such thing as an average child. As you consider your child's development through the school years, it's helpful to remember that "average" is a statistical term and not the description of a person. The unit called *average* is arrived at by lumping together all of something and finding the mathematical mean. The average of anything is nothing more than the abstract quality of the middleness. Some aspect of each child's being may happen to fall on the mark called *average,* but it's unlikely. Each child is going to be more of this and less of that. Your child is a unique individual.

He got that from your side of the family! In the academic world, this topic is called "nature versus nurture." Much study has been devoted to this topic, but as far as this book's approach to parenting is concerned, there is no *versus* at all. Both elements, our own combination of genes and our environment, play their roles together in how we grow into adulthood.

For parents concerned with how development affects their children, however, the most significant differences among school age children are those of developmental timing, for instance, the more than six-year range between the earliest normal onset of puberty for girls and the latest beginnings for normal boys!

Some people with political agendas make endless efforts to prove that there are racially significant differences in intelligence. There is no valid scientific evidence to support the claim of genetic inferiority or superiority in intelligence. There is, however, extensive evidence that children with the loving support of their families and the society around them will do better in school.

Theories of Development In earlier times, folks didn't think about human development much. There were occasional introspective geniuses (St. Augustine is one example) who left autobiographical records of their childhood and gave thought to education and development, but children were generally thought of as little adults who just got bigger and (most of the time) smarter.

The growth of science in the eighteenth and nineteenth centuries changed how we viewed ourselves. The knowledge and techniques of study learned from the natural sciences were applied to human beings, and the result was the growth of psychology and the study of human nature. Sigmund Freud, Erik Erikson, and Jean Piaget are the three most notable recent thinkers in this area. People may agree or disagree with their particular theories, but we all owe them a debt for stepping in to take a closer look at how the curious creatures we call humans develop.

The theorist who has had the most influence on education is a Swiss psychologist, Jean Piaget, who devoted much of his life to carefully examining how children think. Most contemporary western educational programs are built on aspects of his findings and theories. His observations of children led him to conjecture that our intellectual abilities increase through qualitatively different stages from infancy through adulthood. The infant who begins life by putting together only the simplest and most immediate or tangible facts grows through several intellectual stages into an adult capable of building and using powerful abstractions.

Seeing the Whole Child No matter what particular theory of development rings truest to you, there is an important lesson to be learned from child psychologists, developmental specialists, and scientists of human behavior and learning like Piaget. This lesson is that thoughtful observation is the basis of understanding. In the case of the experts, it has led to understandings about large patterns of human nature. In the case of you, the parent, it is your understanding of an individual, your child.

All of us get caught up in the trap of comparing our child to other children (after all, Mozart was only three when he started to compose). Our parents probably did it to us and we know we shouldn't do it, but there we go again! One way to short-circuit this pointless exercise is to keep in mind that developmental age and chronological age are two different things!

MEAN AND HORRIBLE?

Children really want boundaries. It's a major sign of caring on the part of a parent. Children usually feel a lot more comfortable knowing that there's a set of standards and rules that a family needs to abide by. "I love you and I want the best for you; I'm not setting up these rules because I'm mean and horrible!"

SEE WHAT DEVELOPS

Jerome Brunner, Robert Coles, Herbert Kohlberg, and Carol Gilligan are among the many contemporary specialists in different aspects of child development who are worth looking into. Their insights into the development of thinking, moral development, and valuing are fascinating. In this speculative field, there are no absolutes and lots of controversy and excitement.

LEARN LIFE'S LESSONS

I want my daughter to be happy and enjoy life. Education is really important, but the education life gives you is even more important. That's where my daughter will have to learn to communicate with people, to accept changes in life, and through what she and I cover together, I think that will help her. If she's not a doctor or professional or famous person, that's fine. I tell her to do what she feels like doing. Be somebody that can get along with others and strive hard in the areas of your choice.

I HAVE CONFIDENCE IN YOU

At Score@Kaplan, I admire parents who are less stressed-out about their kids. They're the ones who have confidence in their child's abilities, and they usually take a more active interest in their kids' education. They try to convey to their children their confidence outwardly and visibly, and it impacts the kids as to how well they're able to do.

At any particular age, any three children can be at three very different stages of mental and physical development within a general range. Given our wildly different genetic makeups and the different timetables those genes set for our physical development (and don't forget to throw in the role that different environments play), there's really no accurate way to compare children on a point-by-point basis. The best that we can do is observe closely, try to understand, and do the best we can to support our children's growth and development.

"I need new sneakers!"

First, let's talk about your child's physical growth and development. Human bodies don't grow at a sedately slow and steady pace. Different parts of us grow at different speeds and at different times. Our heads and the brains inside grow very rapidly until sometime between the ages of four and six and then continue to grow, but more slowly, until adolescence. Our height and weight increase tremendously from birth until around age three and then slow down until puberty when there is a second growth burst. Our lymphoidal tissue (the tonsils, adenoids, and parts of the intestines) grow quickly through about age ten and then taper off, still growing, but at a slower rate until maturity. Our reproductive organs grow very slowly until the onset of puberty and then grow rapidly. The muscles and our skeletal frame develop a little unevenly; feet, hands, and head reach adult size before the rest of us, and our legs lengthen before our trunk stretches out. (Hey, look! He's wearing high waters!) Kids outgrow their pants before they outgrow their shirts.

Quiet! Child Thinking

Mental development in children alternates between incremental growth and great leaps. Whereas the physical and emotional changes that our children experience can't be missed, mental growth can be less obvious. Ankles erupt out of pant legs, hairs sprout, doors slam, and last year's obsessions suddenly become little-kid stuff. Mental growth appears to be just as obvious at first. There is a clear, measurable increase in how much your kid knows.

Vocabulary grows (not always the words we want), skills increase, and children acquire more factual information. These are quantitative differences and they are substantial, but there are changes in your child's mental ability that are subtler and much more profound.

IT'S A BIG JOB!

I admire any parent out there because it's such a tough job. There are times I think I want to have ten kids because kids are the greatest, then I see how much work parents have to put into their children and I think, Whoa, can I do that? It's a lot to be a successful parent and raise happy kids!

From Collecting Facts to Spinning Theories Students of human development have come to realize that, as we mature, the very ways in which we do our thinking change. The differences between a toddler and an adult are much more than size of vocabulary and the accumulation of factual information.

Children start school being very specific, concrete thinkers. Their thinking is based on the manipulation of objects and immediate events and the relationships among them. In the later elementary and early middle school years, this kind of thinking is mixed with a more abstract ability. In this middle stage, they are able to generalize. They can consider a group of objects and think about them in terms of an abstraction that sums them all up. In late middle school and high school, they make a third transition. They become able to take generalizations and conjectures and think about them quite separately from real objects. They can theorize about tyranny, democracy, and relativity, and they can argue (and they do love to argue) about the general advantages and disadvantages of either of the first two or the philosophical fallout of the last.

TRYING OUR BEST

I wouldn't have had children if we didn't try to do the best job we could to make sure that they're secure, in an environment that's conducive to learning, and where they can flourish—but not to the point where we won't let our children take their own falls.

Characteristic Questions If you were to characterize children at different levels of mental development in a rough-and-ready way, you might separate them by the kinds of questions they ask. *What* is the question that belongs to the earlier years. *How* is the question for the middle school years. *Why* and *what if* are the questions of adolescence and beyond. Of course, these questions get asked at all ages, but the ability to fully understand them and appreciate the answers grows and unfolds as we mature intellectually.

There is no exact timetable for development. No one can say, "At half-past seven years of age your child will be able to do thus and such or think in this or that way." In fact,

EVENTFUL

Score@Kaplan emphasizes learning as an "event." For instance, "We learned the times tables today," and boom—we have a learning event! We hear many children say, "This is division, and I can't do division," and they categorize what they're not comfortable with. We help teach kids that they can "do division," and it's a revelation to them. It becomes this event for kids. "Oh wow, I just did division!" They feel like they just ran the 100-yard dash in under 10 seconds.

Learning moments between parents and children should become learning events. "We're going to practice 5 times 5," and make it an event at home. Then when your child masters 5 times 5, it's like it's up on a billboard: "This is what I can do!" When your child can say, "I get this science assignment," that should become an event too. And so on and so on.

developmental specialists are very careful to make a distinction between developmental age (the age at which certain things generally happen) and chronological age (the actual age). Every child develops in her own way and at her own pace depending on environmental factors and her own genetic nature.

Looking at It Another Way If children were squirrels, in grades two, three, and four, they'd be gathering and sorting nuts and enjoying the climb; they'd spend their next three years finding more trees of similar types and organizing nuts (while worrying, of course, about whether they were wearing the same thing as the other squirrels); and in grades six, seven, and eight, our squirrels would be planning storage facilities, worrying about how many nuts to set aside, and wondering how many they could eat right now because they're really hungry.

"Leave me alone!"

When it comes to emotional and social development, we also find varying rates of growth. You could speculate that this is nature's way of keeping parents on their toes. You get used to your child's behavior during a nice period of consolidation—life is going smoothly, your kid looks and acts the same from day to day (ignoring sudden external changes in fashion and hairstyle). Then, just when you were feeling relaxed, comfortable, and like maybe you were doing a good job as a parent, suddenly you're faced with a whole different person. It may be that the teddy bear gets demoted to a spot in the closet, or a certain food is only for babies, or you'll hear, "I'd never wear that" about yesterday's favorite garment. Whatever it is and at whatever the age, you scramble to quickly learn the habits and customs of what almost seems like a whole new species.

5th and 6th Graders—A Snapshot

We've called this section a snapshot. It has to be a bit blurry, however, because the subject of the picture is always in motion! Development, whether physical, mental, or emotional, is a process. There is no moment where everything comes to rest and you can describe the static moment and the particular child and say this is exactly how it is.

No snapshot can accurately catch the qualities of each child, because every child is unique. Within any group of children, there is an enormous range of development. Since children at any one chronological age stretch across the entire range of what is normal and appropriate for each particular stage of growth, we have tried to provide a general picture knowing that you will flesh out the portrait through observation of your own child's individual details.

At School The later elementary years were a time when skills were mastered and consolidated. In the beginning middle school years, grades five and six, these skills are put to use. These school grades coincide with a period when new intellectual abilities appear. As children enter puberty, their minds as well as their bodies begin to undergo qualitative changes.

Children were intellectually oriented towards facts in the earlier years; gathering facts, making collections of facts, and (along with sports cards and collectibles) trading facts. Now, they begin to be able to think more abstractly, and they begin to do things with facts. In grades five and six, kids begin to make generalizations based on specific cases. Laws, for example, are now considered in a new way—as more than just a set of specific commands governing specific behaviors. Kids at this age now come to understand, for example, that laws are written by people for specific purposes, and that there are reasons behind the laws, reasons that unify them. The concept of what is fair now extends beyond their immediate lives and classrooms and into the world. As they begin to grapple with concepts like fairness and equality of treatment, they still personalize things, but the generalizations they make encompass a larger social universe.

The traditional three Rs remain very much a part of school, but more and more they are incorporated into work in other subject areas such as the sciences and social studies. Work on skills development continues, but it is more often in service

AT GRADE LEVEL?

There are oftentimes two different kinds of parents. One is determined to get their child in line with the skills needed for a certain grade level. For instance, "By a certain grade, my son needs to learn to read well, or he has to have certain division and multiplication skills." And then there are the parents who are less interested in making sure their children have attained certain skill levels but are more concerned with what skills their children do have. I tell parents that I'm not into gearing their child into being a "typical fifth grader" because there is no typical fifth grader—they're all over the spectrum. Students should be given the freedom to move ahead, catch up to their grade level, or whatever keeps them motivated and excited to learn.

The best a children can hope for is to have some sort of structure within which they have the freedom to explore their own strengths and weaknesses, personally and academically.

IT STARTS EARLY

Learning begins in the first days of life. Scientists are now discovering how young children develop emotionally and intellectually from their first days, and, therefore, how important it is for parents to begin immediately talking, singing, even reading to their infants.
—from the 1997 State of the Union Address, President Clinton

THE WRITE WAY

Penmanship or handwriting is a subject undergoing serious reconsideration by contemporary educators. Technology has created profound changes in the emphasis on good penmanship in schools and even on the role of handwriting. In the late 1940s, students used to suffer through hours of dipping a scratchy steel-nibbed pen into an inkwell; today's '90s child is moving from a brief try at script into keyboarding. Expect lots of changes and some controversy in this realm (as in the realm of calculator versus knowing your number facts) over the next few years.

to other topics. This change in their schooling is consistent with their growing intellectual abilities. In writing, they communicate in longer and more thoughtful forms and learn that style, grammar, and punctuation are skills that enable them to further larger goals.

Physical Development The rapid changes in body size and maturity that occur during the years of puberty are not always easy for children—or for their parents! There are three significant facts about the physical changes that take place during puberty. First, growth, which had been slow and steady for several years, takes off again. Children have not grown this quickly since they were in their twos. Second, people start puberty at different times. Some children will begin puberty before they turn ten, and some will not begin until they are fourteen. Third, girls tend to begin puberty a couple of years before boys. These three facts have significant consequences for the school and social lives of middle schoolers.

As you no doubt recall from your own childhood, it's hard enough keeping up with your own changing body and then you see what's happening to all your friends. Or not happening—yet. The growth in stature for girls begins to take off around age ten, and they soon outstrip the boys in growth rate and often in size. Since girl's bodies are maturing faster, there are times when they are muscularly better developed and even stronger than boys on certain physical tests. Within each sex, of course, there are also very large individual differences. Some children will have already achieved sexual maturity and accomplished much of their growth while others are just entering puberty. Because of the uneven beginnings of maturation for girls and boys and for individual children, this time of rapid physical, emotional, and mental change stretches across some four or more years, from the 5th through 8th grade years.

Social and Emotional Concerns At around age eleven, a time of rebelliousness and restlessness typically sets in, often more at home than at school. This moodiness is not typical of all children and it will ebb and flow with things calming down a little for the twelves. Social life (or the lack thereof), self-image, and peer relationships all become big issues. Friendships still tend to be with members of the same sex and are often built around shared interests.

Collections are not as important as they were and there is a growing fascination with how things work. Girls typically tend to put their most intense energy into relationships with their peers. Games are very important, often more so for boys than girls: board games, fantasy games, card games, and computer games. Games may be treated with the same intensity that collecting was in the previous elementary years.

So much is going on for children at this stage that it is sometimes a wonder that anything gets learned at all. Surprisingly, quite a bit does get done. Some of the pride in competence carries over from the earlier years and is coupled with newfound skills and abilities. It's as if the awareness of approaching maturity adds luster to new intellectual skills. For many kids, increased confidence and skill will grow through this period, especially if supported and encouraged at home.

A Group Portrait and a Last Thought

Imagine a 3rd grader, a 5th grader, and an 8th grader playing a game of Monopoly™. You see their obvious differences in size and physical maturity, and, by being observant, pick up on the less obvious differences in their interests and abilities. The 3rd grader is fascinated with all the houses and hotels, eager to get the right token, attentive to collecting and stacking the money and (although deeply interested in the rules and fairness) mightily concerned with winning. Meanwhile, the 5th grader loves to be the banker, is zealous about the rules and how they affect fair play, and makes quick moves without a lot of planning. And there's the 8th grader—knowing exactly the best property to own (and will argue with you about it), thinking in terms of strategy, and, although playing steadily and seriously for most of the game, occasionally exploding in tears or anger and remonstrating with the other players about being unloved and not respected.

PRACTICE THE LEARNING

Success for children can take any form: sports, academics, playing an instrument. Whatever the passion is, use it to create an academic goal. Ask your child if it's always fun at soccer practice? No, of course not. Sometimes it's raining and your child would rather be inside eating macaroni and cheese. Or your child would rather be anywhere else than at practice because she or he is making so many horrible mistakes. But rather than thinking, "I don't want to be doing sprints any more," your child needs to be thinking, "Sprints will really help out my game!" Practice really does make perfect—in sports, studies, and life. So practice practicing academics at home, and bring some excitement to your child's mastery of a skill by celebrating the learning that takes place.

WINNING THE LOTTERY

When my son completed his first home workbook, he showed it to me and you would think he had won a million dollars. It was the biggest thing. He took his workbook to school and showed it to everybody. It was really awesome!

It's almost as if they were playing three different games. In one way, they are. Although they are playing together, each child plays a game appropriate to that child's own developmental level. As they mature, they will pass through new stages and enter new versions of the game, just as we have done.

How Do Children Learn?

Have you ever heard these comments before? "Kim is so good with her hands, but she just doesn't enjoy reading." "Jack remembers every little thing he reads, but he's not real well coordinated or good at sports." "Even when she was a baby, Julia could sing along with the radio, right on key." "Martin is a real people-person. He just knows how to get along with everyone, from the kids in his Scout troop to the cranky guy in the apartment upstairs."

ONE OR MORE WAYS

Not every child understands things from the same learning approach. There are several different approaches for each child. It's finding the way to teach the material to the child that's key for parents in helping their children learn. There are many ways to teach a concept, and parents will have to experiment with approaches and find one or more that work.

For generation after generation, parents have been having those kinds of conversation about their kids. And although they weren't trained educators, these parents had made an important discovery: People learn in different ways!

Many Kinds of "Smarts"

It's not just kids. People in general have multiple intelligences—ways of perceiving, knowing, and understanding the world. Recently, experts have identified "seven kinds of smarts"—seven different types of intelligence. And, as people have always sensed, in most people, one or two or more of those intelligences are usually stronger than the others. That blend of traits makes each person unique. But the experts also point out that everyone can work on developing the other kinds of intelligences as well.

Your child's learning style—just like your own—makes it easier for him to learn and do certain kinds of things, from reading novels to doing gymnastics to playing the guitar. With your help, your child can also develop some of the

PACE, NOT PUSH

I see all types of parents. Some are really strict and totally into the academic progress their children are making. Some parents really push their kids hard. I personally like to see parents allowing children to work at their own pace, knowing that the progress will happen without pressure. The parents who really monitor their kids so closely tend to freak out their kids a lot; if the kids miss even one problem on a lesson, it becomes a very stressful event.

SUPPORT SUCCESS

It was a real success for me as a parent to realize that my challenging son is not going to necessarily "like" school, but he can still succeed in school. I believe in supporting his school and his education as much as possible, while at the same time letting my son find his own way.

other ways of learning that will be useful both in school and in real life.

Learning Styles in School

Most traditional school courses, such as math or science or language arts, do draw on specific types of intelligence—mainly verbal, visual, and logical. In the classroom, skills in reading, writing, analyzing, computing, thinking critically, and learning from books are emphasized. The kid who is naturally strong in those kinds of intelligence may have an advantage in the classroom.

Modern textbooks, however, usually try to give teachers suggestions for activities and approaches that will help children who have other styles of learning. And, as the experts note, children (with the help of their parents) can also work to strengthen the specific learning styles that are emphasized in school. That is what many of the activities described in this book are designed to help you accomplish with your child.

Seven Ways of Learning

How does *your* child learn? Look for the characteristics described here and apply them to what you've already noticed about your child. What are her strengths? Her weaknesses? What types of intelligence are stronger in your child? What types need encouragement?

Take note of some of the general approaches mentioned here to encourage the development of each kind of intelligence. Then look through the specific Learning Adventure activities described in Section III of *Making the Grade*. These will help you work with your child to strengthen the kinds of intelligences that are needed to be successful in school, while still keeping the unique blend of traits that make up your child's personality.

Verbal/Linguistic If your child is strong in this kind of intelligence, he may have started to talk early and in complete sentences. Probably he learned to read early and easily, too, and has a wider vocabulary than many kids his age. He likes books, puns, word games, and puzzles and probably enjoys writing. He may have more trouble taking in spoken information, such as from a lecture, than he does, for instance, in reading printed directions. This is the kid "whose nose is always in a book," who may ignore the scenery during a car ride and read a book instead.

Verbal/linguistic intelligence is one of the ways of learning that is very important in many school courses. You can encourage your child's verbal/linguistic intelligence by making reading and its associations fun and pleasurable. Many kids who are good readers and writers learned by imitating their parents, so show that you enjoy reading.

Make reading material—books and magazines—easily available at home. Encourage trips to the library and take an interest in the books your child likes. (You may be surprised to find how enjoyable some so-called kids' books can be.) For younger children, storytelling, poetry, and reading aloud are especially important.

Logical/Mathematical Logical/mathematical intelligence goes beyond being "good at math." Perhaps your child has a good dose of this kind of smarts. Strength in this type of intelligence includes thinking in clear, logical ways and liking to analyze problems and situations. These kids are good at finding patterns and sequences, and they may frequently point out logical flaws in other people's actions. They are curious about new ideas and developments in science and may enjoy "brainteasers" that demand logical solutions. They can reason their way to solutions and think abstractly.

Most kids who are strong in this type of intelligence like science and most kinds of math. You can encourage logical/mathematical intelligence by giving your child a chance to use these skills outside school. Learn about science by star watching or hiking in the woods. Build "what if" experiments, math computation, or logical

AUTHOR, AUTHOR!

Parents can tell their children that they're soon going to be a "published author!" Kids love to write stories, type them up, add a byline and artwork—and parents can collect writings that they've done over the year and make it a fun home project to bind them together. And there are so many writing games that parents can use at home. There are travel games related to poetry, reports, and stories, and many other games kids can play with to help build a more powerful vocabulary and comfort with the language.

PRAISE FOR PARENTS

I love working at Score@Kaplan. The program is great, but every child who succeeds here does so because of their parents. The parents make a commitment to their child's education. Without that commitment, nothing will succeed.

Allow your children to keep learning throughout the summer so they can jump right in at the beginning of the school year.

CLEAR THE AIR

Support your teacher's plan for your child's learning, but if you see a problem, discuss your concerns with the teacher—but not in front of your child, at least to begin with. A parent and teacher may view a child differently. Be patient, but upfront with your concerns and questions.

FAMILY TIME

We do not allow a lot of sitting-around time at home. We stress "do something." As a family, we go to the beach, we go on hikes, we go for walks, we go to bookstores, we go to the library, we go to the pool and do swimming together. We spend a lot of family time together, especially on the weekends. That's the way we foster a learning atmosphere for our child.

problems into everyday situations. For instance, ask your child to figure out (with mental math) the comparative price per ounce of two different brands of breakfast cereal in the supermarket. Or when you are buying gas, ask, "Can you figure out how many miles per gallon we got with that last tank of gas?"

Visual/Spatial This intelligence includes both artistic vision—sensitivity to color and imagery—and a sense of space and spatial relationships. These kids often like to draw and doodle and they have a good visual imagination. If your child is strong in this kind of intelligence, she may enjoy jigsaw puzzles. She's likely to be good with maps and location and can probably find her way around unfamiliar places. In math, she'll probably think geometry is fun, but may have more trouble with algebra, which is more symbolic and abstract.

Encourage visual/spatial intelligence by supplying your child with tools and materials: a camera or camcorder, drawing and painting equipment, and well-illustrated books. A younger child will enjoy manipulatives and design blocks. Give your child a taste of good art and design, not just by visiting art museums and galleries but also by looking at buildings and surroundings, and sharing an interest in good architecture, furnishings, cars, gardens, and houses.

Body/Kinesthetic People as varied as athletes, inventors, and dancers have this type of "hands-on" intelligence. They are aware and confident of their own movements and physical self and are generally well coordinated. This characteristic also makes them restless—this is the kid who "can't sit still for a minute."

Since action and activity are so important to this kind of kid, parents need to make sure these kids have a chance to do what they are good at. A kid like this is likely to want to spend time actively outdoors or to work at handicrafts and activities such as pottery or woodworking. He may be interested in sports, hiking, dance, or gymnastics. Remember that this is a kid who learns best by doing—by practicing an activity rather than just watching or reading about it.

Children who are not strong in this kind of intelligence can be encouraged to develop their physical skills and abilities.

Musical/Rhythmic Your child's musical/rhythmic intelligence can show itself in different ways and to different degrees. Even very young children show a good sense of rhythm and an ability to sing along or imitate a song they have just heard. They may hum to themselves, tap out rhythms, or make up their own songs and tunes.

In many schools today, music and art programs have been eliminated or cut back because of budget cuts. You can make up for this problem to some extent at home. No matter what her musical ability or formal training, you can help your child enjoy and appreciate different kinds of music through tapes, CDs, radio and TV, and live concerts or performances.

If your school system offers instruction on musical instruments, you'll be doing your child a favor by enrolling her. Music as recreation can bring immense pleasure to people throughout their lives, even if they do not have the skill or inclination to perform professionally. Real involvement in music has even been shown to enhance acquisition of traditionally academic skills such as mathematics, literature, and writing.

Interpersonal Interpersonal intelligence includes "people skills," the ability to get along, communicate, and work together. While hard to quantify, these skills are usually quite obvious. Your child may be the one who almost always gets along with others, whether in school or at play. He likes to be involved in social activities or group sports and is often a leader or the center of a group of friends.

If your child is strong in this type of intelligence, you will not have to work at encouraging him to be active and sociable. In fact, you may have to work to keep him from becoming overscheduled. He may need to develop the ability to enjoy his own company and solitude. For a shyer, less outgoing child, one who has less of this kind of intelligence, it is important to encourage and support social activities while not pushing too hard.

MORNING ROUTINE

When my son was younger, part of my morning routine with him was to get up, put on some fun music, and color and paint with him. He still loves to do it.

GOOD FOR YOU

My husband and I love Score@Kaplan from the standpoint that they give kids goals. It's not just this fun place where kids go and play on the computer. They learn, but it gives them an educational, fun format where they can reach and attain goals and be commended. Kids love that! Kids love to be patted on the back. They like being told, "That was great! Good job. Look how hard you worked." They might not be getting this praise somewhere else, and if they're not, what a great experience for them to get it here. Our daughters love it, and they tell us, "I'm almost to my goal!" "I got a Score card!" "I've got 25 Score cards and I'm going to get a gold one." This has been a healthy, good, fun experience for our girls.

EXPRESSING YOURSELF

Give your children the tools to succeed. My mother bought me a blank journal. It said "My Book" on the outside of it, and every day I wrote a poem in it. This was like a little assignment that my mother and I did together each day. A year later, I had a full book of poems that I can't imagine having done on my own without my mother's encouragement. But she gave me the tools to express myself to do it.

ENHANCING SMARTS

Many studies suggest that early stimulation of a child's brain and body can enhance general intelligence. When the child's natural curiosity is encouraged and fostered, and learning is made fun, intelligence is enhanced.
—*The Parent's Answer Book* by Gerald Deskin, Ph.D. and Greg Steckler, M.A. (Fairview Press, 1995)

Intrapersonal While interpersonal intelligence looks outward, intrapersonal intelligence looks inward. Children strong in this kind of intelligence are likely to be thoughtful, and they are generally more aware of their feelings and emotions than children for whom this is not a strong intelligence. Not necessarily a loner, this child is probably self-reliant and independent and enjoys solitude and her own company. She is likely to have a firm idea about what she believes and what her goals are. She is self-directed and will explore ideas on her own.

Keeping a journal is one way for your child to develop intrapersonal intelligence and self-awareness. A child who is already strong in this type of intelligence may need encouragement to reach out to new friends and join in group activities.

Playing to Your Strengths

Your child is a unique blend of different intelligences—and so are you. Your own interests and ways of learning will inevitably have an influence on the kinds of activities that you can and want to do with your kid. Not surprisingly, it will probably be easiest to encourage the kinds of activities and approaches that you yourself are most comfortable with.

After you've analyzed your child's different kinds of smarts, take a look at your own. You may want to make a checklist for both of you.

- What are the areas in which each of you are strong?
- Do your strongest learning styles differ much?
- Do you share weaker learning styles?
- Or do your areas of weakness and strength complement one another?
- Which are the kinds of smarts that are the easiest for you to work on with your child?
- Which kinds are the hardest?

"We're so different!" After thinking about the seven kinds of smarts, you may come up with this conclusion. One of the challenges parents face in helping their kids do better in school occurs when there are differences in their learning styles. Just because you and your child belong to the same family, you aren't necessarily alike in interests or learning styles. If you have more than one child, chances are that they're not exactly alike, either.

Before you can cope with these differences, you have to recognize them. Think of things you've noticed in everyday life—you love sports, your kid thinks they're boring. Your kid is a whiz at math; you can't balance your checkbook without a calculator. You work on a dozen different handcraft projects; your kid would rather read.

Paradoxically, it can be hardest to help your child develop the kinds of smarts that you already have. For instance, if you're very verbal and a great reader, it's easy to become impatient and critical with a child who isn't. You may find it hard (even frustrating) to understand just why this stuff is hard for her.

On the other hand, you have an advantage because you like and appreciate books and reading or the constant discoveries of science. Here you have an opportunity to pass on some of that appreciation to your child. It just may take a little more patience. And remember, she may never be the book lover or science whiz that you are. But you can be a terrific role model.

"That's not what the book says." Another pitfall of being skilled or knowledgeable in a certain area or way of learning is that you may try to explain things to your middle-school child in college-level terms. If you're an engineer or accountant, for instance, your math skills and knowledge are much greater than what your child needs to know—for now, at least. A too-rich explanation could make things harder for him.

When trying to help, check out what kinds of solutions or answers the textbook or homework assignment is actually asking for. Give your child just the help that's needed. Think

PROBLEM SOLVER

There are at least ten different strategies for your child to use to solve math, word, and other homework problems (from *The Problem Solver* by Shirley Hoogeboom and Judy Goodnow). Every parent should know them and teach them to their children—they're not necessarily going to be covered in school!

1. Act out or use objects.
2. Make a picture or a diagram.
3. Use or make a table.
4. Make an organized list.
5. Guess and check.
6. Use or look for a pattern.
7. Work backwards.
8. Use logical reasoning.
9. Make it simpler.
10. Brainstorm.

Bring your family together to work on a "family mission statement." Every parent and child has goals. Write them all down, then work together to make them all happen.

MUSIC FOR THE MIND

Relaxation induced by specific music leaves the mind alert and able to concentrate. The music found most conducive to this state is baroque music, like that of Bach, Handel, Pachelbel, and Vivaldi .... Most baroque music is timed at 60 beats per minute, which is the same as an average resting heart rate.

— from *Quantum Learning* by Bobbi DePorter (Dell, 1992)

back to when you were first learning these facts and processes. Then use the Learning Adventure activities in Section III to work on the skills he needs to know this year.

Learning Together On the other hand, through family ties and influence, you and your child probably have some similar learning styles, along with similar areas in which you're both less comfortable. You may both be good musicians and athletes, not so good at verbal or visual skills. As a result, you may both have to work in areas of less strength, rather than avoiding them.

Maybe mathematical/logical intelligence isn't your strongest area—or your child's, either. But as you help your child to make the grade, you may find yourself developing new kinds of smarts yourself. As you work through activities in math and science together, for instance, you'll find that both of you are building new skills and strengths.

How Are Children Evaluated?

From the moment of birth, we start measuring and sizing up our kids. At first we have only their physical characteristics (birth weight and length is just the beginning) to work with, but right away we begin to compare them to some norm. How is my child doing compared to others? We keep asking ourselves this question. As kids begin to walk and talk and learn—the hundreds of little skills they do before entering school—the comparisons fly. All through the toddler and preschool years, we watch, we read, we talk, and we wonder, Is my kid doing okay? Before we know it, our baby is off to school and this evaluating stuff goes big time. When schools judge how well your child is doing, the process is called *assessment*.

TEMPORARILY TOUGH

Many parents say negative things around their children. It destroys the confidence and motivation of children with each utterance of "He can't do this" or "She can't read that." Parents should rethink their delivery to express a concern about the level of their children's academic work. Try "This concept is very challenging right now." That way, kids recognize that the tough lessons are temporary and achievable, not permanently out of their reach.

Assessment Is . . .

Few topics on the school reform agenda have generated as much discussion and scrutiny as assessment has—after all, how well your child is doing has been at the core of the school experience since the beginning of time, hasn't it?

Simply put, assessment is the systematic and purposeful method of looking at where students are and where they should be going in their classroom and in their school system. The measurements are made about all development aspects of your child—emotional, social, cognitive, physical, and intellectual. The results can be used for several purposes:

KEEP TRYING

I have a video of Mary Lou Retton, the Olympic gymnast, working out before the 1984 games. She was doing a switch from the parallel bars, and she was doing a very tough move. She missed it 20 times in a row. She got back up and kept trying. That's physically and mentally exhausting to do, but she kept getting up and trying again. She got it on the twenty-first try, and went on to big achievements in her sport. Parents need to help children be patient and persevere. And parents need to have faith, to give their children the space to fail and encourage them to keep trying and learning until they finally understand.

WEAVE IN THE COLOR

Conceptualization starts with the imagination! Expose children to as many artistic and colorful activities as often as possible. Weave the imagination into any educational activity and it will click faster for your child.

- To tell you and your child how she is doing
- To give teachers information to plan what and how to teach your child
- To provide school districts with the data they need to see how well they are doing their teaching job

Changes Underway Along with the many current efforts to make schools more relevant to kids, educators are making some big changes in how they assess kids. They are

- Moving away from something that teachers do to students towards more of a partnership between teachers, students, and their parents
- Moving away from a single letter grade on a quarterly report card towards a more continual process involving a series of tests, observations, and work samples
- Moving away from single events treated separately from the learning process ("Stop what you are learning and take this test . . . .") to an activity that is interwoven into the lesson plans

As a parent, you need an understanding of these kinds of assessment. Here's a closer look at some of the old and the new ways schools are evaluating children's educational growth.

Traditional Assessment

Remember the joys of this kind of testing! You'll recall that it

- Is mostly paper-and-pencil based
- Is given formally—every child has to do the same thing at the same time
- Often is required by the district or state (as in the case of a standardized test like the California Achievement Test, or CAT
- Usually involves a multiple-choice format that emphasizes memorizing facts
- Is almost always subject specific (ah, those weekly spelling tests, reading pop quizzes, and history unit tests)
- Involves comparison of a child's progress to that of other students

- Is based on what a child is able to remember at the time of the test

Values of Standardized Testing Nationally distributed tests, like the Iowa Test of Basic Skills (ITBS) or the CAT, can help teachers and administrators learn a number of things. Standardized achievement tests measure how much your child has already learned about a school subject, and teachers can use the results to plan reading, math, and science lessons that match what the test defines as your child's ability level. These tests may focus on verbal ability, mechanical ability, creativity, clerical ability, and abstract reasoning—the aptitudes considered important to success in school. The results from such tests help teachers to plan lessons that are neither too hard nor too easy for your child.

Alternative Assessment

A wide variety of other ways of evaluating students' progress is now available. Alternative (as opposed to traditional) assessment is more of a process than a single event. It puts the emphasis on your child's progress over time rather than on individual test scores. Alternative assessment:

- Is an ongoing picture of the work a child does in a variety of contexts
- Is focused on a child's work compared to his own previous work
- Is meant to show how kids apply what they know, not just facts they memorize
- Is able to show progress not just in single subjects but also in interdisciplinary projects (where subject matters, like reading in social studies, are combined)
- Is often conducted informally such as through observation or conversation
- Is commonly referred to as *portfolio assessment,* since the notes and work samples are usually kept in a manila folder

THE SCOOP ON TESTS

Remember that all tests have their limitations. They are not perfect measures of what your child can or cannot do. They are at best one entry in the overall picture of your son or daughter.

Some tests may not measure just what we think they do. For example, in an assignment to copy spelling words from the blackboard, we may learn this about students:

- How well they can print
- How well they can copy
- How long they can sit still
- How quickly they can work
- How willing they are to do work that may seem meaningless to them

"Not everything that counts can be counted and not everything that can be counted counts." —*Albert Einstein*

TESTER TALK

achievement test—an objective exam, often given to groups of students at a time, that measures educationally relevant skills in subjects such as spelling or math

diagnostic test—an in-depth evaluation of a specific skill area in order to identify specific learning needs of an individual student

norms—performance standards that are established by a reference group and that describe average or typical performance

percentile—the percentage of people in the testing sample whose scores were below a given score

raw score—the number of items that are answered correctly

standardized test—a form of measurement that has been normed against a specific population; an individual's score is then compared to the norm group's performance

Here's a look at some of the specific types of portfolio assessment. Notice how these methods typically include much more information than what a child writes on paper.

Performance Tasks These are assignments (whether student-initiated or teacher-planned) that are designed to measure your child's skill in a certain area; for example, being able to write a persuasive essay or to follow written directions to build a specific kind of birdhouse. Looking at the entire process rather than just the end result takes into account each child's individual learning style.

Observation By paying attention to how students approach a problem, interact with other students, or use their free time, teachers and parents can build the complete picture of your child's success in learning. Teachers may take notes in checklist form or in more of a narrative, anecdotal fashion.

Self-Evaluation When children are encouraged to make thoughtful evaluations of their own work, they begin to accept responsibility for their own learning—a key element in their educational growth.

What's a Parent to Do!

The ways you can help your child succeed in school can be changing too. It used to be that test scores and grades were sent home without much explanation. But now it's increasingly possible for parents to talk with teachers about what certain grades and scores mean. In these discussions, you can also contribute to your child's success in school work by helping the teacher get the big picture of the your child. These are opportunities for you to offer unique information about your child's likes and dislikes and way of doing things that are important for the teacher to know.

What Those Test Scores Mean Standardized testing is still in the picture as a somewhat efficient and objective way to collect data about groups of students, so you will likely have sets of grades or scores to interpret. Once again, keep in mind that test scores are just one factor in the assessment of your child's progress.

Supporting Your Child in the Assessment Process
Do you remember how your folks reacted to your report cards? The attitudes about test taking and report cards that you take send a message to your kids that can help or hinder their school progress. You can help your child by

- Not being overly anxious about scores or grades
- Not judging your child on the basis of a single score
- Using mistakes as a focus of discussion rather than reasons to punish
- Using all modes of reports as opportunities for discussion (along with praise and encouragement)

Staying in touch with teachers about your child builds partnerships for the benefit of your child. These partnerships are important to help your child get the best education possible.

How You Can Use Assessment

Assessment is not for schools and teachers alone—you and your child should get involved too! *Making the Grade* includes a special pull-out section, "The Home Learning Quizzes," because the whole point of assessment is to use it as a learning tool. Our parents' quiz provides strategies for you to use to learn how your child is doing—what he knows and can do, what is difficult for him, what helps him progress, and so forth. It also provides a way for you to discover what you know about home learning and how aware you are of your child's progress, growth, and habits. Use the kids' quizzes to help you choose appropriate Section III activities to fill in your child's knowledge gaps. But, above all, use The Home Learning Quizzes to have fun with your child and develop a "big picture" of your child's progress. Self-assessment is important to everyone's learning, and so the pull-out section encourages you and your child to see what you already know and explore some new ground.

NOT STILL BEHIND

When kids are behind in a subject, they're not fully aware of how far behind they are. They may have started out being a year behind and maybe they work up to only three months behind, but in their mind, they're still behind. They don't realize they've made much progress. Parents can help out so much just by encouraging students and pointing out how far their child's hard work is carrying them.

WHAT'S WRONG HERE?

America's schools spend more per pupil than virtually any of the countries that routinely trounce us in international scholastic comparisons.
—*Beyond the Classroom,* Laurence Steinberg, Ph.D. (Simon & Schuster, 1996)

How Can Parents Affect Their Children's Success?

Parents are the single most important factor in a child's educational success from the earliest months through the school years. Our shoes may be scuffed, our wallets thin, and our gasoline tanks running on empty, but it is our effort, energy, and support that make the difference.

We all look back on that time when our toddler first held up a bug or a blade of grass and proudly named it for us. We cherish being a part of that moment of learning and hold on to the hope that every moment of learning in our children's lives will be as exciting and as important.

Children make those first discoveries both for themselves and for the loving adults around them. Your presence, your pride, your support, and your enthusiasm were an essential part of that moment and will continue to be a part of their learning moments for as long as they live with you. As children mature, enter school, and continue up through the higher grades, the intensity of their learning experiences changes and their public expectations of us change (try gurgling excitedly over your 13-year-old's mastery of the square root), but our basic role remains the same.

GO BACK TO SCHOOL

When parents take the time to attend a school function—time off from an evening activity or time off from their own jobs—they send a strong message about how important school is to them, and, by extension, how important it should be to their child. When this sort of involvement occurs regularly, it reinforces the view in the child's mind that school and home are connected, and that school is an integral part of the whole family's life. —from *Beyond the Classroom*, Laurence Steinberg, Ph.D. (Simon & Schuster, 1996)

Spend Learning Time Together

We may do more supporting and less teaching once our children hit school, but there are many opportunities for support that have nothing to do with textbooks or classroom lessons. These are the times when you and your child can build a wonderful relationship around learning together.

ENSURE THEIR HEALTH

Children who are physically and emotionally healthy perform better in school, have higher self-esteem, and enjoy positive relationships with their family and peers.

• Make preventive health care and education a priority for your family. Schedule routine check-ups, health screenings, and immunizations to provide early detection and treatment of health problems.

• Serve a low-fat and high fiber diet that includes five servings of fruits and vegetables each day. Choose nourishing snacks to round out a well-balanced diet.

• Encourage and participate in age-appropriate physical activity and exercise with your children.

• Promote your children's self-esteem and emotional health by understanding their needs, encouraging their independence, setting standards, and sharing your feelings and experiences with them.
—The National PTA®

One parent may discover a local garden club's edible-plant walk to take with his seven-year-old botanist. Another may share her skills with carving tools and linoleum blocks with her son. Others are willing to join a teenager under the car. All are engaged in learning with their children. These are the parents and children who are joined in a learning process that transcends the ordinary routines of living together.

Parents Can

We are sometimes intimidated by schools and schooling. This happens most frequently in later years when the more advanced mathematics, language, or science curriculum can leave us scrambling for reference books as we try to help our struggling young chemists or geographers. It can also happen in earlier years, particularly if our children have problems with specific skills like reading and if the school is using teaching techniques different from the ones used when we were in school.

At such times, it's important to keep in mind that no one person and no single institution can possibly provide all of the care, support, and expertise that are required to educate a young human being. We, as parents, may not have the pedagogical skills or knowledge to teach a particular subject, but we are the primary support team, the cheerleaders, the enforcers, and, when necessary, the champions of our young students. As you read this book, you will also find that there are many ways to supplement and support your child's education that require only our energy and enthusiasm for learning (of course, knowing how hard parents already work, that is a big *only*).

Provide the Taste of Success

Good educators (good managers, successful politicians, and great generals as well) all know that success breeds success and that nobody thrives or learns in situations in which there is frequent failure. To learn well, we all need to build on successful experiences.

Learning should be tailored so that children can taste success. A fact, a skill, or a concept successfully acquired will stick—and contribute to *more* learning. This doesn't mean that learning won't be work. Learning, as we all know, often takes lots of work. Stumbles, guesses, and trials occur all along the way. These are part of the process and part of the learning. When something becomes too full of stumbles and sulks and tears, however, it's time to take a break.

A break is also a good idea when there are tears of frustration over a homework assignment. If your child is stumped and it's appropriate for you to help, lead him back to a simpler level. Try to break the present task into smaller steps. If the steps lead to small, recognizable successes, the original, frustrating task can be easily accomplished.

If you are working with your child and using the activities in this book, avoid situations in which defeat and disappointment seem likely. This is not always easy to do, but learning to read your child's reactions will help you know when to halt an unsuccessful attempt. While you pause, consider the child and the task, and then rethink the task. Can you break it into smaller units or subtasks? Can you try teaching in a different way? Or should you abandon it and try something totally different?

Providing tastes of success is like carefully laying a new course of bricks in a wall. If you have crumbly bricks and lumpy mortar, there'll be trouble higher up. When each brick is even and snug and the mortar satisfyingly set, you have laid the perfect foundation for a new course.

Learn to Listen

Good listening skills are necessary for learning, but they are equally (or perhaps even more) necessary for teaching.

The First Level of Listening There's an old educational maxim, "He who does the talking, does the learning." Talking requires putting your thoughts together. The more your child talks about something that she's learning, the more putting together—learning—she does. This is a simple and extremely useful thought, but it's very easy to forget, even for the most experienced teachers.

DO IT!

Parents can show kids how learning basic skills applies to everyday life. Use the tools you have around the home, and have a lot of fun too. Do projects with your children. Focus on one child or all siblings. Turn measuring food ingredients into the lesson of the day. Split a recipe in half or double it. Whoa—there's a huge math lesson going on there! Do it. Use the measuring cups. Use the flour and the sugar. Break some things, make some mistakes along the way. Have fun. What do you have at the end of the "lesson"? Chocolate chip cookies, and the kids get to brag about how they got to make them. My mom's not the best cook in the world, but we really had fun cooking together.

PARENTS TEACH!

Parents are educators too. By the time your children enter school, you will have taught them more than they will learn during their entire school experience!

FREAKING OUT

One mother told me that her daughter was really amazing at math and other subjects, but she hadn't opened her mouth in school the whole year. This was a big issue for her and the teacher. I told her that at Score@Kaplan we interact with the children, and her mother said she didn't think that could really happen. I told the girl to raise her hand and say "I'm done," because when you do, you'll get a Score incentive card, which children can use to redeem for prizes or gifts. The mom was surprised she even opened her mouth.

The mom called me a few nights later. Her teacher freaked out because the next day in class the girl raised her hand and said, "I have a question." The teacher thought, Oh my god, Lazarus has come out of the cave, because she never spoke up before. That's what's going on at Score. We're teaching life things here, beyond what you learn in a textbook. We're teaching kids how to be people.

If *you* are quiet enough, you'll get the thrill of watching those miraculous moments when your child's learning takes place. The sound of the penny dropping can be the most important (and satisfying) sound in the world.

The Second Level of Listening This level of listening is a bit harder. It requires you to be both quiet and as completely aware as possible of everything about your child. We use this skill unconsciously in conversations with our friends. We are sensitive to their facial expressions, read their body language, and monitor the tone of their voices. With your child, make this a more conscious process. Deliberately watch her face as an exercise is being written. Notice the enthusiastic posture (or discouraged or bored slump) as your child talks to herself during a hands-on activity. Pay attention to changes in behavior. These and many other subtle signals will help you determine how well, or how poorly, a particular educational activity is going.

Learn Something Yourself

We know a parent who began learning Hebrew at the same time as his child was learning to read. His child was having a struggle. Because this parent had to learn a new alphabet from scratch as well as how to read right to left, he was especially sympathetic with and supportive of his child's struggles.

Learning something new yourself has two other benefits (besides having a good time learning ballroom dancing or car maintenance or whatever). The first is that it makes you an observer of how your own learning process works, and that *always* makes you a better teacher. The second is that you are providing your child with an excellent model.

Remember Your Own Learning

Everyone who engages in teaching touches a lot of old hot buttons. There were subjects you loved, subjects you hated, teachers who helped you, and teachers you just couldn't please. These are useful memories, but they are primarily useful to you as an adult engaged in education. They can help you think about what works or doesn't work, but they can also bog you down while you're working with your child. As much as possible, keep your memories to yourself while you are working with your child at the homework table or using the activities in this book.

This is not an iron rule, though—nothing in education should be ironclad. If an old feeling or experience makes helpful sense at the moment, share it. All children are curious about their parents' lives as children, and you should share whatever you feel comfortable about sharing. Usually, however, it's better to do it at some other time.

MANY INFLUENCES

If you are a good parent and you live in a neighborhood with other good parents, chances are that the lessons you have tried so hard to teach your child at home will be reinforced when your child comes into contact with other children, and other adults, in the community. —from *Beyond the Classroom* by Laurence Steinberg, Ph.D. (Simon & Schuster, 1996)

Finding More Educational Resources

Beyond this book lies a whole world of educational opportunities. Like most parents, you are probably the phone book, resource manager, librarian, transportation officer, executive secretary, and personal assistant in your child's education right now. Here are a few ideas of resources to make your job more rewarding and easier.

Use the institutions around you. Almost all areas of our country are within range of a college, university, research field station, or county extension service. Such institutions often sponsor a variety of public educational events staffed by young, eager graduate students or professionals who are happy and proud to show and talk about what they do. Call them up and find out what they have to offer and get on their mailing lists.

Meet interesting neighbors. Ham radio operators, retired people with exotic hobbies, the guy who raises parakeets or poodles for sale, and many others like them live somewhere nearby. They are usually happy to share their stories and skills with interested families.

LEARNING SITES

Factories, farms, greenhouses, fire stations—any place of business—can be a learning site for your child. Call these businesses up and see if they can handle family or small group tours.

Plug into the Web. It can be confusing and it can be maddening, but the possibilities of finding facts, books, articles, connection resources, and you name it are so great that tuning into the hum of information on the World Wide Web is worth the effort. Having your own computer helps, but it isn't necessary. Libraries all over the country now offer

LEADER OF THE PACK

Use your child's friends to help out with home learning projects and keep everything fun and exciting. Sometimes older siblings can be great role models to younger children. I wanted my older sister to read to me all the time; have older brothers and sisters read to younger children. Parents need to encourage this kind of positive experience in the family.

TOOL TIME

Teach your children how to use a dictionary, encyclopedia, or different kinds of software reference tools. Many kids don't know how to look up the meaning of a word because no one's helped them or shown them how. You don't learn some of these skills until late in school, so it's a big headstart if your children learn at home first.

access to the Internet as a resource and will be happy to help you search.

Make your own connections. Everyone seems to work harder and have less time these days.This is very isolating for parents who have the added responsibility of child rearing. You can be sure, however, that there are lots of people out there just like you. Use your PTA, visits to the park, church, or synagogue, membership in organizations, and contacts with other places where you meet adults with children to raise issues about children and education. This connecting can be as simple as finding enough interested families to organize a modern dance class or as complicated (and important) as galvanizing parents to take action against a program cutback in the local schools.

Contact home-schooling groups. Home schoolers have taken on the whole burden of their children's education and usually have done extensive research into the educational opportunities in the communities around them. Subscribe to any publications they produce and talk with them about what they've found useful.

Check out professional and trade associations. Many of these groups have extensive educational and public relations resources that you can use to supplement hobbies or educational activities. Offerings range from posters and booklets to some quite sophisticated educational materials. Many libraries have indexed directories for professional and trade groups.You and your child could spend a pleasant time browsing through one of them looking for areas of interest together (and you'll be amazed at the variety).

Use the library with your child. Libraries not only offer special programs for families, they are increasingly defining themselves as community information and resource centers. Their bulletin boards reflect this and will guide you to unsuspected educational opportunities ranging from reading programs and book clubs, to arts and crafts classes, to author readings. And, of course, take advantage of the professional skills of the children's librarian.

Finally, don't forget your mother! Members of your extended family make wonderful resources. We often overlook the richness of wisdom and experience available in our own immediate circle. An aunt who crochets, a cousin who loves to do woodworking, or a grandparent who cooks some special food all have skills to share. Older relatives may have personal experiences like military service, life in another country, or skills in an occupation that no longer exists that they would be happy to share for oral history projects.

Making the Most of Small Moments

Teaching moments exist all around you. It's easier with younger children because their defenses aren't up and they ask great questions. But, in fact, older children are as curious and eager to explore if you open up situations. An example might be stopping by the road to read a notice board about an area of reclaimed prairie and then researching this at home. Budgeting for throwing a party is a natural. And minilessons don't have to be complicated. A game of "subway-stop bingo" (looking for all the letters of the alphabet on a subway station map) can change a tedious wait into a language arts lesson.

Remember—You Do Make a Difference

Whether you work on the Learning Adventure activities in this book, share your child's enthusiasm for all the right answers she got on The Kids' Home Learning Quizzes, zealously support your children's homework efforts, seek out exciting field trips, drive your child to an enrichment program, or do all of these, your support makes a big difference in your child's educational success. Everything you do, no matter how small a beginning, encourages and strengthens your child's learning. Thanks for making the effort.

A TASTE OF SUCCESS

One boy in our center was not expected to walk or talk after a severe accident. He made a great recovery, but still has a bad vision problem and needs to sit very close to a computer screen. I told his mother that I had a good friend who also had poor vision and hearing problems, and he got accepted to a top college. He had to sit in the front row of class and tape lectures and use his laptop to record what he heard, but he adapted just fine to higher education. And I told this boy's mom that he could go to college—Berkeley, for instance, has an extension service for students who have challenging physical problems—and just to be aware of the opportunities out there. She started crying. "Nobody ever talked to me before about my son going to college. Nobody has ever made that a reality." If your child, under any condition, is given a taste of success, like moving forward in his skill levels, it's a good thing. Then it's not a matter of *if* the child is going to college, but *which* college he should attend.

What's Being Covered in School?

What's My Child Studying in Language Arts?

Depending on where you live, grades five and six in your child's school may be called upper elementary or intermediate grades, or either or both of them might be a part of middle school. Your child may be entering a new building and be among the youngest students there or stay put and be among the oldest in the building, where new responsibilities and leadership opportunities abound. In these grades, kids or teachers may begin to travel between rooms for different classes within a building. The very arrangement of the classroom may change from grouped desks or tables to individual desks in a new (or old-fashioned) layout. Suffice it to say that there are likely to be changes in your child's basic learning structure. Paired with the physical and emotional developmental changes going on for 5th and 6th graders, you are in for a couple of lively years!

KEEP ON TALKIN'

Talk to the teachers and to other parents about what your child is learning. And, of course, talk to your children about school. Look at their homework and make sure they understand it and know how to do it. Volunteering in your child's classroom is very beneficial to understanding what is being taught.

All of this has a significant impact on your child's language arts program, which will likely change as well; in some areas it may even have a new name: English. Reading will become literature study. At the very least, there will be a remarkable increase in the quality *and* quantity of language-related work expected of your child at this level.

Language Arts and Reading in the previous school years focused on the introduction and mastery of rules and conventions for reading, writing, listening, and speaking. Now, during these middle school years, a shift takes place from basic skills instruction to using and applying the skills in an ever-widening range of ways. Kids ten to twelve can be expected to absorb information through reading and listening more widely and extensively and be capable of more in-depth analysis. They will be engaged in fine-tuning their language skills. The interest in playing with language that kids this age demonstrate can expand their range of creative expressions and enliven communication of their understanding and ideas.

Not all expansion is outward, however, as 5th and 6th graders typically become much more self-aware. Journal writing and portfolio work typically increase noticeably at this level. Opportunities to work on projects that combine social studies, science, math, and reading/language arts really lend themselves to this age group. The weaving together of formerly distinct subjects is more reflective of real life and suits these kids' new connection to their world.

NEED TO READ

I loved to read while I was growing up, and there's nothing better a child can do than to read a lot. Sometimes your child may not have a natural interest in reading, but you just have to get the right books. Reading can greatly improve grammar and spelling. Does your child's natural interests involve motorcycles or sports or dinosaurs? Focus on these subjects and get materials on the subjects that your child will enjoy—any reading is productive.

Ten Core Areas in Language Arts Despite differences in approaches to the teaching of language arts and reading, the following nine core areas form the basis of most language arts programs in grades five and six:

1. Grammar and Usage
2. Mechanics
3. Spelling
4. Composition
5. Vocabulary
6. Reference and Study Strategies
7. Thinking Skills and Strategies
8. Listening, Speaking, and Viewing Skills and Strategies
9. Literature and Reading

READ ALL ABOUT IT

Try to find books you and your child both can agree upon. Kids may not think they like to "read," but all kids want to learn about their favorite place, their favorite animal, their favorite sport, and so on. Let books satisfy their curiosity.

Approaches to Language Arts Teaching The *how* and *when* of language arts instruction in grades five and six may vary considerably from state to state and from class to class depending on curriculum structure, teacher passions and knowledge, school district standards, and testing programs. The following instructional approaches may also influence language arts instruction in your child's school.

Team Teaching and Specialist Teachers During the middle-school years, teachers often work in teams to cover instruction in the basic curriculum areas. Rather than teach all subjects to a single classroom of kids, in many schools individual teachers now focus on math/science or humanities (language arts and social studies). A team might consist of two or three such teachers who plan together so that the English teacher's classes are coordinated with the lessons taught by the math and science teacher, for instance. Depending upon the degree of coordination, there can be more emphasis on cross-discipline study—sharing a theme across subjects—and language arts is integrated all the time and everywhere possible.

In addition, teachers with a special learning focus, such as foreign language, are found in many middle school settings. Your 5th or 6th grader reaps the benefits of working with several different teachers and styles, serving as preparation for the multiteacher reality of secondary school.

Curriculum Integration and Cooperative Learning The mingling of previously separate subjects is a common feature of many middle schools. The greater resemblance to real life is an important motivational element for ten to twelve year olds. One example of an integrated unit would be that while kids read and discuss *The Phantom Tollbooth* (Do you know this intriguing story about traveling backwards in time and about language, logic, and lunacy?), they may also learn how ancient cultures kept track of time for social studies, make a water clock in science, and do math problems and explorations that involve time.

Teamwork becomes common for students as well as teachers. Learning to study together and how to collaborate on long-term assignments are skills that prepare students for survival and success in today's workplace as much as or more than a straight learning of facts.

Portfolios The collection of students' work over the course of a year or several years is called a portfolio, and portfolio assessment is used as part of a student's evaluation. Examples of your child's work from his portfolio may well be part of your parent-teacher conference. In middle school years, this collection of work over time becomes especially important

WHERE ARE YOU GOING?

Parents always want their kids to have more than they had. It gets to a point where it has to level off. My dad didn't have skates and other things we had growing up, and we would like our children to have even more. For me, growing up wasn't a question of "Will you go to college?", it was "Where are you going to college?" Neither of my parents went to college, and I knew I was going and there was no question about that. We encourage our children to think about where they're going, even though they're still in the middle grades.

as students can begin to evaluate and plan for their own progress or identify areas that need strengthening.

The Writing Process Much research has been done recently on the steps that writers take when they write. For the teaching of writing, that process has been subdivided into five general phases or steps:

- Prewriting
- Writing (drafting)
- Revising
- Editing
- Postwriting/publishing

During the middle school years, students begin to take more extensive responsibility for using the skills involved in each step in order to communicate in a meaningful way. They become able to make a fairly detailed writing plan, then execute and refine it for a specific purpose. The amount of time and attention devoted to each stage varies from phase to phase and from writer to writer, but attention to this process helps kids (all of us for that matter—you too!) become more fluent, happier writers.

Using Technology Perhaps nothing varies as much in classrooms across the country as the amount of access teachers and their students have to equipment such as computers, modems, VCRs, TVs, and the like. Some schools aren't able to get the hardware; others have it, but scheduling becomes a burden to already overloaded teachers. During the school day, there's an increasing likelihood of your child's being engaged in any of the following technology-based activities in grades five or six:

- Using a computer for word processing, perhaps even having keyboarding lessons
- Exchanging letters with an electronic pen pal
- Using software programs for practice with spelling, grammar, vocabulary development, or writing
- Research via a CD-ROM or online service
- Using a VCR for viewing videos related to language arts activities

HOME PC BUYING TIPS

Newsweek's Computers & the Family newsmagazine (Fall/Winter 1996) advises you to get the best-performing machine for the money, and here are the specifications they recommend:

- **Audio:** 16-bit stereo 3-D sound, Soundblaster-compatible sound card, speakers (some models have microphones and speakers built into the monitor)
- **Monitor:** 17-inch Super VGA is best, followed by a 15-inch with a dot pitch of .28 or less (skip the 14-inch monitors!)
- **Upgradable:** your new PC should have extra bays and slots for adding components; at least a couple of bays for inserting hard drives and two to five slots to plug in additional video and graphics cards
- **Warranty:** 3-year warranty, including a year of onsite service, 3 years of parts and labor, and a 24-hour toll-free technical support line

- Listening to books on tape or other audio presentations
- Watching TV programs with an educational focus

What's Taught in Grade Five?

During the intermediate school years, children in grade five become increasingly confident and independent learners. Their view of the world becomes wider and their curiosity seems to intensify as they begin to initiate and talk about various self-directed educational pursuits.

Fifth graders can read for both information and enjoyment. They can feed their curiosity about the outside world by reading literature that covers a wide variety of genres, periods, and multicultural perspectives. The study of literature in grade five is often organized around themes such as responsibility, friendship, and self-reliance. The themes may also be the focus for research in specific content areas as well. With increased reading and writing assignments, you can expect to see your child doing more homework several nights a week.

Your 5th grader will continue to write for a variety of purposes and probably be asked to use feedback from peers to improve her work. Typically youngsters' ability to express themselves exceeds their grasp of (or concern for) the mechanics, so teachers often use a two-part grading system: half for content or ideas, and half for spelling, punctuation, and grammar and usage. Such an approach helps youngsters see more specifically how their problems with grammar, usage, or mechanics interfere with their success in writing. Handwriting may be less emphasized and word processing increasingly used. In fact, in some schools, the computer can become quite commonplace by grade five.

Language arts and literature study begins to include a focus not only on language construction, but also on the power of the spoken/written word as people continue to experience it at home, in their communities, and through the media.

Core Area 1: Grammar and Usage

- Identify predicate nouns and adjectives

FUN AND GAMES

Many times parents can find great learning games at Toys R Us or other children's retail outlets, but also check out educational supply stores. Most cities have them, and that's where teachers go to add extra resources to their lesson plans. Look in your yellow pages under "Educational Supplies" for the nearest outlets.

WE DO IT TOGETHER

Education is very important to both my husband and me. We recognize we cannot depend solely on the public school system to provide it all, so we sit down with our son and we read a lot and do homework with him—also adding things that we've made up or borrowed from outside educational sources. We spend about an hour and a half of work a day on school subjects, and we do this together.

SUPPORT AND INTERACTION

If a parent is just dropping off children and picking them up from school, and there is no support or interaction at home, and nothing at school in between, I think their children's education will definitely suffer.

- Find direct objects in clauses and objects of prepositions
- Recognize uses of prepositional phrases and place them correctly
- Differentiate between abstract and concrete nouns
- Identify demonstrative adjectives and use them correctly
- Use correct pronoun agreement with antecedent
- Identify coordinating conjunctions and use them correctly
- Use irregular adjectives and adverbs correctly
- Recognize interjections
- Begin mastery of several problem words usage

Core Area 2: Mechanics
- Use capitals in abbreviations, outlining, and proper nouns
- Punctuate interjections
- Use comma in series, compound sentences, and with appositives and introductory elements
- Use a colon correctly
- Punctuate direct speech
- Use quotation marks or underlining for titles

Core Area 3: Spelling
- Use word families to increase spelling ability
- Develop a study plan for frequently misspelled words
- Spell theme-related words correctly

Core Area 4: Composition
- Write a business letter in correct form and style
- Prepare an outline and develop a paragraph from it
- Write effective introductions and conclusions
- Follow the steps of the writing process
- Use persuasive language in writing
- Write a paragraph on a topic from a curriculum area
- Expand creative writing techniques

Core Area 5: Vocabulary
- Use context clues to aid in understanding words
- Expand use of base words and root words to find meanings
- Expand understanding of idiomatic expressions
- Recognize content-specific words

Core Area 6: Reference and Study Strategies

- Use the dictionary to find pronunciation, syllabication, etymology, and part of speech for words
- Use thesaurus to vary language used in writing
- Fill out forms and applications
- Ask for information in writing, by phone, or in person
- Seek information through card catalog and online searches
- Identify theme-related nonprint media
- Skim and scan passage for information
- Take notes from reading and lectures

Core Area 7: Thinking Skills and Strategies

- Practice critical thinking skills such as making inferences from details, identifying cause and effect, detecting overgeneralization
- Recognize propaganda techniques

Core Area 8: Listening, Speaking, and Viewing Skills

- Listen to tell fact from opinion
- Listen to take notes
- Participate in a debate
- Recite memorized passage
- Do a dramatic reading
- Conduct an interview
- Describe how art of persuasion is used in TV programs
- Watch and listen to media for evidence of the use of bias

Core Area 9: Literature and Reading

- Read a variety of types of literature (poetry, drama, biography, novel)
- Identify the theme of a written passage
- Analyze passages for mood and tone
- Differentiate between formal and informal language
- Identify story elements
- Analyze characters based on speech or action
- Extend understanding of figurative language such as personification
- Share, review, and recommend books and other written materials to others

"HEY, TEACH!"

At a parent-teacher conference, Score@Kaplan wants you to find out the teacher's perception of your child's learning progress and get the teacher's recommendations for activities and projects that will help reinforce classroom learning. Share your perceptions of your child's schoolwork at home and ask, "What do you see in school?" Ask the teacher "What can I do?" rather than "This is what you, the teacher, need to do."

Teachers deserve respect and they probably know what they're doing. Parents won't get anywhere if they lecture teachers, say that the teacher is doing something wrong, or make accusations. "I just need more input from you. I've noticed this at home, and I want to keep the lines of communication open with you." The more a teacher knows about what parents are doing with their children at home, even whether they're feeling challenged or frustrated by a personal event, the better the likelihood of designing a proactive approach to a child's learning challenges.

ARE YOU ON A HOTLINE?

Many schools are going tech with automated phone systems that call and leave messages for busy parents who work during school hours. One such system, U.S. Telecom International's PhoneMaster 2000 (call 800-835-7788), allows schools to notify parents of:

- Absentees and tardies
- Homework assignments
- School events
- Invitation to meetings
- Bond issues
- School cancellations
- Report card announcements
- Fines due reminders

Information hotlines also give students and parents instant access to an electronic bulletin board of important information for the home, including homework hotlines, attendance policies, sporting schedules, lunch menus, bus routes, and school policies.

What's Taught in Grade Six?

By the time they enter grade six, children understand that language can be used in a wide variety of ways; they have many choices about how to learn about and communicate with their ever-expanding world. Their curiosity about the world and their place in it propels an independence in language learning and specific content areas. Youngsters in grade six often discover a favorite author or read everything in print about some topic of particular interest to them.

Reading selections at school come from around the world and from many points in time. Some of the literature for 6th graders is often grouped around themes such as mythology or heroes. Themes often become the focus for writing assignments, group discussion, and research in other content areas as well. An increased number of reading and writing assignments mean that you can expect your child to have homework most nights, and long-term projects are fairly standard 6th-grade fare.

By grade six, youngsters have been introduced to all the basic mechanics of good writing and been exposed to a wide range of writing styles and purposes. At this age, they generally possess the motivation, skills, and opportunity to choose and use language in its many forms to communicate for many different purposes. Perhaps even more than in grade five, teachers in grade six may use the double-grading system when marking your child's written work to evaluate her content and her mechanics separately. Submitting a paper that has been done on a computer rather than handwritten is frequently acceptable; in fact, the use of computers for many purposes can become quite commonplace at this level.

Core Area 1: Grammar and Usage

- Identify and use complex sentences
- Recognize inverted order of subject and predicate
- Understand use of independent and dependent clauses
- Identify transitive and intransitive verbs
- Identify indefinite and interrogative pronouns and use them correctly
- Use correct pronoun case

- Place adjectives and adverbs correctly
- Understand the use of prepositional phrases as adjectives and adverbs
- Choose the correct preposition
- Continue to focus on problem word usage

Core Area 2: Mechanics
- Apply knowledge of capitalization and punctuation rules to current writing assignments
- Use comma to set off interrupters, words in series, compound sentences, and with appositives and introductory elements
- Use comma with nonrestrictive phrases and clauses
- Use semicolon and colon correctly
- Use quotation marks, commas, and end punctuation in quoting or writing dialogue
- Use quotation marks or underlining for titles

Core Area 3: Spelling
- Identify and generate specialty word lists
- Focus on frequently misspelled words
- Hyphenate words correctly

Core Area 4: Composition
- Write nine types of paragraphs
- Apply language arts skills to writing in other curricular content areas
- Compare and contrast an issue in an essay
- Make use of a wide range of creative expressions
- Use the five steps of the writing process with increased attention to revision

Core Area 5: Vocabulary
- Use clipped words and blended words
- Apply connotation and denotation to word meanings
- Generate and apply specialized vocabulary

MULTIAGE CLASSROOMS

Kentucky has mandated that every school in the state offer multiage classes for kids from age 5 to 9. Cincinnati is planning to have all their city classes be multiage from Kindergarten through 10th grade by 2001. As part of the school reform movement, many areas are experimenting with putting a variety of grade levels together into a single classroom setting—like the old frontier one-room schoolhouse! Some experts hate the concept; others say students can move from easier to more difficult material at their own pace, without having to wait until they're promoted to a new grade level.

If learning is part of the everyday, it can be fun—kids like participating in real life.

QUALITY TIME

It's hard being a single parent and trying to find the time for learning activities and personal time with your child. But you know what—I've got to make the time. I have to say, "What's more important: Do we have to eat dinner at 6:00, or first can we spend some time doing homework together?"

Core Area 6: Reference and Study Strategies

- Do more intensive online searching
- Use periodicals for current information
- Summarize
- Expand understanding of book classification system
- Obtain information from detailed illustrations, diagrams, timelines, and maps
- Take notes

Core Area 7: Thinking Skills and Strategies

- Practice critical thinking skills such as making judgments, drawing conclusions, predicting outcomes, making analogies, and identifying bias and false reasoning

Core Area 8: Listening, Speaking, and Viewing Skills

- Listen for bias, motive, and point of view
- Discriminate between fact and opinion when listening or viewing
- Do an oral summary of media presentation
- Present a character analysis orally
- Compare and contrast written and filmed versions of a story or event

Core Area 9: Literature and Reading

- Recognize use of denotation and connotation
- Identify use of irony, sarcasm, and symbolism
- Identify use and effects of narrative techniques of foreshadowing and flashback
- Continue written and oral responses to reading various types of literature
- Infer author's purpose and unstated points and cite evidence
- Identify and discuss point of view in works of literature

What Language Arts Content Should I Review?

It's clear that lots of language learning goes on informally before kids even enter school. They listen and then begin to speak. From an early age, exposure to all sorts of visual information makes them aware of print and its impact on communication. Soon they pick up a pencil and start their own messaging.

Once in school, they go through many mostly teacher-directed language experiences. So by the time they are ten, kids are ready to cast off the classroom training wheels and do a solo. Middle schoolers have a great need to communicate in every way. Their connection to real world events, combined with ever-emerging emotions, make them need to reach out in many directions.

WORLD WIDE WAIT

With Internet education being a hot political goal in the United States, there is a major push to get each classroom plugged in. With the current problems, however, including major online traffic jams and peak hours that delay log-ons, the Info Superhighway needs to move faster and somehow accommodate the millions of new users each year. Stay tuned!

Use the following skill areas as a review for yourself, and then just go for it! But remember it's two years' worth of content. Don't try to go through the whole thing at once. Take it in chunks. Think of as many ways in a day as you can to talk, listen, watch, and write with your child. After all, how did you learn to ride a bike? By riding, of course, not by just reading the manual.

Core Area 1: Language and Grammar

This is the meat-and-potatoes section of our written and spoken language. By grade five, kids are looking at language skills in greater detail and learning the specialized rules that will enable them to accomplish their loftier purposes in writing.

QUESTIONS GET ANSWERED

I recommend encyclopedias, in book form, for the family. It was exciting when my son had a question and first went to the encyclopedia by himself and started reading.

QUITE AN IMPACT

Want to make more informed choices about the media your children are watching? Look up useful "Children's Impact Statements" to check age appropriateness, violence, language, sexual content, and character traits for various TV shows, movies, and video games. These statements from The National Institute on Media and the Family. For more information, contact them toll-free at (888) 672-5437 or visit their Website at: www.mediaandthefamily.org

Sentence Types and Structures In your everyday conversations, you probably communicate a lot without using complete sentences. You might say:

no more ice cream for me
over there

Your meaning is usually clear to the listener, though, isn't it? In written English, however, you must use a complete sentence in order for it to make sense to the reader. A complete sentence is a group of words that expresses a complete thought. Look at some of these examples:

the crowd outside the building (not a sentence)
The crowd rushed into the rock concert. (sentence)

a television program (not a sentence)
I got home just in time to watch my favorite television program. (sentence)

Sentences fall into four categories, each with a different purpose; that is, you use them for different reasons:

- A statement (also known as a declarative) is a sentence that tells something. It ends with a period.

  Ellen is a good athlete.

- A question (also known as interrogative) is a sentence that asks something. It ends with a question mark.

  What is her favorite sport?

- A command (also known as an imperative) is a sentence that tells someone to do something. It ends with a period or an exclamation point.

  Bring all your equipment to the game!

- An exclamation is a sentence that shows some strong feeling. It ends with an exclamation point.

  I am so glad that team made it to the play-offs!

Predicate Nouns and Adjectives These are words in a sentence that help describe or explain something about the subject. They usually follow a being or linking verb (Remember that one? It is forms of the verb *to be* such as is, *am, was, were, are*) that links them with the predicate in the sentence. Here are some examples of a predicate noun. They rename the subject of a sentence.

Kevin will be my partner.
That building is a school.

In the following cases, the italicized word describes the subject. It is called a predicate adjective.

That dog looked *sick*.
The candy is too *sweet*.

Independent and Dependent Clauses Sentences are made up of groups of words that we call clauses. *Independent* clauses have their own subject and verb and express a complete thought as in the following:

Miss Pritchard cut up all the vegetables, and Fred put them in the bowls for the salad bar.

Each clause could actually be written as its own sentence, couldn't it? Now look at this one:

Before the game started, Brian and I ate lunch in the stadium.

Can the italicized part stand by itself in a sentence? No. That's because it does not make complete sense on its own. These kind of clauses are called dependent (or also subordinate) clauses.

Transitive and Intransitive Verbs There are two groups of action verbs: transitive and intransitive. A verb is transitive when the action it expresses is directed towards a person or thing named in the sentence. For example:

The bride cut the cake.

PARENT RIGHTS AND RESPONSIBILITIES

Your involvement as a parent in a child's education takes many forms. From helping children with homework to attending school board meetings, your participation is important. One significant avenue for your involvement is through shared decision making, since this addresses the most basic elements of a child's school experience. As a parent, you should contribute to making decisions on issues affecting your child's education, health, and safety.

Parents have the *right* to

- Have a clear understanding of the processes to gain access to the appropriate school officials
- Participate in decisions that are made
- Appeal matters pertaining to your children

Parents have the *responsibility* to

- Know, help, and interact with your child's teachers and school administrators
- Communicate with and participate in the selection/election of school officials (e.g., school board members, superintendents, school councils)

—The National PTA®

The action of the verb *cut* is directed toward *cake*. So the verb is transitive. Now read this sentence and pay attention to the verb:

This morning I overslept.

Nothing in the sentence receives the action, so this verb is intransitive.

Just to muddy the waters a little, as English is prone to do, you should know that the same verb may be transitive in one sentence and intransitive in another.

John speaks French. (transitive—the action applies to French)
John speaks fluently. (intransitive)
John speaks his words slowly. (transitive—do you see why?)

When you see verbs in a dictionary, they are listed as *v.t.* for transitive and *v.i.* for intransitive.

Demonstrative Adjectives Adjectives (you know—the words that describe or tell something special about nouns) that tell *which one* in a sentence are called demonstrative adjectives. They point out a specific person, place, or thing. For example:

Do you think this table by the window has better light than that table by the door?
These red grapes taste better than those green grapes.

Notice: *this* and *that* point out a single person, place, or thing while *these* and *those* point out more than one person, place, or thing.

Indefinite and Interrogative Pronouns Pronouns take the place of nouns. And the nouns that they replace are called their antecedents. Well, there's a type of pronoun that doesn't have an antecedent—it's an indefinite pronoun. Words like *somebody*, *anyone*, and *everything* don't refer to a specific person, place, or thing.

Everybody is waiting for the movie to start.
Does anyone want to go get popcorn?
Something is wrong with the projector.

Then there are interrogative pronouns (*which, who, whom, whose,* and *what*) that are used in questions. Interrogative pronouns do not refer to a specific person, place, or thing either. (If you know the antecedent, why would you need to ask the question, right?)

Who is running for office?
Whom do you believe? (Are you confused about *who* or *whom*? Make a statement out of the question to check.You do believe *whom* is fine; so *whom*, not *who,* is correct here.)
Whose vote will decide? (Be sure not to confuse *whose* with *who's*—the contraction of the words *who is*.)

Direct Objects An action verb is often followed by a word that tells who or what receives the action.These words are called direct objects. See if you can find the direct objects here:

Cheryl played the piano loudly.
The music annoyed Mr. Roberts.

Did you pick out *piano* in the first sentence? That's the word that receives the action of the verb *play*. How about the next one? Did you pick *Mr. Roberts?* He is the one whom the music annoyed. (A transitive verb is one that has a direct object.)

Prepositional Phrases You might remember that prepositions are words that show relationships between other words; they are always followed by some noun or pronoun. *Over, under, around,* and *through* are all prepositions. The noun or pronoun that follows a preposition is called the object of the preposition.

The baby woke up several times during the night.

In this case, *night* is the object of the preposition because it follows the preposition *during*. When you put together the

WHO'S SORRY NOW?

My husband and I make mistakes sometimes, but we always apologize to our children and let them know that we're sorry. It's also part of being a good role model, acknowledging our errors. It allows them to understand that people are not always right and it's good to apologize.

COMMON PREPOSITIONS

about
above
across
after
around
at
before
behind
below
by
during
for
from
inside
into
of
on
over
through
under
with
without

preposition, its object, and all the words in between (it can be just one or many words), you have a prepositional phrase. (Remember, too, that phrases are groups of words that can't stand alone because they don't have a subject and verb.) Check these out:

near the earth (prepositional phrase)
Sirius is the brightest star near the earth. (sentence)

Conjunctions Ever wonder what our language would be like without conjunctions? (No? Well, read on anyway.) Here's a sample:

Jeff went to the mall. Kate went to the mall. He bought three CDs. She bought only two cassettes.

Pretty boring stuff, right? Well, by using conjunctions—that is, words that connect other words together—we can make it a little more interesting:

Jeff and Kate went to the mall. He bought three CDs whereas she bought only two cassettes.

By connecting ideas together using conjunctions like *and, but, or, because,* and *since,* we can write things that are more interesting to read.

Interjections An interjection is a word or words that show feeling. If the interjection stands alone, it is followed by an exclamation point. If it begins a sentence, it is set off by a comma. For example:

Oh, no! I can't believe I missed the train!
Well, I did oversleep again this morning.

Core Area 2: Usage

Kids in middle school continue to refine and fine-tune their written and spoken language skills. Learning and applying knowledge of the following issues help kids to write in a way that is more interesting to the reader and more personal to themselves as authors.

SO MANY KIDS!

According to *Newsweek* magazine ("Standing Room Only," September 16, 1996), administrators and teachers are swamped trying to take care of a record 51.7 million elementary- and secondary-school students. These numbers top even the peak baby-boom years. The surging birth rates and immigration numbers are giving districts more students to cope with. Many voters are defeating school-construction bond issues, so schools are teaching students in trailers, busing some kids to less crowded districts, and converting any available space into classrooms. In the West and Southeast United States, it's a problem finding enough teachers for the kids.

Avoid Sentence Fragments and Run-Ons If a group of words does not express a complete thought, it is called a fragment. Here are some examples:

popcorn and drinks
talking in his sleep
after we left the game

These groups of words can become sentences only when other words are added to make the thoughts complete:

I sell popcorn and drinks at the theater.
Randy is talking in his sleep again.
We relaxed only after we left the game.

If a sentence contains more than one complete thought and doesn't contain the right punctuation, it is called a run-on sentence.

Where are Gadget and Gizmo those cats won't come when I call them.
Last summer we went to California, this summer we plan to go to Maine.

Run-ons can be made into two separate sentences or into a compound sentence using punctuation and a conjunction like *and* or *but*.

Where are Gadget and Gizmo? Those cats won't come when I call them.
Last summer we went to California, but this summer we plan to go to Maine.

Use Pronouns with Correct Antecedents A pronoun must always agree with its antecedent—the word it replaces—in number and gender. For single antecedents, *he, his,* and *him* are used if the antecedent is masculine and *she, her,* and *hers* are used if the antecedent is feminine. *It* and *its* are used if the antecedent is neither masculine or feminine. Look at these sentences:

Alison made her presentation yesterday.

POCKET PAL

Ask at your bookstore for one of those great little, pocket-sized speller's books. American Heritage's is called *Word Book II.* The whole family will be glad you got one.

FASTEST-GROWING DISTRICTS

The U.S. Department of Education, National Center of Education Statistics, lists the fastest-growing enrollments for the nation's schools:

District	Increase	% Change
LA Unified (CA)	91,223	16.6%
NYC (NY)	87,163	9.5
Dade County (FL)	86,407	38.9
Broward Co. (FL)	64,118	51.0
Clark County (NV)	55,647	62.1
Palm Beach Co. (FL)	51,327	72.5
Gwinnett Co. (GA)	38,263	100.1
Orange Co. (FL)	34,893	44.3
Guilford Co. (NC)	30,214	124.7
Fresno Unified (CA)	27,127	55.1

Herb wants to take his own car to the show.
I chose a gift and put it on the counter.

Sometimes, though, we are dealing with more than one person, place, or thing. Two or more antecedents joined by *and* should be referred to by a plural pronoun.

Diana and Charles were giggling because they knew a secret.
The boys made up their own minds.

Distinguish between Adjectives and Adverbs Here's a quick reminder about these two parts of speech: Adjectives describe nouns, but adverbs describe verbs. Depending on how and where they appear in a sentence, many words can be either an adjective or an adverb.

fast car (adjective) drives fast (adverb)
loud horn (adjective) beeps loudly (adverb)

Notice that adverbs are often formed by adding *-ly* to an adjective.

The words *good* and *well* are often confused. *Good* cannot be an adverb. You should use it before a noun or after a linking verb. Don't use it to mean healthy.

Maya Angelou is a good writer. Her poems are good.

Well is the adverb that means "in a good way."

Maya Angelou writes well. (never *good*)

When the word *well* is used as an adjective, it is a different word (that sounds and is spelled the same way) and it means "healthy."

The hamburgers were not cooked very well. Todd ate one and is not well now.

Place Prepositional Phrases Correctly Here's one that's fun. What's funny about the following sentence? Why?

PLUG-IN WRITING

Many newer reading and writing software programs give tools, but children have to figure out how to use them. Children are naturally active learners, and this is a plus when it comes to writing. Kids feel liberated at the computer. When they write a story by hand, much of their time and energy are spent on perfecting penmanship. Computers free them to concentrate more on the actual writing, according to Douglas H. Clements, a professor at the State University of New York at Buffalo, because pecking away at the keyboard can be less stressful than holding a pencil. The computer also allows kids to revise easily; they're less afraid to make mistakes and more likely to take some creative risks. —from *Newsweek's Computers & the Family* newsmagazine (Fall/Winter 1996)

Brad figured out how to get the stuck car out of the mud by using his head.

Did you picture Brad putting his head in the mud and lifting the car out? What's going on here? It has to do with where the prepositional phrase *by using his head* is in the sentence. Prepositional phrases need to be near the words they modify.

By using his head, Brad figured out a way to get the stuck car out of the mud.

Now the sentence makes clearer sense because the phrase *by using his head* is near *Brad figured*, the words it describes.

Continue Mastery of Problem Word Usage English is full of exceptions to the rule, as you know. The usage of some words is hard for children and adults alike to do correctly every time. In grades five and six, attention is given to pairs of words that are often confused. Here are several examples.

Will you bring your camera with you?
Yes, I will take it with me.

Bring means to come carrying something. *Take* means to go carrying something. Think of *bring* as related to *come* and *take* as related to *go.*

Please teach me how to bowl.
You must learn how to knock the pins down with the ball.

You can see now that *teach* means to give instruction and *learn* means to receive instruction.

Scott, can you reach the jar on the top shelf?
Yes, you may invite Alex for supper.

May means to be allowed and *can* means to be able to. This pair has been the focus of many a discussion, hasn't it?

NET NECESSITIES

I think parents need to set limits, particularly with tools like the Internet. Children are naturally curious. We've sat down with our daughter and talked about things we've read about regarding the Internet and how she needs to be careful. I've told her to let her mom know who she's writing to. Parents have to let go of their children a little bit so they can learn, but children need to know they can't surf certain areas. I also won't leave her totally alone. I'll go in periodically and check up on her and see what she's doing. I also set up time limits with her too. "First you have to do your homework, then you have 20 minutes for going on the Internet."

Core Area 3: Mechanics

Fancier bridges require fancier nails. As the sentences that kids write become more complex, so do the details needed to support them. In these grades, kids focus on some new and advanced uses of punctuation that add meaning to their writing assignments.

Apply Knowledge of Capitalization Rules As kids begin to use a greater variety of written offerings, they need to learn how to present their compositions correctly. During these middle-school years, kids expand their knowledge of capitalization rules to include:

- Proper adjectives
  We ate dinner at an Italian restaurant.
  The American Team won three gold medals.

- First word of main topic and subtopic in outlines
  I. Types of libraries
  A. Large public library
  B. Bookmobile

Use Commas Correctly Commas tell readers where to pause. Many kids tend to sprinkle commas whenever and wherever. Here are some of the legitimate places they belong as far as middle schools are concerned:

- With appositives (words that follow a noun and identify it in some way)
  Our summer party, a barbecue, was a great success.

- To set off interrupters (a group of words that expresses a feeling)
  Oh, we forgot the theater tickets.

- With nonrestrictive phrases and clauses (a group of words that is not necessary to the main idea in the sentence)

  I am very proud of my son, whose athletic talent impresses everyone.

THE PARENTING SPECTRUM

After a great deal of systematic study, we now know that there are three fundamental dimensions of parenting that differentiate good parents from bad ones, and accordingly, that differentiate the home environments of children who are successful in school from those who are not: acceptance versus rejection, firmness versus leniency, and autonomy versus control. Psychologists conceive of each of the three dimension (acceptance, firmness, and autonomy) as a continuum along which parents vary (e.g., from extremely accepting to extremely rejecting, or from very firm to very lenient). Most parents fall somewhere between the two extremes of each range. —from *Beyond the Classroom* by Laurence Steinberg, Ph.D. (Simon & Schuster, 1996)

Use Colons Correctly Fifth and sixth graders begin their use of the colon in a very specific place: after the greeting in a business letter.

Dear Mr. Thomas:

Kids learn to differentiate between this more formal type of writing and the casual letter, in which they use a comma after the greeting.

Use Semicolon in Compound Sentences A semicolon looks like what it is part period and part comma. It says to the reader, stop here a little longer than you stop for a comma but not so long as you stop for a period.

Semicolons can be used in place of the comma and conjunction in compound sentences. (Remember them? They have two or more independent clauses and are joined by a comma and a conjunction.)

I washed the dishes and swept the kitchen, and then I went to the grocery store. (compound sentence with comma and conjunction)
I washed the dishes and swept the kitchen; then I went to the grocery store. (compound sentence with a semicolon)

Hyphenate Correctly As you know, some compound words are hyphenated (such as *soft-spoken*); some are written as one word (such as *airport*); and some are written as two words (such as *real estate*). As your child's language grows, new compound words enter the vocabulary, and she needs to know what their corrects forms are. Dictionaries are a big help since they list each word and whether it is hyphenated or not. Here are some general rules that middle schoolers learn:

- Use a hyphen to divide a word at the end of the line. A word must be divided between syllables.

  He spoke politely, but it was obvious that he didn't re-cognize me. (incorrect)
  He spoke politely, but it was obvious that he didn't recog-nize me. (correct)

COACHING EVERY STEP

A huge thing Score@Kaplan offers is our environment. It's not just our unique learning software system and the rewards of Score cards and basket shooting—it's the coaches too. We're the most important part of Score. Fifty percent is academic and the rest is building kids' confidence and helping them learn from their mistakes and keep trying. We're there to help them every step along the way. Parents, too, can provide a positive "coaching" environment for their children and turn their home into a dynamic place for learning.

AMERICA READS!

We must do more to help all our children read. Forty percent of our eight year olds cannot read on their own. That's why we have just launched the America Reads initiative—to build a citizen army of one million volunteer tutors to make sure every child can read independently by the end of the 3rd grade. We will use thousands of AmeriCorps volunteers to mobilize this citizen army. We want at least 100,000 college students to help. And tonight, I am pleased that 60 college presidents have answered my call, pledging that thousands of their work study students will serve for one year as reading tutors.
—from the 1997 State of the Union Address, President Clinton

- Use a hyphen with some prefixes and suffixes
  Sam was the all-American quarterback last year.
  The new catalogs will be released in mid-September.

Core Area 4: Spelling

With the advent of word processing programs with spell checkers, your 5th or 6th grader may try to convince you that these skills are less important than in the olden days. However, many middle schoolers routinely still have weekly spelling tests, and having marks deducted in written assignments for misspellings is to be expected. The emphasis on spelling is apt to vary from teacher to teacher, so you should check out your child's particular situation. Here are some global strategies that your middle schooler may be asked to employ.

Use Word Families to Increase Spelling Ability If your child can spell the word *urge,* for example, then he has a good chance of spelling *urgent* and *urgency* correctly. In other words, he can use what he already knows about words to help him with the ones he is just learning. If your child asks you how to spell a word that is new to him, help him determine if he already knows another word that is spelled like it, and use that knowledge as a spelling aid. Identifying a word that is like it can help locate it in the dictionary, too.

Identify and Generate Specialty Word Lists As kids begin to read and write in specific content areas, they come across new words that can be grouped by category. For example, a social studies lesson in careers might introduce the words *architect, engineer, dietician, pharmacist,* and *programmer.* Learning these words may require your child to recall many of the spelling rules he has learned during elementary school. Words like these theme-related ones can be the focus of some pretty interesting conversations for the two of you. Try it!

Develop a Study Plan for Frequently Misspelled Words Spelling demons might have been the name for these nasties when you were in school; words like *though, absence, friend, guess, wear, where,* and *yield*. Everyone seems to have a few words that are just hard for them to remember. The basic way to approach learning a word is to pronounce it, study it (read the letters to yourself and out loud several times), and then write it. (The more you write it, the more your hand has the chance to remember the feel of the letters in order.) The point to make with your child is that with a little extra attention (written and oral), even his personal spelling demons can be mastered. Some kids might enjoy the challenge of trying to use the words that are difficult for them as much as possible—in other words, on purpose—in order to get in the extra spelling practice.

Core Area 5: Composition

Fifth and sixth graders are really making their entry into the world at large, and so their need to communicate in writing in real ways increases. They begin to see writing as a legitimate tool for achieving some purpose they have in mind, not just a classroom activity assigned by their teacher.

Follow the Steps of the Writing Process This acknowledged series of five steps that help writers (new and old!) to produce quality writing are now commonly used throughout elementary and middle school classrooms.

- *Prewriting* means getting ready to write by thinking about what you want or need to do, deciding on a topic, or finding resources for an assigned topic and making some notes.
- *Writing* a first draft means starting to get information down on paper without too much attention to spelling or punctuation for the moment. The focus is on getting the ideas in logical order and providing supporting details.
- *Revising* means rereading what you wrote and letting others read it and make comments about the content of it and then making the changes in order to improve the composition, style, clarity, etc.
- *Proofreading* means doing a review of your work specifically to check the spelling, grammar, and punctuation.
- *Publishing* means making a final copy of a composition and sharing it with others.

CRITICAL VIEWING SKILLS

Set rules for TV viewing and adhere to those rules. Set a weekly limit for the amount of time children are permitted to watch television. At the start of each week, help your children select the programs or videotapes they want to watch. When the selected program is over, turn the television off and get involved in another activity.

Turn what you see on television into positive and educational family discussions and activities. Television can inspire creativity and educate and inform children and youth. When a topic on television sparks your child's interest, go to the library or museum and explore the subject further.

—The National PTA®

Prepare an Outline and Write a Paragraph Starting in grades five and six, kids are asked to prepare and present assignments that require the research and development of a somewhat lengthy composition. How should they approach the organization of all the information they collect into a logical report? By writing an outline first, of course! Forget how? Here's a quick refresher:

- The outline consists of main headings with subheadings under them.
- You can use phrases and words instead of complete sentences.
- Use the format below to set up your outline.
- Begin each heading with a capital letter.

Things That Bug Me
I. At home
  A. Hearing "I told you so"
  B. Arguing about TV
  C. Going to bed early
II. At school
  A. Boring assemblies
  B. Homework
    1. Assignments on Friday
    2. Making oral reports

As with many of the composition-related skills, the impact of computers and word processing is felt here. Whether or not your child follows the above guidelines to the letter is less important than his awareness of a process that can help him organize information in an effective way on or off a computer.

Write Good Introductions and Conclusions Sometimes when kids (or all of us for that matter!) write, they forget that someone is meant to read the words, and so they may pay little or no attention to how interesting it is. For example, let's start with this statement:

I would like to write about lawn mowing.

Doesn't really make you want to keep reading, does it? How about these variations for opening statements?

CONTENT DECISIONS

Just as parents are best suited to selecting reading materials for their own children, they can exercise similar judgment as regards educational computer content. You do not need to understand bookbinding and typesetting to select books for your child. Neither is technical knowledge required to select interactive programs. Remember: Focus on the content, not the technology. If you're the kind of parent who buys beautiful picture books and illustrated guides to wholesome educational activities for your child, there is some beautiful interactive content available for use on your computer. On the other hand, if you are the kind of parent who tolerates your child reading comic books, watching lots of TV, and playing mindless, repetitive games, there is an astonishing variety of computer-based material for you to choose from.

> Most people think of lawn mowing as an arduous chore to be done only under the threat of bodily injury.
> What is there about lawn mowing that compels otherwise lazy individuals to tackle this weekly chore?
> Lawn mowing can be fun if you have the right lawn, the right tools, and the right attitude.

Don't these three opening sentences motivate you to keep reading a little bit more? Grabbing a reader's attention and drawing him into the passage should be a goal for your young writer.

A good closing is as important as a good introduction. In the final several sentences of a composition, your child needs to make a statement that leaves the reader thinking about something or that relates to his everyday life. The writer can also recap the ideas presented in the composition as part of his conclusion. The point is to wrap things up in an interesting way for the reader.

Compare and Contrast an Issue in Writing These assignments will involve a topic in which your child shows how some things are similar (comparison) and how they are different (contrast).

> As sisters, Sarah and Jane are similar in many ways. Both are tall, thin, and have long blonde hair. Both like to read a lot. On the other hand, Sarah is quite different from Jane. She excels at math, sings in the choir, and has many friends. Jane, on the other hand, dropped out of math in the 8th grade, can't carry a tune in a bucket, and is on the shy side.

Use Persuasive Language Effectively One of the new kinds of writing assignments your 5th or 6th grader will have is to write in a persuasive fashion. Strong, exact words that appeal to the senses are usually more persuasive than others. When your child really thinks about what words make a greater impact on the reader, her writing will improve greatly. Read these two sentences and see which has the greater impact.

WHAT DID YOU DO TODAY?

Parents always have to ask their children what they did in school, or their children just won't talk. They also just forget everything they did in school without being asked—they have too much on their minds. If you don't talk it over with them, then forget it!

WELL DONE

Make sure to reward kids for being good. Good kids often receive no attention from their parents. If a child is acting up and you give her attention, that's a reward for negative behavior. Telling kids you think they're great and you're proud of them is so important. It's important to be recognized, and to take time out to do that.

Join the PTA. It will be good for you as a parent.

Join the PTA to learn about what is going on in your child's classroom and how you can help your child.

YOU'RE INTERESTED

At Score@Kaplan, we tell our children that we're really interested in what they're studying in school, and set up an expectation that what's going on in school WILL be talked about. Parents can set up that same situation at home. Make it clear that if your child needs any help, she can always come to you—you will be involved in her learning process. The more you can reinforce and reiterate that, like scheduling a check-in each day, the better it will be.

Don't fall back on the attitude that your child's school will do everything, so you can count on them to get the job done. You can't know what's going on at school and not get involved in your child's learning at home—the two must go hand in hand. Get your child intrinsically motivated to communicate with you about school. Make talking about school part of your home culture.

Write a Business Letter with Correct Form Fifth and sixth graders may find that they have reason to correspond with people they don't know in order to get information, and so they learn about business letters. They learn about the correct formats for the heading, the inside address, the greeting, the body text, the closing, and the signature. They may also learn about addressing the envelope with a return address.

Expand Creative Writing Techniques Besides communicating to others through writing, 5th and 6th graders are becoming acutely aware of the power of writing to express themselves. At the same time, in most classrooms they are reading a wide variety of literary genres: plays, biographies, speeches, essays, and many kinds of poetry. Encourage your middle schooler to experiment with all sorts of creative writing—it's like trying on a variety of clothes to see which fits best and is most suitable to the occasion.

Core Area 6: Vocabulary

Kids learn vocabulary informally on a daily basis—words that define what they are into (*surfin' the Net*) and words that express their reactions and understanding of things (*cool*). Here are some strategies for vocabulary learning of a slightly more formal nature.

Use Context Clues This skill involves getting the meaning of a word you don't know from the other words you do know in the sentence. Here's an example:

The self-stick paper *adhered* firmly to the shelf.

Say your child doesn't know *adhered*, but she does know *stick* and *firmly*, so she figures out that adhered means *stuck*. She just used context clues to help determine the meaning of a word. Good for her!

Expand Use of Base and Root Words Base and root words are the core of a word to which beginning (prefixes) and ending (suffixes) are added. Like:

wait, await, waited, waiter
direct, direction, redirect

These beginnings and endings may change the meaning of the word slightly but you can usually get pretty close to the meaning of a word using roots and base words.

Use Clipped and Blended Words Sometimes new words enter our vocabulary because words that we use frequently seem to take too long, and we are looking for shortcuts. Fifth and sixth graders learn about:

- Clipped words like *flu,* for *influenza, plane* for *airplane, phone* for *telephone, hippo* for *hippopotamus*—which are shortened versions of the original word
- Blended words, called portmanteau words—*telethon* from *television* and *marathon*; *brunch* from *breakfast* and *lunch*; *smog* from *smoke* and *fog*; and *moped* from *motor* and *pedal*—which are two words made into one

Expand Understanding of Idiomatic Expressions Idioms are so much a part of our everyday speech that we forget that they too are part of learning language. An idiom is an expression that has a special meaning that is different (sometimes *very* different) from the usual meaning of the words in the idiom. You'll find them throughout this book ("giving your gut response," "shooting from the hip," "copycat behavior"). You might be surprised at the number of idioms used in everyday conversation. Your 5th or 6th grader should be able to recognize idioms like these:

- How come the game was canceled?
- I waited on pins and needles to hear from the doctor.
- Jim turned up at 3 o'clock.
- Sarah turned down my offer.

Apply Connotation and Denotation to Word Meanings The feelings and associations that a word has in

TRICKY ENGLISH

Of TOUGH and BOUGH and COUGH
and DOUGH.
Others may stumble, but not you,
On HICCOUGH, THOROUGH, LAUGH
and THROUGH.
Well done! And now you wish, perhaps,
To learn of less familiar traps.

Beware of HEARD, a dreadful word
That looks like BEARD and sounds
like BIRD.
And DEAD—it's said like BED, not BEAD.
For goodness sake, don't call it DEED!
Watch out for MEAT and GREAT
and THREAT.
They rhyme with SUITE and STRAIGHT
and DEBT.

A MOTH is not a MOTH in MOTHER,
Nor BOTH in BOTHER, BROTH in
BROTHER,
And HERE is not a match for THERE,
Nor DEAR and FEAR for PEAR and BEAR.
And then there's DOSE and ROSE
and LOSE—
Just look them up—and GOOSE
and CHOOSE.
And CORK and WORK and CARD
and WARD.
And FONT and FRONT and WORD
and SWORD.
And DO and GO, then THWART and CART.
Come, come, I've hardly made a start.

A dreadful language? Man alive,
I'd mastered it when I was five!

—Anonymous

STUDENT REFERENCE LIBRARY

Many students want to dig deeper and learn more for their creative writing and school research papers. For younger students, there's a need for a tool that parents and children can use together to explore any subject. Mindscape's *Student Reference Library* combines a lot of writing and research resources for students, plus other multimedia help, into one CD-ROM: an encyclopedia, dictionary, thesaurus, manual of style, U.S. history guide, famous quotes, atlas, photos, maps, videos, animations, audio, and a Lycos search feature (hooking up with your Web browser) on the World Wide Web. Contact Mindscape at (800) 234–3088.

addition to its dictionary meaning (its denotation) are called its connotations. The words *demand* and *request*, for example, both mean to ask for. However, think about what it feels to have someone make a demand as opposed to a request, and you will see the difference the connotations of a word can have. Words may have a negative or a positive connotation, a friendly or unfriendly connotation, a calming or frightening connotation, etc.

Generate and Apply Specialized Vocabulary A typical day with a 10- to 12-year old brings many opportunities for vocabulary development. Look around as you go through your day: current events, a trip to the mall, soccer games, going to the dentist, what's going on at your office. All these things can spark the introduction of new words for conversing with your children.

Core Area 7: Reference and Study Strategies

During the middle school years, the quantity of work assigned begins to make planning how to get it done a necessity. Knowing where to look and how to look in order to use time effectively are key strategies to learn for living in this Information Age.

Use the Dictionary and Thesaurus Effectively Kids who are writing as much as should be expected in these grades need to see these reference books as tools to write well, not crutches that only poor writers turn to. Help your child use them comfortably to search for

- What particular word to choose
- What word to use to avoid repetitiveness
- How to say a certain word
- How to hyphenate it
- How to spell a plural form

Fill out Forms and Applications It may seem to be too soon for your 5th or 6th grader to be filling out forms and such. But by the age of ten or so, kids encounter opportunities to request information (for a certain product or catalog), to sign up for a club or library card, or the like.

Most kids (and many adults) tend to rush through and fill out the blanks without attentive reading. A helpful hint you can give your child is to read through the entire form first and then go back and fill things in.

Ask for Information in Writing, by Phone, or in Person
Somewhat related to the item above and to the business-letter category is the skill of requesting information in an effective manner. What this requires of your kid is the ability to state succinctly what it is that he wants from the person across the counter, on the phone, or reading the letter. Most people who receive requests these days (that is, if you get a live person and not voice mail) appreciate a clear question followed by a thank you.

Seek Information through Card Catalog and Online
More and more information is being made available to us every day, like it or not. Besides traditional sources—books, encyclopedias, almanacs, readers' guides to periodicals—we have access to new, very dynamic sources on CD-ROMs and online by computer.

In the same way that you learned to poke through the card catalog by subject before going into the book stacks, your kids will be learning to search through some electronic source by keyword (that's like the main category or subject being looked up). They may then go into the book stacks or periodical room to retrieve what they need, or they may be able to view it right online from some library file.

Skim and Scan for Information Not everything kids read is meant to be read carefully and studied deeply. Sometimes they don't need to decode every word, and sometimes there just isn't time to. In either case, your kids will be learning a couple ways to locate information quickly. They can skim a passage to get an overview of it and then scan it to get specific facts. Skimming includes:

- Reading the title and any headings
- Reading all of the first and last paragraphs
- Looking at any illustrations

MONITOR THE MESSAGE

In our Score@Kaplan centers, we have great learning software systems specifically designed to raise a student's grade level abilities in specific subject areas. Of course, not every parent has access to a Score center, but there are tons of great educational games and materials that you can load onto a home computer. Many of these can play the same way video games play, and they are so much more productive than *Mortal Kombat* or programs your child might be playing otherwise.

These actions help you get the general idea. Scanning includes:

- Looking for key words (things that have to do with the topic you are looking for)
- Paying attention to information that is called out by being in boldface, in numerals, with capital letters, etc.

At a fast food restaurant, when you look up at the big menu full of words and numbers and pictures, to order quickly, you are skimming and scanning (whether you realize it or not).

Take Notes from Reading and Lectures Note taking is basically a shortcut for writing down information you want to remember. There are lots of opportunities in our lives to do this casually—especially when it comes to answering the telephone (which no one ever does well enough—especially a 5th or 6th grader!). In a more formal setting like the classroom, kids are expected to take notes when they are studying a subject, like history, or are preparing to do some research and then write a report. Taking notes means writing key words and phrases, not entire sentences (but enough for the writer to remember the point when she goes back to read her own notes). Here is the start of some notes taken in health class:

Four dimensions of wellness
- Physical
  bones and muscles
  circulation and respiration
- Social
  importance of friendship
- Emotional
  avoiding stress
- Intellectual
  alertness

Based on these notes, your youngster would be able to write a topic sentence for a composition about wellness. She would also have some keywords to use for research purposes to complete her composition.

NEVER TOO OLD

We always read stories before bed. We still read to our fifth grader. He likes being read to. We just lie on the bed together and read, and my daughter likes it too. They each get one or two stories. With my son we read a novel, and we do a chapter a night.

GOING, GOING, GONE

According to the International Reading Association, we retain:

- 10 percent of what we read
- 30 percent of what we hear
- 50 percent of what we see and hear

Use Visual Materials for Information A picture is worth a thousand words, as the old saying goes. This is particularly true when it comes to learning things in school. Enhancing text information with visuals of many types offers kids of all abilities and learning styles another way to get at what they are supposed to learn. By 5th and 6th grade, kids should be used to seeing a wide variety of visual material, including:

- Cartoons
- Charts and graphs
- Drawings and paintings
- Detailed illustrations
- Diagrams/floor plans
- Timelines
- Maps

Core Area 8: Thinking Skills and Strategies

Everything we do involves thought, of course. The key to effective thinking is not *what* you are thinking about, but *how* you are thinking about it. That critical thinking leads to solutions, effective study, and answers.

Practice Critical Thinking Skills Basically critical thinking skills involve the processes you and your child go through whenever you read or hear something and want to make a thoughtful response. It's sort of the opposite of giving your gut response or shooting from the hip. With regard to school subjects, it is very much a part of developing reading and writing skills. Your child is likely to be asked to practice critical thinking skills such as:

- Making inferences
- Making judgments
- Drawing conclusions
- Predicting outcomes
- Making analogies
- Detecting propaganda
- Identifying cause and effect
- Solving problems

GOOD GOALS

We go to a Cal alumni camp, and all of the counselors are college students. They're great role models for my children. I take my son through the college campus where I went to school, I take him on the double-decker bus, show him the bowling alley, and all those fun things. It's motivating for him. He's also taking music lessons because he wants to be a camp counselor, and he knows that they have to have a music background and be a university student. My husband and I helped set some goals with our son that he's excited about.

Core Area 9: Listening, Speaking, and Viewing Skills and Strategies

We've outlined specific strategies for teaching and learning reading and writing skills, and there is also a specific approach to the other key elements of communication. The skills of listening, speaking, and viewing, though not based on the written word, can be practiced and acquired through careful planning and evaluation.

PERFECTLY POSITIVE PARENTING

Make education fun and exciting, not "Oh, do I really have to study those words again?" Make your child excited about her teacher at school. You can be negative about the teacher, but you have to curb it in front of your child. When you're negative, your child becomes negative. But be open to hearing your child's complaints and negativity because she may have a valid problem that needs to be addressed. When your child shares what she is learning in school, tell her how exciting that is and how proud you are about what she is doing.

Apply Comprehension Strategies to Listening This ability can be a challenging one for kids of any age since it generally means sitting still and concentrating on what's being said. Auditory learners (kids who understand and remember best what they hear) may seem to have the advantage here, but your child can train himself to learn from listening by listening with a purpose—that is, he should listen for the

- Topic
- Main idea
- Important details

If your child learns to look at any speaker and to think of and ask questions, he will increase his listening comprehension. Some specific listening goals in these grades are:

- Listen to tell fact from opinion
- Listen to take notes
- Listen for bias, motive, point of view
- Listen for persuasive words

Apply Composition Strategies to Speaking Since he has been speaking for about a decade now, it may be hard to convince your 5th or 6th grader that he needs to work on his skills in this area. Although attention is given to children's everyday conversation, of course, this skill focuses on a somewhat untapped part of oral communication—more formal, public speaking. And here, the same strategies that your youngster is learning to apply to his written work will help him to plan, organize, and deliver an effective oral presentation. Some specific speaking goals might be:

- Participate in a debate
- Recite a memorized passage
- Do a dramatic reading
- Conduct an interview
- Present character analysis orally

Apply Comprehension Strategies to Viewing Activities It's hard to pick up a newspaper or magazine without seeing a reference to couch potatoes or to an act of copycat violence from a TV show or movie. We all know what an impact TV has on our lives. It doesn't have to be a completely passive influence on your child, though. More and more schools are beginning to include skill training for kids in evaluating what they watch on TV.

Helping youngsters realize that they can and need to watch different shows for different purposes is the first point to make—*how* they watch and listen to the news is different from the attention they pay to cartoons (or it should be, anyway!). At the pace we keep these days, it is likely that your child is seeing much more information than he is reading, so being able to tune in to and make sense of information is a valuable skill. Some specific viewing goals to keep in mind are:

- Describe how persuasion appears on television
- Watch and listen to media for evidence of the use of bias
- Do an oral summary of a media presentation
- Compare and contrast a written account and video presentation of a story

MEDIA INFLUENCES

Monitor the media influences on your children that are within your control. Forbid certain programming if necessary or "talk back" to your radio and television when media depicts lack of respect for life and property and use of foul language. Do not give your children the impression that you approve of or tolerate behavior that is inconsistent with your own family values and beliefs.
—The National PTA®

Core Area 10: Literature and Reading

In these grades, kids move into longer pieces of prose and begin to look more closely at their reading and try to figure out what authors were up to when they were writing. They examine literal and figurative language and appreciate and begin to harness the power of words. They are beginning to feel the connection between reading and writing.

Read and Respond to a Variety of Types of Literature Kids in these grades are ready to devour just about any kind of reading, including biographies, essays, plays, poems, mysteries, research reports, and personal narratives. Their response can come through book reports, journal entries, and discussion groups.

Identify Theme in a Written Passage What used to be called the *main idea* in earlier grades grows up a little to become the *theme*. Kids should be able to read a piece of literature and tell in general terms what point the author is presenting.

SMALLER IS BETTER

A small group reading experience in school (1:4 ratio) made the big difference for our son when he was learning to read.

Evaluate Author's Purpose and Point of View At this level, kids begin to differentiate between works written in the first person (the "I" point of view) and third person (the "he" or "she" point of view). They can discuss the different impacts each kind of point of view makes, as well as the author's intent in using one or the other.

Analyze Passage for Mood and Tone Here your child learns to identify the emotional tone of a passage; that is, she can identify the feelings that the author hopes the reader will experience.

Analyze Characters Based on Speech or Behavior Characters—whether people, animals, or imaginary beings—are generally the most important part of a story. Being able to focus on what a character says and does and then make judgments about what the character is like is an exercise your 5th and 6th grader should be able to do comfortably.

Differentiate Between Formal and Informal Language Careful, correct use of language, usually in complete sentences, is called formal language. Casual speech, often used with friends or in relaxed settings, is called informal language. Kids at this age can identify the two types and tell the author's reasons for using one or the other.

Extend Understanding of Figurative Language Literal language is the use of words with their ordinary meanings. Figurative language goes beyond the regular meaning in order to create another image in the reader's mind. Some common types your 5th or 6th grader will come across are:

- *Personification*—the use of human qualities to describe something that is not human

  Every time Carol went to the mall, her money cheerfully abandoned her wallet.

- *Simile*—a comparison of two things using the words *like* or *as*

  My science teacher has a voice like a tuba.

- *Metaphor*—a comparison of two things without using *like* or *as*

  The trees on the hillside were a colorful, patchwork quilt on the sunny autumn day.

Recognize use of Writing Techniques As kids read a wider range of literature by a wider variety of authors, they are exposed to a growing number of literary techniques—ways of writing that authors use to make certain points or get certain reactions from their readers. The following is a sampling of techniques encountered in grades five and six.

- *Irony* involves opposites. A situation that contrasts sharply with what is naturally to be expected is ironic.
- *Foreshadowing* involves giving the reader a clue about what is yet to come in the story.
- *Flashback* involves interrupting the current action to return to the past (a technique your kids are very familiar with because of television).

HOOKED ON BOOKS!

Every parent would like to encourage their child to read more. Here are two books that fit the bill: *Hooked on Books!: Activities and Projects That Make Kids Love to Read* by Patricia Tyler Muncy and *Books on the Move: A Read-About It, Go-There Guide to America's Best Family Destinations* by Susan M. Knorr and Margaret Knorr. The first title has over 160 games, projects, and activities to help kids form a good reading habit. The second title helps parents and kids plan a weekend adventure, a quick day trip, or a long family vacation by taking an armchair tour of hundreds of great destinations across the United States (with hundreds of related children's books to read before, during, and after the trip). Contact Free Spirit Publishing at (800) 735-7323 or E-mail them at help4kids@freespirit.com.

My daughter is lucky. When she's at school, she has very high-quality learning time. As a result, we don't have a lot of materials in our home for learning—except life itself!

IN A JAR

Why say *pale* when you can say *etiolated?* Is a cow a "grass-eating animal" or a "graminivorous beast"? *Wondrous Words in a Jar* by Deborah Stein is a plastic jar filled with 365 fortune-cookie slips of colored paper, each with unusual words and definitions. Pull out a new word each day with your child, and you'll liven your speech, build up a distinctive vocabulary, and have a terrific home-learning day-starter. Other "In a Jar" products include *Riddles in a Jar, Curiosity in a Jar, Attitude in a Jar,* and *Inventions in a Jar.* Contact Free Spirit Publishing at (800) 735-7323 or E-mail them at help4kids@freespirit.com.

Share, Review, and Recommend Written Materials
Kids in this age group are very much involved in the personal side of reading; it both stimulates their intellectual curiosity (I can find out stuff I want to know!) and meets their emotional needs (Wow! That kid is going through the same stuff I am!). At the same time, they can be expected to talk and write about their reactions to various reading experiences and to listen to their peers do the same.

What's My Child Studying in Math?

The elementary mathematics curriculum is designed around the essential math concepts and skills that are the foundation of all mathematics. Students in grades five and six learn from many of the same topic areas that they studied in earlier grades.

Nine Core Math Areas The following nine core subject areas form the basis of most schools' elementary mathematics curriculum:

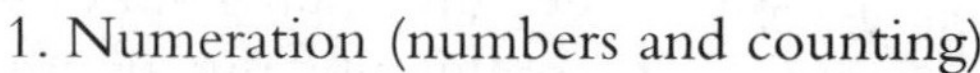

1. Numeration (numbers and counting)
2. Computation (addition, subtraction, multiplication, and division)
3. Money and Time (units of money, money calculations, clocks, and calendars)
4. Geometry and Measurement (two- and three-dimensional shapes, area, volume, and units of measure)
5. Fractions and Decimals
6. Graphing (bar graphs, pie charts)
7. Statistics and Probability
8. Problem-solving (solving word problems, estimation, spatial reasoning, recognizing patterns, experimenting and inventing new strategies, and other analytical skills)
9. Algebra

What's Taught in Grade Five?

Math in grade five could be entitled "More Fractions and Decimals." Students in 5th grade usually learn more about multiplying and dividing fractions and decimals. Your child will find the common denominator of two fractions and

THE BIG PAYOFF

Mom and I had really neat things everyday that we could do together. When I was in middle school, my mom made up a checkbook for me and I did my own checking account. I used to get my own bills in the mail and pay them myself, and that was exciting. Show your child what you as a parent are doing, make it all less mysterious, and give your child a sense of excitement and anticipation. They'll think, Wow, I want to be older and do that all my myself!

will add more complicated fractions. Your 5th grader also will work intensively with decimals. She will add, subtract, and multiply many decimals, and she will begin to learn how to do some simple decimal divisions. Your child also will put these operations into action when she learns about percent, ratio, and proportion. Fifth graders also learn from the nine core areas, but the primary emphasis is on fractions and decimals. Core area work on money and time is not usually emphasized, but keep practicing these skills at home.

A new core area, algebra, is introduced typically in 5th grade. Although many preliminary concepts related to algebra are used in earlier grades, algebra is formally introduced in 5th grade. Many 5th graders start to work with variables and solve equations for the first time. A solid introduction to algebra in grade five will ensure success in math in later grades. Encourage your child to practice these skills regularly at home and share the activities for 5th grade math with her.

The following outline represents the content of the typical 5th grade mathematics curriculum. Since each district designs its program of study to meet the needs of the local community, this summary may not describe your child's mathematics curriculum precisely. These topics are organized according to the nine core areas of the elementary mathematics curriculum. For descriptions of the topics and skills, refer to the next chapter.

Core Area 1: Numeration

- Read and write up to fifteen-digit numbers (trillions)
- Compare and order billions
- Find the common factors and greatest common factor of two numbers
- Find the prime factorization of a number
- Find the common multiples and lowest common multiple of two numbers

Core Area 2: Computation

- Multiply a three-digit number by a three-digit number
- Divide by a three-digit number

Core Area 3: Money and Time

MATH FOR GOOD SPORTS

In *Major League Math*, you can take your child (ages 9–13) out to the ballpark for a 3-D virtual major-league baseball game, complete with rowdy fans and an organist! There are drills and helpful workshops with over 4,000 math questions mixed with baseball trivia that will fascinate most kids. It's a great way to play the game, learn the math, and make good use of your home PC.

For more info on this title, and other fun math titles—*Math Ace/Grand Prix, NFL Math,* and *Real World Math*—contact Sanctuary Woods at (800)943-3664, or visit their Web site at www.ah-ha.com

Core Area 4: Geometry and Measurement

- Identify and measure acute and obtuse angles
- Identify and classify polygons
- Make scale drawings
- Recognize congruent line segments
- Identify space figures and count their vertices, faces, and edges
- Find the surface area of a three-dimensional figure

Core Area 5: Fractions, Decimals, and Percents

- Find the common denominators of fractions
- Add and subtract fractions with unlike denominators
- Multiply fractions
- Write and compare decimals through hundred thousandths
- Add and subtract decimals through hundred thousandths
- Multiply decimals
- Divide decimals by whole numbers
- Learn the meaning of percent
- Find the percent of a number
- Convert percents to decimals and vice versa
- Convert percents to fractions and vice versa
- Estimate percents
- Learn the meaning of ratio
- Identify equivalent ratios
- Learn about and solve proportions

Core Area 6: Graphing

- Read and draw circle graphs
- Read and draw line plots
- Read and draw stem-and-leaf plots

Core Area 7: Statistics and Probability

- Find the median, mode, and range of some numbers
- Take samples
- Find the probabilities of simple events having probability 0 or 1
- Calculate permutations and combinations
- Interpret statistics

MATHEMAGIC

Parents should never just say, "Okay, tonight we're going to practice our math facts!" If you put a bunch of neat math facts materials and games out, then your kids can explore them independently (or play games with friends or parents). Kids have a blast with these things.

Have your child find the least expensive applesauce, pizza mix, or peanut butter on the grocery store shelves—do the little everyday things that make learning math fun and practical.

BE A PROBLEM SOLVER

Parents need to understand the problem-solving process. There are so many different ways for children to solve math problems or other homework exercises. Children have different learning styles, so these processes will vary from child to child. There are at least TEN different ways that children solve problems, and different strategies work for different kids! Sometimes one strategy won't work for your child, and that's okay. Let that strategy go and move on to another one when you're trying to provide some helpful guidance.

KEY MATH YEARS

Many students fall behind in math because they don't grasp or practice the new skills taught in 5th and 6th grades. Nurture your child through these key math years! Practice the skills together with enjoyable workbooks, games, software, manipulatives, and the activities in this book.

Core Area 8: Problem Solving

- Use inductive reasoning
- Solve percent problems
- Solve ratio and proportion problems
- Use problem-solving strategies to solve word problems involving decimals

Core Area 9: Algebra

- Represent a number by a variable and solve equations
- Learn and use order of operations

What's Taught in Grade Six?

In grade five, your child completed his trip through whole numbers up to trillions, and now he is moving on to even greater things. Grade six introduces many new and different topics: integers, exponents, and functions. Having a solid background in 5th and 6th grade math will provide your child a strong foundation for success in later grades.

Your 6th grader will learn why he has been studying those amazing negative numbers—they are an important part of the numbers called integers. In addition, 6th graders typically study exponents, that is, the powers of a number, such as 5^3. Learning about integers and exponents is important because they are used to solve many problems in the real world, and they play important roles in algebra.

By the end of grade six, your child will have been taught all the basics about fractions, decimals, and percents. He will learn how to divide decimals, estimate decimal divisions, and work with percents less than 1%.

In grade six, your child also will learn why he has been working with number patterns, tables of numbers, and other patterns. It turns out that these provide the basis of an understanding of function. A function is just a relationship (or pattern) between numbers. For example, one common function is the doubling function that takes a number such as 4 and doubles it to get 8. Since most curriculums have talked about functions in many ways in the earlier grades without using the term, your child will apply his prior knowledge to make the transition to functions.

The following outline represents the content of the typical 6th grade math curriculum. Since each district designs its program of study to meet the needs of the local community, this summary may not describe your child's mathematics curriculum precisely. The topics are organized here according to the nine core areas of the elementary mathematics curriculum. For descriptions of the topics and skills, refer to the material in the next chapter.

Core Area 1: Numeration
- Identify and write integers
- Compare and order integers
- Read and write numbers with positive exponents
- Read and write squares and square roots

Core Area 3: Money and Time

Core Area 2: Computation
- Add and subtract integers
- Multiply and divide integers

Core Area 4: Geometry and Measurement
- Construct the perpendicular bisector of a line segment
- Identify complementary and supplementary angles
- Construct and bisect angles
- Use area formulas
- Use volume formulas
- Find the surface area of a cylinder and cone
- Learn about and use milliliters and milligrams
- Estimate capacity

Core Area 5: Fractions, Decimals, and Percents
- Divide fractions
- Divide mixed numbers
- Terminating and repeating decimals
- Divide decimals by powers of ten
- Divide decimals
- Round decimal quotients
- Use percents less than 1%
- Find what percent one number is of another
- Use ratios with similar figures

GOALIES

A major part of our Score@Kaplan program is helping students and their parents develop and reach academic goals. And we encourage parents to set academic goals at home with their kids. Parents need to ask children how they're doing with their goals. Many parents have had no experience helping their children reach goals. They can adopt something like our goal program, using visual images of how children are doing as they reach their achievements. We have kids record their progress on paper—skiing down a hill, climbing a mountain, etc. These goals don't have to be only educational; they can be anything in life. There can be a serious or outrageously fun reward at the end of every goal. Every day parents and their kids can evaluate how they're doing.

DISCOVERY QUESTIONS

Ask your child questions about what they're learning. Kids will get that glazed look in their eyes when you start telling them answers or give them long explanations. Show them how something works and explore a problem together. Ask questions that might get them to discover the answer on their own—that's key.

Core Area 6: Graphing
- Read and draw double bar graph
- Graph integers in the coordinate plane
- Draw the graph of a linear equation

Core Area 7: Statistics and Probability
- Use the fundamental counting principle
- Perform simulations

Core Area 8: Problem solving
- Write and use equations to solve word problems
- Solve word problems involving integers

Core Area 9: Algebra
- Learn about functions that follow a rule
- Study linear functions
- Identify and write geometric sequences

What Math Content Should I Review?

In this section, you can find descriptions of each concept and skill in the outlines of 5th and 6th grade mathematics. The concepts and skills for both grades are organized together according to core area. For example, both multiplying by three-digit numbers (a 5th grade skill) and multiplying integers (a 6th grade skill) can be found under the head "Core Area 2: Computation." You can use this section as a reference to review concepts and skills.

TIMING IS EVERYTHING

It's important for parents to find the right times for doing things with their kids. I find that my daughter is too tired later in the evening to do complicated things. The best time for memorizing, we've found out, is before dinner, after dinner, and just before she goes to sleep. Then she gets up a bit early in the morning, and she has it.

Core Area 1: Numeration

Numeration is a word for the system of numbers that we use. This core area is devoted to learning about numbers and comparing and rounding numbers.

Read and write up to 15-digit numbers (trillions) We're talking about really big numbers—numbers that are too big to get a handle on. How can we grasp the distance between the earth and the star Alpha Centauri, which is about 23.5 trillion miles (written 23,500,000,000,000)? Or, try thinking about the value of all the products and services provided in the United States in 1992, a whopping $5,950,700,000,000 (almost $6 trillion)!

Compare and order billions Even when you're working with huge numbers, you still compare them place by place. For example, 60,001,070,000 > 10,115,000,707 because the 6 in the ten billions' place of 60,001,070,000 is greater than the 1 in the ten billions' place of 10,115,000,707. (Recall that > means "greater than.")

Find the common factors and greatest common factor of two numbers A common factor is a factor that factors two numbers. Oops, let's try THAT again. A common factor is a number that is part of the factorization of two numbers. Here's how it works. To find the common factors of 75 and 105, for instance, first find the numbers that you can multiply to make up each of the numbers (75 and 105); those multipliers will be the factors for each number:

$$75 = 5 \times 15$$
$$105 = 7 \times 15$$

Then compare the factors of the two numbers. Since both numbers have a factor of 15, 15 is a common factor of 75 and 105.

The greatest common factor is the greatest number that is a common factor of the two numbers. To find the greatest common factor, just multiply together all the common factors. To find the greatest common factor for the numbers 63 and 84, for example, first get your common factors and then just multiply them:

$$63 = 7 \times 3 \times 3$$
$$84 = 7 \times 3 \times 4$$

Since the common factors are 7 and 3, the greatest common factor is 21, that is, the product of 7×3.

If your child understands the concept of the greatest common factor, using a calculator can help test for factors. Using calculators is one of many strategies that students use to help with numerical operations. Other strategies include using concrete objects, recording with paper and pencil, and using estimation.

Find the prime factorization of a number A prime factorization of a number is the product of prime numbers that equals the number. For example, to find the prime factorization of 308, first write any factorization of 308 (for instance, 2×154). Then factor the numbers in that

FACTOR FACTS

Writing a number as the product of some numbers is called a *factorization* of a number. Examples of some factorizations: $12 = 4 \times 3$, $12 = 6 \times 2$, $12 = 12 \times 1$, and $12 = 2 \times 2 \times 3$. The *factors* are the numbers that when multiplied equal the other number. When we make a factorization, we say we factor a number.

WE'RE IN THIS TOGETHER

Parents have to work one-on-one with their child's teacher in order to help their child learn. It's not Them vs. You, or they do it all and you do nothing. You have to work together with them.

factorization that are not prime until you get $308 = 11 \times 7 \times 2 \times 2$, that is, 308 is the product of the prime numbers 11, 7, and 2 (used twice). To get this prime factorization we must use the factors 2×2 because 4 is not prime.

Find the common multiples and lowest common multiple of a number A multiple is the opposite of a factor. For example, whereas a factor of 24 is a number (such as 6) you multiply by another number to get 24, a multiple of 24 is the number obtained by multiplying 24 by another number. Therefore 48 (2×24) is a multiple of 24; so is 72.

A common multiple is a multiple that two numbers both have. For example, 36 is a common multiple of 6 and 9 because $36 = 6 \times 6$ and $36 = 9 \times 4$.

The least common multiple is the lowest number that is the common multiple of two numbers. In the case of 6 and 9, the least common multiple is 18 (3×6 and 2×9).

Identify and write integers The integers are the numbers that include positive numbers and negative numbers. Positive numbers are numbers greater than zero; negative numbers are numbers less than zero. Look at some examples of negative numbers in our lives:

- The average temperature in January in Fairbanks, Alaska is –13°. (Brrrr! That's 13° below zero!)
- A checking account has a balance of –$140 (not good!).
- The elevation of Death Valley, California is –282 feet (282 feet below sea level).

Compare and order integers It helps to think of integers in terms of temperature. Since a positive temperature is higher than a negative temperature, positive numbers are greater than negative numbers. If you think of negative numbers as the temperature below zero, then $-40 < -10$ because –40° is a lower temperature than –10°. (Recall that $<$ means "less than.")

Read and write numbers with positive exponents An exponent is the little number hovering above and beside

PRIMO

A prime number is a number whose only factors are itself and the number 1. For example, 7 is a prime number (only $7 \times 1 = 7$). Here are some more prime numbers: 1, 2, 3, 5, 11. . .

PLAY DAY

While it is true that American youngsters spend a considerable amount of time watching television (somewhere close to 15 hours weekly), this figure is comparable to that reported by youngsters in other countries. This international comparability is not the case when it comes to "playing," however; elementary school children in America spend twice as much of their free time playing as Asian children, for example, and American adolescents spend about twice as much time socializing as do their Asian counterparts. —from *Beyond the Classroom* by Laurence Steinberg, Ph.D. (Simon & Schuster, 1996) a number, such as 2^4. The exponent indicates the number of times the bottom number is multiplied by itself. For example, the number 2^3 has an exponent of 3 and means you should multiply the number 2 three times. Thus, $2^3 = 2 \times 2 \times 2 = 8$.

Read and write squares and square roots Besides being the four-sided figure having equal sides, a square is a number raised to the second power (that is, with the exponent 2). To square a number you multiply it by its own value. For example, the square $3^2 = 3 \times 3 = 9$.

A square root is the reverse of squaring a number. For example, since 32 = 9, then the square root, denoted $\sqrt{9} = 3$. Here are some other examples:

$\sqrt{49} = 7$ because $7^2 = 49$
$\sqrt{144} = 12$ because $12^2 = 144$

Many calculators have a square root key.

CELLULAR LEARNING

I think that parents should function as a nucleus in a cell when it comes to their children's learning. Parents have to foster the entire learning process.

Core Area 2: Computation

Computation refers to addition, subtraction, multiplication, and division. This core area also uses estimation to help perform the calculations and to check answers to calculations.

Multiply a three-digit number by a three-digit number We multiply 747 × 285 by placing one of the numbers on top of the other and following these steps:

- Multiply 747 by the ones' place of 285: 747 × 5 = 3,735 (see the first row under the horizontal rule).
- Since the 8 in 285 is in the tens' place, it represents 8 tens

or 80. Multiply 747 × 80 = 59,760 (see the second row under the horizontal rule).

- Since the 2 in 285 is in the hundreds' place, it represents 2 hundreds or 200. Multiply 747 × 200 = 149,400 (see the third row under the horizontal rule).
- Add the three rows.

$$\begin{array}{r} 747 \\ \underline{\times\ 285} \\ 3{,}735 \\ 59{,}760 \\ \underline{149{,}400} \\ 212{,}895 \end{array}$$

Thus, 747 × 285 = 212,895.

Divide by a three-digit number To divide 11,178 by 243, follow these steps:

- Since the divisor 243 has three digits, try dividing it into the first three digits of 11,178; that is, try figuring 111 ÷ 243. Since 243 does not divide into 111, we try the first four digits of 11,178 (1,178).
- Dividing 1,117 by 243, we find that 4 × 243 = 972 is the largest multiple of 243 that is less than 1,117. Write 4 above the horizontal rule above the tens' place (the place above the 7, the last digit in 1,117).
- Since 4 × 243 = 972, write 972 under 1,117 and subtract. The answer is 1,117 – 972 = 145.
- Write the remaining digit in 11,178 that has not been used yet, which is 8, next to 145 to form the number 1,458.
- Divide the new number 1,458 by 243. The answer is 6, which is written above the rule next to the 4.

Thus, 11,178 ÷ 243 = 46.

$$\begin{array}{r} 4 \\ 243\overline{)1117} \\ \underline{-972} \\ 145 \end{array}$$

$$\begin{array}{r} 6 \\ 243\overline{)1458} \end{array}$$

11,178 ÷ 243 = 46

AIMING TO PLEASE

My child had a great experience with Score@Kaplan. A neutral person, the Score coach, related to my son much better than either my husband or me because our son was trying so hard to please us with his schoolwork, and he ended up becoming defensive! Parents might consider tutors or study buddies (fellow classmates) to help kids who are having tough times relating to well-meaning parents.

OPPOSITES ATTRACT

The opposite of an integer is the same number with the opposite sign. For example the opposite of –5 and +5 (normally written as 5) are opposites; the opposite of 22 is –22.

Add and subtract integers Add and subtract integers using a number line. The positive direction on a number line is to your right; the negative direction is to your left. To add 5 + (–3), first go 5 units to the right (the positive direction) and then go 3 units to the left (the negative direction). You get 5 + (–3) = 2.

Another example: add –2 + (–5) by moving 2 units to the left and then another 5 units to the left. You get –2 + (–5) = –7.

Subtraction is done in a similar way. To subtract two integers, replace the integer after the subtraction sign with its opposite and add. For example, to subtract 2 from -3 (-3 – 2), replace the number 2, the number after the subtraction sign, with -2 and then add, that is, -3 – 2 = -3 + (-2) = -5.

-7 -6 -5 -4 -3 -2 -1 0 1 2 3 4 5

Integer Line

Multiply and divide integers Multiplying and dividing integers is just like multiplying and dividing whole numbers—except that you have to remember the + or – signs. When multiplying or dividing integers, recall these rules about the signs of the two numbers:

Sign of first number	Sign of second number	Sign of product or quotient
+	+	+
+	–	–
–	+	–
–	–	+

BEING THERE

The type of parental involvement that makes a real difference is the type that actually draws the parent into the school physically—attending school programs, extracurricular activities, teacher conferences, and "back to school" nights. —from *Beyond the Classroom* by Laurence Steinberg, Ph.D. (Simon & Schuster, 1996)

Here's how the rules apply: Let's multiply first. To multiply (–4) × (–5), first multiply the numbers without the signs: 4 × 5 = 20. Since the two numbers are both negative, the product is positive. Thus, (–4) × (–5) = 20.

To multiply (–6) × 8, multiply 6 × 8 = 48. Since we are multiplying a negative number by a positive number (the two numbers have different signs), the answer must be negative. Thus, (–6) × 8 = –48.

Dividing is a similar process. To figure −72 ÷ (−12), divide 72 ÷ 12 = 6. Since we are dividing a negative number by another negative number (both are negative), the answer is positive. Thus, −72 ÷ (−12) = 6.

MATH'S GREATEST HITS

According to *Newsweek's Computers & the Family* newsmagazine (Fall/Winter 1996), there were quite a few bestselling math computer software titles in 1996, including:

- *Math Blaster: In Search of Spot* (Davidson & Associates) for ages 6 to 12; (800) 545–7677
- *Math Blaster 2: The Secret of the Lost City* (Davidson & Associates) for ages 8 to 13
- *Mathematics* (boxed set by SofSource) for ages 10 to adult; (505) 523–6789
- *Math Heads* (Theatrix Interactive) for ages 10 to 14; (800) 955–TRIX
- *Major League Math* (Sanctuary Woods) for ages 9 to 13; (800) 943–3664

Core Area 4: Geometry and Measurement

Students in grades five and six study plane figures (two-dimensional figures) and solid figures (three-dimensional figures) in more depth. They learn about angles, and they use them to classify polygons. In grade six, the formulas for area and volume are taught.

Identify and measure acute and obtuse angles

- An acute angle is an angle whose measure is less than 90°.
- An obtuse angle is an angle whose measure is more than 90°.
- Recall that an angle whose measure equals 90° is called a right angle.

Students measure angles with a protractor, although it is not needed to identify an acute or obtuse angle. Look for angles in your home or neighborhood, such as a slice of pizza or the angle formed by two intersecting roads.

Identify complementary and supplementary angles Complementary angles always involve two or more angles. So do supplementary angles.

- Complementary angles are angles whose measures add up to 90°.
- Supplementary angles are angles whose measures add up to 180°.

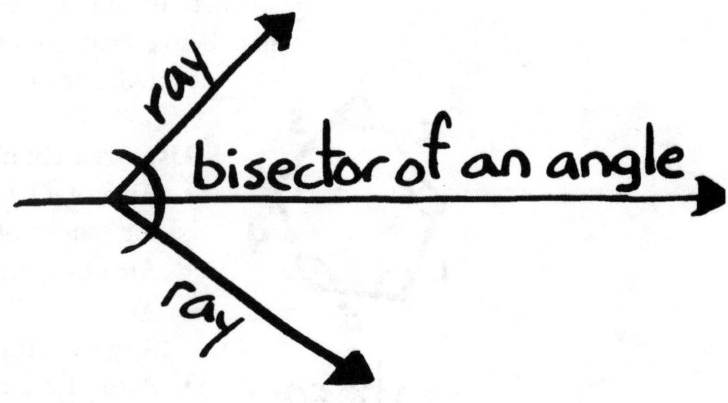

Construct and bisect angles An angle is formed by two rays. Use a protractor or ruler to draw angles. The bisector of an angle is a ray that divides the angle into two equal angles.

Recognize congruent line segments Two lines are congruent if they have the same

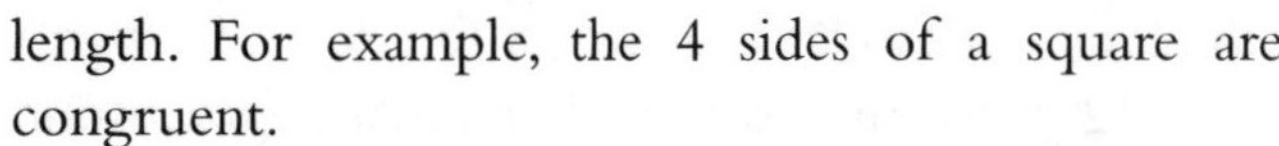

length. For example, the 4 sides of a square are congruent.

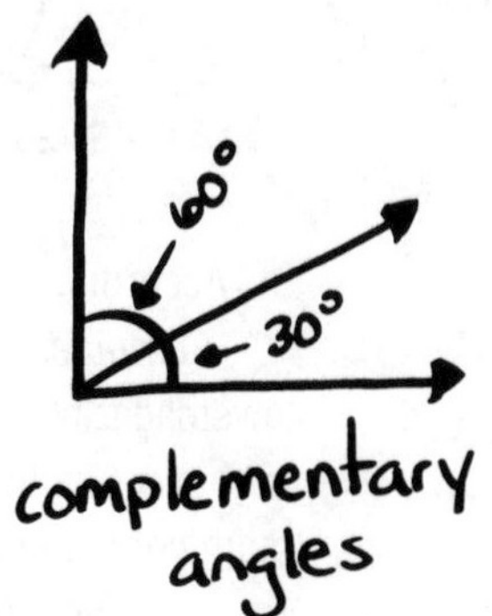

Construct the perpendicular bisector of a line segment A perpendicular bisector of a line segment intersects the line segment at a right angle and splits the segment into two equal parts.

Identify and classify polygons A closed figure formed by line segments is a polygon. Following are some facts that can be used to identify polygons.

Polygon	Number of Sides	Number of Angles	Sum of Angles
Triangle	3	3	180°
Quadrilateral	4	4	360°
Pentagon	5	5	540°
Hexagon	6	6	720°
Octagon	8	8	1,080°
Decagon	10	10	1,440°
Dodecagon	12	12	1,800°

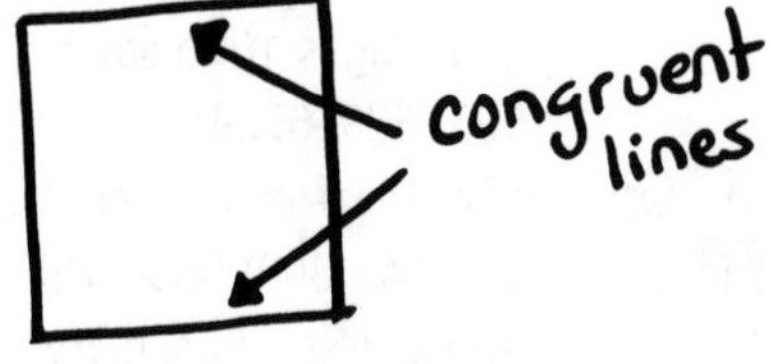

A regular polygon is a polygon that has equal sides and equal angles. What is the measure of each angle of each of the preceding polygons?

Make scale drawing Architectural drawings and street maps are scale drawings that are exact but smaller copies. Each measurement in the real object is translated into a smaller measurement using the same conversion rate. It's like being beamed up onto the Starship Enterprise and arriving at one-tenth your normal size.

Use area formulas

- Area of a triangle = $(1/2)bh$ (b is the base and h is the height of the triangle)
- Area of a square = s^2 (s is the side of the square)
- Area of a rectangle = $l \times w$ (l is the length and w is the width)
- Area of a circle = πr^2 (π is the irrational number called *pi* that is approximately 3.1415, and r is the radius of the circle)

Identify space figures and count their vertices, faces, and edges The space figures include the following:

- Rectangular prism
- Cube
- Pyramid
- Cylinder
- Cone
- Sphere

For space figures that have polygonal faces,

- A vertex (plural: vertices) is a corner where three sides meet.
- A face is a side of the figure.
- An edge is the line where two faces meet.

Name	Number of Vertices	Number of Faces	Number of Edges	Type of Face
Rectangular prism	8	6	12	rectangle
Cube	8	6	12	square
Pyramid	4	4	6	triangle
Pyramid with square base	4	4	6	triangle with square base
Regular Pyramid	4	4	6	equilateral triangle

Use volume formulas

- Volume of a rectangular prism = $l \times w \times h$ (l is the length, w is the width, and h is the height)
- Volume of a cube = s^3 (s is the side of the square)
- Volume of a pyramid = $Bh/3$ (B is area of the base, and h is the height of the pyramid)
- Volume of a cylinder = $\pi r^2 h$ (π is the irrational number called *pi* that is approximately 3.1415, r is the radius of the circular base of the cylinder, and h is the height of the cylinder)
- Volume of a cone = $\pi r^2 h/3$ (π is the irrational number called *pi* that is approximately 3.1415, r is the radius of the circular base of the cylinder, and h is the height of the cone)
- Volume of a sphere = $4\pi r^3/3$ (π is the irrational number called *pi* that is approximately 3.1415, and r is the radius of the sphere)

BEING IRRATIONAL

An irrational number is a number that cannot be written as a fraction. Decimals that never end and do not repeat are irrational numbers. The square root of many numbers (such as $\sqrt{2}$) are irrational numbers.

Find the surface area of a three-dimensional figure

- Surface area of a rectangular prism = $2B + Ph$ (B is the area of the base, P is the perimeter of the base, and h is the height of the prism)
- Surface area of a cube = $6s^2$ (s is the side of the square)
- Surface area of a pyramid = $B + (1/2)Ps$ (B is the area of the base, P is the perimeter of the base, and s is the slant height of the face, that is, the length of the edge from the base to the tip of the pyramid)

Find the surface area of a cylinder and a cone

- Surface area of a cylinder = $2\pi r(r + h)$ (π is the irrational number called pi that is approximately 3.1415, r is the radius of the circular base of the cylinder, and h is the height of the cylinder)
- Surface area of a cone = $\pi r^2 + \pi rs$ (π is the irrational number called *pi* that is approximately 3.1415, r is the radius of the circular face of the cone, and s is the slant height of the cone, that is, the distance along the outer face from the circular face to the tip of the cone)
- Surface area of a sphere = $4\pi r^2$ (π is the irrational number called *pi* that is approximately 3.1415, and r is the radius of the sphere)

OVER AND OVER AGAIN

In helping your child with a math problem, you can explain something the same way over and over again, and sometimes your child won't understand. You then need to step out of the situation and focus on "How can I relate this better to my child? My child loves soccer, so maybe we'll try this math problem with soccer balls rather than cups of baking flour." Just drawing an analogy from something that means a lot to your child may often be enough to really help.

Learn about and use milliliters and milligrams A milliliter (abbreviated ml.) is a metric measure for fluids. A milliliter isn't much; it takes 5 ml. to fill a teaspoon. Cooking oil, cough syrup, and paint thinner can be measured in milliliters. For example, a small bottle of cough syrup is about 240 ml.

A milligram (abbreviated mg.) is a metric measure of weight. A milligram is about the size of a grain of sand; it equals 1/29,000 of an ounce. Milligrams are used to measure tiny amounts of chemicals and medicines. For example, some aspirin tablets contain 250 mg. of the active ingredient. Most of the tablet is other stuff that holds the medication.

Estimate capacity Suppose a family friend gives your child a fish tank and you need to find out its capacity to select the correct water filter. Instead of filling the tank with water and making a sopping mess, you can estimate its capacity, that is, the amount of fluid the tank holds.

One way to estimate capacity is to use cubes whose capacity you know. (You can buy or borrow snap cubes, or you can make cubes out of Styrofoam, wood, or paper.) Lay the cubes on the base of the tank. The total number of cubes that cover the base of the tank gives you the area of the base. Now find the height of the tank in cubes. The capacity in cubes is the product of the height × the area of the base. Multiply the capacity in cubes × the capacity of one cube to find the capacity of the tank.

Core Area 5: Fractions, Decimals, and Percents

Understanding the concept of a whole and its division into equal parts is essential to understanding fractions, decimals, and percents. (Recall that percent is just the part of 100. For example, 80 percent of a 100 gallon drum means 80 out of the 100 gallons.) Students in grades five and six work extensively with fractions, decimals, and percents and learn the relationships among them.

Find the common denominator of fractions Recall that the denominator is the number under the bar of a fraction (2 is the denominator of the fraction 1/2.) A common denominator of two fractions is the number that is a denominator of two fractions. For example, the fractions 1/6 and 7/6 have a common denominator. To find the common denominator of two fractions, find the lowest common multiple (see Core Area 1) of the denominators. For the fractions 1/3 and 1/5, the lowest common multiple of 3 and 5 is the product of 3 × 5, that is, 15. Rewrite the fractions with the denominator 15:

WE'RE HERE TO HELP

Teachers aren't scary. We want to teach your kids; that's why we're teachers. If you have a good rapport with your child's teacher and let himm know what you're doing at home, it's going to make their job a lot easier. He'll be more willing to talk to you because he knows that your child is getting support from you at home. Teaching children is not just a teacher's job. You're doing your part, too.

$$\frac{1}{3}\times\frac{5}{5} = \frac{1\times 5}{\,} = \frac{5}{15} \text{ and } \frac{1}{5}\times\frac{3}{3} \times \frac{3}{15} = \frac{3}{15}$$

Add and subtract fractions with unlike denominators The fractions 2/3 and 1/8 have denominators that are not alike. To add or subtract unlike denominators, rewrite them with a common denominator. Since the lowest common multiple of 3 and 8 is 24,

$$\frac{2}{3}\times\frac{8}{8} = \frac{2\times 8}{\,} = \frac{16}{24} \text{ and } \frac{1}{8}\times\frac{3}{3} \times \frac{1\times 3}{\,} = \frac{3}{24}$$

Add or subtract by adding or subtracting the numerators of these fractions that have common denominators.

$$\frac{2}{3} + \frac{1}{8} = \frac{16}{24} + \frac{3}{24} = \frac{16+3}{\,} = \frac{19}{24}$$

$$\frac{2}{3} - \frac{1}{8} = \frac{16}{24} - \frac{3}{24} = \frac{16-3}{\,} = \frac{13}{24}$$

Multiply fractions Multiply the fractions 5/8 × 2/3 by multiplying numerators and multiplying denominators:

$$\frac{5}{8}\times\frac{2}{3} = \frac{5\times 2}{\,} = \frac{10}{24} = \frac{5}{12}$$

Divide fractions To divide 5/8 ÷ 2/3, invert the fraction after the ÷ and multiply:

$$\frac{5}{8}\div\frac{2}{3} = \frac{5}{8}\times\frac{3}{2} = \frac{5\times 3}{8\times 2} = \frac{15}{16}$$

Divide mixed numbers To divide $1\frac{1}{5} \div 1\frac{2}{3}$ first, rewrite the fractions as improper fractions,

$$1\frac{1}{5} = \frac{5}{5} + \frac{1}{5} = \frac{6}{5}$$

$$1\frac{2}{3} = \frac{3}{3} + \frac{2}{3} = \frac{5}{3}$$

Now, invert and multiply as before.

$$\frac{6}{5}\div\frac{5}{3} = \frac{6}{5}\times\frac{3}{5} = \frac{18}{25}$$

HANDS-ON LEARNING

In Score@Kaplan's Learning Adventures, we provide children with hands-on learning to introduce key concepts in academic subjects. These are one-week seminars, and in that short time we inspire kids and spark their curiosity and desire to study subjects further. That is good advice for parents too. You can provide little learning experiences for your children at home, just to spark their intellectual curiosity. There are so many opportunities at home to learn.

SWITCHEROO

To invert a fraction, just give it a flip so that it stands on its head. For example, inverting $\frac{2}{3}$ gives you $\frac{3}{2}$.

Write and compare decimals through hundred thousandths The decimal 0.00001 is one hundred thousandth, and it represents a teeny, tiny amount. For example, 0.00004 inches is the diameter of the smallest living cell, something that can be seen only with a powerful electron microscope.

The decimal 1.27519 has a 9 in the hundred thousandths' place. The number is read "one and twenty-seven thousand five hundred and nineteen hundred thousandths."

To compare decimals, compare the whole number parts first, and, if necessary, compare the decimal parts. For example, 1.72015 is greater than 1.72001 because 72015, the decimal part of 1.72015, is greater than 72001, the decimal part of 1.72001.

Terminating and repeating decimals Decimals come in two flavors: terminating and repeating. A terminating decimal is a decimal that ends neatly, such as 5.46 or 7.1555. A repeating decimal is a decimal that keeps repeating, such as 1.16161616... (the dots mean the numbers 1 and 6 repeat forever). It can also be written $1.\overline{16}$.

Add and subtract decimals up to hundred thousandths You add and subtract decimals just as you add and subtract whole numbers. The only trick is to make sure that you keep track of the decimal point. Always place one decimal below the other, making sure the decimal points line up.

$$\begin{array}{r} 14.647 \\ +7.196 \\ \hline 21.843 \end{array} \qquad \begin{array}{r} 14.647 \\ -7.196 \\ \hline 7.451 \end{array}$$

TEACHABLE MOMENTS

Parents shouldn't be giving kids all the answers when they do schoolwork together. Kids won't understand what's going on if this well-intentioned spoonfeeding happens on a regular basis. Focus on providing "teachable moments" for your child, rather than forcing the information down. Teachable moments are times when you can tell that something new has really clicked for your child. Maybe she's struggling with Roman numerals, then all of a sudden, you know she gets it!

GETTING INTO THE FLOW

Set up a home culture where it's expected that "we are a family unit, we want to learn more about each other because we care about each other, and we will have certain ways we interact all the time." Practices like having regular meals around a table together with a common sharing time are key to establishing a home culture. It's hard in an age when adults work harder and longer, but we all need to make time for our children, and other commitments to our children's lives will flow from that.

Multiply decimals Multiply decimals as you multiply whole numbers. But, there's a wrinkle. The number of decimal places of the answer must be equal to the sum of the decimal places of the two numbers you are multiplying.

$$
\begin{array}{r}
12.19 \\
\underline{\times\ 1.66} \\
7314 \\
73140 \\
\underline{121900} \\
20.2354
\end{array}
$$

Notice the answer has 4 decimal places because 2 + 2 = 4 (the sum of the two decimal places in 12.19 and the two decimal places in 1.66).

Divide decimals by whole numbers Divide decimals by whole numbers the same way that you divide whole numbers. Just keep track of the decimal point in the number being divided.

Divide decimals by powers of ten To divide a decimal by a power of 10, all you need to do is move the decimal point in the decimal to the left the number of times that there are zeroes in the divisor. For example, 10^2 is 100; since 100 has two zeroes, 14.57/100 = 0.1457 (move the decimal point two places to the left).

28.12. → 28120.

14.582. → 14582.

Divide decimals To divide a decimal by another decimal, first move the decimal point in the divisor to make it a whole number. (For example, suppose you were to divide 28.12 by 14.582. First you move the decimal point three places to the right to make 14.582 the whole number 14,582.) Then you move the decimal point in the dividend the same number of places to the right, making it 28,120. (Notice that you had to add a 0 to move the decimal point three places.) Now, divide as you normally would.

14.582 → 14582.
189.566 → 189566.

14582)189566

14582)18956 = 1
−14582
3374

14582)33746 = 3
33746
0

Thus, 189566 ÷ 14582 = 13

Round decimal quotients If you divide 9.36 ÷ 2.43, you get the repeating decimal 3.851851851... (or $3.\overline{851}$). This decimal may be rounded just as whole numbers are rounded.

- Rounding to the nearest hundredth, we get 3.85 because the next digit in the thousandths' place is 1.
- Rounding to the nearest tenth, we get 3.9 since the next digit in the hundredths' place is 5.

Learn the meaning of percent A percent is a part of 100 which can be expressed either as a decimal or a fraction. We see percents used often in our daily lives. Here are some examples:

- A jacket is on sale at 25% off.
- The unemployment rate is 5.9%.
- A tennis player placed 40% of her first serves in play.
- There's a 60% chance of rain today.

Convert percents to decimals and vice versa Change percents to decimals by placing the decimal point before the second digit from the right. For example, to change 100% to a decimal, place the decimal point to the left of the two zeroes and drop the percent sign: 100% = 1.00.

To change a decimal to a percent, move the decimal point two places to the right: 18.91 = 1,891% and 1.245 = 124.5%

Convert percents to fractions and vice versa Since percents are parts of a 100, to change a percent to a fraction, write the percent (without the sign) as the numerator of a

BIGGER, BETTER, FASTER

The PC has changed a lot in just six years, allowing homes to have powerful tools for learning. Here's a quick comparison:

	1990	1996
Chip	Intel 80386SX	Intel Pentium
Speed	16 megahertz	166 megahertz
RAM	2 megabytes	16 megabytes
Hard-disk	30 megabytes	2 gigabytes
Monitor	12-inch VGA color	17-inch SVGA color
Specials	Internal modem, 2,400 baud	8-speed CD-ROM, 33.6 bps modem, microphone
Cost	$2,600	$3,300

Dull beige boxes for PCs are out. Sleek black is in, complete with extras like tuner cards to watch TV and full-screen video graphics. —from *Newsweek's Family & Computers* newsmagazine (Fall/Winter 1996)

fraction having the denominator 100: 65% = 65/100, or 13/20 when we reduce the fraction.

To convert a fraction to a percent, first write the fraction with a denominator of 100. For example,

$$\frac{3}{4} = \frac{3}{4} \times \frac{25}{25} = \frac{75}{100}$$

Now, convert 75/100 to a percent by writing the numerator with a percent sign: 75/100 = 75%.

Find the percent of a number To find 15% of 60, change 15% to 0.15, then multiply:

$$15\% \text{ of } 60 = 0.15 \times 60 = 9$$

Estimate percents To estimate what 12% of 350 is, round 12% to 10%, convert to 0.10 and multiply: 0.10 × 350 = 35. An estimate for 12% of 350 is 35.

Use percents less than 1% Percents less than 1%, such as 0.1% or 0.009%, are just the same as other percents. For example, to convert 0.009% to a decimal, move the decimal point two places to the left by inserting more zeroes: 0.009% = 0.00009.

Find what percent one number is of another What percent of 120 is 24? To find the percent, first divide 24 by 120 and write a fraction with the denominator 100:

$$24 \div 120 = \frac{24}{120} = \frac{1}{5} = \frac{20}{100}$$

Now, convert to percent: 20/100 = 20%. So, 20% of 120 = 24.

Learn the meaning of ratio A ratio is a way of comparing numbers. For example, we say the ratio is "2 to 9" or 2/9. For example, a recipe for a real sweet dessert might ask for 2 cups of sugar for 9 cups of flour. The ratio of sugar to flour is 2 to 9 (or 2/9 or 2 : 9).

Identify equivalent ratios Continuing with the recipe

example, if we double the recipe, then there are 4 cups of sugar to 18 cups of flour. The ratio 2/9 is equivalent to 4/18 because the fractions 2/9 = 4/18.

Ratios are equivalent if the numerator of the first fraction is a multiple of the numerator of the other, and the denominator of the first fraction is the same multiple of the other denominator.

Learn about and solve proportions A proportion is an equation that says one ratio is equal to a second ratio. To solve a proportion, use your equation-solving skills to isolate a variable on one side of the equation and a number on the other side. (Equations are discussed in Core Area 9.)

Use ratios with similar figures Two rectangles are similar when the ratio of the sides of one rectangle is equivalent to the ratio of the sides of the other rectangle. For example, a rectangle with a length of 8 inches and a width of 5 inches (ratio of sides = 8/5) is similar to a rectangle with a length of 24 inches and a width of 15 inches (ratio of sides = 24/15 = 8/5).

GOING FOR GOLD

One of my Score@Kaplan moms is on a Nike poster! She started training after her twenties, and she kept training until she made the Olympic track team. She's a great reminder to kids that we all have goals, adults as well as kids.

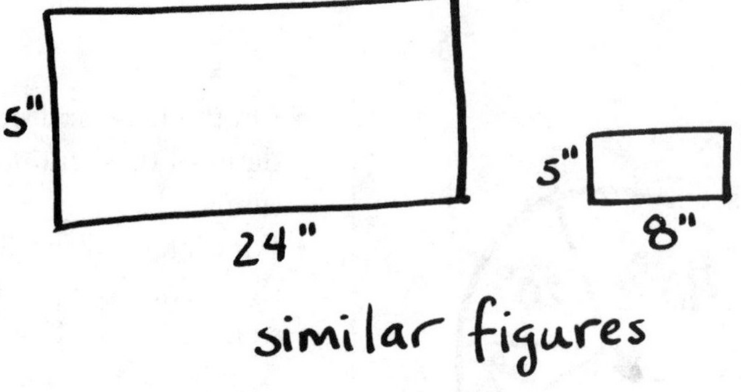

Core Area 6: Graphing

Graphs are an effective way to organize and display data. The shape of the graph and how it organizes data provides a great deal of information about the data.

Read and draw circle graphs Circle graphs are also called pie charts because they resemble the slices of a pie. Circle graphs show how each category compares with other categories and with the whole. Circle graphs are useful for graphing percents, because the total circle represents the whole (or 100%). The larger the size of the slice, the greater the share of the whole.

Read and draw line plots Remember those connect-

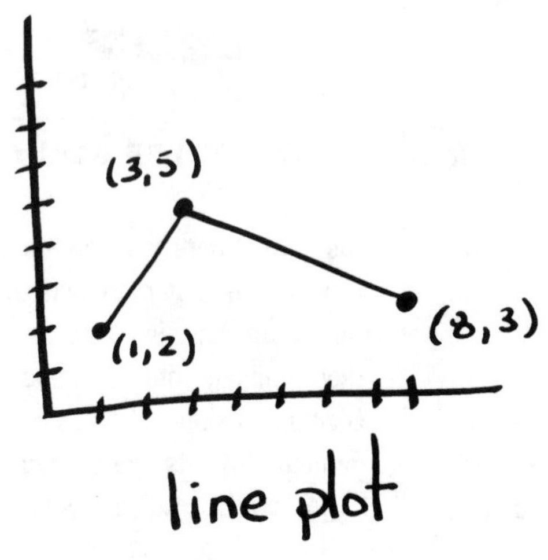

the-dots puzzles that create a picture when you finish? Well, the same principle works with line plots. A line plot is a collection of points connected by lines.

To draw a line plot, first plot some points, such as (1, 2) by moving one unit along the horizontal axis and then go straight up two units. Plot a point. After plotting several points, connect them by drawing a line from one dot to the next.

Read and draw stem-and-leaf plots A stem-and-leaf plot is a kind of graph that classifies data according to the following system. To graph the numbers 12, 14, 24, 25, 26, 23, 33, 45, 39, 33 on a stem-and-leaf graph, follow these steps:

- First organize the numbers by tens:

12	24	33	45
14	25	33	
	26	39	
	23		

- On the left-hand side of the graph, list all the possible first digits of these numbers (1, 2, 3, and 4). These are called the stems.
- For each stem, list all the second digits the appear with this stem. For example, for the stem 1, the numbers using this stem are 12 and 14. Beside the stem 1, write the numbers 2 and 4. Continue this for the other 3 stems. These numbers are called the leaves.

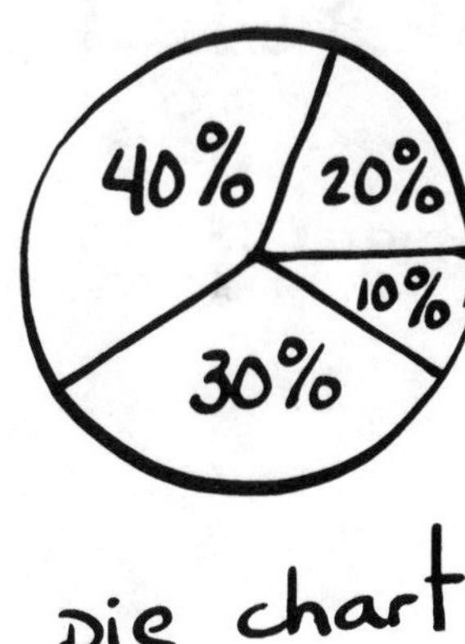

The length of each leaf shows the number of numbers in this category.

Read and draw double bar graph A double bar graph is a bar graph with two sets of bars which represent two cases. For example, in this double bar graph, one set of bars displays the income in the United States and the second set of bars shows the income in Japan.

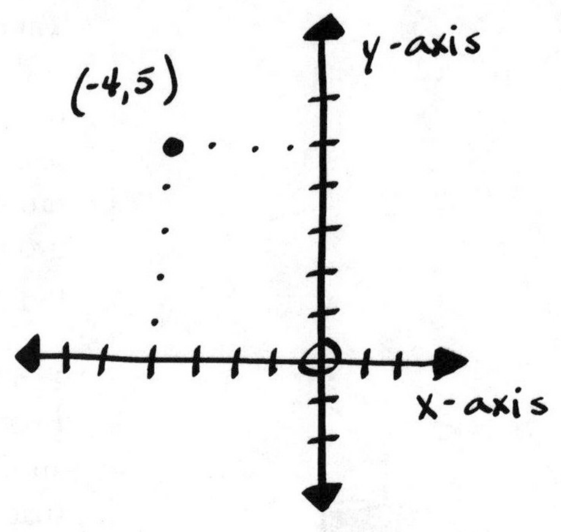

Graph integers in the coordinate plane A coordinate plane is two perpendicular number lines, usually called the *x*-axis and the *y*-axis. To graph the integers (–4, 5), move 4 units to the left of zero (negative side) and then go up 5 units (positive direction).

Draw the graph of a linear equation Two numbers are a solution to a linear equation $ax + by = c$ if you replace the two variables by the numbers and get a true statement such as 9 = 9. If you get 6 = 9 when you substitute, then the numbers are not solutions to the equation.

To draw the graph of a linear equation, you graph some numbers that are solutions to the equation. Plot a point for each pair of numbers that are solutions. Draw a line through the points.

Core Area 7: Statistics and Probability

Statistics and probability are the tools used to analyze problems in our world. They are used to take surveys of attitudes on smoking and to find the chances of winning the lottery. Frequently students choose the kinds of issues they wish to investigate. Since many topics for study are problems that students wish to learn about, they become involved and interested in learning the concepts.

Find the median, mode, and range of some numbers

- The median of some numbers is the middle of the numbers. There are as many numbers less than the median as there are numbers greater than the median. For example, 50 is the median of the numbers 22, 50, 57, 44, 60, 83, and 7.
- The mode of some numbers is the number that occurs most often in the group. For example 9 is the mode of the numbers 4, 9, 6, 7, 9, and 12.
- The range of some numbers is the difference between the greatest number and the lowest number. For example, 8 is the range of the numbers 4, 9, 6, 7, 9, and 12 because 12 (the highest number) minus 4 (the lowest number) equals 8.

THE ADULT WORLD

Whenever I set goals with students, I say two things. I tell them that when I was their age, I wanted to be on the cross-country team in school, and in order to get good enough, I had to practice and practice. Then I ask them if there's anything like that going on for them, and I try to get them to talk about their goals and dreams. Share something cool from the "adult world" that shows you had to practice and practice to master or understand something. Kids love to see adults as people who make mistakes and aren't born perfect.

Take samples Instead of interviewing *every* man, woman, and child in the United States about which cola they prefer, researchers take a sample of *some* men, *some* women, and *some* children. They select the people by calling phone numbers randomly or by some other means so that the group of people they interview represents the entire population of the United States.

Find the probabilities of simple events having probability 0 or 1 An event that has a probability of 0 is an event that cannot happen. For example, the probability that the month of July follows the month of May in some year is 0.

An event that has a probability of 1 is an event that is certain to happen. For example, the probability that the sun will rise tomorrow is 1.

Calculate permutations and combinations You must choose 6 numbers from the numbers 1, 2, 3, 4, 5, and 6 for the personal identification number for your bank card. Arrangements of these numbers are called permutations. To calculate a permutation of these 6 numbers, we would need a long time!

Let's take a simpler example: How may permutations of the numbers 1, 2, and 3 are there? Begin by making a list.

123	132
213	312
231	321

There are 6 possible arrangements of the numbers. Here's another way to calculate this. To form the three-digit number from the numbers 1, 2, and 3, you have

- 3 choices for the first digit. Say, you choose 3.
- 2 choices for the next digit, either 2 or 1. Choose 1.
- 1 choice left: 2. The number is 312.

Now, the total arrangements are $3 \times 2 \times 1 = 6$.

What if you choose 3 digits from the numbers 1, 2, 3, 4, and 5 and the order doesn't matter? This means that 123 is the

DARE TO COMPARE

Children deal with comparisons all their lives. That's part of the world. Everyone always compares themselves to others. Parents should downplay making negative comparisons, but you can't ignore that comparisons will always happen.

Parents often like to compare siblings. Kids can be so completely different or the same in terms of their levels of learning. Kids will already be comparing themselves to their brothers and sisters, but it's important for parents not to dwell on the comparisons. Even in school, kids get the sibling comparisons all the time, especially from teachers. I have an older brother, and I did really well in school but he didn't. My parents didn't make any comparisons between us, and we achieved things in different areas as a result.

same as 321. (Think of choosing three numbered pool balls from six pool balls numbered 1–6). Such arrangements are called combinations because you combine the three numbers in any order. The possible choices are

123	124	125	134	135
145	234	235	245	345

The number of combinations is 10.

Interpret statistics Students read articles that use some statistics such as the mean (or average) and median, and they evaluate the writer's conclusions based on the statistics. For example, if the median family income in Reverton is $25,000, then you cannot say how much the top 10% of the families earn, but you can say that half the families in Reverton earn more than $25,000 and that half earn less than $25,000.

Use the fundamental counting principle The fundamental counting principle says that the number of possibilities of some events taken together is the product of the choices of each event. Calculating the permutations of the personal identification numbers is an example of the fundamental counting principle.

MOTHERS MATTER

Here's a social message that needs to be proliferated: Mothers at home are not being rewarded. They've never been financially rewarded, and they have not been rewarded in terms of respect. They're not considered professionals, but the skill levels for mothering are getting more challenging day by day. It's a challenge to keep up the family and kids and nurture our children's educational process. There are complex issues we have to face every day.

Perform simulations Using a model, such as a coin or a spinner to estimate the probability of a complicated event, is called a simulation. For example, we can estimate the probability that a family planning to have two children will have a boy and a girl using a spinner. Let the even numbers equal a boy and odd numbers equal a girl. Spin the spinner two times for each trial and record the result. Perform many trials and estimate the probability.

Core Area 8: Problem Solving

Problem solving in math consists of a set of strategies for tackling word problems in an organized way and includes the following characteristics:

- Understanding and exploring the problem
- Thinking creatively and trying many approaches to the problem
- Persevering until the problem is solved or a new approach is discovered
- Answering the question and explaining how the problem was solved

As your child solves problems successfully, she will gain confidence in her problem-solving abilities and will develop her thinking and reasoning skills. Problem solving is a key part of elementary math that improves student achievement and helps students build self-confidence.

Use inductive reasoning Inductive reasoning makes conclusions based on a large number of objects or numbers. For example, let's look at the numbers 10, 11, and 12. Adding them, we get 10 + 11 + 12 = 33. Now add the digits in 33: 3 + 3 = 6. Try this yourself for the numbers 34, 35, and 36, always adding the digits of each total sum. The answer should be 6. Doing this with many groups of 3 numbers such that the last one is divisible by 6, you use inductive reasoning to conclude that this process always yields 6.

Solve percent problems Percent problems appear in almost every walk of life. For example, calculating the savings on a sale item or the sales charge for some shares in a mutual fund involve percents. These are some common parts of a percent problem:

- Find the percent in the problem.
- Figure out what number you should take the percent of.
- Check what the question asks.

Solve ratio and proportion problems A ratio problem compares two quantities having the same units. For example, your child might be asked to find the ratio of the average price of a single-family home in your town or city

ASSISTIVE TECHNOLOGY

If your child has a disability, check into the possibility of assistive technology to help make learning easier. The Individuals with Disabilities Education Act (IDEA) says assistive technology is any device that helps a student with disabilities function better—like a talking laptop computer that "reads" papers and books to students through earphones. The law requires that schools make it available to students who need it to obtain the free, appropriate education IDEA guarantees.

Some insurance companies will cover assistive technology devices, as well as community groups, corporations, foundations, and state governments, and they can be costly—from $10 for a used cart to $15,000 for electronics that convert type into spoken words. You should check all possible resources to maximize your child's learning opportunities.

and the average price of a single-family home in a neighboring community. To find the ratio, write the two numbers as a fraction:

$$\frac{\text{price of average single family home in your town or city}}{\text{price of average single family home in another community}}$$

A proportion problem involves writing equivalent ratios. For example, a proportion problem might ask whether the ratio of the prices of single-family homes is the same for multiple-family homes.

Solve word problems involving decimals Solving word problems is an art that requires patience and persistence. Suggestions like these for developing good problem solvers, also apply when decimals are involved.

- Encourage your child to think clearly and logically and suggest that he ask many questions.
- Listen to your child to see if he understands the problem.
- Encourage your child to explain his thinking.
- Ask "what-if" questions to explore the problem and extend your child's understanding.
- Encourage your child to try different strategies to solve the problem.
- Help your child persevere, encourage him to be flexible, and praise him for taking risks and trying new approaches.

Write and use equations to solve word problems Writing equations that represent the information in a word problem is a key part of solving word problems. Practice with your child the following skills:

- Identify the data in the word problem that you are given.
- Figure out what you must find, and represent this quantity with a variable.
- Write an equation using the variable and the other data in the problem.

Learning how to translate the information in a word problem into an equation takes practice. Here are some guides to help you (we use the variable x for the unknown quantity).

LET GIRLS GAIN GROUND

The American Association of University Women put out an eye-opening report called "Girls in the Middle: Working to Succeed in School" (September 1996). Boys and girls enter school with roughly equal skills, but girls lose ground. The AAUW urges schools to recognize the gender gap in U.S. schools by breaking schools into smaller units that consider girls' personalities in assigning them to teachers, bolstering school support for adult women role models, provide professional development for schools on gender sensitivity, conduct research on gender issues in our schools, and foster leadership opportunities for all girls. Outspoken or confrontational girls can become peer mediators and quiet girls can be encouraged to participate in student government, for example.

The word problem says	Write the quantity as
The sum of something and 3	$x + 3$
3 more than something	$x + 3$
Seven added to something	$x + 7$
Something minus 2	$x - 2$
Two minus something	$2 - x$
Double something minus 2	$2x - 2$
Two times something	$2x$
The product of 5 and something	$5x$
One-fourth of something	$\frac{1}{4}x$
Two percent of something	$0.2x$
The quotient of 4 and something	$\frac{x}{4}$

Solve word problems involving integers When you read "below zero" or a negative balance, think negative integers. Some common uses of negative numbers are

- –25° Fahrenheit
- –124 ft. elevation
- –$4,000 balance in a checking account; watch out for those bouncing checks!
- –5 yards rushing by a football running back (get a new running back!)
- –$2 change in the price of a mutual fund

FAIR, BUT FIRM

Some parents let their children make all the decisions about what's right for them. Some children will give up on goals and parents will say, "My Tommy just doesn't want to do this any more." A child may need help or need practice and may get a lot of good out of it, but he may decide to pull back. And his parents may not fight their child about it. This often sends a message to kids that it's okay to quit. It's great to make a decision with a child, but to give them too much control at a young age isn't great. As a parent, I try to be fair, but firm.

Core Area 9: Algebra

Algebra is the study of variables. It is an essential part of problem solving. To be a successful problem solver, your child should have a good understanding of algebra. Remind her that she has seen things that are like variables in previous grades, such as an open box ( ) and a good, old blank line (____), other ways of representing unknowns. For instance:

( ) + 7 = 10
8 – ____ = 3

Also, she saw some variables in the formulas she used to find area (*lw*) and volume (*lwh*). Practice working on variables with your child. Emphasize that working with variables is the same as working with numbers. All the rules for numbers also work with variables. Encourage her to see a variable as just another number, only for the present you don't know what quantity it is.

Represent a number by a variable and solve equations Variables are used in formulas, such as the area formula for a square: area = s^2. Here, *s* represents the length of a side of the square. Variables are also used to represent unknowns. Variables are letters in italics.

An equation is a math statement that says that two quantities are equal. Some equations are statements about numbers, and some involve variables. Here are some examples of equations:

$$2 + 3 = 5$$
$$7x - 3 = 60$$

Sometimes an equation is shown using a balance. To solve the equation $7x - 3 = 60$, follow these steps:

- First add 3 (the opposite of –3) to both sides to get $7x = 63$.
- Divide both sides by 7 to get $x = 9$.

Learn and use order of operations Following are the rules for figuring calculations that have more than one operation. Always do the operations in the following order.

1. Do operations above a fraction bar first.
2. Then figure calculations inside grouping symbols, such as parentheses or brackets.
3. Next, simplify exponents.
4. Then do multiplications and divisions working from left to right.
5. Finally, do additions and subtractions working from left to right.

For example, let's calculate $(6 + 15) \times 3 - 4^2/8$.

- Do operations within parentheses: $(6 + 15) = 21$.
- Simplify exponents: $4^2 = 16$.

PARENTS' PICKS

We surveyed scored of parents for this book, and here are some of their recommended educational resources:

- Art materials
- Books and software tailored to a child's interests
- Home encyclopedia, dictionary, and thesaurus
- Public TV programs and educational programs
- Card games and flashcards for learning everything from math concepts to another language
- The Internet
- Musical instruments
- Neighborhood libraries
- Outdoors and any natural environment
- Classics in literature
- Science museums
- Youth groups
- Sports activities
- Art galleries
- Theaters and plays (to inspire a love for stories and characters)
- LEGOS™ and other toys requiring the imagination

- Now do the multiplication: $21 \times 3 = 63$.
- Do the division: $16/8 = 2$.
- Finish by doing the subtraction: $63 - 2 = 61$.

These rules also apply when you are working with variables.

Learn about functions that follow a rule A function is a relationship between two sets of numbers. For example, the doubling function takes a number and doubles it. The rule for the doubling function is $y = 2x$. For each value of x, double it to get y.

PEMDAS

Remember PEMDAS, and you and your child will never forget the order of operations: Parenthesis, Exponents, Multiplication, Division, Addition, and Subtraction.

We can represent a function with a function table. Following is a function table for the doubling function.

x	$y = 2x$
−3	−6
−2	−4
−1	−2
0	0
1	2
2	4
3	6

Study linear functions A linear function is a rule of the form $y = ax + b$ for the numbers a and b. Some examples of functions are

$$y = x + 9$$
$$y = 2x - 19$$
$$y = 1x$$
4

You can write function tables for linear functions.

Identify and write geometric sequences A sequence is a list of numbers such as 1, 2, 4, 8, 16, etc. A geometric sequence is a sequence in which each term is the same multiple of the previous term. The sequence 1, 2, 4, 8, 16 is a geometric sequence because each term is the product of the previous term times 2. For example, $16 = 8 \times 2$. A geometric sequence can be written as a, ar, ar^2, ar^3, ar^4, etc. with a being the first term and r being the common multiple. In the sequence in the previous paragraph, $a = 1$ and $r = 2$. Check this for yourself.

New Ways of Teaching Mathematics

Sometimes, parents discover that their children's math is being taught in a new way, a way they worry they won't understand. Teachers seem to place less emphasis on addition and multiplication, and they are teaching mathematics in unusual ways. Students don't have math homework as much as their parents were accustomed to. What's going on here?

A Response to Problems In recent years, innovative math programs have been written in response to the serious problems in math education. Clearly, in many schools, the success rate in math has not been high. Test scores are lower, and students have trouble learning and using basic arithmetic facts.

In study after study, students have shown that they are not interested in mathematics and have not been engaged by the subject matter. Many are frustrated and have difficulty understanding the purpose of the math facts. What has been going wrong?

Researchers have learned that

- Standard teaching methods do not always reach all students. Children learn in many different ways. The memorization of arithmetic facts does not compute for students whose learning styles do not fit this approach.
- Learning arithmetic facts does not ensure that students can solve problems. Knowing how to begin to solve a problem and which operations are appropriate for the problem requires a level of understanding different from and beyond the number facts.
- Memorization of math facts does not stimulate the creativity that is necessary to be a good problem solver. Students have difficulty applying arithmetic facts flexibly in different situations.

MASTER MOTIVATION

I heard something on National Public Radio that somebody finished a longitudinal study of children through college, and the biggest determiner of success is not IQ level, it's how well parents motivate their kids. This is an area I as a parent would like to learn more about!

FORMULA FOR SUCCESS

Having students believe that it is worth investing time and energy in school is a necessary condition for academic achievement, but it is not sufficient by itself. In order to succeed, students also must believe that they have some control over how well they do in school, that their performance is somehow related to their effort, and that trying harder will lead to an improvement in their grades and test scores. —from *Beyond the Classroom* by Laurence Steinberg, Ph.D. (Simon & Schuster, 1996)

FUN AND CREATIVE

There are many exciting innovations going on in mathematics and the way it's being taught right now! This is something that parents should know: You should no longer tell children how to do math problems. Rather than say, "This is how you borrow" or "This is how you multiply" or "You go through these steps and this is how you get the answer," have your children articulate for themselves over and over again "What is the question and how do I solve the problem?"

It's exciting for kids to get together to work on a problem, explaining what the problem is and how they can tackle it. There will be many different ways that kids use to come up with the answer, and it's fascinating for them to see how everyone thought differently in the problem-solving process. It's also valuable to articulate the process—that's the real moment of learning, where it all starts to gel for them. Math can be fun and creative!

Many new programs to deal with these issues have been developed, based on the recommendations that mathematics professionals have come up with.

Characteristics of a Strong Math Program The new methods of teaching math are centered around problem solving. What, you may ask, does that mean, and how does it relate to familiar addition and subtraction? It means that problem solving is a set of strategies for describing and solving a problem in ways that are meaningful to a child. A good problem solver studies a problem by

- Talking about it with others
- Using reasoning skills to explain and justify their thinking
- Making graphs or drawings that describe the problem
- Trying a variety of approaches to attempt to solve the problem
- Using concrete objects to represent numbers

Students investigate extended problems involving things within their world. For example, they estimate the time it takes to get to school or distances in their neighborhood. By solving real problems, they learn that math is important and is used frequently in life. In addition, they come to appreciate that mathematics is more than just number facts. Just as reading is more than learning the meaning of each word, mathematics is more than reciting arithmetic facts.

Talking with others Usually students work in small groups to explore a problem. Each group member brings his own information and talents that others may or may not possess. As students share their ideas and ways of thinking, they develop their mathematical vocabulary and explain the relevant mathematics in their own words. Teachers assist them by asking questions and modeling other exploration strategies to promote investigating and describing the problem.

Use reasoning skills Students are encouraged to question and to elaborate on suggestions made by others. Teachers ask students to explain how they came up with the answer, why the solution worked, and how the solution is similar to other related problems. Students are encouraged to recognize patterns and relationships so that they learn that solutions may be used in numerous contexts.

Making pictures One important way to express mathematical ideas is with a picture. For example, students represent the heights of classmates using a bar graph. The number of children who are a certain height is shown by a bar on the graph. Graphs and other drawings are important ways in which data is organized and information in a problem is represented (such as the dimensions of a rug). Organizing information visually promotes clearer thinking and helps students get started.

Trying different approaches Teachers encourage students to take risks and explore different ways to solve a problem. Unlike what we learned, there is no right way to solve a problem. Some might solve a problem using blocks, and others might solve it by drawing a picture or pacing it out.

Using objects Children are tactile beings. They effectively express and work with mathematical ideas using objects. At age 2, they learned about numbers by counting their fingers. At age 6, they practiced addition by grouping objects. Manipulatives are specialized objects that teachers use to teach mathematics. Following are some common ones.

- Unifix cubes are interlocking cubes that connect in one direction. These cubes are used for counting, addition, subtraction, and many other kinds of work with numbers.
- Pattern blocks are colorful, geometric shapes that usually are triangles, squares, trapezoids, and hexagons. These are useful for studying geometry, exploring patterns, and working with fractions.
- Snap cubes that connect on all six sides are used to explore three-dimensional figures.
- A hundreds board is a square grid showing the numbers from 1 to 100. This is useful for addition and multiplication, skip counting, and learning about patterns in the number system.

MORE MATH, PLEASE

Improve your child's arithmetic skills. Learning to calculate will improve your child's concentration, as well as his or her reasoning skills. —*The Parent's Answer Book*, Gerald Deskin, Ph.D. and Greg Steckler, M.A. (Fairview Press, 1995)

NEW-FANGLED MATH

In some schools now, we have the "new-new math," and the difference between that and what they've taught in the past is more of a problem-solving approach. Rather than focusing on memorizing math facts, like multiplication tables, they might take all the kids out to the playground and have them figure out the area of the soccer field or how much grass they'd need to purchase to lay sod down in a certain area. In many schools, there's more of a focus on the logical and problem-solving approach than ever before. I think, however, that critical math skills are also important for kids to have.

NEWSWEEK PICKS CHOICE TITLES

A number of math software products "made the grade" with the folks at *Newsweek* magazine. Here are some of their 1996 "Editor's Choice" titles:

- *Go West* (Edunetics Ltd.) includes some practical budgeting and planning experience for kids
- *Major League Math* (Sanctuary Woods) combines the fun of big-time baseball with math drills and skills
- *Math Heads* (Theatrix Interactive) is a virtual TV Land filled with math fun and attitude
- *Mega Math Blaster* (Davidson & Associates) is an arcade-style romp that teaches math concepts while blasting through a colorful universe
- *Mighty Math Number Heroes* (Edmark) combines entertainment with geometry, fractions, probability, and computation.
- *Chessmaster 5000* (Mindscape) teaches critical thinking and problem solving, key math skills.

If your child is having trouble learning math facts using paper and pencil, you too can use manipulatives to practice. Ask your child's teacher which manipulative would be appropriate to teach the skill. Refer to the Resources section for companies that sell these items. Usually the manipulative kit comes with complete instructions on how to use them.

How Parents Can Help Having some information about the purposes of the program is not enough. We're all familiar with the experience of trying to help our children and being told, "But that's not how my teacher does it!" To provide your child with support and assistance, first and foremost, approach this endeavor with a sense of adventure and curiosity. Fostering an inquisitive attitude will help your child see the value and excitement of doing mathematics. In addition, we recommend the following:

- Always read the letters and other notices sent home.
- Do math homework along with your child.
- Have your child teach you how it is done.
- Go to math night at your child's school.
- Talk to your child's teacher.
- Talk to the math curriculum coordinator.
- Read the sources listed in this book's Resources section.
- Enjoy the activities in this book.

These new math programs are best understood by doing them. Take every opportunity to participate in workshops and to do activities with your child, so that you can share the sense of accomplishment that comes with becoming a skillful problem solver.

What's My Child Studying in Science?

If the question is "What are our children being taught in science classes?" the answer, alas, is "Not anywhere near enough." Science education in American schools is spotty and erratic. This is both surprising and discouraging for parents in a country that is seen as a world leader in scientific thinking and technological innovation.

WEIRD SCIENCE!

Science students sometimes come up with "quirky" explanations. Here are a few, courtesy of *Popular Science* magazine (© 1996 Times Mirror Magazines, Inc.):

- Mushrooms always grow in damp places and so they look like umbrellas.
- Blood flows down one leg and up the other.
- A vacuum is a large, empty space where the pope lives.
- A magnet is something you find crawling all over a dead cat.

Some schools excel at science education and others, at the dismal end of the spectrum, lump science in with the extras. Although most schools fall between these extremes, we feel that being vaguely in the middle is not good enough for your child. If there is one area where parents can make an enormous difference in helping their children make the grade, it is in science education.

The Importance of Physical Experiences Elementary educators who are comfortable with science enthusiastically incorporate physical exploration and experimentation into their teaching. Unfortunately, others who are less comfortable with science themselves or who are in less well equipped schools, rely on stories, readings from textbooks, and worksheets to meet their system's requirements.

Large differences between individual classrooms, schools, and even between states means that there is much for you to do. You can be alert and outspoken about your particular school's situation, and you can do a lot as a parent to encourage, supplement, and expand your child's curiosity about the world. The most important thing you can do for your child is to restore science to its roots in the world of physical exploration.

Making Science Easy and Pleasurable There's no need to force your child to spend time memorizing science vocabulary and abstract descriptions of science concepts. This is actually a waste of time. Advanced ideas and obscure terms sound impressive, but they are beyond the conceptual ability of most children at this age and are more appropriate for high school or college students.

Memorizing advanced material leads to confusion and frustration more often than to illumination, and time spent on rote learning takes time away from more useful physical experiences. Building a simple device that converts solar energy to electrical energy to kinetic energy (a solar-powered car, for example) has much greater value than memorizing the First Law of Thermodynamics. The student with that concrete experience will bring much more experience to the more appropriately abstract considerations of high school and college physics.

As parents we can feel intimidated by the rapid and complex advances in contemporary science. But the doing of science, the actual work of learning and achieving, has its base in simple, enjoyable physical exploration. Dr. Myron Fiering, an engineering professor and pioneering computer scientist at Harvard University, took great pleasure, even as an adult, working on model trains and their switching systems. Science can often begin with this kind of playful exploration.

How We Wrote These Curriculum Outlines We have combined what is currently taught in our better schools with what scientists and science educators generally agree should be at the heart of the best science learning in order to provide you with a picture of the kinds of learning that your child should be experiencing in the 5th and 6th grades.

You will find that most of the topics and skills listed here are at least touched upon in all schools. But in each individual

WHAT DO ADULTS WANT?

Kids learn an unfortunate message from many adults—parents and teachers—that what adults want is more important than what they as kids want. In exploring which breakfast cereal is most nutritious, most kids don't care about the nutritional value, but they think that's what *you* want them to investigate. Which breakfast cereal tastes the best? Shouldn't chewing gum in class help you relax and do better on assignments? Who is the strongest kid in class? Do different colored M&Ms taste different? Most kids don't see these as scientific questions because they're not the kinds of things you find in science textbooks. The trick is to get kids to investigate a question they want answered rather than one they think adults want answered!
—The Wild Goose Co.

child's case, how thoroughly and usefully they are presented depends on the efforts and commitments of individual teachers and school systems.

Newer Curriculum Models Some American schools have begun to adopt what is called the *integrated unit* curriculum in their elementary and middle-school classes. In this type of curriculum, a central unit of study is built around a single topic or theme, and much of the classroom work revolves around it.

A typical example of an integrated unit might be "From Sheep to Shirt." In this particular unit, a student's science lessons would focus on the characteristics of the animals and plants providing material for fabrics; the properties of plants used for dyeing fabrics; the chemistry of dyeing; and the technology of weaving and clothing manufacture. You won't find these exact topics in our outline. However, integrated units are usually thoroughly researched and prepared, and they will incorporate most of the concepts and skills you'll find here.

Science in the Middle School Years Children's mental abilities grow at a rapid pace similar to that of their bodies. The changes are both quantitative—they know more information—and qualitative—how they know things changes as well.

In the elementary grades, students are involved with the collection and integration of information. In the middle school years, about the time of puberty, children begin to acquire the ability to generalize. They start to be able to draw new information out of information that they have already acquired. Fully adult thinking, the ability to move from generalization to generalization and think abstractly, will in most cases not appear until the late middle school years or at the beginning of high school. In grades five and six, children are at this learning crossroads.

Science teaching in these years needs to respect these changes and also be sensitive to the range of abilities that children are in the process of developing, each at their own

EXPLORATION, PERSPIRATION

The more freedom we give children to explore, the more they learn—we've observed that in our Score@Kaplan Learning Adventures program. One of our coaches set up something innovative for the kids in our chemistry classes. Instead of providing a lab for them, he taught them the five steps of scientific thinking and then gave them the chemistry lesson plan. He said this end result is what you want to look for; he handed the lessons over to the kids, and they went for it! For about an hour and a half, they explored and worked super hard and afterwards, they presented their findings. It was so much more creative than a controlled classroom environment would have been.

CYCLE THE LEARNING

Use the Learning Cycle when doing science with your kids. Coined in the 1960s by the Science Curriculum Improvement Study, the Learning Cycle is three stages:

• **Explore**—First do some exploring with your child by doing hands-on activities, uncluttered by vocabulary and such.
• **Explain**—Then you can explain the concept, connecting it to the hands-on experiences your child just had.
• **Apply**—Most children don't fully understand the concept at this point, so they need to apply the concept in new hands-on situations.
—The Wild Goose Co.

rate. You will find that as your child's learning abilities increase, the kinds of tasks that she has in school science will begin to broaden and be more intellectually demanding.

Six Core Areas The following six core subject areas form the basis of the science curriculum for upper elementary to middle school grades:

1. Life Science
2. Physical Science
3. Earth and Space
4. Technology
5. Health science
6. Inquiry Skills

What's Taught in Grade Five?

The changes in the complexity of thought mentioned above are most likely to begin occurring in 5th grade. It's possible that girls will begin to demonstrate this change a bit earlier than boys.

The range of topics in this outline is wider than that of the outlines for earlier grades. This scope reflects both the wider range of science that becomes available for older children's study and the large variations in school science programs.

Core Area 1: Life Science

- Animals: distinctions between vertebrates and non-vertebrates, how animals' body plans differ inside and out, how animals obtain food, and tracing the sources of this food
- Plants: essential elements for life and successful growth
- The cell: how the basic cellular life functions are similar to ours, cellular reproduction of yeasts
- The life cycle in human beings—birth, growth, aging, and death (sometimes covered in special Human Growth and Development classes)
- Essentials of life: basic needs and processes that living organisms have in common such as respiration, food, elimination, and reproduction

- Differences between inherited and learned behaviors and characteristic actions
- Interdependence of living organisms, particularly in relation to the sources of food

Core Area 2: Physical Science

- Properties of matter: heat and cold cause changes in materials, conducting properties of simple materials, weight of an object equals the weight of the parts of an object, compound materials have different properties than their ingredients
- Forms of energy: how energy is transformed, different methods for producing electrical energy and how electrical energy can produce different types of energy
- Position and motion of objects: how changes in speed and direction of an object's motion are caused by forces acting on the object

Core Area 3: Earth and Space

- Geological history of our planet, fossils, methods of dating the age of our world
- Physical properties and formation of soils, weathering and the actions of plants and animals
- Weather: measuring the properties of the atmosphere, air pressure, humidity, temperature, precipitation, wind (speed and direction)
- The role of solar energy in our lives and in the lives of all organisms
- The solar system in relation to our galaxy and the known universe

Core Area 4: Technology

- The role of computers in business, science, the military, and telecommunications
- Personal use of computers: elementary touch typing, use in homework, basic operating procedures
- Inventions and the people who invent, the stories behind particular inventions
- Making and using plans to create devices to solve technological problems

HAVE FUN AT HOME

Use the Learning Cycle to help do fun science stuff at home! Here's a real-life example:

• **Explore**—Give your children a microscope and have them start looking at pond water, human skin, onion skin, or anything that can be called an organism and has a definite cell structure they can see under the microscope. Don't tell your kids about cells and then have them look for cells in the organisms. Just have them describe what they see and compare one thing with another.

• **Explain**—Focus on the similarities between the organisms, and sooner or later, your child will latch on to the similarities in structure. Then you're ready to introduce the word *cells* and explain that all life forms contain these little chunks.

• **Apply**—Modify the "explore" phase of the activity. For example, instead of looking at a piece of onion skin under the microscope and describing what she sees, have your child look at a completely different organism and draw a picture of the cells in it.

—The Wild Goose Company

Core Area 5: Health

- Personal health: personal grooming, first aid, personal safety and protection, safe use of tools and materials
- Inside the body: nervous system, reproductive system, begin viewing body as a system of interrelated systems and parts
- Nutrition: current best knowledge of healthy nutrition, effects of harmful substances
- Mental and social health issues and, in some localities, education about HIV and other public health problems

Core Area 6: Inquiry Skills

- The representation of data collected from observation with tables, models, demonstrations, and graphs
- Noting and describing relevant patterns, details, and relationships within and between objects and processes
- Planning and executing investigations and experiments and presenting the results with a variety of presentation methods, using multiple lines of inquiry
- Increase in the use of specialized measuring and observational tools such as microscopes, micro balances, and specialized thermometers
- Categorization: materials and the properties of materials, such as listing the characteristics of living and nonliving things, the characteristics of mammals and insects, or the properties of different minerals

BENCHMARKS

The American Academy for the Advancement of Science, in collaboration with some of the best science teachers in the country, published an important resource for all parents seriously interested in their children's science education called *BENCHMARKS for Science Literacy* (1993). This very thorough and readable report establishes guidelines for what children should know at the completion of all grades from kindergarten through high school. Your library can probably get access to it for you.

What's Taught in Grade Six?

In grade six, science learning begins to be focused on the skills and factual knowledge that underlie the later middle school years. Some topics listed here may be taught in grades five or seven in some schools. In some locations, human growth and development is specifically incorporated into the science curriculum, since many students at this age are passing through puberty.

Core Area 1: Life Science

- Relationships of living organisms, predator-prey, parasite-host, producer-consumer
- Animal behavior: the role of nature and nurture in animal and human behavior

- The cell: inside the cell, the basic unit of organic life, all complex organisms develop from a single cell, sexual and asexual reproduction
- Plants: how plants adapt to and survive in different environments
- Ecosystems in greater detail, different kinds, the different components, how matter is repeatedly transferred, over time, between organisms and their environment

Core Area 2: Physical Science

- Properties of matter: changes of state in matter are accompanied by a change in molecular motion, the concept that equal volumes of different substances may have different weights
- Properties of energy: further study of energy and the transference of energy, detailed study of light and the spectrum of visible radiation
- Experiments creating simple compounds and studying their properties—the relationships of energy in these investigations
- Properties of motion: the effects of unequal forces on motion, discussion of gravity as a force
- Further study of properties and ways in which they are formed, discussion of the concept of the particulate model of matter

Core Area 3: Earth and Space

- Interactions of geology, oceanography, meteorology, and astronomy
- Long-term changes in climate and their causes and effects, glaciers, global warming cycles, role of the sun
- Role of water in all three states—solid, liquid, and vapor—on our planet
- Formation of igneous, metamorphic, and sedimentary rocks
- Gravity and our planet's relationship to the sun and the rest of the solar system

Core Area 4: Technology

- Use of computer to apply problem-solving skills, model, and predict

AMAZING SUCCESSES

Some parents pay a lot of good, positive attention to their children, while some need to pay more attention. I run into grandparents who give me a laundry list of problems their adult children are having at home with their youngsters. All children are capable of amazing successes. At Score@Kaplan, we encourage parents to look for success and recognize it in the home with their children.

MAKING A LIST

Parents and teachers should help kids realize what kinds of things they can investigate in science projects by having kids list questions they have whenever the questions come up. Start with a poster or bulletin board on which you list any kinds of questions about the natural world (including humans), whether the questions come up over everyday things or during homework or lessons in science, math, art, or whatever.
—The Wild Goose Co.

"REAL" SCIENCE

The National Science Standards strongly recommend that adults get students involved in their own science projects so they can get a feel for what real science is all about. So you announce, "Today we're going to begin working on a science project. You can investigate anything you want. Get started figuring out what kind of question you'd like to answer with a scientific investigation." Kids get worried by this—it seems that doing their own investigations is intimidating. They think they'll have to do a lot of background reading in an encyclopedia in order to come up to speed on some unsolved problem in genetic engineering and then come up with a cure for cancer and the common cold. They have a view of what science is, and it usually has little to do with their everyday lives. What can you do to get kids involved? Let them know that almost any kind of question can be addressed—and not necessarily answered—with a scientific investigation.
—The Wild Goose Co.

- Personal use of computers: studying and using different technologies for data storage and retrieval, CD-ROM, disks, online systems, use of telecommunications between classrooms and schools
- History of technological development and the effects of technology on human life
- Making and using plans to create devices to solve technological problems

Core Area 5: Health
- Personal safety and protection, importance of safety equipment in school, sports, and occupations; first aid; in some schools, an introduction to first aid techniques such as the Heimlich maneuver
- Nutrition: vitamins, minerals, and basic food requirements for good health
- How to be an informed food consumer, learning to thoroughly read food labels
- Smoking, drug, and alcohol awareness instruction
- Human growth and development, sex education, HIV education
- Inside the body: function of specialized cells in the human body, effects of malfunction—diabetes, sickle-cell anemia

Core Area 6: Inquiry Skills
- Extending measuring skills: knowing the difference between, and being able to use, both digital and analog measuring devices, using more sensitive devices
- Observing with tools that change the scale of observation such as binoculars, microscopes, and magnifying glasses
- Continuing to develop methods and vocabulary for classification and description
- Planning and executing investigations: considering whether something can be investigated through direct observation or not, applying multiple lines of investigation to solve problems

What Science Content Should I Review?

Science teaching in grades five and six is usually built around five core content areas and a core skills area. In this section, you will find a discussion of the content generally covered in grades five and six in each core area. Because of the great variations found in science teaching for these grades, there are likely to be differences between the number and presentation of topics discussed here and what you will find in your child's school.

JUST A TOOL

A word to parents: Don't be overwhelmed by the hype. It's hard to pick up a newspaper or magazine these days without reading something about how technology is going to transform everything from shopping at the mall to performing brain surgery. While there's no question that computers are slowly becoming a valuable tool in the classroom, they are just a tool—like books or paper or pencils. And they're useless without good software and teachers who know how to make the most of the material. —from *Newsweek's Computers & the Family* newsmagazine (Fall/Winter 1996)

You will also find some variations in science education that reflect particular school settings. Elementary school students in urban, suburban, and rural areas tend to have materials and science units that may reflect their immediate school environment. There will also be regional differences. Students in southern coastal areas may spend more time on tropical storms and marine life than students in the Pacific Northwest, who may learn more about volcanoes and the movements of the earth's surface than children elsewhere in the country.

The Excitement of Doing Science

As parents, we are sometimes intimidated by science. Does science seem to bristle with obscure vocabulary, incomprehensible formulas, and complicated concepts? There are moments when we feel at a loss when it comes to helping our children with their homework, and we hastily consult dictionaries and reference books to refresh ourselves on the difference between deciduous trees and evergreens, or try to work out whether the earth moves clockwise or

THE SCIENTIFIC METHOD PART ONE

Here's a version of the Scientific Method that is fun and clear for parents to share with their children. The first three (out of six) points appear below; the next sidebar contains the other three.

Think of an Idea: The first thing you need to do is think of an idea. It may be something you want to explain or do in an experiment or something you just want to study. The best way to get started is to adapt an existing experiment in a way that's unique to you. Ask a question that needs an experiment to get an answer.

Research Your Topic: Find out what's already known about the topic. See what you can add to the general body of knowledge. It's a good idea to take some notes.

Plan Your Experiment: This part of the Scientific Method is called the *procedure.* You make a game plan of when, where, how, what, and why you're going to do what it is that you're going to do and what you need to do it.

counterclockwise around the sun (counterclockwise, if you're sitting at the north pole).

Some of this discomfort is probably the result of the inadequate science teaching that many of us received. But we must remember that the dull lectures and demonstrations of the past have nothing whatsoever to do with the reality of science—that pleasantly messy and exciting process of exploring the natural world. This exploration and the opportunity to be freely curious is the core of science and the heart of good science education.

Building on Facts Science depends on using our senses. Physical exploration lays the intellectual groundwork for all higher science learning. Children who spend their science time doing science instead of memorizing it will come out way ahead. In the earlier grades, your child gained some basic factual knowledge as she explored her world—that gathering of core science facts was a major part of the science curriculum of the early years. In the middle to upper elementary years, children continue this process and, at the same time, start to use their factual knowledge to build theories and conjectures. They begin to move from collecting and classifying rocks to testing them and making conjectures about their origins.

Of course, the level of abstract thinking of the practicing scientist is different from that of the 5th or 6th grade geologist, but the basic human impulse to fiddle around with something and wonder, "Why?" or "What will happen if . . . ?" is the same. Good teaching reflects this understanding of science and encourages a questioning mind while providing the physical and intellectual tools necessary to begin finding the answers (or more likely, as scientists know, the next questions).

Core Area 1: Life Science

Life science is the study of things that are living or were once living. Like all of modern science, the life sciences are undergoing constant change and revision. Nowhere else has this been more dramatically illustrated than within the field of biology. College students in the late 1950s and early 1960s had to unlearn much of their textbook high school and college biology when the discovery of the role of DNA and RNA revolutionized the life sciences. You can be sure that much of today's scientific truth will be revised or rewritten.

The details may change and the theories transform and deepen, but the basic skills and motivations of science remain the same. This is why students who are exposed to practical physical exploration in the life sciences and whose curiosity is nurtured will benefit the most.

Animal Studies By the time students are in middle school they will have learned many of the particulars of the distinctions between plants and animals. One of the most important of these is the different ways in which these two divisions of living things obtain their energy; green plants depend on sunlight to fuel the internal process that makes their food and animals consume external sources of energy-rich foods. In 5th and 6th grade, youngsters are ready to spend time exploring the particular mechanisms that animals use to feed and grow.

What an animal uses for food and how that food is obtained is often used as a trigger for exploring the differences among animal forms.

- What is this animal's food?
- Does the animal go after its meal, or does it wait for the meal to come to it?

THE SCIENTIFIC METHOD PART TWO

The Scientific Method continues. After your child has (1) thought of an idea, (2) researched a topic, and (3) planned an experiment, then:

Do Your Experiment: Party time! This is where you get right down to the nitty gritty of doing the experiment, collecting of the data, rolling up the sleeves, and diving in to the science fun. Remember to always follow safety rules!

Collect and Record Data: This is all the information that you're seeking. You'll include all your information in charts, data tables, lab notes, and records of observations.

Come to a Conclusion: Compile the data that you've collected, evaluate the results, answer the question you asked at the beginning, write a law describing what you observed, then . . . collect your Nobel Prize!

—The Wild Goose Co.

Both strategies work, and sometimes we find examples of both within just one species. Some spiders, like the jumping spiders that you might surprise on a garden wall, are aggressive hunters, while the orb weavers spin webs and patiently wait. How are these spiders physically different? What is it about a worm that makes not having a backbone make it easier to get food?

BE LIKE MIKE

I tell students that Michael Jordan misses half of his basketball shots. If his first shot of the game doesn't go in, does he stop shooting? Nope. We have all these sports stars achieving great things, things in the Olympics no one's ever done before, and yet somehow academically we don't continue with the "try until you succeed" mentality. Why in sports do we know you can fail so many times, but in school, you can't fail?

One of the great divisions in animal classification is between animals with backbones (vertebrates) and animals without backbones (invertebrates). All animals share certain basic functions—respiration (breathing), reproduction (making more of your kind), and the need for nourishment (eating), and elimination (getting rid of what the body doesn't use), but how they accomplish these tasks and the body structures they have are extraordinarily varied.

As children in the middle school years move beyond simple classification and categorization, they are intellectually ready to begin looking at the reasons why animals have evolved in specific ways. They can begin to ask why certain body structures work and in what kinds of situations they are most successful. A starfish is superbly equipped to flourish in its shallow oceanic world and would be lost on the steppes of central Asia where horses thrive. What is it about each creature that equips it so well to live in its environment?

Watching animals usually leads to discussions of animal behavior. Students are ready to think (and generate questions) about the differences between behaviors that result from inheritance and those that are learned.

- What is the difference between a beehive and a human society ruled by a king or queen?
- Are some animals smarter than others?
- What does *smart* mean? You can teach a dog tricks, but can you teach something to an earthworm? Such discussions open up a wonderful world of experimental possibilities.

Plant Studies Plants exhibit the same basic life functions as animals, but have some totally different answers to the problems of life. The principle difference, of course, is the use by all green plants of the sun's radiant energy to make food—the process of photosynthesis.

The range of ways that plants have adapted to their environments is as great as that of animals and, if you use the length of individual lives as a standard, some plants have done much better than animals. Plants do not aggressively seek food, but they have developed very efficient techniques for obtaining it. When you compare our relatively crude attempts to capture the sun's energy using photovoltaic cells with the wonderful arrays of miniature green solar panels that plants deploy, you begin to understand why they are so successful.

When the nutrients that they need are not available, plants have developed techniques for capturing insects to balance out their diets of sun and water. Although no plant is quite as ambitious or demanding as the voracious Audrey in *The Little Shop of Horrors*, students are fascinated by the snares and traps that insectivorous plants have evolved. Other plants have developed complicated relationships with microscopic life forms that live with them in symbiotic (mutually beneficial) relationships. In 1996, a massive die-off of bees distressed farmers because of the important role bees play in pollenizing blossoms that only then can yield their fruits or vegetables.

Relationships Among Living Organisms Middle school science builds on the factual and experiential base laid down in the elementary years. An extensive knowledge of animals and plants makes it easy to begin the more serious and generalized consideration of the relationships of all living things.

These relationships have many forms. They can be mutually beneficial as in symbiotic relationships or beneficial to only one partner as in the predator-prey or parasite-host relationships. Scientists are beginning to understand that the boundaries of these relationships are not always clear. For example, the predator-prey relationship (think, for instance, of fox and rabbit) is definitely not beneficial to the individual who happens to be the prey (poor baby rabbit)!

PRESSURE COOKER

I think some parents put too much pressure on kids. Education is very important, but I see some of my daughter's classmates consumed by learning all the time. It's the only thing they're allowed to do. In our house we try to achieve a good balance for our children, including down time.

NATURE'S BUDDIES

Symbiotic relationships can be so close that the two partners seem to the naked eye to be one organism. Lichens are a symbiotic relationship between a fungus and an algae. Reef-building corals are a symbiotic relationship between an algae and a small polyp related to the sea anemone. On a larger scale, you could argue that human beings and their domesticated plant and animal partners have developed a similar interdependent relationship.

However, having predators may, in the long run, help the survival of the prey species, since populations are kept at a level that can be sustained on the land (too many rabbits = too little tasty veggie matter left for them to eat = starvation).

The same set of complex interrelationships exists between humans and plants. While we happily (some of us) harvest and eat various members of the *Brassica* plant family—everything from cabbage to brussels sprouts and broccoli—the success of this plant family and its spread through the world is a result of human cultivation. Is this a predator-prey relationship, a symbiotic relationship, or a host-parasite relationship? Perhaps, from the plant's standpoint, humans are just a convenient way of getting around.

TAKE A BREAK

When your child is angry or upset and can't get something accomplished when you're doing homework or some other home learning activity, there's a focus on the problem and his hurt feelings. Talk about something fun your child has done and focus on the positive. Let your child forget about the frustration. Don't go back to what you just did, but take a good break from it. Show your child that it's good to be positive and optimistic. Show how things will work out.

Students at this age are beginning to be able to think larger thoughts, but they still benefit from and need lots of opportunities to work with living things. The study of small animals, invertebrates such as meal worms, and plants of all kinds continue to be useful. The emphasis in these grades usually shifts from close attention to the obvious physical details of particular life forms to internal structure and the observation of behavior and development.

Microscopic Life The cell is studied as the basic unit of life. Single-celled organisms have the same basic life functions as multicellular ones, and the cells that make up more complex plants and animals display this truth as well. Yeasts are familiar, often-studied unicellular organisms whose life processes have been used by humans since ancient times. The byproducts of their prodigious biological activity—carbon dioxide, alcohol, and certain vitamins—

have nourished us since ancient times. Anyone who bakes bread has learned, at least on an intuitive level, that happy yeasts are well fed, allowed to breathe, and encouraged to reproduce. Farm families are familiar with that distinctive aroma of the fermenting silage that cattle thrive on through long winters.

Cells produce new cells either by sexual or asexual reproduction. In sexual reproduction, elements from different individuals are combined to produce new individuals. In asexual reproduction, one individual cell produces an exact copy of itself. Asexual reproduction, by the way, is not limited to unicellular creatures. More complex life forms such as the whip tail lizards of the American southwest are all female and reproduce asexually.

The Interdependence of Life In grades five and six, animal and plant study units often lead to considerations of the planetary ecosystem that sustains our lives. The cycle of food production and food consumption, and the cycling of energy and matter back and forth through the food chain complement the study of the water cycle in the physical science core area. They provide the first steps in understanding the complex relationships upon which all life depends. The nitrogen cycle and the movement of carbon and oxygen through our ecosystem will be studied in greater detail in high school and college. The principle concept that children learn is that matter is repeatedly transferred, over time, between organisms and their environment.

Core Area 2: Physical Science

By the time children have reached the 5th and 6th grades, they have had lots of experience with bodies in motion (and not just in science class!). Physical science can be a very exciting area of study because of the increased observational abilities and greater thinking power children have by this age. The opportunities to be involved with physical experimentation are great, and the rewards of thinking things through to a conclusion can make each challenge satisfying.

THRILLER

My Score@Kaplan experience has been wonderful. I've gotten a lot of good ideas for home education from the program, too. I work more closely with my girl when she does homework, and we turn learning into quality, enjoyable time together. I was surprised how much I could contribute to her positive attitude about school! In just a few months, she's reading better, she's comprehending better, the math is so easy, she loves science—my daughter and I are just thrilled.

STARTED YOUNG

Robert Goddard has been called the father of modern rocketry. His inventions included patents on most of the basic features that have carried astronauts, satellites, and probes into space. His early interest in physics and things mechanical grew out of a childhood fascination with machines and tools that was supported by both his father and his uncle.

CLASSROOM TECH STATS

Spending on computers has increased, but there's room for improvement, according to the *Newsweek Computers & the Family* newsmagazine (Fall/Winter 1996).

- **Big budgets:** Schools shelled out $3.3 billion during the 1994–95 school year. But it will take at least $50 billion more over five years to give every seven students a PC.
- **Limited experience:** Nearly half of the nation's teachers have little experience with technology in the classroom.
- **The Internet:** Only half of the country's schools had access to the Internet in 1995.
- **Multimedia:** The ratio of students to PCs is ten to one. But many don't have modems, sound cards, or CD-ROM drives.

ENVIROLINK

Spend time with your child surfing the World Wide Web for cool science sites. There are many great ones that will give you and your child hours of fun science experience. For instance, look into Envirolink for their environmental library, articles from *OneWorld* magazine, and teacher lesson plans on great science projects: http://www.envirolink.org

If you could compare the science student in the earlier elementary grades to great collectors of the past like James Audubon and Louis Agassiz, you could compare middle school students to the great trial-and-error and dreamer inventors like Thomas Edison and Robert Goddard.

Properties of Matter Solids, fluids, and gasses are the states of matter that really matter in daily life and in the classroom. They are studied in a variety of ways, the commonest being experiments that involve water. At this grade level, hands-on experiences with different combinations of fluids or of fluids and solids lead to experiments that involve planning and predictions.

Combining various oils, water, and other liquids raises the question of why some liquids sink below or rise above others. These liquids can be weighed in equal volumes and the volumes of equal weights compared to explore the different properties of these substances.

Weight is also a consideration in studying the properties of solids. Most children at this grade level know that the weight of the individual components of an object add up to the weight of the whole. They are ready to wonder why, when you add a cup of water to a cup of sand, you get a weight equal to the sum of the weights of the sand and water, but not two cups of volume. This kind of mind-teasing experiment (and its physical component) is part of students' preparation for the concepts of higher level courses in high school.

Studying the properties of materials occupies a large portion of some school science programs, but memorizing abstract, adult definitions of atoms and atomic interactions is not the focus. Rote work like that is confusing and unnecessary. The distinctions between atoms and molecules and between different atoms of the same substance (still the subject of intense scientific study) may be generally referred to, but the important task in these grades is to build an experiential base for later learning.

The same is true for the molecular composition of compound substances. The general concept to learn is that combinations of materials can produce materials with new and different characteristics. We know on the experiential level that flour, water, sugar, chocolate chips, and a pinch of salt combine in the presence of heat to make something that tastes a lot better than the cup of flour by itself. Children at this age are being asked to think about this reality in more generalized ways and to begin to ask why and wonder what if (even if it's sometimes "What if we used even more chocolate chips?").

Forms of Energy Those chocolate chip cookies don't become cookies without the presence of heat energy. When middle schoolers experiment with mixing and making things, they are led to consider the role of energy in these investigations. Science educators generally agree that observing energy in all its forms and working with it in as many ways as possible has tremendous value. They also agree that it can be harmful to frustrate children with concepts that are too abstract or that depend on mathematical or scientific skills that they have not yet acquired. The essence of the study of energy in the 5th and 6th grades lies in providing lots of room for experimentation and speculation.

Light and heat are the two commonest forms of energy studied in the middle school years. Studying and experimenting with the visible portion of the electromagnetic spectrum and with that portion of the spectrum that we perceive as heat leads to all of the wonderful learning that will take place in high school chemistry and physics.

"Energy is conserved" is the terse statement of the First Law of Thermodynamics. Students encounter the physical expression of this law every time they talk about the different forms of energy they encounter when they experiment with materials, machines, and processes that involve the transfer of energy.

The cartoonist Rube Goldberg loved drawing hilarious devices that accomplished simple tasks with outrageously

SLIME AND A WHOLE LOT MORE

Introduce your child to a variety of hands-on science activities. This series of science kits will help kids grades 5 through 8 learn the laws of physics, play with colloidal chemistry, uncover Earth's mysteries, and show that questions are the beginning of all discoveries. Check out:

- *Oh, Mr. Newton*—Cruise through different fields of science and see how they're all related!
- *Newton on the Earth*—Explore the geologic layers of Earth and the gaseous layers of the atmosphere.
- *Newton on Slime*—Discover colloids, polymers, disappearing water, and the science of root beer foam.
- *Newton's Greatest Hits*—Use springs, ball-bearing roller coasters, and a math teeter-totter to understand Newton's Three Laws.

Contact The Wild Goose Co. at (800) 373-1498.

complicated equipment. A cat on a treadmill (mechanical energy) chasing a mouse suspended on a string might power a generator (mechanical to electrical energy) that lit a bulb which heated a match (electrical to heat energy) which burned through a string (chemical energy) which released a weight (kinetic energy) which dropped on the head of a sleeping subject (very little energy—probably a parent). It's a ridiculous alarm clock, but a superb demonstration of the transfer and interplay of energy in physical systems.

Making devices and inventions and experimenting with bulbs, bells, and batteries are some of the ways that middle schoolers approach the concept of the transference of energy.

GO WITH YOUR GUT

It wasn't until my son was in the fourth grade that he was diagnosed with ADHD and also having a learning disability. I felt the school missed this and should have answered my earlier concerns. For two years I was told nothing was wrong with him. Parents need to demand answers sometimes, go with their gut feelings, and be involved. Our son is now in the sixth grade and although we still struggle with his attention, understanding how he is and how he learns has helped us. There are many different ways to help children learn, and parents just need to find the right way!

Position and Motion of Objects Basketballs, jump ropes, baseballs and bats, inline skates, and soccer games probably don't seem like the stuff of classical physics, but they are all examples of objects in motion and in motion in relation to one another. When you begin to wonder why it is that an aluminum baseball bat connects differently with a ball than a wooden one does, or why spins make a difference in a pitch, a pass, or a soccer kick, you have crossed the line into science.

Studying pendulums or free-rolling balls (even pool or billiards) are useful ways of studying how changes in speed and direction of an object's motion are caused by the forces acting on the object.

- What happens to a large ball rolling on a field directly into the wind compared to a wind coming from the side?
- Why do commercial jets need constantly updated information about the jet stream?
- Why do sailors need to learn how to tack?

Gravity is something we all take for granted and something very few of us understand. Even scientists who have a deeper mathematical understanding of this force are still hard at work both explaining it and trying to work out its relationship to other forms of energy. Fifth and sixth graders should be able to recognize gravity as a potent and ever-present force in their world and should be encouraged to experiment with its effects. Parents (and teachers) need not mutter and stumble around with complicated and poorly understood textbook definitions. It's much easier to say, "It's a force. I don't know exactly how to explain it, but let's play with it and see what we can find out."

Core Area 3: Earth and Space

We occupy a very thin habitable layer over the surface of our planet. Here we are cozily sandwiched between the active and inhospitably hot planetary interior of Earth and the cold and equally inhospitable vastness of space. Our comfortable environment is the product of the interaction between the hot bulk of our planet, the cold of space, and the great radiating energy of our star, the sun. All the familiar landmarks and geographical features, as well as the life-sustaining chemistry of our physical environment, are shaped by the interaction of these three.

Variations in Local Curricula The eastern coast of North America is regularly visited by the great seasonal storms known as hurricanes; the western coast knows volcanism and earthquakes firsthand; and our continental interior periodically suffers the weather extremes that produce droughts, floods, and tornadoes. Since different regions of North America suffer different examples of the more severe effects of our planet's dynamic processes, you may find that the emphasis in your child's earth science lessons at school differs somewhat from this general presentation. Since kids are legitimately concerned with the events that directly affect them, it makes sense to focus their learning around the particular phenomena that directly affect their lives.

TECH SELECT

The folks at *Newsweek* magazine are making it easier for you as a parent to select high quality, effective learning tools for your home computer. Whether you're looking for socko science titles, hot math games, or cool creativity tools for your PC, check out the "Editor's Choice" titles on *Newsweek's* Parent's Guide Web site: www.newsweekparentsguide.com

The site features multimedia reviews of new software titles and expert commentary on a weekly basis, along with searchable archives. You'll find reviews of the fifty Editor's Choice software programs, plus nearly 500 past reviews! *Newsweek* rates each set of software using a set of criteria, including educational lessons, degree of interactivity, and entertainment value. Use this great guide to make knowledgeable educational software purchases.

THE DATING GAME

Rocks change very slowly on the atomic level, but scientists are able to analyze and measure these changes and roughly estimate their ages. Samples of the oldest rocks from different locations on our planet have yielded an approximate age of four and one-half billion years (very approximate!).

Closer to us in time, the carbon absorbed by living organisms can be identified, and the amount that it has changed since the organism died will roughly determine its age. The sequences of layers in tree rings and their thicknesses, the position of bones or artifacts in layers of soil or sediment whose age is known, and the presence of microscopic bits of pollen in archaeological sites all contribute to the dating of ancient finds. None of these methods is so precise that you could say, "Ah-hah, this arrowhead was dropped here 10,472 days ago at noon," but when used together, they can give useful approximations of age.

Geological History of Our Planet The oldest known rocks on our planet all date from about four and a half billion years ago and scientists generally agree that this is a reasonable rough estimate of the age of our planet in its present consolidated state. As our planet formed, the interior continued to radiate heat while a thick crust formed on its cooling surface, and the forces that still shape our world got down to work.

Caution, Planet at Work Until quite recently, most people believed that the surface of the earth, while not always calm, was a fairly stable place. Continents were assumed to have been always more or less the same shape and size and always located pretty much where they are today. In the last few decades, we have realized that this stability is definitely not the case! Our planetary surface has turned out to be more like the skin on the surface of a hot, thick pudding that never completely cools.

The study of the movements of the vast masses of crust is called plate tectonics. The earth's continents are actually plates of cooler crustal material that float on the surface of the earth's more molten interior layer. Material from deep within constantly wells up along cracks (hidden in the depths of the sea) that lie between the enormous continental plates. The plates are slowly pushed apart as new material is added. And we do mean slowly! The movement of our continental plates is almost imperceptible. Only recently has modern instrumentation and incredibly sensitive satellite observation documented this phenomenon. In North America, we creep westward at a pace that can be measured in just centimeters a year. To earth scientists, however, a year is a mere wink in time. They see the movements in terms of hundreds of thousands and millions of years. Over the span of geologic time, the motion has been dramatic and has had powerful results.

The resistance that the plates encounter as they push against one another causes the buckling and wrinkling that show up on our topographical maps as mountain chains and the deep valleys among them. In their slow drifting, plates override one another, pushing one of them down and under into the deeper regions of the mantle. The pressure, cracking, and sliding that this overriding causes results in earthquakes and also, scientists now think, the volcanic activity that occurs along the edges of the plates.

Some other volcanic activity occurs where there are either thinner areas of crust or deep, hot currents welling up from the interior. The Hawaiian islands seem to be an example of this phenomenon. If you look on a globe, you can see the chain of these volcanic islands marking the passage of a portion of a crustal plate across an area where molten material works its way to the surface.

Crusty Old Planet The crust of our planet is composed of a most bewildering variety of that substance we call rock. Rock can be sorted into three main categories.

- Igneous rock is formed directly from the molten material in the earth's mantle. (The name comes from the Greek word for fire, just like the word *ignite.*)
- Sedimentary rock forms as layer upon layer of sand, silt, and clay (sediment) settle out of the earth's rivers and seas, and time and pressure compress that sediment into rock.
- Metamorphic rock is rock whose form has been changed. (Its name comes from the Greek *meta* for "change" and *morphe* for "form.") As the earth's crust is pushed and folded under by the movement of the continental plates, layers of sedimentary rock that were once on the surface are squashed and heated. The loose, crumbly sedimentary layers are compressed and melted together to form metamorphic rock. Igneous rocks that are folded back under are also transformed into metamorphic rocks.

You can see that among all the cycles being considered by modern science, rocks have a cycle, too, although a much slower one. An igneous rock can be worn and abraded by ice and wind into small particles of sand. The sand collects in an ancient sea bed and compacts and solidifies into sedimentary rock. This is eventually folded beneath the surface and is heated and squeezed into a metamorphic form. Eons later, pushed to the surface, this too is worn and abraded down . . . we could go on, but you get the picture.

UP ON THE REEF

Although corals do grow in colder waters, the reef-building corals are limited to warmer tropical seas. Compared to the dramatic outpourings of volcanoes and the massive upliftings of the continental plates, these corals don't contribute a great deal to Earth building, but they do make a major difference in our lives.

Coral reefs function both as a protective barrier for coastal ecological zones and as a rich environment for sea life. Because this kind of coral requires sunlight to feed its symbiotic algae partner, it grows only in relatively shallow depths. Scientists are able to study the older sections of coral reefs and determine the rise and fall of sea level during past geological periods.

Forces at the Surface Even as continental forces are pushing mountain ranges up and building volcanic mountains up, other forces are at work wearing them down. *Erosion* is the general name given to this second process. The constant motion of our atmosphere and the constant action of our watery surface environment are both incredibly slow, but amazingly powerful agents of change. The force of the wind and the action of falling rain and running water are the most obvious causes of erosion.

DUMB DUMBER DUMBEST

Studies suggest that the average intelligence of the population has been increasing, not decreasing, over time, most likely as a result of improvements in early nutrition, prenatal care, and health, all of which affect IQ-test performance for the better. Despite the widespread belief that Americans have gotten "dumber," there is no evidence to suggest that they have—at least with respect to the sorts of skills measured on standardized intelligence tests. What Americans have become is not less intelligent, but less interested in being educated. In concrete terms, although today's students appear less interested in school than they were in previous generations, they are no less smart.
—from *Beyond the Classroom* by Laurence Steinberg, Ph.D. (Simon & Schuster, 1996)

Another eroding force is the action of water as it changes state from liquid to solid. As a liquid, it seeps into rock at the surface, expands as it freezes, and then splits the rock. As snow, it forms the centuries-deep accumulations that become glaciers. Glaciers with their hundreds and thousands of feet of heavy ice can scrub towering mountains into gentle hills. Water with enough heat changes into vapor. Ground water also percolates deep below the surface as a liquid and then is changed to steam by the interior heat. That steam can force rock apart or even dissolve it.

Biological forces are also at their break-down work. The interaction of the oxygen and other gases given off by life forms of all kinds have a role in the alteration of our planet's surface. On a smaller scale, the action of tree roots and other vegetable action, and the artifacts and byproducts of human life create change as well.

Water Cycle Life could not exist without water. Even the recently discovered microbes that dwell in the seemingly solid rock miles below the earth's surface depend on the presence of water for their lives. Beyond our need for the basics of life, the essential processes, our familiar environment is completely bound up with what is called the water cycle.

The cycle itself is relatively simple. Water is changed from its liquid form to its gaseous form by increases in temperature at the earth's surface. The vapor rises until higher altitudes cool it enough to return it to its liquid (or if it gets cold enough, solid) state. Now heavier, it floats or falls back to the earth. If it falls on land, it flows downhill until it is either turned back into water vapor along the way (through evaporation) or it reaches the oceans. As water passes through this cycle, it nourishes crops, fills reservoirs, carves out deep canyons, fills the oceans, and sustains life.

Weather Station Earth Two elements make studying the weather rewarding for 5th and 6th graders. The first is their increased sophistication in the use of measuring devices, and the second is the increased development of their intellectual abilities. The appearance of deeper thinking skills at this age allows them to imagine and work with more complicated general systems. Even beginning to understand the constantly active and complex behavior of our atmosphere requires both.

Simple weather stations have instruments that simultaneously measure different aspects of the atmosphere. Wind speed and direction, air pressure, humidity, precipitation, and temperature are all variable qualities of local atmospheric activity. Reading the instruments that measure these variables, keeping records, and using the data to attempt predictions puts science skills to the test and provides many opportunities for learning. Meteorological studies have the added benefit of using an ever-changing and ever-present resource. No matter where your child's school is, there's always weather just outside the door!

Tracking local and immediate weather conditions usually brings students to the consideration of long-term weather changes. Computers may be used to gather, analyze, and visualize data that covers great sweeps of time and vast distances; they are powerful tools in the hands of students. Experiments in physical science that give students concrete experiences with the properties of fluids and gases demonstrate their value in these kinds of studies. Watching the swirl of pressure zones displayed on a computer monitor is much more meaningful when students have had plenty of chances to work with water and other liquids in preparation and have actually set fluids in motion themselves.

With a background in local, short-term weather observation behind them, middle schoolers can learn about larger, more

KNOW YOUR CHILD'S PACE

Nothing is more important than your children and what they are working on right now. If they're working on their addition tables, then focus on that and not on comparisons that make children feel inferior or behind other children. Some children may be doing astrophysics in fifth grade, but you have to remember that each child is an individual and will be working at his or her own pace. Parents have to support their children and where they're at. Negativity and unfavorable comparisons reinforce inferiority complexes.

SOMETHING TO CHEW ON

Try dinner conversations in which each family member needs to share or teach one fact with everyone. It can be silly or serious, significant or trivial!

general systems that are not immediately observable. Even in the relatively brief amount of geological time that we and our ancestors have walked the planet (and hurried to get out of the weather), the global climate has oscillated through several major cycles of heating and cooling. The evidence of these cycles is all around us. The smoothed mountains, loose boulders, and gravel hills of northeastern America; the slowly rising beaches along the Great Lakes; and the notches of stopped-and-started growth in the corals of the Caribbean are all physical evidence left by the immense glaciers that grew and then shrank during these cycles.

- What caused these cycles?
- Are we in the middle of one of these cycles right now?
- What contributes to these cycles?

We don't have any definite answers to such questions. Perhaps your child will be one of the scientists who helps unravel this particular meteorological mystery.

If our planet were not spinning and were uniformly heated from just one direction, our weather would be a lot easier to figure out. You can watch a cup of hot tea with milk sitting on a steady surface and see the slow rolls of fluid as warm and expanded portions of the liquid rise and cooler and contracted portions sink. This process is called convection. On a global scale, convection is the principle engine that drives our weather. Weather in a teacup is simple. Unfortunately for meteorologists, we don't live in a teacup; we live on a rapidly spinning globe whose rotation brings it under the intense radiation of the sun for a part of each day and exposes it to the coldness of space for the other part. The sun's heat provides the energy for the evaporation of water and the rise of heated and expanded air, while the earth's rotation keeps the whole brew in constant motion. When you add to this the enormous currents of frigid suboceanic currents flowing from pole to pole and the temperature-regulating effects of our vast oceans, you get an idea of how hard our weather is to predict.

Our Furnace in the Sky It's a big one, and, like all furnaces, it will eventually exhaust its own fuel. (Since the

STILL LEARNING

"It is unclear whether the shift in large-scale atmospheric circulation that has brought more severe northeasters to the Middle Atlantic and New England states is a result of natural variation in the climate system or is related to changing global temperature patterns that accompany global warming. 'The outright honest answer is that we don't know what is behind the change,' said Dr. Robert E. Davis, a climatologist at the University of Virginia."
—*New York Times*, October 29, 1996

sun's burnout will happen millions of years from now, you can go right on worrying about how to afford college instead). Our star radiates a tremendous amount of energy into space. Although we perceive only a very small portion of this energy with our senses—the light and the heat—we are affected by its entire spectrum.

The sun's energy drives our atmosphere, provides the energy that supports our food chain, and fuels the processes that shape and sculpt the surface of our planet. Until very recently, the sun was seen as completely beneficent and the source of all life. We have now come to realize that this benign view doesn't quite describe the case. Technology has increased the scope of our senses far beyond the limits of our eyes, ears, and skin, enabling us to become aware of the force and hazards of the entire range of radiant energy that our star sends us. The sun washes our planet with intense levels of this radiation, and it is only the interaction of our atmosphere and our planet's daily rotation that keep the levels of exposure to solar radiation at tolerable levels (but don't forget that sunscreen!).

One Furnace Among Many The sun is the energetic center and gravitational focus of a system of planets, their satellites, and vast rings of debris (the asteroids and comets) that stretch far out into space. Our solar system is several billion years old and, although the pace has slowed since its youth, it is still in the process of change. We are just at the beginnings of our understanding of both our own system and our immediate galactic surroundings. As we sweep through space on the outer rim of a spiral galaxy, that galaxy itself is in motion in relation to other galaxies. Without the benefit of wormholes, teleporters, and the other apparatus of science fiction, we can only use the instruments we have and our own imaginations to speculate about where we came from and where we are going. Nonscientist adults can find all of this a little daunting, but most 5th and 6th graders find it exciting to think about. They are at an age when they can put all of the factual knowledge they have gathered so far at the service of wonder.

GOOD SCIENCE DOUBTS

Here's some advice for parents on kids and doing science:

- Cut your kids some slack. Don't tell them they have to believe something like Newton's First Law just because it's the "right" way to look at things. There's no better way to turn kids off to learning.
- When you're talking about science concepts with kids, and the concepts don't jive with everyday life, encourage kids to be skeptical. That's what scientists do. Tell them NOT to believe anything unless they're convinced. But make it clear that you don't have to believe in something to understand it. This amounts to an end-run around those kids who will claim they don't have to get something right on a test if they don't believe it. Clever, but too sneaky!
- Use sentences like, "According to Newton's First Law, what should happen here?" That way, you make it clear that the purpose is to understand the concept and how it applies to a situation rather than to believe the concept.
- Show kids that even though it tends to contradict common sense, something like Newton's First Law helps predict a lot of things. In other words, it works. If it didn't work, we wouldn't use it.

—The Wild Goose Co.

YOUR CHILD'S BIRTHRIGHT

To prepare America for the 21st century, we must harness the powerful forces of science and technology to benefit all Americans.

This is the first State of the Union carried live over the Internet. But we have only begun to spread the benefits of a technology revolution that should be the modern birthright of every citizen.

Our effort to connect every classroom is just the beginning. Now, we should connect every hospital to the Internet, so doctors can instantly share data about their patients with the best specialists in the field. And I challenge the private sector to start by connecting every children's hospital as soon as possible, so that a child in bed can stay in touch with school, family and friends. A sick child need no longer be a child alone.
—from the 1997 State of the Union Address, President Clinton

Core Area 4: Technology

The difference between science and technology is largely a difference of purpose. Technology is generally considered to be the use of tools, materials, and scientific knowledge to solve human problems, while the purpose of science is the study of all aspects of the natural world. However, even in the adult world, the distinction between science and technology is fuzzy. A contemporary entomologist might be involved in the purely scientific study of bee flight patterns to determine how they navigate, or he might be using computer simulations to construct a practical portable housing system for beekeepers who transport their hives for commercial crop pollination.

For elementary and middle school students, the distinction is worth knowing; but since much of the science work in these years is concerned with physical exploration using tools, machines, and the beginnings of scientific concepts, the distinction is not always important except as an introduction to how we put our knowledge to practical use.

Bits and Bytes In the mid-1960s, Harvard University maintained an entire floor of a specially air-conditioned computer lab to house an enormous computer costing thousands and thousands of dollars. Today, 30 years later, a computer just as powerful gets slung over the arm of a young executive as she catches her bus to work. The extent to which the information revolution has altered our world is hard to assess because we are still right in the middle of it. New computer applications, technologies, and devices are appearing so quickly that it is hard to keep up and even harder to pin down in a school's curriculum. Even so, it is useful for children (most of whom seem to be at least as comfortable with computers as we are, or more so) to spend some time thinking about computers in a more general way.

In grades five and six, kids learn that computers are operated on sets of instructions, that these instructions have rules and a grammar, and (as many of us have found out) computers can be even fussier than English teachers about getting those rules and that grammar exactly right. Your child should also be learning that the tired adage "garbage in, garbage out" is both true and important. Sometimes the world of movie and television fantasy, peopled (or should we say machined) by invincible robot creatures and all-knowing electronic brains, makes it a little hard to see the computer as just a piece of equipment that depends on how humans use it.

In the earlier grades, the use of computers in science education is of dubious value. What matters most for elementary science students is tangible experience. In middle school, however, youngsters are ready to use the computer as an adjunct to their science work. It is a powerful tool for record keeping, problem solving, model making, predicting, and communicating.

In schools that provide practical computer skills training, you will find instruction being offered in elementary touch typing, homework applications, and basic operating procedures. Students are expected to know and understand how to use different technologies for data storage and retrieval such as CD-ROM, disks, and online systems. Many schools are beginning to install networks that allow telecommunication among classrooms, different schools, and educational services.

Eureka! The history of technological development and the effects of technology on human life often supplements science education in these grades. The personalities of inventors and their unique (and sometimes eccentric) working and thinking styles are excellent examples of creativity at work. Their stories also teach the importance of unfettered imagination modulated by the disciplined use of basic science skills.

The Wright brothers are a perfect example. They had a vision, a purpose, and the diligence to experiment over and over again. During the years in which they developed their flyer, they drew upon the scientific knowledge available at the time, such as the research already done by the German Otto Lilienthal; they built and tested models using scientific equipment such as a wind tunnel; and they kept detailed and accurate records as an aid to their problem solving.

LOG ON AND LEARN

There's a classroom service for your child that doesn't require field trips, school bus rides, lunchboxes, or teacher conferences. It's a cyberservice that goes right into your home via the Internet. A group called OnlineClass has offered some fascinating courses taken by thousands of kids. Class samplings: Blue Ice (all about Antarctica, including actual links for students directly to scientists and explorers in Antarctica), U.S. politics (specially timed to coincide with the presidential elections), and Student Ocean Challenge (kids follow sailing fleets around the world). To register and obtain more information, reach OnlineClass at: http://www.usinternet.com/onlineclass

CYBERSCHOOL MAGAZINE

Go to this site and you'll be hit with a variety of educational information. The articles here are fun and different and slightly disorganized, but the real prize is the Surfin' Librarian page, with loads of links to museums, libraries, maps, and education sites on the Web. Check out this cool tool at: http://www.infoshare.ca/csm/index.htm

Contemporary technological achievements also make excellent case studies for middle schoolers, either as the basis for projects or as subjects for research activities. The completion of the tunnel under the English channel or the Fort McHenry tunnel underneath Baltimore's harbor are two examples. The Fort McHenry tunnel used the immersed tube technique, which involves digging an enormous trench, floating in prefabricated tunnel sections weighing tens of thousands of tons, and then sinking them so they join up end to end with tolerances of just a few inches. Extraordinary achievements like this (that wed skills and knowledge of science and mathematics) are all around us, and all of them are worth studying.

Middle schoolers themselves thrive on opportunities to create. Good science programs provide them with the time and materials to solve problems with technology in their own creations. Making plans and then using them to create devices that solve specific problems puts many science skills into practical focus—and it's fun to dream of things, build them, and make them work!

NO GARBAGE

Be an active advocate in your school district for good, nutritional lunch programs for your child and fellow classmates. The Physicians Committee for Responsible Medicine just surveyed 20 large U.S. school districts to find the nutritionally best and worst lunch programs. **Best:** Miami's Dade County Public School District, serving low-fat salads and fruit plates, salad bars, and daily vegetarian options. **Very good:** New York City, Houston, Atlanta, and Charlotte. **Worst:** Chicago Public Schools, with no options for low-fat or vegetarian meals. **Other "bottom feeders"**: Los Angeles, Washington, D.C., Cleveland, and San Francisco. For a full copy of the PCRM report, write to them at 5100 Wisconsin Avenue, Suite 404 NW, Washington, D.C. 20016, or call them at (202) 686-2210.

Core Area 5: Health

Although health is an aspect of science, schools vary in how they integrate health education into the 5th and 6th grade curriculum. In some school systems, for instance, health programs are defined and taught separately, while in others, health topics are covered not as a separate science core area but as a part of other core areas, such as life science.

Health education often involves less experimentation and exploration than the other sciences, because some health issues make it necessary to provide straight factual information and lay down clear-cut rules. Simple experiments like growing cultures from material scraped off hands fresh from the playground might make important visual points about cleanliness, but no one wants to actually swallow the results! This is even more true when the hazards are unseen, like viruses or the lead in soil and paint, when the threat is invisible and the risks can be even greater.

Personal Health Given the intense interest of children at this age in personal appearance (even for those who won't admit it), personal grooming and cleanliness are topics of great interest. Other aspects of personal well being that are covered are first aid, the safe use of tools and materials, and the importance of safety equipment in school activities, after-school sports, and occupations. Some schools also provide an introduction to more sophisticated and valuable first aid techniques such as the Heimlich maneuver.

Inside the body Earlier learning about our body systems and some new learning at this point about the nervous and reproductive systems often form the basis for more advanced thinking about the whole human body as a larger, integrated system.

Given the physical sensitivity of youngsters at this period in their lives, it helps to focus on characteristics of humans that don't carry a particular emotional or societal charge, but whose study can lead into thinking about genetics and the role of heredity. Left and right handedness is one such characteristic. A steady proportion of humans (roughly ten percent) are left handed—a fact that has been documented through time by studying ancient Egyptian murals, ancient cave hand prints, as well as the flaking patterns of stone tools that humans created over a million years ago. All three of the candidates for president in the 1992 American election—Bill Clinton, George Bush, and Ross Perot—were left handed. Students can do statistical studies of their classmates and families to explore handedness and use libraries to research this subject and its link to heredity and habits.

Students continue to learn about the organisms that cause disease and how the body defends against them, and how the skin, digestive system, and immune system act to protect them. Teaching is provided about specific infectious diseases and the methods of infection as review or as new material depending upon how the school system has handled the subject in earlier years. Some diseases are of short duration and not very serious, like the common cold; other infections may be fairly short yet severe, like influenza, and some are of longer duration, like tuberculosis. Chronic diseases, which

ENERGY LEVELS

At Score@Kaplan, I see a lot of kids who have an extracurricular activity almost every day of the week—musical instruments, sports, gymnastics, martial arts. Part of these after-school projects work out well. Many kids have extra energy, and it helps to work it off every day after school. Some kids can maintain that schedule and still have enough energy to go home and do well on their homework, and to interact well with their friends and family. But that's not every child!

NOT ONLY IN SCHOOL

Parents are often disappointed with their children's schools. Their expectations may be exaggerated. They expect a teacher to teach their kids everything. But when a kid is learning to read or add, there are many different stimuli in our environment that contribute to a children's learning—it doesn't all happen at school. Parents have a key role in their child's education. The more active role they take, the more their children will get out of school.

NEED TO KNOW

Kids hear so many health rumors—about AIDS, drugs, etc.—and parents need to know there is misinformation floating around. Offer to help your child look up solid, reliable health facts!

THE WHY FILES

The National Institute for Science Education has a nifty Web site with topics lifted from the headlines. Questions like "Is there life on Mars?" are addressed in fun, readable essays accompanied by charts and illustrations. Message boards and a great science image library make this a site worth exploring with your child: http://whyfiles.news.wisc.edu

affect the patient for much longer or are permanently debilitating, are also covered. Kids in these grades are also at a stage at which they can draw upon other aspects of their science learning to discuss how some disease conditions are the result of cellular or organ dysfunction—sickle-cell anemia and diabetes are two examples.

Some kinds of essential health education specific to particular regions of North America are taught or reviewed. For instance, learning about the ticks that carry Rocky Mountain spotted fever and Lyme disease and how to minimize one's exposure are vital in areas where these diseases are a risk. Rabies is another concern that should make education about how to avoid infection extremely important.

What You Put Inside Most schools do the best they can to provide the current best knowledge of healthy nutrition in general and our physiological need for certain amounts of vitamins and minerals. This is an area that nutritionists and medical scientists are constantly refining, and so the best teaching is that which emphasizes the need to be constantly aware of what you consume. How to be an intelligent consumer (and learning how to read those labels!) is a vital part of every middle school child's health education. Learning the effects on the body's systems of harmful substances such as tobacco, alcohol, and drugs is a necessary part of this education.

Obesity is a difficult subject for schools because of the physical changes and social pressures students encounter at this age. However, obesity is being recognized as a major health problem and one that can possibly be resolved by early intervention. The combination of nutritionally poor (but heavily advertised) food, the decrease in physical education programs in schools, the decrease of physical activity in general, and the increase in time spent plopped in front of one kind of screen or another have combined to cause an alarming increase in overweight adults and children. Health programs that focus on nutrition will probably be increasing the focus on good eating and exercise habits.

Two other disorders that involve denying the body food or binging and purging, anorexia and bulimia, may be touched upon in school health programs, since it is most often in these years that these problems may start, primarily among girls. These are serious and specific health problems that are recognized as primarily psychological disorders, and should be treated by medical professionals. The physiological consequences of these eating disorders range from severe to dreadful because the attending malnutrition affects bone development, sexual maturation, and, in extreme cases, causes death. Helping children to accept their bodies and providing opportunities to talk about the baleful effects of advertising on young people's images of themselves are preventative measures that any family can take, along with avoiding activities that subordinate a child's health and well being to external goals such as sports activities that can damage their healthy development and affect future health.

Some schools offer health education programs that cover mental and social health issues, and, in some regions, education about HIV and other public health problems. These topics are usually taught by specially trained personnel. Sex education, another appropriate topic for this age, is sometimes handled in a separate course on human growth and development and is often taught by specially prepared teachers.

Core Area 6: Inquiry Skills

All of the topic areas of science draw upon a basic set of investigative skills. These scientist's skills, in their simplest forms, are part of our basic intellectual equipment as curious human beings. In addition to skills practiced in earlier years, the skills outlined below are refined and practiced in the middle school years and, if encouraged, grow into the more sophisticated analytic and predictive skills needed in high school and college science (and life).

Observational Skills Increased dexterity and intellectual development extend the ability to make observation possible beyond the range of our immediate senses:

SCIENCE HAS LIMITATIONS

Scientists spend their lives asking WHY this or that happens. Most people assume that a good scientist will be able to answer a few WHY questions for them. Why is the sky blue? Why do things fall to Earth?

"Why do things fall to Earth?" Everyone knows it's because of gravity. Then you can ask, "Well, what is gravity?" Well, it's the thing that makes stuff fall to Earth. Duh! You see, the answer isn't really an answer at all, it just gives a name to something. Now a physicist will give you a different answer. She will talk about a force that acts between all things, and she'll write down a formula that describes how the force behaves. But you can keep asking WHY questions, like Why does this force exist?

If you're looking for the "ultimate" answer to your WHY questions, science is the wrong place! Why do we bring all this up? Because we believe that if kids understood some of the limitations of science, they may not be so scared of it and may be willing to tackle those limitations head-on to find even more. —The Wild Goose Co.

BALANCING ACT

Some parents boast, "I'm not one of those parents who overschedules their children. I make sure my kids have time for their friends, time for their schoolwork, and maybe one other activity." It doesn't seem that learning is a burden for these kids. Schoolwork is fun, not just another activity on their list that needs to be crossed off. They also seem to have a great relationship with their parents because they spend time together. Certainly the kids who seem the happiest and the kids who do the best in school are kids who have time to spend with their families and time to explore school.

LEARN ALL YOU CAN

Our philosophy in Score@Kaplan is that children need to have all the learning experiences they can, and you can't learn if you're missing out on some.

- Increase in the use of specialized measuring tools such as microbalances and specialized thermometers
- Extending measuring skills: knowing the difference between, and being able to use, both digital and analog measuring devices, using more sensitive devices, keeping appropriate records of measurements
- Observing with tools that change the scale of observation, such as binoculars, microscopes, and magnifying glasses

Descriptive Skills Students begin to move far beyond the simple groupings of earlier years and can work with complicated groups and subgroups. An increase in general word skills extends the richness of scientific description:

- Categorization extended to include multiple subdivisions for materials and the properties of materials, as well as for the families and characteristics of living things
- Beginning to use mathematical and other scientific vocabulary to describe physical processes
- Continuing to develop methods and vocabulary for classification and description using more specific and accurate terminology

Experimental Skills Science investigations begin to become more complex at the 5th and 6th grade levels:

- Planning and executing investigations and experiments and presenting the results with a variety of methods and techniques, reports, posters, slide shows, and computer graphics and displays
- Considering whether a problem or process can be investigated through direct observation or not and applying multiple lines of investigation to solve problems

Interpretive Skills Middle school students are ready to make more sophisticated uses of data such as:

- The representation of data collected from observation with tables, models, demonstrations, and graphs
- Noting and describing relevant patterns, details, and relationships within and among objects and processes

The Unity and Diversity of Science

Today's scientists work back and forth among many disciplines. The older, rigid idea of separate science disciplines has been crumbling for some time, and school curriculums have begun to change to accommodate this tendency. A modern biologist will draw upon mathematical statistics to work out population questions, chemistry to determine nutritional needs, and computer science to keep track of it all. There has been a greatly increased interest in crossdiscipline collaborations within research science. A recent and very exciting study of heart circulation, for example, was undertaken by an academic mathematician with an interest in fluid dynamics and a research pathologist.

This interdisciplinary trend is reflected in the schools by the increased attention being paid to what is called *crossdomain study*. Educators have an unfortunate tendency to apply learned names to simple concepts. What they mean by crossdomain is that science doesn't exist in tight-fitting and well-labeled drawers in a library. It sprawls all over the place, and the really good scientists draw skills and information from whatever field has what they need.

When students consider the effects of weather on the surface of our planet and the role of the sun, they shouldn't have to draw boundaries in their minds between this and that field of study. What is important are the interactions of what we know from geology, oceanography, meteorology, astronomy, and mathematics. Learning how to think flexibly, how to draw from as many intellectual resources as are available, and how to adapt and use our constantly growing technology are the skills that will take our young scientists into their very challenging and exciting future.

JUST BORN THAT WAY

Some kids don't get a lot of parental pressure about school performance, but they put a tremendous amount of internal pressure on themselves to succeed. It's important for parents to recognize this and come up with a plan to combat it. Some students start crying when they don't get consistently perfect or high marks on a test or assignment. When these kids get into high school, they're going to have nervous breakdowns. When they get into college, forget it! If they're in a class with other bright students, and they're perhaps not in the top of the class, they are going to freak out. Parents often feel self-conscious about their stressed-out child—they wonder if it's something they did. Kids have personalities from the day they're born, and some kids are just born like this.

What Can We Do at Home?

Learning Adventures— 5th Grade Language Arts

IS YOUR CHILD ENGAGED?

Emotionally engaged students try hard in school, believe that doing well in school is important, and have faith that what they are learning there is valuable. —from *Beyond the Classroom* by Laurence Steinberg, Ph.D. (Simon & Schuster, 1996)

WHAT'S MORE

If your child has written a letter that could go to more than one person in government, make additional copies, changing the inside and envelope address and the salutation for each, and send it to as many people as she wishes.

CAPITOL CAPITALS

Letters to political figures are a time-honored way of letting off steam, expressing a concern, exercising political pressure, or saying thanks for a job well done. And they are heeded. You may not always get much of a response, but when someone takes the trouble to write, it is noticed.

Writing formal letters to political figures gives students the opportunity to practice almost every possible use of capital letters. Capitals are used in the addresses, titles, salutation, closing, and body of such letters. If you and your child pick a topic close to your hearts, the letter will have an urgency and purpose that makes this much more than an exercise.

At a Glance

Grade/Subject: 5th/Language Arts—Mechanics
Skills: capitalization, writing formal letters
Materials: pencil and draft paper
pen and better paper
envelope
Time: 1 hour

Getting Ready

Talk with your child about something that concerns her about the government, the environment, the law, or any other issue that

WHERE DO I SEND IT?

United States

President:
President William Clinton
The White House Office
1600 Pennsylvania Ave. NW
Washington, DC 20500

Member of Congress:
Congressman (Full Name)
United States House of Representatives
Washington, DC 20515

Senator:
Senator (Full Name)
United States Senate
Washington, DC 20510

Canada

Prime Minister or Member of Cabinet:
Prime Minister or Honorable (Full Name)
Office of (Prime Minister or Cabinet Post)
Langevin Block
80 Wellington
Ottawa, Ontario KIA03A

Member of Parliament:
Honorable (Full Name)
Langevin Block
111 Wellington St.
Ottawa, Ontario KIA0A4

Senate:
Honorable (Full Name)
Langevin Block
111 Wellington St.
Ottawa, Ontario KIA0A4

involves your elected representatives. When you've picked a topic, have her write down or dictate to you some rough notes of what she'd like to say on the subject.

Step One

In the body of a formal letter it's important to observe all the basic rules of punctuation. Sentences begin with capitals, and capitals are used for titles, proper names, the official names of governmental bodies, and places. Have your child use her notes to write a rough draft of her letter, and then the two of you can edit it together. Don't write a final version yet, though.

Step Two

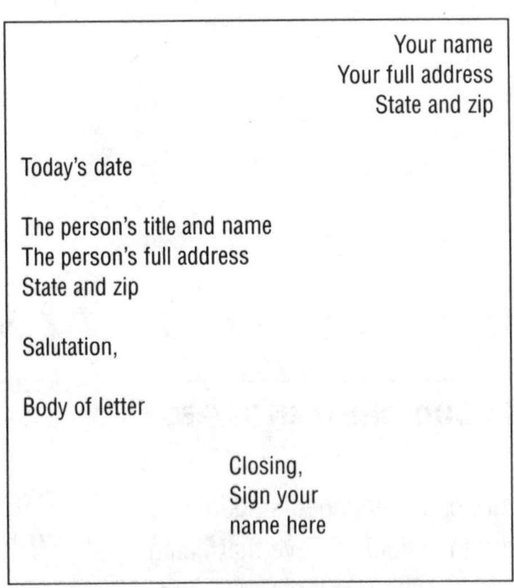

Formal letters from a single person usually have the addresses of the writer and the receiver at the top. Most often the writer's address is first and on the right-hand side. The receiver's address is next and on the left-hand side. Write out a rough version of both addresses, and edit them with particular attention to capital letters. The salutation (Dear . . .) is capitalized, as is the closing (Sincerely, Yours, or Thank you).

Your name
Your full address
State & zip

The Person's title and name
The Person's address
State & zip

Step Three

When your child has given her letter a final look over, she's ready to write it up on better paper. Typing or printing it out from a computer is okay, but a hand-written letter is good practice for your child.

Step Four

When she addresses the envelope, your child should use the same amount of care in punctuating and capitalizing. She could do a rough draft first, but since it's easiest to just copy the addresses from the heading of the letter, this isn't really necessary. That's it. All that remains is to seal and stamp the envelope and mail it.

WHAT'S MORE

If your child writes on behalf of an individual or cause, have her send a copy to the person or group she is writing to support. They will appreciate knowing that someone cares.

Letters to the editor of local papers about local topics is another way to polish writing skills. Well-written letters from young people about current local issues are frequently published.

DEAR PREZ

Start a letter to the president with "Dear Mr. President," but for Congress, it's "Dear Mr. X, or Dear Ms. X," (for Representatives) or "Dear Senator X."

▸ Dictionary Doodling

A dictionary is perhaps the most basic book for kids in middle school language arts. It can help them find out what an unfamiliar word means, how to pronounce it, and what other meanings the word has. The dictionary is important for their writing too, telling them how to spell different forms of a word and where to break a word into syllables.

This activity gives your child practice in using the dictionary for all those different skills and, at the same time, will build up his repertory of useful and usable words.

At a Glance

Grade/Subject: 5th/Language Arts—Reference/Study Skills
Skills: using the dictionary to find pronunciations, syllabication, parts of speech, word derivations; building vocabulary
Materials: dictionary
newspapers or magazines (changing daily or over time)
diary, weekly calendar, or small notebook
pencil or pen
Time: 1/2 hour each evening (if possible) or at least twice a week

Getting Ready

Be sure your home has a good dictionary for your whole family to use—inexpensive paperback editions are available. For general family use, the so-called "collegiate" editions are okay. At some point, you may want to invest in a larger, more comprehensive dictionary.

Step One

Use a newspaper or magazine as your main source for choosing words to investigate in the dictionary. Each evening—or at least a few times a week—sit down with your child and skim through

UN BUEN IDEA

For native speakers of other languages, the dictionary can help in choosing the best English word to use in a given situation.

WHAT'S MORE

As you continue the activity, encourage other family members to bring in mystery or problem words that they've met in their own reading. You can turn exploring the dictionary into a family project.

You need a firm grasp of alphabetical order to use the dictionary well. If this is a problem for your kid, build in some extra practice on the alphabet, using the guide words on a dictionary page.

Take a trip to the library to explore some of the unusual dictionaries available—slang, rhyming words, scientific terms, cooking terms, and the like.

news stories looking for five words (more or less) that he doesn't know well.

Have him write those words on his page for the day in his diary, calendar, or notebook. Then, before looking the words up, ask him to try to figure out the meaning of each one from its context or other clues. Also have him try to pronounce each word and say whether it is a noun, verb, adjective, adverb, or other part of speech.

Step Two

Now have him turn to the dictionary entry for the first of the words. In the first few sessions, go over the different parts of the dictionary entry with him. The entry word, usually in boldface type, shows how the word is divided into syllables. That's followed by the pronunciation, which is written using one of several different special systems of symbols (which are generally found at the front of the dictionary).

Point out where the dictionary entry uses abbreviations to tell what part (or parts) of speech the word can be. If any changes in form—plurals or different tenses—have unusual or problematic spellings, the dictionary lists those, too.

Step Three

Review together all the definitions (usually numbered) that are given for the word your child is looking up. Remind him not to assume the meaning in the context where he found the word fits the first meaning he reads. He should try out each meaning in the context of the sentence. Discuss which meaning seems to work best.

To keep building a working vocabulary, have him write the original sentence along with the word and its meaning in his notebook. Have him then make up a sentence of his own using the word, and have him write his sentence in as well.

Step Four

Repeat the Dictionary Doodling process with the other words for the day. Encourage him to use the same process with words that crop up in school reading assignments, conversations, TV programs, and recreational reading. Make "looking it up" an automatic response to meeting an unfamiliar word.

▸ Getting Down to Business

A skill that lasts a lifetime is the ability to write a good business letter. Your 5th grader can be delighted to discover that a well-prepared letter can yield a response from the world out there. As your child goes on through school, carefully prepared letters will help her in getting jobs, scholarships, and other benefits.

This activity jumps off from your child's interests to focus on writing a business letter that expresses an opinion or asks for information or action. You can also adapt it to many situations of interest to your child and your family.

At a Glance

Grade/Subject: 5th/Language Arts—Composition, Reference and Study Strategies
Skills: writing a business letter in correct form, asking for information in writing
Materials: typewriter or word processor
standard-size (8 1/2 × 11) white typing paper
Time: 1–2 hours per letter, in addition to preliminary research

Getting Ready

Lead up to this activity by starting family discussions about events in the news that you or other family members care about. These might range from activity at a sports stadium or shopping mall to a current election campaign or questions about human rights or child labor.

Step One

Focus on a topic or issue that your child cares about or is curious about. Talk about it and the kind of letter she could write and what she would like to say in the letter. Does she have an opinion about an issue—say, community activities for kids or actions that affect wildlife? Does she want to ask for information about something? Does she have a complaint about a product or the desire to congratulate someone? Decide together on the person (or organization) to whom she will write her letter. Have her find out the correct address, using the telephone book or library resources.

ORDER ISN'T EVERYTHING

Dictionaries vary in the order in which they list the different meanings of a single word. Some go from oldest to most recent meaning, others from most common to least common meanings.

SEND THEM OUT

Encourage your child to send her thoughts and opinions out into the world. The Getting Down to Business activity is full of ideas for writing other kinds of formal letters as well.

Step Two

If the letter is going to express an opinion, have your kid jot down a short list of the points she wants to include: Why does she think this issue is important? What are her thoughts or opinions about it? What actions does she want taken or want to know more about?

To get the right information, she needs to think out clearly what questions she wants to have answered. Does she plan to ask for informational pamphlets or other materials?

Step Three

Help your child draft the letter. Talk about the differences between a business letter such as this and a friendly letter—not just the tone and style of the letter itself, but also the inclusion of a formal inside address, which a friendly letter doesn't have. The closing and signature style also differ from friendly letters. Remember that a business letter should state its purpose up front and be short and to the point.

Go over the correct forms for the inside address and the formal salutation. The letter should be written on a typewriter or word processor if possible. If it is handwritten, be sure it is neat and well spaced on the page.

Step Four

Continue to look for more opportunities to write letters in correct business form. Besides opinion letters, your child might want to write for information to organizations such as the following: science or sports equipment companies, tourist information offices (local, state, or foreign) for family vacations, schools or museum programs in other locations, and collectors of stamps, cards, or coins.

WHAT'S MORE

Acquiring interesting foreign stamps can motivate kids to write to organizations or people in other countries.

Letter-writing follows the steps of the Writing Process. Editing and proofreading are especially important stages. Neatness counts!

Now that your child is in the letter-writing groove, check out the classic kids' activity book *Free Stuff for Kids* (published in annual editions by Meadowbrook Press/Simon & Schuster) for a great collection of places your child can write to for free or inexpensive items from a variety of clubs, organizations, sports teams, and manufacturers.

"HALF" TIME

Lots of familiar words are compounded or blended from two independent words. Often a compound word actually combines the meanings of the two base words—like *headache* (*head* + *ache*) or *rattlesnake* (*rattle* + *snake*). But sometimes the two halves just don't add up—like, for instance, *butterfly*!

Here's a rummylike card game that helps build awareness of how such words are put together. The aim of each player in this game is to acquire a hand of six cards that all can be paired to make words. Bringing together the parts that make up such compound words can also be a big help to your child in spelling those words.

At a Glance

Grade/Subject: 5th/Language Arts—Vocabulary, Spelling
Skills: using base words and roots, spelling difficult words
Materials: 40 to 60 blank index cards (or smaller cards, which you can make by cutting index cards in half)
colored markers
notebook and pencil
dictionary (to check words)
Time: 1/2 hour once or twice a week

Getting Ready

To get ready for the game, make a list of 15, 20, or 25 compound words. For a game with two people, you can start with 40 cards (that is, 20 words cut in half). For more players—and more challenge—make a deck of 60 or more cards.

Here's some words (divided into halves) to get you started:

air/mail	eye/glass	grass/hopper
cup/cake	rain/drop	star/fish
wild/life	jump/suit	night/fall

Step One

Now create a deck of cards made up of "half-words." Use the markers to print half of each compound word on a slip of paper or flashcard. To add to the fun, include a number of words that share a half—for instance, *headache* and *heartache,* or *rainfall, nightfall,* and *waterfall,* or *raindrop, gumdrop,* and *dropout.*

Shake the cards in a box or shuffle them. Deal six cards to each player. Place the remainder in a pile face down in the center. Toss a coin or roll dice to see who goes first.

Step Two

Each player, in turn, draws a card from the pile. He considers whether it can be matched up with one or more of the other cards in his hand. Then he either discards the new card or keeps it and discards a card from his hand. (Players should always have six cards.)

FROM BUTTERMILK TO BUTTERFLY

One dictionary suggests that *butterfly* may come from a folk belief that these colorful insects actually steal butter and milk!

PRACTICE MAKES PERFECT

Sometimes I find a fifth and sixth grader who doesn't know the months of the year. I had two brothers, and I realized that both didn't know the months. I brought this to their parents' attention, and that's an important part of what we do at Score@Kaplan. We help our parents reinforce lessons at home.

I told the brothers that every time they came in to Score, they could go over the months of the year with me. If they got them right, I'd give them a Score card. I'd put down a month of the year and ask them what comes next and what comes before. Soon they got it down. This was something that took only a week and a half to get down, but it filled in a huge learning gap.

Step Three

Continue playing until one player has brought together a hand in which he can combine all the half-word cards to make words. That player says, "HalfTime!" and lays down the cards in his hand arranged in pairs that make words.

Step Four

To score, players earn two points for each pair of words in their hand, that is each compound word. Players lose one point for each unmatched card in their hand.

If any of a player's cards can be combined with more than one other card to make a legitimate word, the player gets extra points. For example, a winning hand might include these six cards: *night/shirt, rain/fall, egg/plant.* Since *night* can pair with *fall* (*nightfall*) as well as with *shirt*, the player would get an extra two points.

WHAT'S MORE

Your first deck might include words that can be a part of several compound words, such as *ache, air, man,* and *book.*

Decorate your playing cards with sketches illustrating the half-words.

Use a dictionary or little spelling handbook to find a lot more compound words to add to your deck.

Try using the rules of the card game *Go Fish* to play with your cards.

▸ HINKETY PINKETY

Some familiar word games are more than just ways to pass the time—they're also great ways to make your kid realize that language is fun and, at the same time, reinforce Language Arts skills.

A game of Hinkety Pinkety draws on vocabulary, a skill for definitions, and on a kid's ear for rhyming words.

This is an activity game that can involve the whole family. It's one of those games that can be played in the car, while making dinner, or while people are relaxing together after a holiday meal.

At a Glance

Grade/Subject: 5th/Language Arts—Listening Skills, Vocabulary
Skills: recognizing rhyming words, defining words, expanding vocabulary
Materials: dictionary (optional—to help out with definitions or challenges to definitions)
Time: 1/2 to 3/4 hour, whenever the time seems appropriate

Getting Ready

Familiarize yourself and your kid with the concept behind the game:

VISUALIZE THEIR GOALS

Make a picture or drawing with your child that helps him color in his goals, like drawing a mountain with a chapter of a book at each level. Just the little coloring when he works on his goals helps him see how many study steps he's getting done.

- A Hink Pink is a two-word rhyming phrase—usually an adjective plus a noun—that one player gives to fit the definition given by another player. For example, "a scarlet sleeping place" would be a "red bed." (Or, more subtly, "a sleeping place in the former Soviet Union.")
- A two-syllable Hink Pink is a Hinky Pinky.
- A three-syllable phrase is a Hinkety Pinkety.

Step One

With your kid, go over how the game works. The starting player declares the length of the clue—that is, Hink Pink, Hinky Pinky, or Hinkety Pinkety. Then the starting player offers a synonym phrase or a longer clue with that same general meaning.

For instance, an "obese feline" is, of course, a "fat cat." Another approach to this definition would be "what happens when Morris gets greedy." When making up clues, it helps to think of the rhyming adjective and noun first, then make up the clue to describe it. Here are a few examples:

Hink Pink:
"where Disney's Mickey lives"—mouse house
"a candy bar" or "sugary goodie"—sweet treat
"a comfortable college lodging"—warm dorm

Hinky Pinky:
"a gruesome Halloween tale"—gory story
"what you learn at a university"—college knowledge
"the more expensive knit garment"—better sweater

Hinkety Pinkety:
"a way to transport your dog"—terrier carrier
"what you sleep in on your Caribbean vacation"—Bahamas pajamas
"a really great ocean"—terrific Pacific

Step Two

Hinkety Pinkety is a casual, friendly game. Challenges pass back and forth as players give correct answers. Its value, besides fun, is in its challenge to the mind, to the hidden depths of your kid's (and your own) vocabulary and imagination, and to the ear.

WHAT'S MORE

Rhymes and rhyming are especially important in English because the language is so rich in similar sounds. You can hear this in many familiar nursery rhymes: "Higgledy, piggledy. . . . " Check out library books with rhyming lines and enjoy reading them together.

Think of definitions for these Hink Pinks and Hinky Pinkies: stern tern (serious seabird?), fickle pickle (unfaithful gherkin?), soccer locker (where you keep your team uniform?), bee's trees (a yummy arboretum for Winnie the Pooh?).

Try turning your Hink Pink or Hinky Pinky phrases into funny, short poems.

A KINDLER, GENTLER NET

Experts predict that 15 million kids will be on the Internet by the year 2000 (up from 6.3 million in 1997)! Many parents have asked for a management device that allows them to control their children's access to the Internet. One such safe surfing tool is CyberPatrol™. Its administration screen lets parents and teachers control a child's use of a computer by hours of the day and by specific Internet locations. It blocks questionable sites, filters browsing, and limits total time spent online. A CyberNOT List is also included, as well as a subscription service which allows the list to be updated weekly; the list alerts parents to sites with questionable Net content in a number of areas. You can download a free 14-day working demo from www.classroom.net/cyberpatrol, or call Classroom Connect at (800) 638-1639 for more information.

LISTEN UP!

Preteens and teenagers are the focus of many advertising campaigns and techniques, among the most common:

- Endorsements by popular figures in sports, fashion, or entertainment
- Appeals to the almost-universal wish to be popular and attractive
- The bandwagon approach—"Everybody's doing it!"

Help your kid become a more careful listener, developing and sharpening his awareness of these appeals, especially as they are used in TV programs and commercials. He'll also develop ways of recognizing and thinking about ad techniques.

At a Glance

Grade/Subject: 5th/Language Arts—Listening, Speaking, and Viewing Skills; Thinking Skills and Strategies
Skills: listening for persuasive techniques in TV programming, recognizing propaganda techniques used by advertisers
Materials: TV set
TV program guide (optional)
notebook and pen
Time: 1/2–1 hour of TV programs two or three times a week, plus 15–20 minutes discussion of each

Getting Ready

For this activity, both you and your child will probably have to make some changes in your personal routines for watching TV. You need to choose in advance a selection of programs to watch together. Try for a mix of kid-oriented programs on a variety of commercial and/or cable channels (rather than public television).

Plan on an hour of viewing for each session of this activity. Vary the composition of the hour: a mix of two half-hour shows, one hour-long show, or occasionally "channel-surfing" from one commercial to another.

Step One

Have your child set up a notebook, allotting several pages for each of the shows you plan to watch in full. For each program, its first page should list its name, time, and network. For each show, have him also make a note of its regular sponsor or sponsors.

As you watch, at each commercial break, have your child make a note of each product or service or campaign that is advertised in that time slot. Also have him make notes of any products, services, companies, or organizations that are talked about or promoted as part of the show itself.

Step Two

At the end of each listening session, go over the list together and talk about what claims the promotions or advertisements made.

- What techniques were used to make the product/service/ opinion attractive?
- Did the commercial use a spokesperson? Who was it—a model, a sports figure, an entertainer, an animal?
- Why does he think such a spokesperson was chosen?
- What background or setting was chosen? Why?
- What accompanying noise or music? Why?
- What does he remember most about the product/service/ opinion?

Have him make a short list of the features or qualities of each product/service/opinion promoted.

- Did the commercial make him want to buy the product/service or agree with the opinion?
- Does he think his friends would agree? Why?

Step Three

Follow up these first observations by returning to the same program a week or so later. Notice whether the same product/ service/opinion is being advertised. Is the commercial the same one you saw before? Did you remember it accurately?

Compare what you both remembered about the earlier commercial with the one you're watching now. What advertising techniques were most effective for you and your child? Discuss whether those techniques would appeal to lots of people or just a small audience. Why?

WHAT'S MORE

Draw and write a "print" ad for a product, service, or opinion you saw on TV. How is your ad different from the TV commercial?

Make a table that compares types of shows, number of commercials in a show, and products for each network you watched.

Make a separate list of the commercials and products that air between kid-oriented programs.

Watch public television and keep track of how and what products, services, and opinions are promoted there.

CONFIDENT KIDS

Being a director at Score@Kaplan has been a wonderful experience. It is incredibly rewarding to see kids enhance their academic skills, but equally important, they become more confident. It's great to see young children motivated by intrinsic factors. I applaud all the parents who care enough about their children's education to take extra efforts to instill confidence and fun in their learn-at-home activities.

MIND NUMBING?

How much time should a child spend on a computer? If kids are using a computer to write creatively, to analyze biological data for a school project, compose a symphony, or to improve reading and math skills, never fear. As with reading and writing, it's pretty safe to let children set their own limits. There's little danger of their reading and writing too much. On the other hand, your child should not sacrifice a single hour of outdoor play or cozy fireside conversation to play mind-numbing video games.

Step Four

Continue your observations and discussions for several weeks, watching a variety of programs. For each one, keep track of the variety of products advertised and the different commercials used on different dates. Notice whether your child is becoming a more careful and critical listener.

To follow up, have him look through the reports for each program and make a list of the general types and specific brands of product/service/opinion advertised on them. Can he spot ads that are specifically targeted to kids his age?

Patchwork Paragraphs

Learning the different parts of speech may be a problem for kids until they get a feeling for how each part is used in a sentence—the job it does that no other part of speech can do in that sentence.

This activity, for two people, requires both players to identify and supply missing parts of speech in a paragraph or more—out of context. The final results, read aloud, can be very funny.

At a Glance

Grade/Subject: 5th/Language Arts—Grammar, Listening/Speaking Skills
Skills: identifying parts of speech, reading aloud
Materials: access to a photocopier
favorite books
"white-out" correction fluid or correction tape
pens or pencils
Time: about 15–30 minutes for each paragraph (can be repeated frequently with different paragraph selections)

Getting Ready

Before starting, you and your child should each choose several paragraphs from a favorite book. In the library, at the office, or in a copy shop, make photocopies of the two selections.

Each of you will then white out (or cover with correction tape) a number of words scattered throughout your selection, making notes in the blank about what part of speech is needed there: verb, adjective, adverb, noun, plural noun, preposition.

If possible, make a second photocopy of the selections with the words blanked out. A copy will be easier to write on than the original corrected version, as correction fluid may dry in a lumpy blob.

If you want a quick refresher view of the parts of speech before starting, look back at the "Core Area 1: Language and Grammar" section.

Step One

To get started, read through your selection and ask your kid to supply the part of speech needed in each of the blanks. Write his suggestion in each space.

For example, say that the book you chose was *The Cricket in Times Square*. Here's how the beginning of chapter 1 might look after you blanked out key words and defined what was needed in the blanks:

"A [noun] was looking at Mario.
"The mouse's name was [proper noun], and he [past tense verb] in the opening of an [adjective] drain pipe in the [noun] at Times Square. The [noun] was his home. Back a few feet in the wall, it opened out into a pocket that Tucker [past perfect verb] with the bits of [noun] and shreds of [noun] he collected."

But all you would say to your kid is: "Give me a noun for the first sentence, then a proper noun for the first blank in the second sentence, then a past tense verb." And so on through the paragraph.

If necessary, coach your child to make sure he suggests the right part of speech for the blank. The kind of help he needs can help you pinpoint some of his grammar problems.

Step Two

When you've filled in all the blanks in your selection with your child's suggestions, hand him the filled-in page and ask him to read the "revised" paragraph aloud with the new words in it.

The more familiar the original book, the funnier the new version is likely to be.

READING PROBLEMS? PART 1

Does your child have a reading problem? As your child reads aloud with you, watch for these things:

- **Mispronunciation**—This covers saying the word incorrectly or adding or omitting words in sentences. Your child should be able to read eight out of ten words accurately. If your child stumbles over more than half the words, he or she may have a problem.
- **Fluency**—This is the smoothness with which your child reads. Does your child read with emphasis in the proper places so that you can easily understand what he or she is reading? Does your child read in a halting, choppy manner? If your child struggles with too many words, his or her fluency will be poor, and this may indicate some underlying reading difficulties.

—from *The Parent's Answer Book* by Gerald Deskin and Greg Steckler (Fairview Press, 1995)

Step Three

While you're enjoying the humor of incongruous words in a familiar story, also notice whether there's a pattern to your child's mistakes or hesitations. For instance, is he secure with nouns and adjectives but not so confident with verb tenses? How surely and quickly can he identify what part of speech each word in a sentence is?

Step Four

Repeat the same process with your child asking you to fill in the blanks in his selection. Then read that selection aloud.

This repetition offers another chance for you to work with your kid on accurately identifying what a given word does in a sentence. Did he ask you for the correct part of speech for each blank? If not, go over each wrong identification until he's more sure of them.

As you repeat this activity, notice whether your child is becoming more secure both in identifying what kind of word is needed in a blank and in suggesting the correct part of speech.

WHAT'S MORE

You can repeat this game with any paragraph, even a newspaper story or a familiar song or poem.

You can pull some surprises in this activity. Ask your kid, for instance, "What if I had asked you for a substitute word for *at* in the first sentence, or for *in* and *of* in the second sentence—what part of speech would I have asked you for?" (Parental hint: preposition)

Select a larger passage of several paragraphs, and prepare it with a variety of blanks. Gather a group of players together (more than two), and keep going around the group until all the blanks are filled. Try this at mealtime with the family.

Poetry, Please!

In those long-ago days before television—and even before radio—people made their own entertainment at home by memorizing and reciting poems and putting on their own plays. Even people with little education often could recite pages of great poetry and passages from Shakespeare. They absorbed and appreciated the splendor of the language and rhythm.

You can revive this tradition and help your child—and other family members—enjoy and appreciate some of the world's great literature. It also helps your child develop important skills in speaking, reading aloud, and interpreting meaning.

At a Glance

Grade/Subject: 5th/Language Arts—Literature, Listening and Speaking Skills
Skills: reading a variety of types of literature, reciting passages from memory, giving a dramatic reading
Materials: anthology of famous poems or collections by a favorite poet

favorite children's classic poems
access to photocopier
"dress-up" costumes such as capes, hats, etc. (optional)
Time: 1 hour two to three times a week, plus opportunities while riding in the car, at the dinner table, and the like

Getting Ready

The books of plays and poetry suggested under Materials are your source books for this activity. You can either buy inexpensive paperbacks or borrow them from the library. (Buying the paperbacks will add to your library, making sure good literature is always available.)

Don't ignore kids' favorites such as the Dr. Seuss books, *A Child's Garden of Verses* by Robert Louis Stevenson, and other children's classics. You may be surprised to find that your kid—and perhaps you, too—already have memorized pieces of these poems. For example, if you start out, "I do not like green eggs and ham," many people will be able to chime in with "I do not like them, Sam-I-am." Such familiar poems are good starting points for this activity.

Step One

With your child, browse through the books of poetry and look for selections to learn and memorize. Make a trip to the library to look through other collections, too. Look especially for anthologies aimed at young people or teenagers and for pieces from familiar books, such "Jabberwocky" from *Alice in Wonderland.*

Next, choose four or five poems each. They can be serious or humorous or a mix. Read them aloud to one another first before making your choice. Then make photocopies from the book so that you can carry copies with you and your child and study them during free time.

Suggestions for choosing poems to start with:

1. Choose a fairly short poem, with just a few verses. (Sonnet length—14 lines—is a comfortable length.) Later, you may want to take on longer poems, such as narratives with a story.
2. Poems with a definite rhyme scheme and/or meter are easier to memorize.
3. Most important of all, choose poems you each like!

READING PROBLEMS? PART 2

Does your child have a reading problem? As your child reads aloud with you, watch for these things:

• **Skipping lines/losing one's place**—While your child reads, ask him to look up at you, then ask your child a question, especially in the middle of a longer paragraph. Then ask your child to continue reading. Count how long it takes your child to find his place again. If the child takes longer than five seconds, he might have a reading problem.

• **Comprehension**—This is probably the most important area of reading. As your child reads, write down at least seven questions to ask him when he is finished. Your child should get at least five right. If your child has a score of three or less, he most likely has a problem with comprehension.

For more information on how to work with your child and improve reading, check out *The Parent's Answer Book: Over 101 Most-Asked Questions About Your Child's Well-Being* by Gerald Deskin and Greg Steckler (Fairview Press, 1995); contact Fairview at (800) 544-8207.

> **WHAT'S MORE**
>
> You can also revive the old custom of reading aloud as a family—novels, stories, or poetry. Try a chapter a night of an adventure novel.
>
> ---
>
> Techniques for memorizing differ. Some people learn from the printed page, others by repeating a verse aloud over and over. Give your child help when he asks for it.
>
> ---
>
> Enjoy old classics like "Casey at the Bat," "Little Orphan Annie," "The Cremation of Sam McGee," and nonsense poems by Edward Lear and Lewis Carroll.

Be ready to accept an unfamiliar or contemporary poem if it's something that appeals to your kid. Don't force your favorites on him—save them for yourself.

Step Two

After you've each chosen your first poem to memorize, work on learning it. Practice how you will recite it. And set a day and time to present the poems—perhaps just after dinner.

It's important that your child feels that you're participating in this activity, not just waiting to be his audience—he needs to see you make the same effort, even make mistakes as you memorize and repeat your own poem.

Step Three

When the day arrives, set the stage and get other family members and friends to be a cooperative audience as you and your child present the poems you've memorized (another reason for keeping the poems short!). Avoid a sense of pressure—the purpose of this activity is to make poetry enjoyable.

Then set the time and place for your next joint appearance and select new pieces to present. Keep repeating these three steps, perhaps making a regular routine of "Thursday Night Recitals"!

PREFIXES PLUS

The English language is constantly growing and expanding, borrowing words from other languages and inventing new ones. New words often are made by tacking prefixes or suffixes onto existing words.

That's how TV producers came up with *miniseries*:
mini- (small) + *series*
And how car companies came up with *minivan*:
mini- (again!) + *van*
And how fashion designers came up with both a *maxi-* and a *miniskirt:*
maxi- (large) + *skirt*
mini- (small, again!) + *skirt*

By grade five, your child is expected to know and use a variety of prefixes and suffixes. To strengthen that skill, try this game to create words with a group of familiar prefixes.

At a Glance

Grade/Subject: 5th/Language Arts—Vocabulary, Usage
Skills: recognizing prefixes, learning new words
Materials: 10–20 blank index cards (or smaller cards of playing card or flashcard size)
colored markers
notebook and pencil
dictionary (to check words)
Time: 1/2 hour once or twice a week

Getting Ready

You may want to equip yourself with a comprehensive list of prefixes and their meanings, such as that found in most grammar handbooks. It will be helpful once you go beyond your original choices. You don't need to know any other card games to play Prefixes Plus!

Step One

To get started, make yourself a small deck of Prefix Cards with the marking pen and index cards. Here's a list of useful prefixes for making your first prefix deck:

mini, maxi, retro, semi, super, trans, ultra, hyper, inter, post, pre, sub, super, mis, non, multi

Be sure both you and your kid know what each prefix means when it's attached to a word. If you're not sure of the meaning, check it out in your dictionary.

Step Two

Turn the pile of Prefix Cards face down on the table between you and your child. Toss a coin to see who goes first.

The first player draws a Prefix Card and must supply or invent a word using that prefix. An invented word must meet the criteria explained in Step Three.

To get a turn, the other player must supply (or invent) another word using the same prefix. The first player must then supply a

WHAT'S MORE

Prefixes Plus isn't the only way to create new words. Advertising writers and others do it all the time. Encourage your child to look for made-up words in advertisements and to listen for them on TV.

Remind your kid that a solid grasp of prefixes can be a big help in spelling words correctly. He can "read" the dictionary entries for *pre-* words, for instance.

Make a minidictionary for definitions of the new words that have been created playing the Prefixes Plus game.

Super Starters Prefixes

*multi*media
*mis*lead
*semi*sweet
*ultra*violet
*inter*active
*super*ficial
*post*mortum
*trans*atlantic
*tele*pathic
*anti*matter
*mid*way
*over*eager
*un*welcome

TOO MUCH OF A GOOD THING?

It's possible that you have one of those rare children who writes happily and copiously and needs no encouragement. Any enthusiastic middle school writer certainly deserves encouragement and words of praise. Don't worry about your child writing too much. In the middle school years, the excitement of language and first-time authoring can produce extensive journals, elaborate stories, and the beginnings of epic novels. These are wonderful ways to practice and build verbal skills. Soon enough, your young writer will learn the values of economy in writing and when it is important.

third word. If he can supply a third word, he keeps the card in his pile. If he cannot, the second player keeps the card and takes the next turn.

If the second player cannot supply a word with the prefix, the first player keeps the card, draws again, and the process starts over.

Step Three

There are two ways to judge the Prefix Plus word that a player suggests. First, is it a real word? You can both agree that it is or check it in the dictionary.

The second test is more challenging and creative: If it's not yet a real word, is it a useful coinage? For example, *minivan* was a new but clearly useful invention. The inventor of the word must define it and defend it well enough to convince the other player. And here there are lots of chances for laughs and family jokes.

Step Four

When all the Prefix Cards have been drawn, the winner is the person who has kept the most cards. To expand and replay the game, you and your child can create more Prefix Cards. Scour the dictionary to find more prefixes.

Learning Adventures—6th Grade Language Arts

BLOCK THAT METAPHOR!

Some of the most colorful writing and language to be found anywhere is in the sports pages of your newspaper. Metaphors, personification, hyperbole, and other colorful figures of speech abound in sports writing.

Since the sports pages are often favorites with kids anyway, they can be the basis for an entertaining activity that develops and applies writing skills and creative expression. Reading the sports pages can also make your child aware of the colorful, specialized vocabulary of the sports world.

COOL TO LEARN

Older students may hit a place where they don't think it's cool to be learning any more and school's not cool. Parents of older students need to start looking for very positive role models, people who are cool and have accomplished things. This will help students work through the tough spots. Some parents complain that their children don't listen to them any more, so those good role models will help reinforce a parent's positive goals.

At a Glance

Grade/Subject: 6th/Language Arts—Composition, Vocabulary
Skills: recognizing figurative language, applying writing skills in different content areas, learning specialized vocabulary
Materials: sports pages of daily and Sunday newspapers
notebooks, pens, scissors, tape
two highlighters of different colors
Time: 20 minutes–1/2 hour with the sports pages, two or three times a week

Getting Ready

Sports writers use many different kinds of figurative language, or *figures of speech*. Here are some common ones to look out for:

- *Hyperbole*: extreme exaggeration for effect.

  The Rockets *demolished* Cincinnati.
  Jordan Orchestrates *Incomparable* Season.

- *Metaphor*: a comparison in which one thing is described as if it were another.

  The Pats *rolled over* the Colts.
  The Red Raiders *chewed up* the visiting players.

- *Simile*: a comparison of two unlike things, using the word *like* or *as*.

  The football arched over the goalposts *like a rocket in orbit*.

- *Personification*: a way of attributing human emotions and actions to an object or abstract idea.

  Bad luck *has stalked* tennis star Monica Seles all year.

WHAT'S MORE

Sports broadcasters often speak in colorful—though often ungrammatical—language. Tune in to TV and radio to look for ways they use figures of speech.

Your kid may want to try her hand at covering sports for her school paper or as a "stringer" for a local newspaper.

Make a poster for a local team using photos and colorful headlines clipped from the newspaper.

Try rewriting a paragraph or two in literal language, describing the events of a game or other sports event. Discuss how the sentences become ordinary and often dull without the dramatic verbs and figurative language.

Step One

Discuss the examples in Getting Ready (above). Get your child to explain what the writer means literally in each case and what effect the figure of speech has on that meaning.

Step Two

Start an ongoing contest in which you and your child both find colorful writing and figures of speech in the sports pages of several sources (newspapers and magazines) or several days of the same paper. Each of you should have a colored highlighter pen.

Each of you will clip out and tape in the paragraphs or copy the sentences from the paper into your Sports Words notebook (left-side pages for you, right-side for your child). Use your colored markers to highlight each example of figurative language that you find. Compare the examples you've found.

Step Three

Make a special section in the Sports Words notebook to list the lively and dramatic verbs used by the sportswriters. Have your child look up the literal meanings of those verbs and compare them with the way they're used in sports writing.

Here are some typical examples:

- Michael Johnson *streaked* 200 meters to a world record.
- Kentucky *soared* to the national college title.

Step Four

Ask your child to write a descriptive account of some nonsports event, trying to use equally colorful verbs and figurative language. She could describe an event at school, a party, or an activity at home like cooking or cleaning out the garage.

When she finishes, have her point out her figures of speech to you, and talk about them together. Discuss how different types of events may inspire the use of different types of language and figures of speech—you wouldn't, for instance, use the same metaphors or images in writing about a fashion show as you would about a soccer game!

❯ Comma Link-up

The sentence is a wonderfully supple unit of thought. It can be simple, or it can be more complicated. It can shift meaning and tone with just a single word change. As children become more verbally sophisticated, they leave the short, simple sentences of the elementary reader behind. ("Jack threw the ball. Mom caught the ball. Was the ball happy?") Middle school children use and recognize much more complicated sentence forms in both reading and writing.

The more sophisticated they become, the more they need to know how to use commas in their writing and the more fun they can have experimenting with different ways to combine sentences.

At a Glance

Grade/Subject: 6th/Language Arts—Grammar, Mechanics
Skills: using conjunctions and commas in compound and complex sentences
Materials: pencil and paper
magazines or newspapers
Time: 3/4–1 hour

GOOD SPORT

My husband coaches all our children's basketball and baseball teams. He does a newsletter on the computer for the kids' teams, and they all love writing and desktopping it together: Play of the Week, Kids Who Made their First Baskets of the Season . . . . He's big on motivation.

MORE THAN GLUE

A *conjunction* is a word like *but* or *and* that can join two short sentences to make a longer, compound sentence. When you combine "I didn't want to go" and "I went" with a comma and a conjunction like *but*, you get something that says something even more. "I didn't want to go, but I went." The comma is used for indicating pauses and is needed in joining thoughts. It is used just before the conjunction in compound sentences.

WHAT'S MORE

Look through a news story or magazine article with your child. Pick out and circle any conjunctions you find. Read the sentences they are in aloud. Copy some of them on a sheet of paper and try breaking them down into shorter sentences (you might have to change a word or two).

Choose two short sentences from a story (a storybook for young children is a good source). Try rewriting them as many ways as you can by building compound sentences. How do the changes alter meaning in the story?

SOME CONJUNCTIONS

although	for	so
and	if	unless
because	or	while
but		

Getting Ready

Discuss simple and compound sentences with your child. Try making sentences using the list of the most common conjunctions on this page. Discuss what differences in meaning there are in these three sentences:

- I didn't want to go, *and* I went.
- I didn't want to go, *so* I went.
- I didn't want to go, *but* I went.

Try some complex sentences too (sentences with one part that can't make sense on its own because it depends on the other part).

- *Although* I didn't want to go, I went.
- *Because* I didn't want to go, I went.
- *If* I didn't want to go, I went.

Talk about why some of these sentence examples don't make logical sense.

Step One

Here are some (very) simple sentences. Have your child edit each of these two sentence pairs to combine them into one sentence using a conjunction.

I love popcorn. The movie theater didn't have any.
I had an ice cream instead. It was better.
I'm fond of chocolate. I love apple pie.

Take turns with your child thinking up some other short, single-thought sentences. Write them down and splice them together to make compound or complex sentences—if they're outrageous and funny, so much the better; talk about why.

Step Two

Have your child try using a variety of different conjunctions in the new, compound sentences. Some will work, and some won't. Talk about how the meanings change. Take turns to see who can make the most ridiculous compound or complex sentences.

Step Three

Dictate this very short story to your child. Have him write it down exactly as it is, and then read it back to you out loud. Ask him how it sounds and why it sounds that way.

"Worms have their place. They work hard in the ground. They make new soil. Their tunnels carry rain down to the roots of plants. We need them. We need them in the ground. A worm does not belong in my pocket. A worm does not belong in my mitten. Who put worms there? My sister did. She should have left the worms in the ground."

Have your child rewrite this paragraph by combining many of the sentences and adding anything he wants. Not every short simple sentence needs to be eliminated. Having a variety of kinds of sentences makes writing more interesting.

Step Four

Have him read his new version aloud. Check together to see whether or not he has commas where they are needed. Talk about how commas help to indicate how to read the passage.

- How does it sound when you read it out loud?
- Do you think that commas change how these sentences are read?

▸ Dear Aunt Emmeline . . .

During the winter holidays, many families send out annual letters to their friends and relatives. These letters bring people up to date on the year's events; some even include photographs or drawings.

Make this year's holiday letters a family affair! Work with your child to write, illustrate, print, and send the letter. Together, you can get a head start on the holiday season and give a special treat to those far-away friends and family.

At a Glance

Grade/Subject: 6th/Language Arts—Composition Skills
Skills: writing process, creative writing, writing friendly letters, addressing letters
Materials: typewriter or word processor
8 1/2" × 11" paper (with colorful holiday borders, if you wish)
family photographs from the past year
Time: 2–5 hours total (in several shorter sessions), depending on the length of the letter (Allow time for planning, writing a first draft, revising, and proofreading.)
additional time for printing or copying and addressing envelopes

WHAT'S MORE

The list of conjunctions on the last page isn't complete. Look up conjunctions in dictionaries, encyclopedias, or grammar books and list some more.

TALK AMONGST YOURSELVES

We have a lot of discussions at home, in very impromptu ways. We talk during long drives and commutes, at the dinner table—everywhere. Anything that happens to any of us, we just talk about it. We try to get together every evening as a family for dinner. Sometimes my husband is there, and sometimes he's working late, but we carry on discussions at the table. My oldest son has a debate coming up in school about "Are we better off now than we were 1,000 years ago?" and that became a dinnertime conversation.

Getting Ready

This project offers a perfect way for your kid to put into practice the five phases of the writing process that are so valuable to any writer:

- Brainstorming and discussing (prewriting)
- Writing a first draft
- Revising (second and more drafts)
- Proofreading
- Publishing

To review that process yourself, turn back to your content refresher in Section II. If you have a word processor, do even step one (the prewriting) at the computer. If not, just use note paper for gathering your preliminary thoughts and information.

WHAT'S MORE

If there are other kids in the family, have them join in as contributors to the holiday letter. Almost every kid (and many adults) can use the practice in writing and editing!

Instead of commercially printed holiday stationery, you might want to have your child (or a sibling) draw a border or appropriate design on the paper you're using. Use rubber stamps and colored inks, glitter, or stickers to jazz up each holiday message.

Don't make the mistake of thinking that letters like this are just for big families. If you're a single parent, or have a one-child family, you've probably shared lots of fun activities this year. Tell your friends about them!

Step One

Prewriting involves getting together with your child (and other members of the family, if possible), to brainstorm a list of the things that each of you thinks of as highlights of the past year for your family. Your perspectives on the year may be very different, but that's why you're preparing this letter together!

If the list seems too long, decide together which things you'll include in the letter and which you'll probably leave out. Decide also on how to organize the letter. Will you write about the news month by month, season by season, or with some other kind of organization, such as by themes or family members?

Have your child keep the list of brainstormed ideas and topics as well as notes on how the letter will be organized.

Step Two

To *draft* the letter, start it off with an introduction that explains who the letter writers are and what distinguishes each one's paragraphs—different fonts, different color printing, or perhaps both. One of you can write as you work out together what you want to say in this opening part.

To keep the activity interesting and fast moving, you might try writing one paragraph (or section of a few paragraphs) at a time, taking turns at the keyboard. If you're working with a computer or word processor, it might be fun for each of you to choose a "signature" font or typeface. Then, as you write alternating paragraphs or sections, your friends and relatives out there in holidayland will know whose voice they're hearing as they read through the letter.

It's a good idea to write your first draft in several short sessions rather than a long one. Of course, when your child is on a roll, don't stop!

Step Three

When you agree that you have a complete draft of what you want included in the letter, you're ready for what some folks consider the writingest part of good writing—*revising*—along with the important job of *proofreading* and fine tuning. Read each other's paragraphs aloud. Talk about ways to improve them. Make improvements and corrections as you both see fit.

Read the letter aloud to other family members (it's their holiday letter, too). Incorporate any suggestions that you want.

Although your discussion of all parts of the letter is valuable, try to keep hands literally out of the editing of the drafts, especially the parts your kid has written. Give him the responsibility of editing, checking spelling, punctuation, and capitalization. Don't get defensive if he finds things wrong with what you wrote! Talk about it.

Step Four

The final phase of the writing process is *publishing*. How you publish your family holiday letter depends on the kind of equipment and resources you have. With some computers, you'll be able to scan in family photos and perhaps print in color. With other equipment, you may just print or type one copy and depend on a local photocopier.

Publishing also includes distribution—in your case that probably means mailing. Your child can consolidate the skill of properly addressing letters, using the correct style and form on envelopes. Then it's probably time to lure the rest of the family into licking envelopes and attaching stamps and getting them into the mail.

Featuring Films

Moviemakers for decades have drawn on written material for plots and stories. Everything from the plays of Shakespeare and

YOU GO, GIRL!

I had a girl at my center call me over to her desk one day. This girl was starting sixth grade, and she said, "The last two years, I really wasn't good in anything. But at Score, there's lots of things that I'm good at and I'm getting better. Now I'm excited to go back to school." In Score@Kaplan, kids have a chance to succeed, no matter what their academic level.

I'm glad that parents are also trying to give their children chances to succeed in academics while learning at home. Some kids aren't getting recognized in school and aren't able to see that they're getting better. Parents can help them get the confidence to see that they can get better no matter where they're at—and that feels good to them. The kids who are doing well have the confidence to know that they can still get As, but also the kids who are at B and C level can move up too.

the novels of Thomas Hardy to Batman and other comic book heroes have been translated from page to screen. So have many children's classics, from *Gulliver's Travels* and *Pinocchio* to *Pippi Longstocking* and *James and the Giant Peach.*

Tracing changes that occur when written material is transformed into another medium is a great way to explore literature with your child. It can help develop her critical responses to both print and film and add to her enjoyment of both.

WHAT'S MORE

Become a team of film producers! Decide together on a favorite book you'd like to see as a movie and make up a dream cast of the actors you'd choose for the major parts. Choose where to shoot the film.

Make a poster for a film you've seen that was adapted from a written book or story.

The many excellent film versions of Shakespeare's plays are a great way to introduce kids to these masterpieces. While some kids may enjoy reading the play after seeing the film, you may want to select parts of the original play (certain scenes and speeches) for her to read or for both of you to read together aloud.

At a Glance

Grade/Subject: 6th/Language Arts—Literature and Reading, Listening and Viewing Skills
Skills: responding to different types of literature; appreciating point of view, foreshadowing, and flashback; comparing written and filmed versions of a story
Materials: VCR
videotape of a film based on an adult or children's book
two copies of the original written work
notebook and pen
critics' reviews of the films (optional)
Time: about 2 hours viewing time for each video, plus time to read the original book (or skim if previously read)
about 45 minutes discussion time for each film
You might plan on doing one film (and book) a month.

Getting Ready

Visit a video store with your child and choose a film to watch and review. Then obtain two copies of the book to read before watching the film. Be sure both you and your kid have finished reading the book before renting the video. You may also want to read what critics said about the movie.

The first time you do this activity, your film choice should probably be a film aimed at kids. Possibilities include the classic film of *Treasure Island* (the Robin Williams version), the Disney version of *The Jungle Book, The Secret Garden, The Indian in the Cupboard*, or one of the various versions of *Little Women* and the films mentioned at the start of this activity. The TV adaptation of *Anne of Green Gables* is another among many possibilities.

Step One

Before watching the film, discuss the book. Together, make a notebook list of the major and minor characters in the book.

Because movies must often simplify books, discuss which characters you think are absolutely necessary to the story. Talk about which characters you each would especially want to have in a movie and why.

Also discuss the basic plot and try to predict what, if any, changes a filmmaker might want to make. Are there subplots that might be dropped altogether? Have your child make a quick plot outline that summarizes the problem or conflict, the action, the climax, and the resolution.

Step Two

Watch the video together, keeping the notebook handy to write comments or notes. Let your child control the remote, stopping the film whenever she notices changes or wants to write down a comment.

Immediately after seeing the film, discuss comparisons between it and the original story or book. Keep the video handy so that you can go back and look at specific scenes or review the cast of characters.

Step Three

Then go on to look at some specific literary techniques as they are used in writing and in film.

Point of view is an important writing technique that sixth graders often study. It's also one aspect of literature that often changes from book to film. Many classic novels, for instance, are told in the first person. Films are usually shot from a broader point of view. Ask your child to identify the point of view taken in the original story, then later compare it with that of the movie. Talk about the effect that changing the point of view has on how the story affects you as reader or viewer.

Foreshadowing and *flashback* are two other literary techniques studied in sixth grade. They're also very common techniques in film. Discuss with your child whether and how these techniques were used in the film or in the book, or in both. If in both, did the writer and the filmmaker use them in the same way? What was the effect in the film?

EXPLORE THE WORLD

Computers are useless without good software and teachers who know how to make the most of the material. Children still need to explore their world with all their senses. Schools have one mission—to develop children's innate curiosity and desire to learn. Parents can help by lobbying to make sure schools and teachers have the resources they need.
—*Newsweek's Computers & the Family* newsmagazine (Fall/Winter 1996)

BRITANNICA ONLINE

One of the world's most comprehensive reference sources, *Encyclopedia Britannica,* weighs in at 44 million words! There are now online search and retrieval capabilities and linking via the Web to make this a powerful way for your children to research anything under the sun. Browse and search through *Britannica,* plus *Merriam-Webster's Collegiate Dictionary,* the *Britannica Book of the Year,* and more. Try the site for a free visit, but regular searches require a subscriber's fee. Go to http://www.eb.com

Step Four

This activity is likely to add a lot to your enjoyment of movies. Even if you expect—and want—to continue this activity with additional video/book tie-ins, don't try to do too many films in too short a time—probably not more than once a month.

▶ Fishing for Contractions

Most kids and adults know the simple card game Go Fish! In this variation, players must match the right contraction with the words that make it up. For instance, if you have a *cannot* card in your hand, you ask the other player for *can't* as the matching card. And vice versa.

The goal is to have as many matched pairs as possible. Like the original Go Fish!, this activity is more fun with three or four players instead of just two.

At a Glance

Grade/Subject: 6th/Language Arts—Grammar
Skills: making and recognizing contractions of verbs and pronouns
Materials: 30–40 playing-card-sized blank cards (cut 3" × 5" cards in half)
marker
dice or coin
dictionary (optional)
Time: about 20 minutes for each round, depending on the number of players

Getting Ready

To get ready for the game, use the blank cards and the marker to make a deck that includes 15 to 20 sets of paired cards (30–40 cards total). Print the contraction on one card in the pair, its component words on the other card: *cannot/can't, will not/won't, I am/I'm, they are/they're, it is/it's,* and so on. It's okay to have several sets of the same contraction pairs in your deck. If you need more contractions, check a dictionary for ideas.

HELP IS ON THE WAY!

There are some sound books to help students who need a hand, good advice, and some reassurance. Try *Get Off My Brain: A Survival Guide for Lazy Students,* by Randall McCutcheon; *Making the Most of Today: Daily Readings for Young People on Self-Awareness, Creativity, and Self-Esteem,* by Pamela Espeland and Rosemary Wallner; *Stick Up for Yourself! Every Kid's Guide to Personal Power and Positive Self-Esteem,* by Gershen Kaufman and Lev Raphael; and *Bringing Up Parents: The Teenager's Handbook,* by Alex Packer. Contact Free Spirit Publishing at (800) 735-7323 or E-mail them at help4kids@freespirit.com

Step One

Deal each player seven cards (five if only three of you are playing). Place the rest of the cards in a scattered pile face down in the center of the playing area. Throw the dice (or toss a coin) to see who goes first.

Step Two

The first player shows and lays down any pairs already in her hand. Then she asks another player, "Do you have a [xx]?" asking for the match for a card she has in her hand.

Here's how a game might start. The player may, for example, be dealt these five cards: *will not, won't, it is, should not*, and *can't*.

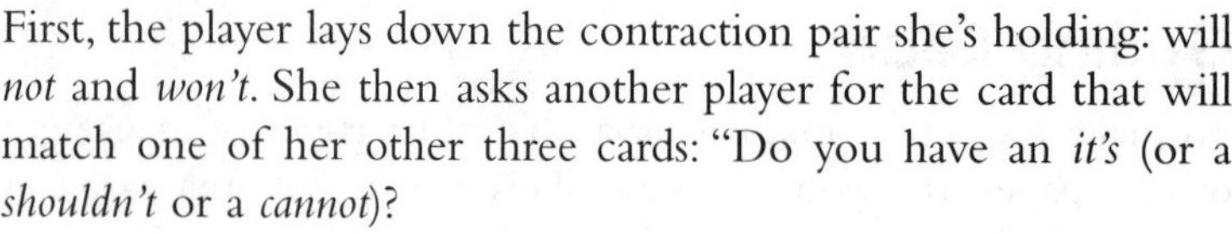

First, the player lays down the contraction pair she's holding: will *not* and *won't*. She then asks another player for the card that will match one of her other three cards: "Do you have an *it's* (or a *shouldn't* or a *cannot*)?

Step Three

If the other player has the card asked for, he must give it up. The first player then lays down the pair of cards (for instance, *it's* and *it is*) and makes another request. Her turn continues for as long as the second player has the cards she asks for to help her make matched pairs.

If the second player does not have the card, he says, traditionally, "Go Fish!" (or "Go Contract!") The first player then "fishes" in the center pile and draws a card. If it provides a match for the card she asked for, she lays down the pair of cards and her turn continues. If she does not draw the matching card, the turn passes to the other player.

Step Four

The game continues until all the cards have been drawn. The player with the most matched contraction pairs is the winner.

WHAT'S MORE

When making up your cards, don't forget some of the less obvious contractions: *you have/you've, we are/we're, shall not/shan't, might not/mightn't, must not/mustn't.*

Let kids draw and color decorative patterns on the backs of the cards. For future games, the cards will look more like "real" playing cards.

Challenge your child to come up with more contractions to add to the deck (*'tis, 'twas*).

JUST BROWSING

To take full advantage of the Internet's multimedia capability, your family computer should have a browser. There are two choices: Microsoft (Explorer) and Netscape (Navigator). Explorer is free with new copies of Windows 95 and downloaded free via the Internet; it filters questionable content on the Web, has special search and home option buttons, and will soon be integrated into the Windows desktop. Navigator is a $49 one-time fee, payable after a 90-day trial. It offers customized E-mail from many sources that can be automatically mailed to you. Both require lots of computer memory, so check your machine's available RAM before browsing. —from *Newsweek's Computers & the Family* newsmagazine (Fall/Winter 1996)

GOING GRAPHIC

While being a good reader is basic to getting information and doing research, other skills are also needed to read important information from graphic devices such as diagrams, cutaway illustrations, and maps. (Remember how Ross Perot counted on it!) Not only does your child meet visual displays in his school textbooks, they are also used widely in newspapers, magazines, and reference books.

At a Glance

Grade/Subject: 6th/Language Arts—Reference and Study Strategies
Skills: reading information from diagrams, illustrations, and maps
Materials: newspapers or news magazines
scissors
scrapbook or notebook
library paste
Time: about 1/2 hour, two or three times a week

Getting Ready

To make the scrapbook, have available older issues of magazines or newspapers that you can cut up. This is an activity that you can also adapt to take advantage of opportunities whenever TV news broadcasts or daily papers use graphics to present information.

Step One

With your kid, leaf through back issues of magazines or newspapers to find graphic displays used to illustrate a point or provide information. See how many he can find and what variety is possible. Then focus primarily on graphics related to subjects that are of interest to your child.

Graphics like the following are useful for this activity:

- Weather maps
- Graphs of record sales of various performers
- Graphs of movie box-office receipts
- Diagrams showing how to assemble a bike, make a birdhouse, etc.
- Cutaway diagrams of plants or animals (including dinosaurs)
- Diagrams of space vehicles, real or imaginary
- Tables of sports statistics

Step Two

Cut out all the graphics of any interest and have your child paste them in the scrapbook. Considering them one by one, have him analyze and discuss each one. Examine points such as these:

- What is the subject of this graphic? What does its title or caption tell us?
- What information can we get from it? How?
- What quantities—weight, dollars, time, movement, miles, batting average, etc.—does the graphic show?
- Does the graphic use symbols? Do we know what they stand for?
- How does this information relate to other things we may know about this subject?

Step Three

Discuss the first graphic until you feel that your child has understood both the information in it *and* the best way to go about getting information from this particular kind of diagram or illustration. Depending on the time discussing each example takes, analyze and discuss just one or several in each session. Don't belabor those of less interest to him.

Have your child make notes on the scrapbook page next to the pasted graphic. Later, you can return to graphics discussed in the past to recap the discussion or compare them to new graphics collected.

WHAT'S MORE

TV offers some graphics, too—weather maps, election graphs. When these appear on screen, they offer a good chance for quick practice and discussion.

This skill is useful in many other curriculum areas, especially science and social studies. Look through school textbooks for examples.

Try drawing a graph or diagram of some interesting information. Making graphics is a great way to understand how graphics are used to convey information.

Step Four

As you explore the graphics you and your child collected, try to find a variety of kinds. For instance, if your child seems pretty skilled at reading cutaway diagrams, you might work with maps for a few sessions or concentrate on regular line or bar graphs for a while.

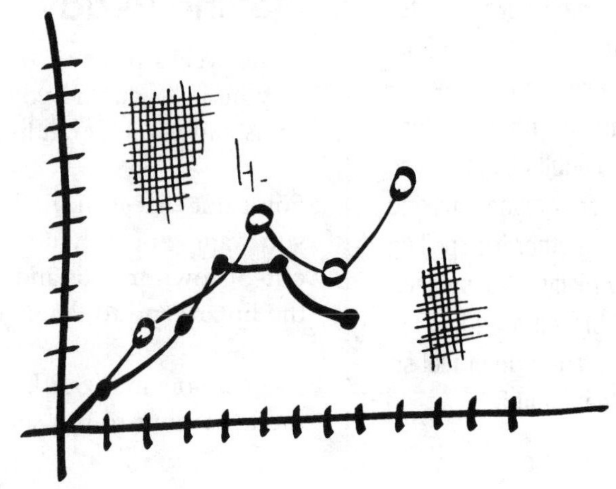

BLOWING IT

When I was a child, I was a perfectionist—and I'm still kind of that way. I had to have everything right, and if I couldn't do it perfectly, it was a disaster. But I had an experience that lessened that. One day a girl raised her hand at a computer terminal and needed my help with some skills. It was the blind leading the blind, but I tried to help her anyway. I tried to be authoritative as I helped her work through her lesson. I was praying that it would work out alright. For me, it was an unabated disaster—we got the wrong answers together.

That was a horrible thing for me and I was so apologetic with the girl. I made a huge fuss. Luckily, another Score@Kaplan Coach came up to me and said, "We need to talk." She told me it's okay for children to see adults make mistakes, and it's not good for children to see adults become very apologetic or angry when making mistakes. So whether it's spelling or math, my really weak subject areas, and I blow it for a kid, I'll admit I blew it and I don't feel so rotten about it.

Happy Birthday!

Is a family member due for a special birthday? Maybe there's an older sibling or a cousin turning 16 or 18 or 21, maybe a parent or aunt or uncle turning 40 or 50, or maybe a grandparent's or great-grandparent's birthday is coming up.

Make the event a special celebration with a custom-made scrapbook and a display reviewing the happenings of the day and year when this important person was born. You and your child can cooperate on bringing careful research and a creative imagination to this Learning Adventure activity.

At a Glance

Grade/Subject: 6th/Language Arts—Composition Skills, Reference and Study Skills, Speaking and Listening Skills
Skills: finding and organizing information, creative writing, making a speech
Materials: old periodicals—newspapers and magazines—from your library (microfilm or actual bound copies)
file folder or scrapbook to hold the research
posterboard
clippings and photographs to make a large wall poster
family memorabilia and objects
Time: 6–10 hours for library research, in several trips
3–5 hours for compiling the scrapbook and displays (Keep focused on the final goal to maintain your kid's effort over time.)

Getting Ready

Some weeks prior to the Big Event, gather your Party Team. It may be just you and your child, or it may involve other siblings, aunts and uncles, grandparents, and other relatives.

Point out that it may take some time to find all the information you want, especially if you're getting information or photos from out-of-town friends and relatives. Expect to make several trips to the library and to family attics or other storage spots.

Even as you and your kid start to research, remember to send out the invitations to this special birthday party well in advance.

Step One

Start by asking the question "What happened on the actual day this person was born?" Let your kid use his library know-how in the periodicals room to find newspapers that report the actual events of the birth day.

- What was the weather like?
- Who was president? Who were local officials and leaders? What were they doing?
- What was happening in your town? in the country? around the world?
- What movie or other entertainment was popular?

Look over the papers together and make photocopies of headlines or articles about local, national, and world events. Or copy the headlines by hand and reproduce them later on the typewriter or word processor.

Work with your kid to unearth other interesting tidbits. Here are some other questions that could be researched:

- What happened on that same day in history?
- Does this person share a birth date with any historical figures?
- What past events happened that day in other years? Your local librarian can help with finding such events in the reference section of your library. (Remind your child to take careful notes and make copies of materials she can't take out of the library). If you have access to the Internet, use it too!

Step Two

Now expand the search to include background about popular culture, fashion, movies, sports, and music during the entire year your birthday person was born. Again, let your kid practice her library skills to find what magazines were being published in that year, then request them from the library stacks.

Discuss how you can use what you find in old picture magazines such as *LIFE, The Saturday Evening Post,* and *LOOK,* if they were being published at the time. Think about including pictures of movie stars, politicians, sports heroes, and fashions in your poster display. What new books were published that year? What songs and singers were popular? Can you locate copies of any of them?

GOLDEN OLDIES

Copies or replicas of back-issue newspapers are also commercially available for some cities and some years. You'll find advertisements for these in the back pages of some newspapers and magazines. Many bookstores also have a series of little paperbacks full of information (like the cost of buying a house, average salaries, and the like) about different decades, even for specific years.

POSITIVE COACHING

All Score@Kaplan coaches read *Positive Coaching: Building Character and Self-Esteem through Sports* by Jim Thompson. Great for anyone working with young people, this book's positive motivational strategies and inspirational stories help parents and educators develop strong communication with young people. Call Warde Publishers at (415) 854-3389, or fax them at (415) 854-0201.

WHAT'S MORE

Have your child write up a mock news story involving one or more of the events referred to in the headlines and insert the Birthday Person into the events, with funny results!

Making a large, bright "Happy Birthday" banner from scraps of cloth or cut-out paper adds a festive feel to the celebration. This is a good project for involving younger kids in the family.

Writing and addressing the invitations to this special birthday party can give your 6th grader good practice in those writing skills, too.

ASK SMART

Parents should do more than just ask, "How was school today?" That might just elicit the response, "It was okay." Ask instead, "What did you do in school today?"

Step Three

As soon as you've begun to accumulate some materials, and even as you continue your research, turn your attention to the scrapbook or display of stuff. Attics, desk drawers, and older scrapbooks may supply birth announcements, school pictures, dry corsages, or pictures from a prom, vacation, or wedding. Maybe there's even a favorite old jacket or dress in a suitcase somewhere.

Step Four

As the Big Day nears, bring it all together. Work with your party team to prepare an oversize multipage birthday card or a scrapbook that includes the headlines, clippings, and news stories.

Make a poster or display with the fashion illustrations, popular culture photos, family photos, and historical information. Add some artifacts or memorabilia to give it color and texture. Arrange to play tapes or records of the music you've found.

Step Five

Have your child prepare to be master of ceremonies for the birthday party. She can write and deliver a special congratulatory speech (or roast!), then present the scrapbook, or huge card to this special birthday person.

JUST AROUND THE CORNER

Giving clear directions—written or spoken—is challenging for most people. Here's a way for you and your child to get better at those skills.

The activity focuses on geographical directions—how to get from here to there and back again. But giving and following directions well is a skill that's useful and applicable in many other situations.

At a Glance

Grade/Subject: 6th/Language Arts—Composition, Listening and Speaking Skills
Skills: expository writing (instructions), giving and following spoken directions
Materials: slips of paper or index cards
two notebooks or tablets and pencils

city or neighborhood map
Time: 1/2 to 3/4 hour for each set of directions

Getting Ready

You may want to make this activity part of a holiday celebration, a birthday party, or some other occasion when people need to be given directions to find their way to your house.

Step One

Sit down with your child and discuss what places in your neighborhood you both know well—his school, a supermarket, a park or zoo, the houses of several friends, a church or synagogue, or a store or mall.

Then write the names of eight to ten such familiar places on small slips of paper or cards. Put the slips in a hat or paper bag.

Step Two

Draw one slip each, without telling the other person which place name you've drawn. Then, separately, each of you will write clear directions for how to get to that place from where you live. Allow about ten minutes for writing.

Step Three

Now, take turns reading your written directions aloud. As one of you reads, the other person listens carefully and then tries to identify the place the directions are leading.

If the listener can't identify the place from the directions given, discuss why. Use the map to check the directions for accuracy in street names, if necessary. If the streets and other places were described and named accurately, then was something wrong with the directions themselves? Were they given in a logical order? Was the listener concentrating?

Step Four

Repeat the activity with other slips from the hat. As you develop proficiency in giving and listening to directions, expand the scope to include places farther afield.

WHAT'S MORE

Another good practice in giving instructions is for your kid to talk you through something he knows how to do—for instance, programming a VCR or playing a video or computer game.

Draw a detailed map of your neighborhood, enlarging the area shown on the main city map. Use it to practice giving directions aloud.

Have your child write directions to your house, a restaurant, or other location for a party or gathering requiring invitations. Include the directions with the invitations—make them a separate sheet to insert (print and decorate by hand or by computer, then photocopy).

GOSH, WHAT'S AN INTERJECTION?

An interjection is a short exclamation which usually expresses some form of emotion. It could be a strong one, like *ouch* in "Ouch, you dropped the dictionary on my foot!" or a milder one like *yes* in "Yes, of course I'll try not to do it again." *Wow, no,* and *why* can all be used as interjections.

WHAT'S MORE

Challenge your child to see how long a list of interjections he can compile. Look in nonfiction writing such as newspaper stories or magazine articles and short stories and longer works of fiction that contain dialogue.

Have your child write a short, short story or a descriptive paragraph and read it to you. Help him add the correct punctuation.

There is a whole class of interjections that are stand-ins for stronger (and unacceptable) words. *Darn, ding it,* and *gosh* are examples. Can the two of you come up with more?

Oh, No!

Life is full of small interruptions—and so are the sentences in the English language! Our patterns of speech accommodate the twists and turns of our thoughts and, fortunately, we have the comma to help our written language keep up. Setting off mild interjections like *well, oh, yes, no,* and *please* is a small, but important supporting role for that master of the pause, the comma.

At a Glance

Grade/Subject: 6th/Language Arts—Mechanics
Skills: using commas with interjections
Materials: pencil and paper, 3"× 5"cards or stick-up notes children's books or magazines (optional)
Time: 1/2 hour

Getting Ready

Talk with your child about the use of the comma that is featured in this activity. It's easy to think of many examples; "Please, can I stay up late?" "Mom, can I have another cookie?"

Step One

Have your child think up some more examples and write them down *without any punctuation* (type or print to be clear). Have your child go add punctuation to what you wrote.

Step Two

Together, brainstorm as many sentences of this kind as you can and write them down on 3" × 5" cards or stick-up notes. Read over your notes and rearrange them so that they begin to tell a (perhaps silly) story. There will undoubtedly be blanks, so think of some more examples that will fit in and round out the tale.

Step Three

Read this paragraph out loud to your child and have him tell you where to place the correct punctuation: "Well there I was Yes fourteen years old and my fingers were stuck in the change return slot Why you'd think I was a toddler with nothing better to do Hey can I help it I wasn't hired to feed the soda machine with silver Why that machine ate one dime after another and gave nothing back Oh I know I was thirsty Oh I wish I'd settled for water"

Learning Adventures— 5th Grade Math

DYNAMICALLY COMMUNICATE

Listen to your children. When they're asking you questions, listen to their questions and give them an answer. If they're doing homework, try to find out what they do know, then help to build on that. Sometimes a child wil ask a question and an adult will start to explain each and every step, when it might be just the last step they needed help with.

Comparing Apples and Oranges

A familiar complaint from kids who don't like math is, "What good is learning this? When am I ever going to need to know how to do this?" Here's an activity that provides one good answer to that question, as well as practical practice in estimating and dividing money and other quantities. In it, you and your child will literally compare apples and oranges, as well as spinach and mushrooms, chicken and hamburger, and different brands of soda and juices.

And your big bonus will be discovering together which food products are good values, ounce for ounce and pound for pound. You may even find that your child begins recommending ways to save money by switching brands to stretch your food budget.

At a Glance

Grade/Subject: 5th/Math—Money and Problem Solving
Skills: dividing money and other quantities
Materials: shopping list
pocket calculator
notebook and pencil
Time: your regular shopping time, plus a bit extra for calculations and discussions (this can be a continuing activity whenever you and your child have time during shopping)

Getting Ready

Before a trip to the grocery store, set up this activity situation with your kid. Discuss the concept that comparing the prices and values of two or more products requires figuring out a common basis for comparing them. In the grocery store, for instance, you'll often compare on the basis of ounces, pounds, or liters. Other products (say, paper towels or aspirin) can usually be compared in terms of feet, sheets, or the number of items in a package.

Step One

With your child, look over your shopping list for this trip. Pick five or six items to focus on to research what is your best buy for each. For instance, you might select orange juice, bread, chicken, coffee, and canned tomatoes. Discuss whether there are other reasons for choosing a more expensive product or whether you should shop just by the numbers. (For example, maybe you think a more expensive brand tastes better . . . but that's another project, doing taste comparisons!)

Remind your child to bring a notebook and pencil.

Step Two

In the store, stop by the shelf or compartment where your first product is kept. Take orange juice as an example. You may see different brands and sizes at these prices: $1.99 and $2.69 for a half gallon (64 ounces); $.89 and $1.29 for a quart (32 ounces). Assuming the brands offer basically the same quality, which is the best buy?

Step Three

Continue down your shopping list, checking out the various prices and quantities of each of the items you selected for this activity. Have your child calculate comparative prices per ounce (or other units) and make notes of them in the notebook.

If he gets intrigued with this activity and wants to make calculations for other products as you shop, congratulations! Unless time is short, go for it. Otherwise assure him you can do more another time.

Step Four

Don't limit this calculation activity to different brands or sizes of

WHAT'S MORE

Practice this calculation skill at home too. Just use the flyers or ads that supermarkets send out to the neighborhood. Ask your kid to use the prices and quantities listed there to calculate what products are good buys to add to your shopping list.

Go metric! Even though few Americans have as yet turned enthusiastically to the metric system, those equivalents are printed on boxes and cans. Have your child recalculate some prices using metric measurements.

Keep track of prices on key items for a number of shopping trips. Plot the price changes on a graph you and your child make—use different colors for different items. Do prices go up or down as a group? What happens when fresh food goes out of season or crops are damaged?

exactly the same product. For example, apples may be $1.49 a pound while oranges are six for 99¢. Aha! Here's a great opportunity to do some mathematical problem solving!

Discuss ways that you could use to decide whether the oranges or apples are a better bargain this week. One approach would be to weigh one pound of apples to see how much one apple would cost ($1.49 ÷ number of apples). Then multiply that by six, to compare the cost of six apples with the cost for six oranges.

Thinking about such different approaches helps your child practice several different operations involving dividing, multiplying, adding, and subtracting money.

▶ Building Blocks

Have some fun being an architect. As you and your child can design and build your own block buildings, she'll get excellent hands-on experience in exploring and understanding spatial relationships and three-dimensional objects. Together you'll consider aspects of the faces and volume of buildings that you build. You'll use cubes to estimate the volume of each building, and you'll use the shadows that the building casts to learn about the front, side, and top views of the building, which show its faces.

It's amazing how much mathematics and geometry is contained in a simple object made from blocks!

YOU CAN TOUCH THIS

Using a concrete object is a learning strategy that's great for helping kids understand mathematics. Such objects touch (!) the kids' tactile sense. Using your sense of size and shape to work with space figures is fun, and you even do a little geometry in the bargain.

At a Glance

Grade/Subject: 5th/Math—Geometry
Skills: learn about space figures and their faces, estimate area and volume
Materials: snap cubes, sugar cubes, wooden blocks, or other toy blocks (like LEGO™ blocks)

flashlight
pencil and paper
Time: 30 minutes

Getting Ready

Since you and your child will estimate the volume of a space figure and the areas of its faces, review the concepts of volume and area with her. Explain that she will use the blocks to estimate volume by assuming each block represents 1 cubic unit of volume. Use the Section II math refresher content to review the concepts with your child.

Step One

Have your child create a building with some of the blocks. You could work together on one building or each make a building at the same time.

Step Two

Ask her to find the volume of her building based upon the blocks. If the building has an open space inside, you can help her find the volume by having her fill the space with blocks. Have her help with doing the same for your building.

Have her draw a diagram of each building and write down the number of blocks used to make the building and its volume (1 block = 1 cubic unit of volume) next to each.

Step Three

Now have your child use the same number of blocks as she used in her first building to build some other buildings of different shapes, then figure out the volume of each new building. Try making the

- Squarest building possible
- Tallest building possible
- Lowest building possible

Have her draw diagrams of her creations and record the volume of each building she makes.

Step Four

Dim the lights and help your child shine a flashlight directly on

WHAT'S MORE

Try building a toy, such as a robot or an animal. Try shining the flashlight on it to make shadows of its faces. Draw a front view and a side view of the toy.

Try making a scale drawing of one side of the object or a floor plan of the building. Help your child decide what scale to use for the drawing and what view to use.

Shine the flashlight on the sides or faces of several household objects such as a tin can, a cereal box, or a clock, and draw the shadows that are formed. Take turns matching the shadow with the object.

the center of one face of a building to produce a shadow on the wall. Ask your child what shape is produced by the shadow. Have her draw the front view of the building, and then tell her to draw the side and top views. Explain that the side of one building block has an area of 1 square unit. Have her find the area of each view of the building (she can count all the blocks and/or count the blocks along the width and height sides and multiply).

READY AND WILLING

Engagement in school is a two-way street—schools need to be interesting, but students need to be willing and able to be interested.
—from *Beyond the Classroom* by Laurence Steinberg, Ph.D. (Simon & Schuster, 1996)

DECIMAL SQUARES

Decimals are a handy way to express parts of a whole. You see them everywhere, and they are used by people from all walks of life. Money, economic statistics, and scientific measurements all use decimals. But you might be surprised to learn that decimals are not always used as numbers.

Working with squares is a fun way to "see" decimals and learn about them using an entirely new approach. This activity calls on your visual and manipulative skills to play with decimals and see that scissors can be just as important to working with decimals as pen and paper!

At a Glance

Grade/Subject: 5th/Math—Fractions, Decimals, and Percents
Skills: adding, subtracting, and multiplying decimals; calculating area
Materials:
sheet of 4" × 4" graph paper
scissors
pen or pencil and ruler
Time: 20 minutes

Getting Ready

Talk with your child about decimals to see how much he understands. Check that he understands that 0.1 is the same as one tenth of a whole. Explain that the activity you will do together uses parts of a whole (a skinny rectangle) to represent a decimal.

Step One

With your child, draw several long rectangles that measure 1" by 10". Using the ruler, draw vertical lines in the rectangle to divide

WHAT'S MORE

Try decimal squares greater than 1 by having your child select a *pair* of numbers for each decimal. The first number is the whole part of the decimal, and the second is the decimal part. Either use the appropriate number of complete rectangles to represent the whole number part, or have your child add the whole number parts on paper.

Use strips to represent fractions in a similar way. Divide each rectangle into equal parts, each of which represents a fraction, and then away you go!

it into ten equal 1" by 1" squares. Since each square is one-tenth of the rectangle, each square represents the decimal 0.1.

Step Two

Have your child pick two numbers between 1 and 9. For instance, suppose he chooses 3 and 7. Thinking of these numbers as the decimals 0.3 and 0.7, cut strips of squares from the rectangles to represent the two decimals. For example, 0.3 will be 3 decimal squares.

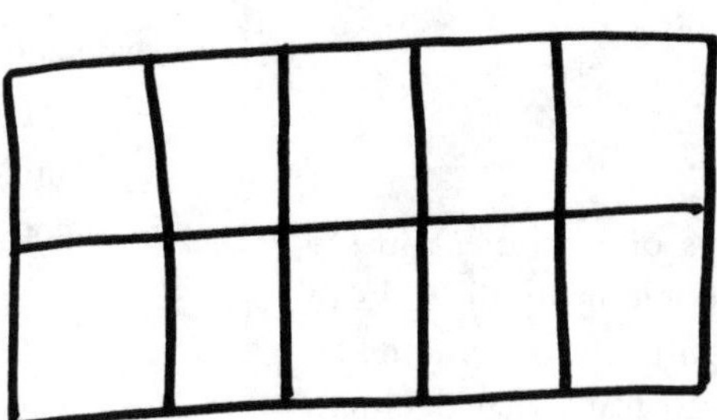

Give the decimal strips to your child and ask him to add the decimals by putting the two strips together. Record the sum. Now have him subtract the smaller decimal from the larger decimal by taking away the number of decimal squares of the smaller decimal from the decimal strip of the larger decimal. Record the result.

CALCULATING KIDS

Should your child use a calculator to do her math homework? If the focus of the assignment is on getting to the answer and thinking how to solve a problem, don't discourage your child from making needed calculations with a calculator. If the lesson focuses on calculating numeric answers to specific math problems, however, encourage your child to set aside the calculator and use the old noggin! Nothing substitutes for knowing your math facts.

Step Three

Now, suppose the length of the side of each decimal square is 0.1. Have him figure the area of the polygon formed when he put the two decimal strips together. First, calculate the area of each square, and then add to obtain the area the polygon. Record this result.

Step Four

How do these results compare? Ask your child to put the three results in order from least to greatest. Ask him to explain why the area of the polygon is less than the other two results.

Step Five

Repeat for several pairs of numbers, and record all the results in a table. You may wish to look for patterns of numbers in your table that represent some number facts.

❯ Fishy Factors

It's amazing how many ways the game of Go Fish! can be adapted. Play this adaptation for some prime practice in thinking about finding the prime factors of numbers.

At a Glance

Grade/Subject: 5th/Math—Numeration
Skills: finding prime factors
Materials: 2 decks of playing cards
paper and pencil (optional)
Time: 20–30 minutes (or as long as your child wants to keep playing)

Getting Ready

Do you remember what *factors* and *prime numbers* are? A prime number is a number that can be divided evenly only by itself and by 1. For instance, 5 can be divided by 5 or by 1 ($5 \times 1 = 5$). A factor is one of two numbers that when multiplied by one or more other numbers equals another number. So 5, for example, and 1 are factors of 5; 3 and 4 are factors of 12. The number 17 is prime because its only factors are 1 and 17; the number 20, on the other hand, has a few factors: 2, 10, 5, 4, 1, and 2.

Now if we combine those two things, and think about *prime factors*, we are referring to numbers that are multiplied by a number to make another number, but have only 1 and itself as factors. Take $3 \times 4 = 12$, for example. Whereas 4 is just an ordinary factor of 12, 3 is a *prime* factor of 12.

Step One

Have your child help you prepare the deck of cards to play Fishy Factors. You will be using sets of cards to represent numbers and their prime factors, like this:

2	= 1(ace), 2	3	= 1, 3	4	= 2, 2
5	= 1, 5	6	= 2, 3	7	= 1, 7
8	= 2, 2, 2	9	= 3, 3	10	= 2, 5
11 (jack)	= 1, 11	12 (queen)	= 2, 2, 3	13 (king)	= 1, 13

Since you can see that you need as many aces, 2s and 3s as possible, combine those numbers from both decks.

BAD IN MATH

One girl was starting sixth grade and she was a good year behind in math. She came from a family that valued education and really supported her, and she was a good student overall. Her mom was really surprised how far behind she was in the subject. The girl came to Score@Kaplan twice a week with a positive attitude, took the feedback and positive comments to heart, and within six months she went all the way through her goal program and was working on seventh grade math. She had advanced two years in her hardest subject! She did practice tests in math at Score before she had to do placement tests for her school. She was confident, having fun, and really excited. Not bad for a "bad math student." This is one of many Score success stories, and I always encourage parents to take a page from this experience and work positively on setting good math goals for their children at home. Improvement will happen with consistent effort.

> **WHAT'S MORE**
>
> You can eliminate some of the cards (like Kings and 7s) in order to focus on certain prime factors, say just 2s and 3s.
>
> ---
>
> Play with more than 2 people to add the need for strategy about whom to ask for cards.

As in the traditional Go Fish!, you will be attempting to put down more *books* of cards than your opponent. In this game, a book means at least three cards: a number and its prime factors (from the list above).

Step Two

Deal seven cards to each of you. Place the rest of the cards face down to draw from when one of you must Go Fish!

Suppose your cards are 2, 3, 3, 7, 10, 10, queen. You might decide to ask your child if he has any 9s because that way you would have a book: 9 plus its prime factors of 3 and 3.

Step Three

If you get your requested card, you go again and request another card. If the card you request is not available, then you draw the top card from the closed deck. Now it's the other player's turn.

Step Two

You may put down books of cards at any time. When you do, you should write down the number and its factors on paper as in the list above. That way you can track interesting things like how often certain numbers are used. And you can also predict how many cards of a certain number are left in the deck.

The game ends when one of you has put down all your cards. Or you might decide to end it when the draw pack is all gone. As in the traditional game, the player with the most books down is the winner.

> **WHAT'S MORE**
>
> You can use the same graph form to record the cumulative total score. Each time you record the total for a set of games, add this total to the preceding total and mark it on the graph just above on the same vertical line. Be prepared to add several sheets to the height of the graph, as the cumulative totals will grow quickly.

Gin Graph

Building and interpreting graphs is a skill that helps prepare students for work in several areas of mathematics. They are important in statistics and are useful in preparation for algebra and other advanced classes in high school and beyond. Preparing and using graphs can be fun and can lead to a lot of good-natured discussion.

Gin rummy is a variation of the many rummy card games. We chose it for this activity because it is simple and quickly played. It requires strategies based on figuring the probabilities of certain cards becoming available, remembering cards that have been played, and building combinations of cards based on number sequences and similarities of kind. This provides a lot of practice in basic number skills.

At a Glance

Grade/Subject: 5th/Math—Graphs
Skills: making and using graphs, problem solving
Materials: deck of 52 cards
paper and pencil for scoring
graph paper (4 or 5 squares to an inch works well)
two pencils of different colors
Time: 3/4–1 hour once a week, as many weeks as the two of you want (The more games you play, the bigger the graph you and your child can create.)

RUMMY RULES

Both players receive 10 cards; the remaining cards are placed upside down in a pile (the stock). The top card is removed and laid face up next to the stack; this is the start of the discard pile.

The goal is to accumulate cards in sets of 3 or more in numerical sequence of the same suit (for example, 9 ♥, 10 ♥, and Jack ♥), or three or more of the same value (7 ♦, 7 ♠, and 7 ♣).

The player who didn't deal goes first and can choose to take the top discard or draw from the stock. This player then discards one card onto the top of the discard pile face up; the next player takes a turn.

The cards are held in the hand until a player has 10 or fewer points left in unmatched cards (these are called the deadwood). The player can then rap on the table with her knuckles and say *knock* (but only on her turn). This ends the hand. If a player has no cards left over at all, then she can say *gin* and end the hand.

Getting Ready

The first task is to learn how to play gin rummy. You can use the rules and scoring described here and on the next page, or follow your own variations. Most card game books list several kinds. Play enough games so that you and your child learn the basic rules of play for one kind of rummy game.

Playing a set of six games is the easiest way to play and keep the graph. You can also play to a fixed number of points, like 100.

Step One

The graph in this activity is built on the data gathered from playing on a standardized set of games. Since the data you are collecting, the final scores, should have a consistent base, you'll need to decide upon the number of hands of rummy you will play each time. As noted above, six hands is a practical number of hands and will usually take about 3/4 of an hour.

Step Two

After you've played your first set of six games, add up the total score and declare the winner. Cheering is allowed!

WHAT'S MORE

Use the information on the graph to see if there are win-lose cycles. If you wrote down the dates for each game played, you could compare the cycles with phases of the moon or the part of the month. Does one or the other player always do better on Mondays, for example?

You can study the graph to work out the averages for total play or for different intervals of play.

WHAT'S MORE

What other things might be graphed? Try graphing time of day: when a parent comes home each evening, when dinner is served. Graph frequencies: phone calls each evening, hours of TV watched.

Step Three

The next step for the two of you is to figure out how to set up the graph. Which axis is going to be for the number of games played and which is going to be for the score? Who will be assigned which colored pencil? How are you going to scale the graph; that is, does each square equal 1 point or 10? (We recommend 10.) When you have laid out your graph, indicate the scores with a dot and jot down the score in tiny numbers near the dot (you could also add the date of the game).

RUMMY SCORING

Both players lay down their cards, matched sets and the deadwood, face up on the table. The values of each player's deadwood cards are added. (The ace equals 1 point, face cards count as 10 points each.) The knocker usually has the lowest total. The lower total is subtracted from the higher total. The remainder belongs to the player who called *knock* or *gin* and is added to her score. A player who goes gin also gets a bonus of 25 points (although you can make the bonus worth whatever you want). Ten points are deducted from the score of a player who knocks, but actually has a higher value in deadwood than the other player.

Step Four

Once you have a few sets recorded, it will be obvious whether your way of recording the scores on the graph is working well or not. If it isn't, redesign your graph and transfer your data. You may want to figure out a different scale or layout. There isn't a single right or wrong way. Depending on how you draw them, graphs represent information in different ways. In thinking about the graph and how it represents your information and making changes, you are engaged in serious mathematics. If your graph works well, play on.

When you've decided on a final graph form and recorded the totals from a few sets of games, you're ready to connect the dots to show the ebb and flow of your fortunes.

WHAT'S MORE

If your graph gets bigger than even you can stand, you can work up a new graph with a different scale and transfer your data. If you and your child decided that one square equals ten points, make the new graph have squares equal to twenty points. Plotting points will require some estimating.

Step Five

Keep your rummy games and graph going for as long as you can. When you run out of graph paper, get some tape and attach another piece. We know one father-son team that played two or three games every week for most of one winter until their outrageous graph unfolded across most of a kitchen wall!

Here's the Scoop

Think about going to the ice cream window to order a double-dip cone. With so many flavors, is it ever hard for you to decide which two to get? There is a way for you and your child to figure out *exactly* how many combinations of two flavors you actually have to choose from. Read on.

At a Glance

Grade/Subject: 5th/Math—Statistics and Probability
Skills: combinations and permutations
Materials: paper and colored pencils
list of ice cream flavors
newspaper circulars
Time: 20–30 minutes, or as long as your child wants to keep playing

Getting Ready

Gather some newspaper circulars that show ice cream varieties. If you can't find any, a listing of ice cream flavors such as you see on a menu is sufficient to start. (Your child might be talked into accompanying you on a "field research trip" to an ice cream shop to write down all the choices.)

Step One

Start the activity with a sort of trick question:

- If you have three ice cream flavors, how many different kinds of *single*-scoop ice cream cones can you order?

Okay, that's easy—three. But . . .. suppose you can have two scoops. That's a more interesting (and fattening?) problem—and a little harder to answer, too.

Step Two

Challenge your child to figure out a way of finding out how many different two-scoop cones you can order when three flavors are available. (Don't forget about two scoops of the *same* flavor!)

This is where the colored pencils and paper come in handy. Pick three flavors and work with your youngster to draw out all the possible combinations. (These arrangements are called

INDIVIDUAL GOALS

I see kids who are feeling bad because the older sibling does well—or worse, the younger sibling is the star learner—and there are constant comparisons of "Why aren't you more like your brother or sister?" Don't tell children that they're working below the grade level of their siblings. Focus on each child as an individual and praise each one for his achievements. "You're doing better and better" should be the line of talk rather than "You're not doing as well as your brother." Set individual goals and praise small victories to keep your child progressing positively.

STAY INFORMED

Most students should have some amount of homework every day. Monitor what your children are doing and if they're understanding the assignments. Ask them when their tests are and follow up with them after the tests are given—"How did you do?"

combinations when it doesn't matter which flavor is on top or on the bottom.)

It can be fun to actually draw each ice cream cone combination; if your child is into the art part, go with it!

WHAT'S MORE

Add sugar cones and plain cones to your ice cream choices to see how many kinds you get now.

Try finding permutations and combinations with a variety of three things: clothing, flower arrangements, models, pizza toppings.

Try finding permutations and combinations of numbers larger than 3 (or with 2 if you need it a bit easier).

Step Three

Now some ice cream eaters are picky about how the scoops are arranged in the cone. For them, which flavor is on the top or bottom makes a difference. (Mathematically it makes quite a difference.) Ask your child how many double-dip cone choices there would be if each variation of "on top" or "on the bottom" is also counted. (When the order matters, the arrangements are called *permutations*.)

Encourage her to talk about her strategy for figuring out all the different permutations of ice cream cones as she draws them. A discussion like that is a great way to learn more about how well your child understands math.

Step Four

Look at the results you have for each part of the activity:

- Single-scoop cones from three flavors
- Double-scoop combination cones from three flavors
- Double-scoop permutations cones from three flavors

Ask your child to predict whether there are generally more combinations or permutations of any set of items.

Test out her prediction. See how many three-scoop ice cream cones could be made with three flavors. How many two-scoop cones can be made from four flavors. Have her think of something other than ice cream to test her prediction on.

POLYIAMONDS

WHAT'S MORE

Try to cover the rectangle with repeating patterns made up of polyiamonds.

Polygons can be made from all kinds of shapes. This activity involves making shapes called polyiamonds from equilateral triangles and discovering their unusual properties. Why *polyiamond*, you ask? Well, if you put two equilateral triangles together, you get a diamond. Polyiamonds are the shapes you get when you grow the diamond by attaching more equilateral triangles (see figure on next page).

At a Glance

Grade/Subject: 5th/Math—Geometry
Skills: making and identifying congruent figures, identifying the properties of polygons
Materials: pencil
several sheets of 4" × 4" graph paper
ruler
scissors
Time: 30 minutes

Getting Ready

Help your child write a definition of an equilateral triangle, a triangle with three equal sides. Explain that equilateral triangles are used in making shapes called polyiamonds. Talk with your child about why some of the figures on the next page are polyiamonds and why others are not. Make sure that your child understands *congruent* figures. Review with him the transformations of a figure, that is, a *flip, turn*, and *glide* of a figure, such as a triangle or hexagon.

Step One

As your child watches, draw a polyiamond on the graph paper with the ruler. Here's how:

- First, draw a triangle with three 1-inch sides.
- Attach another equilateral triangle of the same size to the first one so that the two triangles share a common side completely.
- Then attach a third equilateral triangle to one of the other triangles so that they completely share a side.

Step Two

Now ask your child to draw a different polyiamond made of three equilateral triangles, each with 1-inch sides. Have him cut out his polyiamond and try to fit it on your polyiamond so that his completely covers yours. Ask him which transformation he used to cover your polyiamond.

POLLY WHO?

A *polyiamond* is a shape made up of congruent equilateral triangles, each of which shares exactly one common side with an adjacent triangle.

FLIPS, TURNS, GLIDES

A *transformation* of a plane figure changes its position or orientation without changing its shape or size. A *reflection* (or *flip*) flips a figure over from one side of a line to the other so that the figure is the same distance from the line and its orientation does not change. It's like flipping a pancake from one end of a griddle to the opposite end. A *rotation* (or *turn*) rotates a figure about a fixed point like spinning a pinwheel. A *translation* (or *glide*) slides a figure without changing the figure's shape or size, like sliding a hockey puck across the ice.

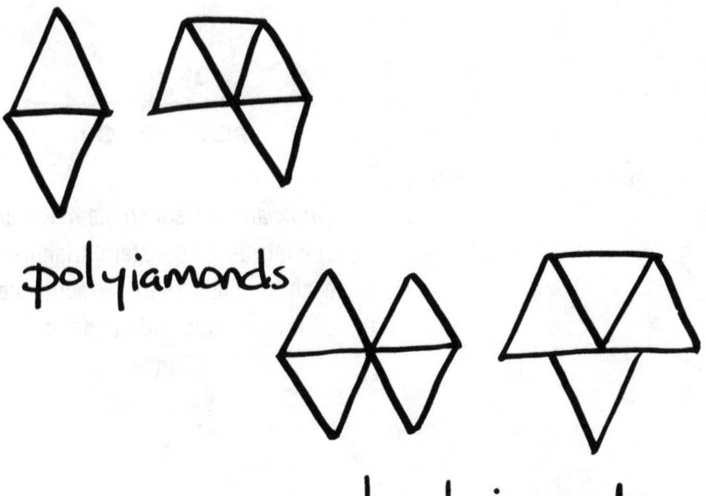

Step Three

Next, have your child draw three polyiamonds, each of which consists of four equilateral triangles, while you also draw three polyiamonds, each of which consists of four equilateral triangles. Both of you cut out your polyiamonds and try to match congruent polyiamonds. Name the sequence of flips, turns, or glides that you use to transform one polyiamond into a congruent polyiamond.

Step Four

There are only three possible four-part polyiamonds. All other polyiamonds can be transformed into one of these basic ones. Work with your child to discover which are the three basic polyiamonds.

- Two of the basic polyiamonds are familiar polygons. Can you name them?
- The third one is part of a hexagon. How many triangles are needed to complete the hexagon?

Ask your child to make a table that shows the number of sides and angles of each polyiamond. What is the sum of the angles in each polyiamond?

WHAT'S MORE

After you have done this activity, you might want to try doing it with polyiamonds made of five congruent triangles. Doing this activity with five-part polyiamonds can take up a lot of time, because they are many more basic five-part polyiamonds.

Draw a large rectangle on a piece of graph paper and try to cover it with polyiamonds.

SNABBLE

In this number-based variation of the traditional board game, Scrabble™, you combine the luck of the draw with practicing computation and a chance to develop great number strategies!

At a Glance

Grade/Subject: 5th/Math—Algebra
Skills: order of operations
Materials: deck of cards
paper and pencil
dried beans (or pennies or some other handy counters)

calculator (optional)
Time: 20–30 minutes, or as long as your child wants to keep playing

SHE GETS IT!

Parents shouldn't be giving their children all the answers when they do schoolwork together. Kids won't understand what's going on if this well-intentioned spoonfeeding happens on a regular basis. Focus on providing "teachable moments" for your child, rather than forcing the information down. Teachable moments are times when you can tell that something new has really clicked for your child. Maybe she's struggling with Roman numerals, then all of a sudden, you know she gets it!

Getting Ready

Think about how Scrabble goes—a first word is put down and all future words need to connect from it and be spelled correctly. In this activity, you will be connecting numbers instead of letters. You see, not just any numbers will do—the numbers you connect have a special requirement: when combined using various operations, these numbers must have the answer of 10. It might be a good idea to try a round by yourself to get a sense of how it works.

This may be a good time for you and your child to review the concept of *order of operations*. Solve these two problems:

$$7 + 6 \times 7 - 6 = 85$$

but

$$7 + (6 \times 7) - 6 = 43$$

What makes the answers different is the parentheses. The parentheses indicate which part of the problem to do first, followed by the other operations done as usual from left to right. Now you are all set to go!

One last thing before starting: Make sure you have a large area in which to lay out cards as you play.

Step One

Deal seven cards to you and your child. The rest of the cards go in a pack face down. As in the traditional Scrabble game, you will put down cards from your hand face up and then build off them in all directions. For each card you play, you pick up a new card from the pack.

Each of you should review the cards in your hand. Aces are worth 1, kings are worth 13, queens are worth 12, jacks are worth 11, and number cards are worth their face value. You are

looking for a series of at least three cards that can be combined using various operations (+, –, ×, /) to get an answer of 10. For example, suppose your seven cards are A, 4, 6, 7, 7, 10, and Q. You could make this problem:

$$6 + (Q/4) + A = 10$$

Start by writing the problem out on paper so you can be sure the answer is 10 and so your child can check it. Then lay out the needed cards in the playing area. On the first turn, they can be arranged horizontally or vertically.

Step Two

When you have finished putting down the cards and checking your math, draw as many cards from the deck as you just played in order to keep seven cards in your hand.

Every time you or your child puts down an equation that equals 10, the player earns a counter.

Step Three

Now your youngster takes a turn. The trick for him is to find a problem that has a number in common with what's on the board already. Have him write the problem on paper with special emphasis on the use of parentheses, as needed, to indicate order of operations. When he succeeds, he earns a counter. Then it's your turn again.

For the first few rounds, you might play with the cards in each of your hands displayed so that you can help each other find the numbers to put together to make problems that equal 10.

When a player is unable to make a problem that fits on the board, the player may trade in as many of his 7 cards as he wants, but then must skip the rest of that turn.

When all the cards in the deck are gone, continue playing for as long as either of you can still make the needed problems. Then tally your counters; the person who has earned the most counters is the Snabble champ.

WHAT'S MORE

Try playing Snabble with a target answer that is higher or lower than 10.

Try restricting a Snabble game to certain operations (like just + and –).

Award more counters depending on the number of cards used—for instance, 2 counters for 4 cards, 3 for 5, 10 for all 7; or you might award one counter for each card used.

ANYTHING BUT TV

My husband and I don't encourage a lot of TV watching at our house, but we will encourage anything creative—cooking, woodworking, building clubhouses, tiling our bathroom.

SPACE TRAVELER

Here's a chance to imagine visiting other heavenly bodies in our solar system. Since the gravity on each planet is different and the pressure of gravity determines weight, the weight of objects changes from one planet to another. Children find it fun to figure out what their weight would be if they traveled to another planet and to imagine what it would feel like to lift various familiar objects.

Invite your child on an imaginary trip to the moon and the planets where, by using the gravity ratios, she can discover how she can gain and drop weight just by standing on different planets or find out how easy or hard it would be to pick up a basketball.

WHAT'S MORE

Your child could figure out how much her luggage would weigh on each planet if her luggage weighed 92 pounds on Earth (you can pick any weight for the luggage).

Your child could figure out how much each member of the family would weigh on each planet. How much would the whole family weigh together?

At a Glance

Grade/Subject: 5th/Math—Fractions, Decimals, and Percents
Skills: ratios, multiplying fractions
Materials: cardboard or construction paper
marker
crayons or paints
paper and pencils
bathroom scale
Time: 15–30 minutes

Getting Ready

Review your understanding of ratios. They represent a comparison of two numbers, using division. For example, the ratio 3 : 4 (or 3:4) can also be expressed as a fraction 3/4, or 3 divided by 4. If you are not that familiar with ratios, check the refresher material in Section II of this book or have your child show you the section on ratios in her math book.

Heavenly Bodies	Gravity Ratio
Mercury	3/10
Venus	7/8
Earth	1
Earth's Moon	1/6
Mars	3/8
Jupiter	2 5/8
Saturn	1 1/5
Uranus	9/10
Neptune	1 1/10
Pluto	7/10

Step One

Use a piece of cardboard or construction paper to make a chart with the different gravity ratios of each planet. Divide the piece of cardboard into two columns. In the fist column, list all the planets and in the second column list the gravity ratios. The gravity ratios represent the difference of gravity on each planet (and the moon) compared to the gravity on Earth.

Use the chart to discuss where in our solar system things would be heaviest and lightest. On which planet would weights be most like on Earth?

Step Two

Prepare for space travel! Ask your child which planet she would like to visit first. By using the bathroom scale and the gravity ratios, have her then calculate out how much she will weigh on her chosen heavenly body. This will allow her to learn how to multiply fractions and learn about ratios. For example, if she weighs 80 pounds on earth, how much will she weigh on Mercury (80 × 3/10)? The answer is 24. Encourage her to discuss with you what she might do when she gets to each planet or have her draw pictures of what it might be like to live on a different planet.

Step Three

Next, have her decide what items she would like to bring with her. For example, she might want to visit Mars and bring a baseball glove, ball, and bat. She can use the gravity ratios to figure out how much each item weighs. That way she will know if she can play baseball on Mars. She will learn whether the baseball bat, ball, and glove will be too heavy or too light for playing a game.

To calculate the weight of objects on various planets, have her first weigh each object then use the ratio to work out its "heavenly" weight.

WHAT'S MORE

How much would the family pet or your child's friends weigh on each planet or on the moon?

Make a chart of information developed during the activity and illustrate it with drawings of people using the objects on the different heavenly bodies.

Learning Adventures—6th Grade Math

LEARN FROM TV?

Just sitting and watching TV won't help kids learn anything of much value. TV is passive—kids quiet down on the outside and inside their heads too. Learning happens when information is used. If the material isn't thought over, refreshed, and processed, it will quickly leae the short-term memory.

Back and Forth to a Hundred

Integers are a handy way to move up and down a scale, much like having a fever that spikes to 104° and then drops to 100° after you take some aspirin. In this card game, you zig and zag through the positive and negative integers until someone reaches 100. Don't be fooled by how simple the game appears. It requires a good deal of strategy to progressively add integers so that you reach 100 without going over 100.

The activity instructions give you the rules for getting started on the basic game. In "What's More," you'll find some variations on the game. Once you have played Back and Forth to a Hundred for awhile, you might want to make up your own variation. This is the kind of game that can grow more and more interesting as your child's mathematical skills develop.

At a Glance

Grade/Subject: 6th/Math—Computation
Skills: adding, multiplying, and dividing integers
Materials: deck of cards
paper and pencil
Time: 30 minutes

Getting Ready

Explain to your child that this game involves adding, multiplying, and dividing integers. Make sure she understands how to work with positive and negative integers. Help your child write the rules for the signs of the product and quotient of positive and negative integers (see Section II for a refresher).

From a deck of 52 cards, take out all the jokers and face cards (jack, queen, and king) and put them aside. You will not need them. In this game, the black suits (spades and clubs) represent positive integers; the red suits (diamonds and hearts) represent negative integers.

WHAT'S MORE

Try this variation: Instead of adding each result to the running total, you could have the choice of either subtracting or adding to the running total.

Another variation is to use jokers as wild cards, that is, they may be any value the player chooses (black +, red –).

To play with more players, set the goal to 250.

Play to 1,000 by using the face cards and giving them the value of 10.

Step One

Shuffle the cards and deal seven to your child and seven to yourself. Tell her to look at her cards and place one on the table face up so that you can see it. Now you choose a card from your hand and play it face up next to the first card.

Form either the sum, product, or quotient of your card and your child's card according to the following rules:

- You have the choice of adding, multiplying, or dividing the two numbers, but keep in mind that the object of the game is to get to 100 without going over it.
- Division is allowed only if one number is divisible by the other.
- An ace has a value of 1; that is, black aces are worth +1 and red aces –1.
- If one or more cards represent negative numbers (that is, if one or more are red), make sure that you attach the proper sign to the product or quotient.

Write your result on the paper. This positive or negative integer is the start of the running total that together you will keep to play the game.

Step Two

Now it's your child's turn. Tell her to play a card from her hand and form either the sum, product, or quotient of the values of her card and the card you just played. Add this number to the running total and record the result.

Step Three

You probably get the idea now. Continue taking turns playing a card and forming the sum, product, or quotient of the values of the card and the previous card. The winner of the hand is the first player who makes the running total closest to 100 without going over it. The first player to win three hands wins the game.

❯ Big Deal

Here's an activity for two that combines the enjoyment of a card game with the very specific calculation of the area of some shapes.

At a Glance

Grade/Subject: 6th/Math—Geometry and Measurement
Skills: finding the area of square, rectangle, triangle (circle?)
Materials: deck of playing cards
paper and pencil
Time: 20–30 minutes (or as long as your child wants to keep playing)

Getting Ready

It might be good for you both to start with a little review of how the areas of common shapes are calculated. You may remember that the area is the amount of space covered within the sides of a shape.

- For rectangles, the area is found by multiplying the length (l) times the width (w). The length refers to the longer side and the width refers to the shorter side. Use $A = lw$.

- For squares, which are a kind of rectangle after all, the area is again length times width. Since the sides of a square are all the same length you can also say $A = s^2$ where s is one of the sides.

- For triangles, the area is one-half of the base (b) times the height (h). The height is the distance from its highest point to its base measured by a perpendicular line (lines that meet and form a right angle, like the corners of a square or rectangle). The base is the side of the triangle that the height is drawn perpendicular to. Use $A = bh/2$.

Now you have a little preparation to do with the cards. Separate them into two packs, putting all the face cards in one pack and all the number cards in the other. Lay them side by side, face down

GOOD STARTING PLACE

We see some parents who are actively involved in home learning doing some marvelous things with their kids. Some parents, however, have a tendency to jump to higher level skills, see their kids struggling, and say their kid doesn't know them. "You've let me down," is their attitude. Our advice is to start with what kids do know and go from there. "You don't know 5 times 5, but you do know 1 times 5. That's great. Let's work from there." Start with the basics and develop a positive attitude and convey that you really believe in your child. At Score@Kaplan, we say, "I totally know you can do this!" and it comes across. If somebody is constantly saying to you, "You may not think you can do this, but I know you can," and this is reinforced by others, it's going to sink in and success will happen.

on your playing table. On a piece of paper, make a sign that shows that the jacks will stand for triangles, queens for rectangles, and kings for squares.

> **WHAT'S MORE**
>
> Use graph paper for your sketching to draw the shapes accurately to make the sides correctly proportional.
>
> ---
>
> Select which numbers you put into the deck of number cards to help your child focus on multiples of certain numbers (like the 6 tables or number squares).
>
> ---
>
> For a bigger challenge, put the aces in the face card deck to represent circles. The area of a circle is $A = (\pi)r^2$. The letter r is the length of the radius of the circle and π is equal to 3.14. When a player draws an ace from the face card deck, two number cards should be drawn from the number deck and added together to represent the radius.

Step One

You can go first to show how the game is played. Draw one card from the face card deck. Since the three kinds of face cards stand for three kinds of shapes, the card you draw will tell you the kind of shape you will need to find the area for.

If the shape you draw is a triangle or rectangle (jack or queen), you then pick two cards from the number deck. If you draw a king (a square), draw one card from the number deck.

Step Two

Sketch the shape you have drawn and use the number cards you drew to calculate the area. The area of your shape will be the score you get for that round. Have your opponent check your calculation. If you are correct, you earn the total and write it down so you can add scores from other rounds to it.

For example, if you drew a queen, an 8, and a 6, you would sketch a rectangle with sides of 8 and 6. The area is then 6×8 or 48, which becomes your score.

Step Three

Now it's your child's turn. Have her draw a shape card and then the appropriate amount of number cards. She should draw the shape and label the lengths of the sides before calculating the area. She records her score, too, in order to add to it each round.

Step Four

The game continues until all the face cards have been drawn. Whoever has the higher total score at that point is the winner. Before putting the cards away, it would be a good review to look at the shapes each of you have sketched to see what a wide range of areas has been covered during the game.

❯ Cast a Net

Have you ever seen a grocery clerk or stock person break down an empty box by unsealing its top and bottom flaps? Did you know that mathematicians use objects shaped like these flattened boxes to study space figures? The two-dimensional shape formed from a three-dimensional space figure is called a *net*. In this activity, you and your child will explore the faces and edges of a rectangular prism by making one from a net. Then you can look for a relationship between the areas of the nets and the volumes of the prisms.

At a Glance

Grade/Subject: 6th/Math—Geometry
Skills: identify edges and faces of a space figure, use area and volume formulas
Materials: pencil and paper (graph paper is helpful)
ruler
scissors
empty box such as for cereal, cake mix, butter, etc.
Time: 30 minutes

Getting Ready

Since you will be working with space figures in this activity, review the ideas of the edges and the face of a rectangular prism with your child. The net illustrated here forms a cube when folded. Explain to your child that you fold the net along the inside edges to make the cube. Tell her that she will work with this and other nets to learn more about rectangular prisms. Also review with her the formulas for the area of a rectangle and the volume of a rectangular prism.

Step One

Have your child draw the net shown at the side. She can draw it at a larger size; just make sure that she makes all its faces the same size.

Have her cut out the net along its perimeter and fold each edge to form a cube. Ask her to use the ruler to measure the edges and find the area of the net (that is, the sum of all the areas of the six squares that form the net) and the volume of the cube (using the fold lines for measurement). Make sure she uses square units for area and cubic units for volume.

EACH KID COUNTS

If you have several children at home, it's very important to provide each one with attention when you reinforce learning. My brother had just graduated from high school and was going to college, he was a national standout in debate, and my father told me, "You know what? I'm really excited about what you're doing." This was a great moment for me, the recognition my dad gave me. He wasn't putting down my brother, but he was taking time out for me. Juggling learning tasks at home with more than one child is tricky, but allocate some time to recognize each child.

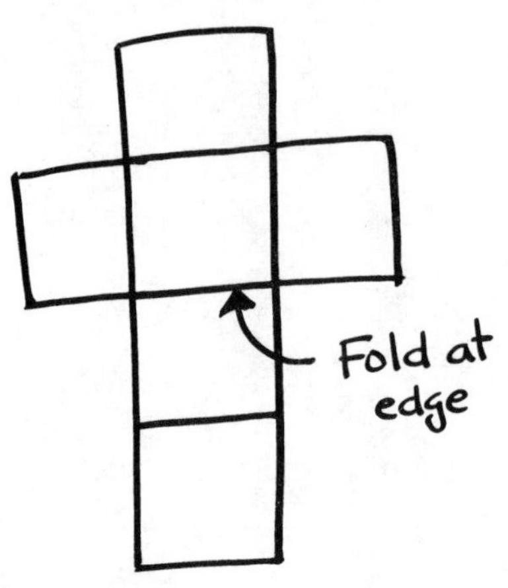

Have her begin making a table that has three columns: area, volume, and shape. Have her put the area and volume of her cube in the first two columns and draw a sketch of the cube in the third.

Step Two

Using an empty box such as a cereal box, help your child carefully separate the flaps and open it until it is in the shape of a net. Since a net does not include any faces that overlap, discard any overlapping parts.

Have her trace the edges of the net to form its outline and then add the inside edges that represent the folds. Ask your child how many different-sized faces are there. (Whereas all the faces were the same for the cube, depending on the shape of the box you've used, it will have 2 or 3 different-sized faces.)

Have your child find the area of the net and the volume of the box and add this information to her table.

Step Three

Now tell your child that she will make an original net of her own that she can cut and fold to form a box. Ask her

- What shape she wants the box to be
- How many different-sized faces the box will have (There can be no more than three.)
- How her choices will determine the shape of the faces and the shape of the net

Help her, as needed, to draw her net, cut it out, and fold it to form the rectangular prism.

Step Four

Have her find the area of the net and the volume of the prism and add this information to her table. Invite discussion of what she has done with questions like these:

- Can you find relationships among the areas of the nets and the volumes of the prisms? For example, as the areas of the nets increase, do the volumes of the prisms also increase?
- Why do you think there are never more than three faces on these nets?

WHAT'S MORE

You can explore nets further by opening up other boxes such as detergent boxes, hand soap boxes, a gift box, or a carton. Remember to discard any overlapping parts before tracing the net.

Another alternative is to make nets of other three-dimensional objects such as a cylinder (try a round oatmeal box) or a cone (a party hat or an ice cream cone). For the cone, it's probably easier to make the net (a triangle) rather than attempt to take an ice cream cone apart!

▶ Color My World

When map makers design a map, they want people to be able to distinguish between two neighboring regions. To do this they color the two regions different colors. If a map has thirty different regions on it, you might think that you would need thirty different colors. If that were true, and you were a printer, you would find printing of maps to be a very expensive operation, since the more colors you need, the more expensive it is to print. Fortunately, however, any two countries that do not share a border do not need to be in different colors.

Here's an activity that challenges you and your child to draw your own maps (designs that cut the paper up into regions) and to try to color each other's maps using as few colors as possible.

At a Glance

Grade/Subject: 6th/Math—Problem Solving
Skills: visual problem solving
Materials: paper
black pens
colored markers
Time: 3/4–1 hour

Getting Ready

Draw a large rectangle covering most of the paper. The inside of the rectangle will be your map area. Keep in mind that two countries are considered to be adjoining if they have any side in common. Sharing a single point in common is not enough (otherwise a map that resembled a wheel with many spokes would require a different color for each region.).

Step One

For the first map you make, construct your regions by starting on the outside rectangle and drawing a line or curve that also ends on the rectangle (see figure at right). You can make the map as complicated as you want as long as you follow the rule about starting and ending on the outside rectangle. Feel free to do more than one of these maps.

Step Two

After you've both drawn your first map, exchange maps, and try

WHAT'S MORE

Many world maps you can find use more than four colors, even though technically they don't need more. If you can get a world map, U.S. map, or other real map drawn with no colors, you can attempt to color them with as few colors as possible. Since we know four colors is always possible, see if you can do it using only three.

Interestingly, if you were to draw a map on a car tire's inner tube (mathematically it is called a *torus*) you could draw a map that would require seven colors. See if you can get hold of one of these inner tubes and some paint markers. Draw a map that requires five, six, or even seven colors.

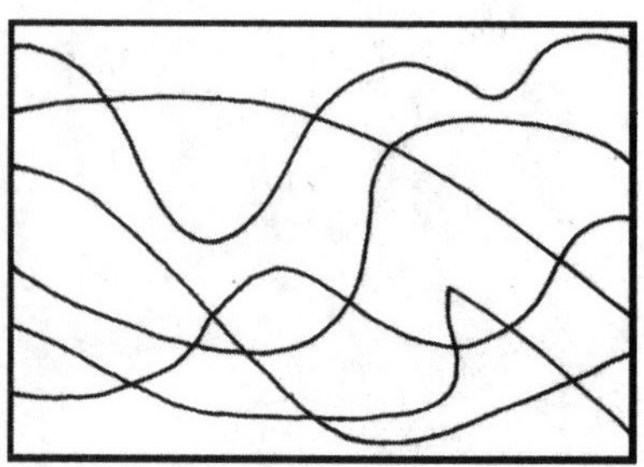

WHAT'S MORE

With the first type of map you drew, try adding circles, squares, or other closed figures anywhere on the map (they can overlap any number of regions) before you attempt to color the map. You should still be able to color the map using two colors. Try it and see!

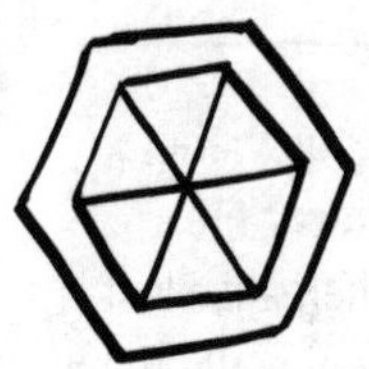

to color the map using as few colors as possible. It may help to put letters or numbers to identify what color you think you'll use in each region using a pencil, before you actually color them with markers. That way you can go back and make changes if you want. It may seem impossible, but mathematicians have proved that all maps of this kind can always be colored using only two colors. Don't be surprised though if you have trouble using only two colors—sometimes it takes a very long time to find just the right combination to make it work.

Step Three

When you've done as many of that kind of map, try a second kind of map—one in which you can draw any map design you want, with no restrictions about always attaching to the edge of the rectangle.

Once you've each drawn one of this kind of map, exchange them and see how few colors you need to color them. You can also try coloring the two maps shown here to see how few colors you need to color them correctly.

Step Four

Were you able to color any map using no more than four colors? The Four Color Map Theorem, which was only recently proven (and is so complex that only a few people really understand it), says that any map that can be drawn on paper or on a sphere can be colored with just four colors.

INTEGER SHUFFLE

Here's a tabletop adaptation of the popular game that offers fun combining a little physical coordination with practice in using positive and negative numbers.

At a Glance

Grade/Subject: 6th/Math—Numeration, Computation
Skills: write, compare, order and add integers
Materials: pencil
ruler
sheets of 8 × 11 paper or larger, if available
checkers or other chip-like markers (6 each of two colors)
Time: 15–20 minutes

Getting Ready

You need to start by making the targets onto which you will shove the checkers. It is a triangular shape that is divided into seven sections, which are labeled with different point values. Use both positive and negative number labels in order to create practice in adding and subtracting integers.

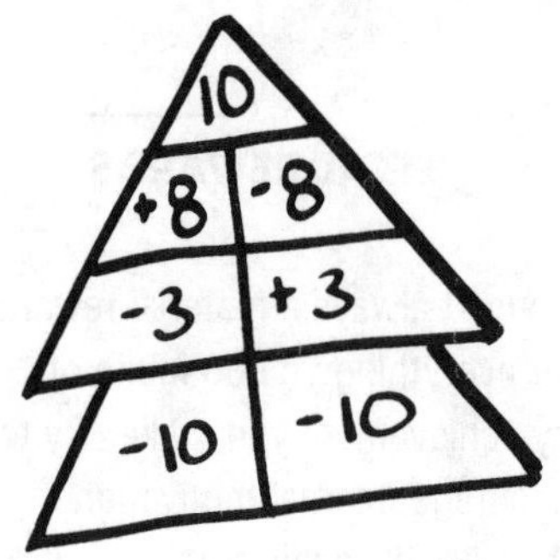

Make one game board to get started. Later, involve your child in helping to make several more target diagrams so that the two of you can easily add some variation to your game-playing.

Review how to add and subtract positive and negative numbers if you feel rusty. (See Core Area 3: Computation in Section II's content refresher.)

Step One

Integer Shuffle involves taking turns with your child using a pencil or ruler to propel a checker across the table top towards the target. The object is to have your checker land in one of the scoring areas so you can accumulate that number of points. Decide with your child what the winning number of points should be; 25 is a good number to start with.

Step Two

Launch two of your checkers, one at a time, towards the target, look at where they land, and do the math to see how many points you have. Remember the tricks involved in adding and subtracting negative numbers!

For example, if you land on the –3 and the +8 your math problem looks like this: (–3) + (+8) = ?

That problem is like subtracting 3 from 8 so you end up with +5.

Only 20 more points to the goal! Leave your checkers where they are. They will contribute to some interesting strategies as you go along.

Step Three

When your child takes her turn, she lands on –10 and –3. Adding a negative number to another negative number gives you a negative number for your total. That makes a total of –13. Bad news—she's got some work to do to reach 25! But look how your next turn may help her out.

WHAT'S MORE

You and your child can make the target larger and include more numbers to aim at.

Make the scoring areas smaller or larger and change to an object that is larger or smaller than a checker in order to increase or decrease the difficulty of landing on certain scores.

Instead of trying to reach a target score (like 25), play simply to see who reaches the highest score after each player propels all six markers.

Keep a running score from one game to the next and watch your fortunes rise and fall as you play off and on over a long period of time.

MATERIAL REWARDS

There isn't always a material reward for everything you do in life or every achievement you make. Try to encourage internal motivation in children. It's a sticky thing, but keep at it with positive encouragement and positive attention to your child and her accomplishments. Avoid instilling in your child the attitude of "What's the world going to give me for doing this?"

WHAT'S MORE

Play Fraction Tic Tac Toe by creating grids with problems using fractions.

Play Decimal Tic Tac Toe by creating grids with problems using decimals.

Play Word Problems Tic Tac Toe by creating grids with word problems in them. (You may need to draw a bigger grid.)

Play Mixed Tic Tac Toe by creating grids with problems of all kinds in them.

When you launch your next two checkers, suppose the first one knocks her out of the –10 spot and into the +3 spot, leaving you in the –10 spot. Your second checker propels her out of the –3 spot into the +8 but leaves you in the –3 spot. This now gives her (–13) + (+3) + (+8) for a new total of –2. On the other hand, you now have +5 + (–10) + (–3) which gives you a new total of –8. What a turnabout!

Step Four

Continue to take turns until one of you reaches the desired goal. After you've each launched your six checkers, remove them and start again. Checkers that land outside the scoring area count as 0.

▶ INTEGER TIC TAC TOE

Tic Tac Toe is a game people of all ages enjoy. This particular Tic Tac Toe is not only fun, but also a good learning tool. It offers enjoyable practice in computing—handy for all aspects of basic math as well as in everyday life. With the chance to create her own game boards, your child can try to stump everyone in the family.

At a Glance

Grade/Subject: 6th/Math—Computation
Skills: adding, subtracting, multiplying, and dividing integers (positive and negative numbers plus zero)
Materials: paper and pencils
two kinds of coins (or other small markers)
Time: 15–20 minutes

Getting Ready

Before you begin playing this version of Tic Tac Toe, check out your own understanding of integers since this activity involves computing them. Integers are positive and negative whole numbers plus zero.

Step One

Explain that to play Integer Tic Tac Toe, the game works in the same way as traditional Tic Tac Toe, but instead of using X's and O's, you will use integers.

Draw a large Tic Tac Toe grid—make two parallel vertical lines about two inches apart and two parallel horizontal lines about two inches and intersecting the lines going down. This should leave nine spaces (about two inches square) to write in.

Step Two

In the nine spaces available, have your child write nine different equations. You can use the following sample equations or you can make up your own equations. These equations are only examples:

$$-84 + 12 =$$
$$23 - (-34) =$$
$$-15 \times 3 =$$
$$7 \div (-4) =$$
$$-67 + 45 =$$
$$98 - (-56) =$$
$$13 \times (-24) =$$
$$-18 \div 23 =$$
$$-16 \times 0 =$$

23 - (-34) =	-18 ÷ 23 =	13 × (-24) =
-84 + 12 =	-15 × 3 =	-67 + 45 =
-16 × 0 =	7 ÷ (-4) =	98 - (-56) =

She should place one equation in each space available. The order of her equations can be random.

Step Three

The object of the game is to solve three equations in a row in any direction on the grid. The person who goes first, picks a space and solves the equation. If the equation is solved correctly, place a coin (or any other item suitable to use for a marker) on that equation. If the equation is not solved correctly, no coin is placed on the space and the other person takes a turn. Continue taking turns until one of you has three markers in a row.

Step Four

Play some more. For each game create a new grid, supplied with new equations. The player with the best out of five games wins.

▶ JUMPING TOADS

Here's a great game that will help your child gain some intuition about probabilities. The more you play this game, the better your child's understanding of the relative probabilities of dice combinations will become.

At a Glance

Grade/Subject: 6th/Math—Probability
Skills: learning about probability, record keeping
Materials: two dice
paper and pencil to make racetrack boards
marker and large sheets of paper to make charts
twelve pennies
Time: 3/4–1 hour

Getting Ready

With your child, make a gameboard (large enough for the pennies to all fit) that looks like the one shown here.

Twelve pennies (the 12 Jumping Toads) should then be placed on the start line, as shown.

Step One

Here is how the jumping toads race: Your child rolls two dice to determine which toad to move after each roll. To know which toad will jump, just add the total shown on the two faces of the dice. After each roll of the dice, move the penny in the corresponding column one space forward on the board. Continue rolling the dice and moving until one of the pennies reaches the finish line. That numbered toad is the winner of the first race. Toad eleven has won the game illustrated here, just nosing out toad number eight.

Before playing, you and your child should each predict which toad you think will be most likely to win. Then hold the toad-jumping race and see how well each of you predicted.

Step Two

After the first race, your child should make up a chart to keep track of how often each toad wins. This chart can be made as a steadily growing bar graph where the numbers one through twelve represent each toad's number of wins.

Continue racing the toads—the more races completed, the better the chart will be. Twenty or thirty games will give excellent results. After playing one, two, or more games you both may wish to revise your prediction about which toads are most likely to win. Talk about what influences your predictions.

WHAT'S MORE

Try conducting two-toad races by flipping a coin to determine which toad jumps each time. How does having just two choices instead of 36 affect the "odds" for each toad.

Knowing about probabilities can help with playing many other games that are based on rolling dice. Backgammon, for instance, is a great game for increasing intuition about dice probability.

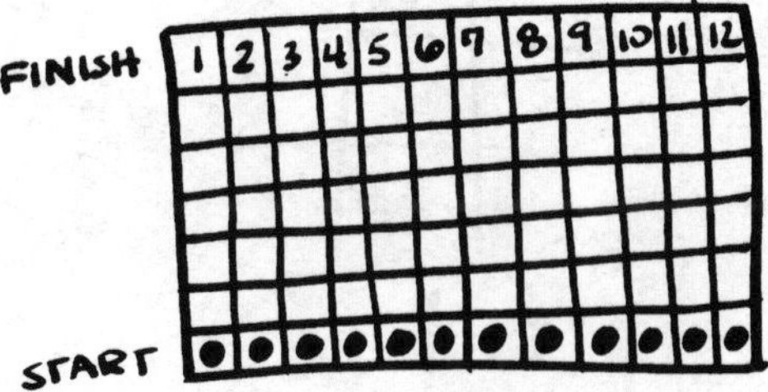

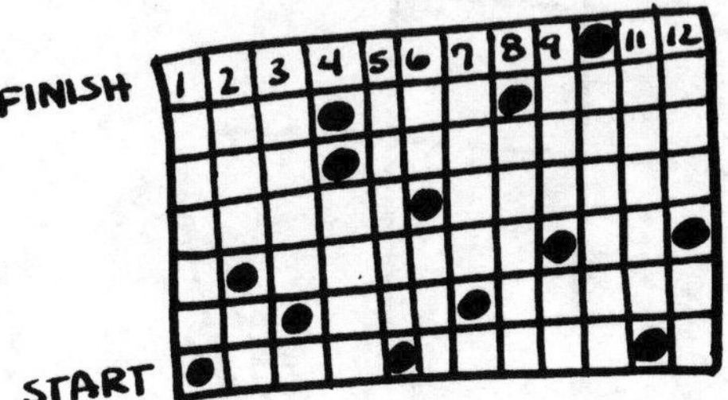

- Does a toad in a certain column seem to do better?
- Can you think of any reason to explain the success or failure of toads in any particular columns?

Step Three

In these two diagrams, a toad needs to have its number come up six times in order to win. Try experimenting with race tracks of different lengths. Start with a one-jump racetrack where a toad needs to have its number come up just once to win. Then lengthen the racetrack by whatever interval you wish.

For each specific racetrack length, at least a dozen or more races are needed in order to have enough results to tell you anything much about probability. Make separate charts for each length racetrack.

Step Four

Make a diagram or other visual explanation of all the possible outcomes that could be rolled with two dice. Since each dice can roll the numbers one through six, there are six possible outcomes when rolling one die. Check to see whether the diagram shows a total of 36 possible outcomes when rolling two dice.

- Why is the total equal to 6 times 6?
- Why does the toad in column one always do so poorly?

Use the diagram to count how many possible ways each of the two dice *totals* corresponding to the twelve toads, could come up. For example, a total of ten could be made in the following ways: 6 + 4, 5 + 5, and 4 + 6. Waiting to make this diagram until after racing the toads many times helps your child articulate the intuitive feeling she develops through the experience of playing.

PITCHING FOR INTEGERS GAME

Graphs do not have to be staid, lifeless tools that only scientists and mathematicians use. This activity uses a coordinate grid for you and your child to have fun practicing your pitching style and learning about integers in a fast-paced game. This easy activity gives practice with integers and demonstrates how integers are used on a graph. It involves plotting integers as well as measuring distances between points on a grid.

WHAT'S MORE

Rolling dice several thousand times would take a very long, tiresome time. But if you could have a computer do the rolling for you, it might take only a minute or two. There are a number of pieces of computer software that allow you to do just that. If you know how to program using computer languages like Basic, you could write a program that picks random numbers many times and keeps track of the results. If you don't know how to do the programming yourself, you might be able to find someone who can do it for you.

DYNAMICALLY COMMUNICATE

Listen to your children. When they're asking you questions, listen to their questions and give them an answer. If they're doing homework, try to find out what they do know, then help to build on that. Sometimes a child will ask a question and an adult will start to explain each and every step, when it might be just the last step they needed help with.

BY THE WAY...

Integers are an essential part of graphing in the coordinate plane. They provide the scale of the axes, and they determine the positive and negative directions in the graph.

WHAT'S MORE

You could track pitching improvements by graphing your scores. Compare graphs to see whose pitching has improved the most. (We're betting on your kid!)

After you and your child have played the game several times, you can add more excitement to the game by playing with more players.

Another way to play the game is to use negative numbers in the scoring. Since left and down are negative directions on a coordinate grid, use negative numbers when counting in those directions.

At a Glance

Grade/Subject: 6th/Math—Graphing
Skills: working with integers, using graphs
Materials: dime
die
sheet of 4 × 4/inch graph paper
pencil
ruler
Time: 30 minutes

Getting Ready

Since the object of the game is to pitch the dime onto a coordinate grid, begin by drawing on the grid paper the coordinate grid shown in the picture. The grid lines should be 3/4 inch apart. Make sure you label each line with the appropriate integer, as shown.

Step One

Explain that the winner of this game will be the person with the *lowest* score. She begins by defining two integers using the dime and the die. Flip the dime to determine the sign of the first integer: heads is positive and tails is negative. Roll the die. Put the number showing on the die together with the sign to get her first integer and write the number. Repeat to get the second integer so that she now has two integers.

Step Two

Talk with her about what point on the grid corresponds to the integer pair. That will be the target she aims for. Have her stand a little away from the table and pitch the dime towards the target on the grid. After her toss, measure the distance between where the dime landed and the target point. That is, count the number of units horizontally until you are directly below the target, and count the number of units vertically to the target point. Add these two distances. This is her score on her first turn. Record the score.

Step Three

Now it's your turn. Flip the coin and roll the die to get the two integers that identify your target point. Make your toss, have your child measure the distance between your target point and the point on the grid closest to your dime by again counting the number of units horizontally until you are directly below the target and the number of units vertically to the target point. Add these two distances, and record your score.

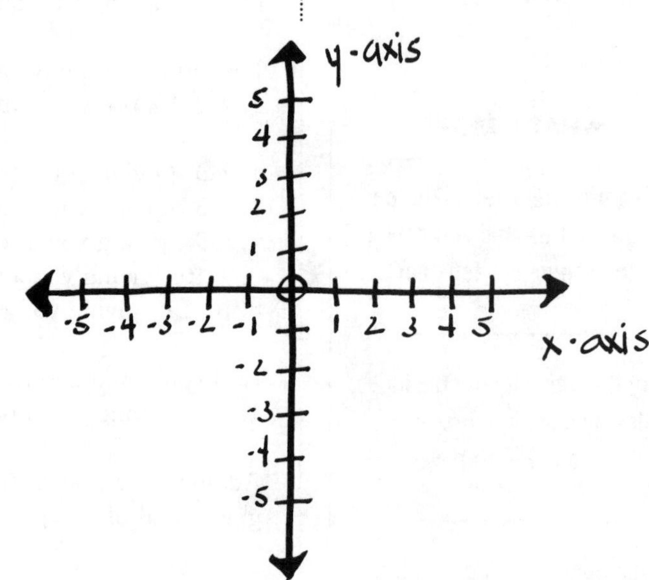

Step Four

Continue taking turns playing until one of you reaches a score of 30 (or whatever number the two of you decide on). Take turns with your child until one of you reaches the winning score.

▸ SEMI-SERIOUS-SERIES

If you've ever played Gin Rummy, this game will seem familiar to you. But there's an interesting new twist on the cards you lay down!

At a Glance

Grade/Subject: 6th/Math—Algebra, Problem Solving
Skills: recognizing geometric sequences
Materials: deck of cards
paper and pencil
Time: 20–30 minutes

Getting Ready

You and your child are going to use the cards dealt to each of you to create some arithmetic and geometric number series. Numbers in an arithmetic series have a common difference from each number to the next in the series (like 5, 7, 9, 11 or 4, 7, 10, 13). Numbers in a geometric series have a common ratio (like 1 : 2 : 4 : 8 or 1 : 3 : 9).

Step One

Shuffle the cards and deal nine cards to both of you. Working with the cards face up on the table, you each try to produce as many number series as possible. The same card may be used in several sequences. Jacks count as 11, queens as 12 and kings as 13. As you make each series, have the other player check whether it is legitimate. If it is, write it down and add up the values of each

TOO HARD FOR YOU?

In the learning process, your child will eventually encounter some high level processes that may be quite difficult. Acknowledge that you may have at one time done schoolwork like this, but you don't quite remember how it goes. Then ask your child to explain what he already knows—get him to teach you about what he can do. (Or you can look up the skill in our skills review section—Section II of this book is a great reference when you're a homework helper!)

card in the series to get your score.

For instance, suppose you were dealt 1 (ace), 5, 9, 12 (queen), 8, 3, 9, 2, 10. You could make the following the arithmetic series:

1, 2, 3 (giving you a total of 6 points)
1, 3, 5 (giving you a total of 9 points)
1, 5, 9 (giving you a total of 15 points)
8, 9, 10 (giving you a total of 27 points)
8, 10, 12 (giving you a total of 30 points)

And you could also make this geometric series:
1, 3, 9 (giving you a total of 13 points)

Adding your points (6 + 9 + 15 + 27 + 30 + 13) gives you a grand total of 100 points.

Step Three

Have your child take his turn. Encourage him to lay out each card sequence and then write the sequence down on paper. (It will be easier to keep track of each sequence made and the totals for each in order to add up running totals for each turn.)

Step Four

Once you have each taken one turn, decide on what target total you want to set for the game. 300 might work best until you have played several games and your child has become so good at making series that you want to aim for a higher ceiling such as 500 or more. The first player to reach or exceed the target number wins.

WHAT'S MORE

Use a timer and set a limit on the amount of time you have to put the sequences together.

Vary the difficulty of creating series by dealing more or fewer cards to each player.

Add a bonus of 10 points if the cards in a series are of the same color, and 20 points if they are of the same suit.

LEARNING EVERY DAY

Parents should tell their kids, "I don't know everything. That's what learning is all about. We learn every day." Parents should remind kids that learning happens every day, and it continues to happen once we leave school. You probably learn even more outside of school because you've got your basics down. Build your child's confidence NOW to prepare her for a lifetime of learning.

Triangle Ratios

Ratios are important in geometry because they show relationship among the dimensions of polygons. For example, if you double the length and width of a rectangle, what happens to its area? This activity uses ratios to take you on an exploration of what happens to the area of a triangle if you change its dimensions. As you explore the figures you create, you use patterns of shaded and unshaded triangles to discover some fascinating results.

At a Glance

Grade/Subject: 6th/Math—Fractions, Decimals, and Percents
Skills: Calculating ratios, drawing similar figures
Materials: pencil and paper
ruler
sheet of 4" x 4" graph paper
Time: 30 minutes

Getting Ready

Explain that this activity uses the ratios of the sides and areas of similar triangles to explore that nature of length and area. Ask your child to write a definition of similar triangles. Make sure he knows the formula for the area of a triangle. (Check Core Area 4 of the Section II math content material if you need a quick review yourself.)

Step One

Have your child draw a figure that is similar to the triangle illustrated here so that the ratio of the side of his figure to the side of the given figure is 1 : 2.

Tell him to divide his triangle into the equilateral triangles that are of the same size and in the same pattern as those in the given triangle. Make sure that the shaded triangles in his figure correspond to the shaded triangles in the original figure. Ask your child to find the ratio of the number of triangles in his figure to the number of triangles in the original figure (it's 1 : 4). Ask him to find the ratio of the area of his figure is to the area of the given figure (it's 1 : 4).

Have him record the ratio of the sides of the two triangles, the ratio of the number of triangles in the two figures, and the ratio of the areas of the two triangles in a table.

Step Two

Now explain to your child that he needs to draw a triangle that is similar to the original triangle so that his triangle is divided into six shaded triangles and three unshaded triangles of the same size and in same pattern as the given triangle. Ask him to explain how he would find such a triangle. What is the ratio of the sides of his triangle and the original triangle? (Answer is 3 : 4.) What is the

CHALLENGED SCHOOLS

Are schools getter harder? I went to a great public school in the Midwest, I had a small class size, I wasn't overloaded with homework, and my classmates and I felt really prepared for the next grade. I look at schools today and kids are crowded into big classrooms, they have tons of homework, and some of them don't know how to tell time except with a digital watch. A lot of educators are struggling to find the best curriculum for reaching kids, and with bigger classroom sizes it's harder to reach all students. Get involved and be an active partner in working with your child, your child's teacher, the local PTA, and other parents to improve your school's effectiveness.

ratio of the areas of the two triangles? (Answer is 9 : 16.) Have him add this information to his table.

Step Three

Now have your child draw another similar triangle so that the ratio of the side of his triangle to the side of the original triangle should be 2 : 1. Have him record the ratios of the lengths, number of triangles, and areas in the table. Does he see a pattern developing? Ask him to explain the relationship between the ratio of the sides of two similar triangles and the ratio of the areas of the two triangles.

Step Four

Observe that the triangle your child found in Step One is the same as the top four triangles of the given triangle, that is, the top two rows. The triangle he drew in Step Two is the same as the top three rows of the triangle. Ask him to find the ratio of the sides and the ratio of the areas using a triangle made by adding another row at the bottom of the given triangle.

Have him predict what would happen if you add two rows to the bottom of the triangle. Try it and see.

• How many rows do you add to get a triangle whose area is four times the area of the given triangle?

WHAT'S MORE

You and your child can do this activity again later using a different shape, such as a rectangle divided into smaller rectangles, or a hexagon divided into equilateral triangles.

Another alternative is to use blocks, sugar cubes, or unifix cubes to make three-dimensional figures and find the ratios of the volumes of the figures.

▶ Table Top Math

The breakfast table may not be the place for advanced mathematical thinking, but in many homes it is a place where the nutritional merits of various cereals is debated. Is Sergeant Sugar's ChocoSweeto Puff cereal better than Mother Nature's Organic Bran Delight?

In this activity, you and your child can collect, interpret, and work with the data provided on cereal boxes, to round up your nutritional facts. This may not resolve your family's breakfast dilemmas, but it may channel the discussion in a useful direction.

WHAT'S MORE

Once your child has worked out the details on one box of cereal, it's not a long step to working it out for another competing brand. To keep things simple, limit the comparison to one or two categories.

At a Glance

Grade/Subject: 6/Math—Decimal Fractions and Percentages
Skills: computations and problems with decimals and percent

Materials: pencil and paper
cereal boxes
Time: 3/4–1 hour

Getting Ready

Pick a cereal that the two of you would like to investigate. Working with fine print is tedious and it's easy to get confused; have your child write out the Nutrition Facts table on a sheet of paper. To keep things simple, stick to just the cereal information; that is, exclude the column of information that details the contribution of milk. If you don't have a cereal box at hand, use the sample panel included on this page.

NUTRITION FACTS
Uncle Jolly's Good For You Cereal

Serving Size 1/2 cup (1oz.) = 30g.
Servings per container 14

Amount per Serving Cereal

Calories 100	Calories from fat 10

% of Daily Value

Total Fat 1 g. 2%	saturated fat 0 g. 0%
Cholesterol 0 g. 0%	Sodium 50 mg 2%
Total Carbohydrates 20 g. 7%	Dietary Fiber 2 g. 8%
Sugars 5 g.	Protein 4 g.

Vitamin A 0%	Vitamin C 0%
Calcium 0%	Iron 2%

Percents (%) of Daily Value are based on a 2,000 calorie diet. Your daily value may differ depending on your needs.

Nutrient Calories = 2,000

Total Fat Less than 65 g.
Saturated Fat Less than 20 g.
Cholesterol Less than 300 mg.
Sodium Less than 2,400 mg.
Total Carbohydrates 300 g.
Dietary Fiber 25 g.

Ingredients: Wheat, soy, oat, buckwheat flour, sesame seed meal, raisins, honey, wheat bran, soy protein, barley flakes, fruit juice concentrate, barley malt syrup, salt, and calcium carbonate.

Step One

You'll notice in the Nutrition Facts chart that right at the top there is an amount of calories per serving. Have your child answer these questions:

- If your total daily caloric need is 2,000 calories, what percent of that need do you get in one serving?
- Look at the top of NUTRITION FACTS, and you'll see how many servings there are in each box. What percentage of your daily caloric need would you get from eating the whole box?
- How many servings would you have to eat to get all the calories that you need?
- Would it be fun to eat that much dry cereal?

Step Two

Have your child pick out one of the following items (ignore any with 0%): Total Fat, Sodium, Total Carbohydrates, Dietary Fiber, or Sugars. Each is listed with the amount in a serving weighed in grams. Answer these questions for the items you picked:

WHAT'S MORE

All packaged foods are required to carry nutritional information. You can extend this activity to such nutritionally hot topics as pizza versus macaroni and cheese, or frozen yogurt versus ice cream.

GOING METRIC

Metric Measurements

GRAM (abbreviation "g"): a small measurement equivalent to .035 ounces

MILLIGRAM (abbreviation "mg"): a very small measurement. It equals 1⁄1000 of a gram (.001)

The *metric standard,* adopted in France at the end of the eighteenth century, has slowly spread throughout the world. The metric system has been legal for use in the United States since 1866, but it has never replaced the old English system of pounds, ounces, inches, and feet—except in scientific work where it is the international standard. Under pressure to standardize and conform to the world economy and science, many American products including cars, farm machinery, and computers are manufactured using the metric system. Most other American products now include the metric measurements. The sooner your child becomes able to use the metric system, the easier scientific measurements will become.

- What amount would be the daily total in grams that you should eat?
- How many servings of cereal would you need to get your daily total?

Step Three

What if your child's entire classroom had only one kind of cereal for its whole food supply for a day?

- How many boxes would they have to consume in order to meet their basic caloric needs ?
- What if that's all they had for an entire week? If they really did eat that much, compute the weight of sodium that would be consumed by the entire class.

Step Four

Have your child invent and name a totally outrageous cereal, design a box for it, and work out a NUTRITION FACTS table. The table can have any amount of just about anything in it. Answer the questions in Steps Two and Three for this new (not necessarily nutritious) cereal.

Learning Adventures—5th Grade Science

CITY SCIENCE

Living in an apartment or in a big city doesn't rule out experiences with nature that encourage your child's interest in science. Even small flats have room for plants and some kinds of pets. Plant a windowsill garden. Try planting the seeds from grapefruit, avocado, or green or red bell peppers (let the seeds dry before planting). Visit parks, zoos, science museums, aquariums, arboretums, or public gardens. Look into hikes run by park rangers or groups like the local Nature Conservancy or Audubon Society.

About Tooling Up

Doing science requires two things—stuff to do it with and a way of keeping track of what you've done. In this activity, you and your kid get some help with the equipment, supplies, and record-keeping paraphernalia that will come in handy for doing science.

You can do the science activities in this book without doing this one, but the steps described here will give you and your child a nice head start!

At a Glance

Grade/Subject: 5th (and 6th)/Science—Inquiry Skills
Skills: planning investigations, setting up shop!
Materials: Each of the science Learning Adventure activities in the following pages list the specific things to use for that activity. To save you the trouble of rounding up everything you need each time, this tooling-up activity helps you prepare some of the general equipment and materials you and your child could have on hand for experiments and record keeping.
Time: Part of an evening—about an hour (a trip to the store may be needed too)

Getting Ready

Browse through the science activities for your child's grade. Notice the kinds of things listed under *Materials* for each. Most of

PETS AND SCIENCE

Getting to know and care for animals—from goldfish to gerbils to golden retrievers—is a great kind of hands-on biology lesson for kids. They can learn firsthand about a pet's life cycle, intelligence and behavior, feeding and grooming habits, adaptation, and reproduction.

Before choosing a pet, have your child read about different animals, birds, fish, and other creatures and the care each requires. Be clear about who will be responsible for feeding, exercising (regular walking, if necessary), and clean up (the aquarium, cage, litter box). Having a pet is a great science learning experience, but parents just might end up with much of the responsibility. Be prepared for a mixture of rewarding learning experiences, some heartwarming times, and a lot of work.

them will be tools and materials that you can find around your house.

Step One

Read through Step Two (Tools of Science) and Step Three (Scientific Record Keeping) with your child. For each, discuss which kinds of equipment you may already have around your home that you can use for scientific studies such as scales, rulers, simple tools, and kitchen utensils. Encourage your kid to think of other things he might use for doing science. Annotate each step with items that either of you thinks of to add, along with ideas of how to get them.

Science activities do take up space and sometimes create a bit of clutter. Talk about where in your home would be the best place to do such science activities and where you might set aside space to store your science equipment, books, and materials. A closet shelf or some storage boxes should provide ample room.

Step Two: Tools of Science

Science for 5th and 6th graders involves lots of doing, and these Tools of Science certainly do not represent an all-inclusive list. You may already have other useful items in your home, and you may think of more as you go along.

Observation Aids magnifying glass, a small but accurate compass, a low-powered microscope (fun, but not essential)

Measuring Instruments ruler, yardstick, small tape measure, thermometers (outdoor and body, if possible), stopwatch or digital watch with timer function, portable postage meter (0–4 oz.), kitchen scale (0–5 lbs.; if it has metric readings as well, so much the better)

Recording Materials small spiral notebook for note taking, jotting reminders, and doodling (a handy tool, but not necessary if you make your own Science Notebook as described below), pencil and pen, set of colored pencils, pocket calculator, calendar with spaces big enough to make reminder notes for observation schedules and for recording events and observations (one that also shows the phases of the moon, if possible)

Miscellaneous Matter a roll of 1/4" or 1/2" masking tape, 3/4" clear tape, small role of duct tape, ball of twine, a few plastic vegetable bags or small earring-sized boxes, white glue, plastic model cement, some rubber bands, pocket knife, assortment of batteries, roll of bell wire from a hardware store, and assorted jars and boxes for holding things

Step Three: Scientific Record Keeping

A large, loose-leaf, ring binder notebook is a valuable tool for recording data, information, and longer reports on science observations. For your child, having his own Science Notebook is a mark of being a scientist. Help your kid get started putting his notebook together—decoration is optional, but fun, takes a bit more time, and can evolve over the period of using the notebook. Some of the items suggested here may require a trip to a store.

3-Ring Notebook A sturdy 8 1/2" × 11" notebook at least 1" thick will serve your child's needs. If it has inside pockets, and you add pocket dividers and a pouch (for a calculator, for instance), so much the better.

Paper Gather as wide a variety of papers as you like—lined, unlined, and graph papers are all useful. Dividers will help with defining sections in the notebook. If you have colored paper or oak tag that you would like to include, just punch out the holes and add them to the notebook.

Other materials Adding a small calculator, paper punch, and a calendar small enough to fit into the notebook would all be useful.

Step Four

As noted, science takes more space and creates more clutter than other areas of study. Talk with your child about the importance of keeping equipment clean and safely out of the way when not in use. Choose and prepare a space where everything can be stored to help focus the clean up that follows many activities.

None of the activities in this book involves very hazardous materials or procedures, but talking over and then practicing good safety practices is important. Such procedures and choices include wearing safety glasses when there is a risk of shattering rock or glass, having adult supervision when working with extremes of hot or cold, and washing your hands well after handling specimens.

SAFETY SPECS

No activity that requires hammers, nails, banging rocks, or has any risk of shattering or splashing should be done without safety glasses. They are inexpensive and worth every penny. Most of the activities in this book involve no risk at all, but it is an extremely good habit for your child to develop now, and excellent preparation for science school lab safety.

A MEANS, NOT AN END

There is nothing inherently beneficial about "getting your child on the computer," unless this is the best way to provide your child with access to content that you have selected. Children should begin "interacting with computers" when they are capable of working with appropriate content. The computer is not an end in itself, but a relatively neutral medium. It can be used for good or ill, much as a book. The content determines the appropriateness for children, regardless of age.

▸ Consumer Stretch

Sometimes dinner table discussions can turn into an opportunity to do a little science. Not all science has to be bold adventure into the unknown. A lot of good work (not to mention practice) can come out of let's-try-it-and-find-out situations. Did you ever notice how hard it is to stretch those wide rubber bands that sometimes hold carrots or broccoli together in the supermarket? The children in one family wondered about them, and this activity grew out of what they did.

At a Glance

Grade/Subject: 5th/Science—Physical Science, Inquiry Skills
Skills: investigation, measurement
Materials: lots of rubber bands, including a few very wide ones (you'll need several that are about 1⁄2 inches wide)
science notebook
31⁄2 foot board
yardstick or tape measure
nail or cup hook
scissors
C-clamp (optional)
several different sizes of canned foods (or other objects weighing around 1⁄2–1 pound)
2 large paper clips
mesh onion bag or plastic grocery bag
Time: 3⁄4–1 hour

Getting Ready

In order to test the strength and stretchability of a rubber band, you and your child will need a test platform and some standard of weights. A test platform can be made from a board just over 3 feet long, a nail, and a yardstick.

Tape the yardstick to the board so that its bottom (the 36 inch end) is flush with the bottom of the board. Screw the cup hook or drive the nail into the board just above the top of the yardstick.

KITCHEN QUIZ

Does water boil faster with the lid on the pot or not? Does hot water freeze into ice cubes faster than cold water? Does salt dissolve faster in hot water or ice water? These kinds of questions often pop up around the kitchen. You don't have to drop everything to check them out, but if you can remember them and make a time when you and your child can invent tests for them, you'll both have a great time doing science and exercising your curiosity muscles!

Your test platform can then be tied to the edge of a table or the side of a chair to keep it upright. (If you don't have a long enough board, clamp a small one to a tabletop along the edge and put the cup hook or nail into its side. You can also substitute a tape measure for the yardstick or use a foot ruler to mark off half-inch intervals on the board.)

You won't need exact weights (although these can be used, of course), but you will need several items that weigh the same. Tuna fish, tomato paste, small vegetable, or pet food cans are all good candidates.

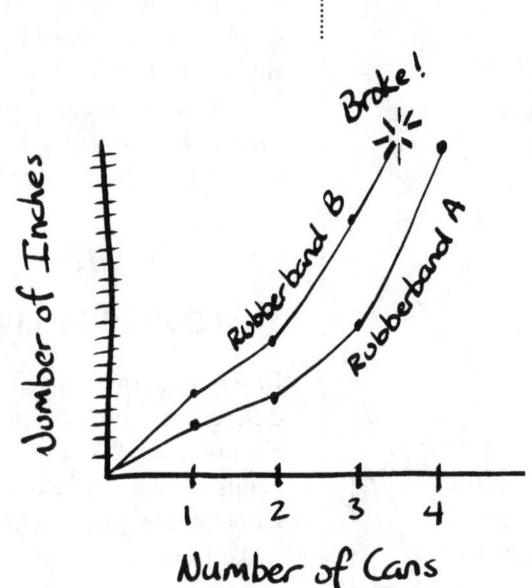

Step One

Pick out several different rubber bands and test them on your apparatus. Loop the top of the rubber band around the cup hook and attach the mesh or plastic bag to the bottom of its loop with a paper clip. Experiment with different weights to see what happens.

Step Two

Now the two of you are ready to be more systematic. Pick one rubber band (but not your widest) and measure its relaxed length (how long it is pressed flat on a surface, but not stretched) and how wide it is. Set up a chart so that you can record exactly how long this rubber band stretches with each amount of weight you try. Does it stretch the same amount each time you increase the weight by one more can? How much weight will it carry before it breaks?

Step Three

Set up a new chart and have your child pick out a wide rubber band (you'll need at least two the same size) and test it to its limit, weight by weight until it breaks. Record the amount of weight and stretch for each trial. Take some scissors and cut the other wide rubber band in half lengthwise. Run the same test on one of these half-width rubber bands. Record the data until it breaks. Then slice the other half again in the same way and test that thinner one in the same way.

WHAT'S MORE

If your child has an airplane model that flies using wind-up rubber band power, experiment with different widths of rubber bands to see which ones work better.

Try testing this: loop several rubber bands of the same size together (you already know how far they stretch individually), and repeat the tests you did with them when they were separate. Do they stretch as far together as the total of their individual stretches?

Use the information from the chart of all the trials to make a graph of each rubber band's behavior and capability. Does a thin rubber band behave the same way as a thin one cut from a wider one? You've thought about width, but if you have any that are thicker, how do they behave? What kinds of things does a wide rubber band hold better? What about the thin ones?

Flowers in Living Color

In science, your fifth grader is learning the basic similarities and differences between plants and animals and what things are essential to all living things. One essential nutrient for green plants is water. They use it to carry food and chemicals to various parts of the plant, where—among other things—it is used to make food.

Water in the stems of plants also helps them stand upright and keeps their leaves from drooping. But this means that water taken in by a plant's roots must travel *upward*. How can it do that?

In this activity, you and your child can explore exactly what goes on inside the stems of plants. (You'll also learn some secrets of the florists' business!)

WHAT'S MORE

Remember those green carnations you saw everywhere last St. Patrick's Day? Now you know how they were made! You and your child can make flowers to match any color scheme.

Experiment with other white flowers and colored water. Do they react in the same way as carnations do?

Have your child keep track of all her osmosis observations in her science notebook. Record daily progress of food color absorption by drawing pictures or taking photographs and by making a chart or graph.

At a Glance

Grade/Subject: 5th/Science—Life Science
Skills: learn how plants live and grow, how water is transported in plant stems
Materials: several stalks of celery
three white carnations
red, green, and blue liquid food coloring
four glass jars (such as those for pickles or applesauce)
paring knife
Time: 15–30 minutes to set up each demonstration
5–10 minutes of observation for a few days following the initial experiment

Getting Ready

Before starting this activity, you may want to review the basic processes of living plants in the section for Core Area 1: Life Science in Section II. Plants make food through the process of *photosynthesis.* Water, which is one of the basic ingredients of that process, is taken in by plants through *osmosis.* That's part of the process you and your kid will explore in this activity.

Step One

Start with a simple experiment that shows the movement of water upward through a plant stem. Have your child make a strong solution of the food coloring in one of the glass jars—any color will do, but red will be most dramatic.

Now stand the stalks of celery in the jar with colored water. Leave them there for a day or two.

Step Two

On the third day, have your kid cut across the stem of one of the celery stalks, an inch or two from the bottom. Notice the pattern of tiny cells filled with colored water. Encourage her to explain to you what the pattern of colored cells demonstrates.

On the same stalk, make another cut nearer the top. How far up the stem has the colored water traveled? Leave the other celery stalk in the water a few days longer, then test it again. How long does it take the colored water to reach the top of the stalk?

Step Three

Did you ever see a single flower that was red, white, and blue? Not in nature, certainly, but you and your kid can make such a patriotic bloom using this same process. Here's how.

Take the other three glass jars. Have your kid use the food coloring to make a blue solution in one jar, a red solution in the other. Put clear water in the third jar.

Step Four

Put a white carnation in water and use the knife to split its stem into three sections. Be sure to cut the stems under water so that air bubbles don't get in.

Put one section of the stem in each of the water-filled jars—one red, one blue, one clear. Keep an eye on the flower to watch the changes that take place.

TREKKIES

The *Ecology Treks* (grades 3 to 9) and *Earth Treks* (grades 4 to 12) software programs involve children in great games, from survival contests to globe-trotting excursions, and offer databases of information, fun facts, and quizzes that can expand your child's understanding of biology, life science, earth's creatures, world languages and cultures, earth history, and the natural environment. Contact Sanctuary Woods at (800) 943–3664, or visit them on the Web at www.ah-hah.com

LEGGO MY LEGO!

LEGO building systems fascinate kids of all ages worldwide, but parents may not know that LEGO's Dacta division has science, math, and technology sets not available at retail stores that are made to help kids K–12 grasp key concepts with hands-on projects. For a catalog or information about what's available, call (800) 362-4308, or visit their Web site at http://www.lego.com/learn

▸ A Pyramid of Food

Ideas about healthy eating habits have changed a lot in the past few decades. Even kids in middle school often are aware of the new emphasis on fruits, vegetables, and grains. Though kids may still love burgers and fries, many know that other things are probably better for them. This activity makes a game out of balancing meals and shopping strategies. Based generally on the current recommended food pyramid shown in the drawing, this game asks players to put together a balanced meal by trading picture cards. The goal of the game is to gather a hand of cards that adds up to a balance among the food groups. The game somewhat resembles rummy. You and your kid can play it as a duo, but involving other family members will add to the fun.

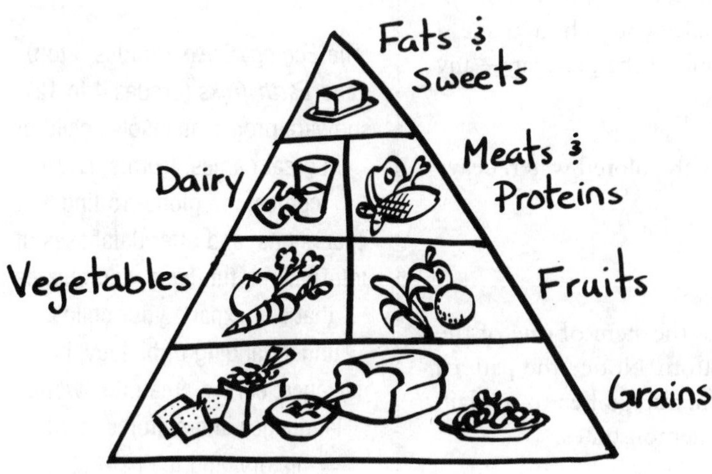

At a Glance

Grade/Subject: 5th/Science—Health
Skills: understanding and applying current nutritional knowledge
Materials: magazines or supermarket circulars' food ads
scissors and paste or glue
30–50 index cards or flashcard-size paper
Time: about 1 hour to get started and make playing cards; then, 1/2 hour two or three times a week

A-OKAY

Parents need to be right on top of their children's education. If I'm not working in the classroom, or if I'm working on a school project but can't be in the classroom, I talk to my children's teachers and ask if everything is going okay. Is there anything I can do to help?

Getting Ready

Before starting, review the food pyramid with your kid. Talk about the different kinds of foods in each group, the foods that you usually eat at home from those groups, and the amounts that are now recommended from each. The combination of cards that you try to get in this game might not represent an ideal meal, but it *will* represent a good balance among the food groups. Here's the goal for a winning hand: two servings (two cards) of foods from the grains group, along with one serving (one card) each of fruits, vegetables, protein (meat, poultry, beans, etc.), and dairy. The foods (and cards) to avoid are fats and sweets.

Step One

First, work with your kid to create your deck of cards. From the magazines or supermarket circulars, cut out illustrations of foods in each group and paste them onto the index cards or other pieces of card stock. Label each with its group: Grains, Dairy, Fruits, Vegetables, Meat/Proteins, Fats/Sweets.

For best results in your games, create about 10 cards for the Grains category, 5 cards each for the other four "good" groups, and two cards for Fats/Sweets—a total of 32 cards.

If you are playing with more players or want a more complex game, increase the number of cards. Always keep a 2 : 1 ratio between the number of Grains cards and those in the other four desirable groups. Since players try to get rid of the Fats/Sweets cards, keep their number low. For example: 16 Grains cards and 8 cards each in other categories, plus the two undesirable Fats/Sweets cards, for a total of 50 cards.

Step Two

Deal six cards to each player. Place the remainder in a pile face down in the center. Cut the deck (or toss a coin) to see who goes first. Each player, in turn, draws a card from the pile. She considers how it adds up with the rest of the cards in her hand. Then she either discards the new card or keeps it and discards a card from her hand.

Step Three

Play continues until one player has brought together a hand whose six cards equal balanced nutrition from the food pyramid. (Players always have six cards.) Players must try to both balance the cards in their hands and avoid keeping the Fats/Sweets cards.

The player who first achieves a balance says "Pyramid!" and lays down her cards. Other players check the balance between food groups in the winning hand: two cards from Grains, one each for the other groups. (No Fats/Sweets!)

WHAT'S MORE

Make a colorful poster for the kitchen wall, showing the food groups and what's in them.

Ask your kid to plan a week of well-balanced meals for the family. Prepare some of them together!

Explore new foods in one of the pyramid groups—for instance, a new kind of pasta, cereal, or bread in the Grains group.

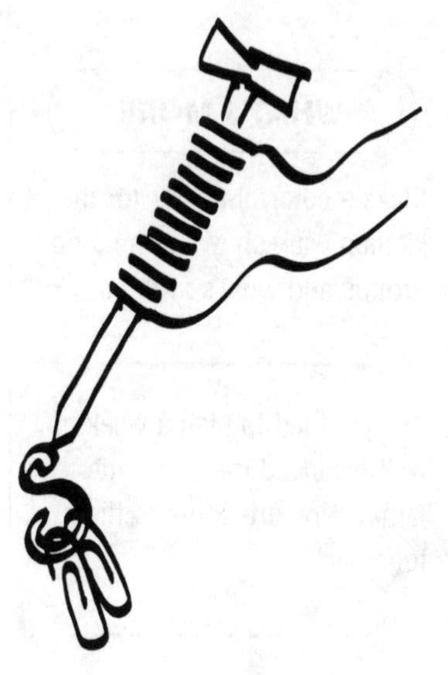

Step Four

Go over each winning hand with your kid. Look at the elements in it and discuss whether they would go together to make a good meal or not.

Use the winning hands from this card game as a springboard to talk with your kid about balanced food combinations that would make good meals. You may have to change just one or two items from the winning card game hands while still keeping a balance.

Give Yourself a Lift

Magnetism is the force that launched a thousand machines—and a thousand discoveries. It was people's curiosity about magnetism and electricity in the late eighteenth and early nineteenth centuries that led directly to our complex, electrically-based lifestyle in the late twentieth century. Your child's curiosity can be a gateway to her own understanding of electricity and magnetism.

It's not necessary to understand the theories behind the operation of the electromagnetic force to play with it. In fact, fiddling with magnets and wires for middle school children is a little like fiddling with simpler materials in the elementary grades. These are the hands-on experiences that flesh out and inform later theoretical studies.

At a Glance

Grade/Subject: 5th/Science—Physical Science
Skills: planning and carrying out investigations
Materials: 9-volt battery (other low voltages will do)
assortment of paper clips, nails, or similar small objects (make sure you have some that are identical)
adhesive tape (masking tape or surgical adhesive tape work well)
plastic model cement
iron nail or spike, 1 1/2"–3" long
3'–4' of single strand cooper wire, such as bell wire from a hardware store

battery connector cap (optional—you can use the battery connector from a discarded electric toy)
other kinds of wire (optional)
stiff cardboard or piece of Styrofoam™ (optional)
science notebook
Time: 3⁄4–1 hour

Getting Ready

Once you have assembled the materials, you and your child can follow the directions below. If your child likes to do things on her own, have her read the directions herself, or read them out loud as the two of you work together. This activity uses lots of wires and bits of metal. For greater stability, have her mount the batteries on stiff cardboard or Styrofoam with model cement or tape.

Step One

Cut off a nine to twelve inch strip of copper wire. Peel off about a quarter inch of the insulation from each end. About two inches in from one end of the wire begin just below the head of the nail and begin wrapping the wire around the nail towards the point. Wrap as tightly and as closely as possible and stop before you get to where the nail starts to taper down to the point.

Step Two

Have your child connect the two ends of wire to the two ends of the battery. (Use a battery cap or adhesive tape.) Try using the wrapped nail to lift some of the nails or paper clips. Find the object that is just a little too heavy to be lifted and set it aside. If you have a number of similar small items, see how many can be picked up at once. You can bend a paper clip to make a convenient hook. Have your child make a note of the quantities lifted in her science notebook.

Disconnect the battery from the nail and take a longer length of wire. Wrap it back and forth on the nail—front to back and back to front, until there is about the same two inch length left over at each end. Reconnect the battery and try lifting an object that was unliftable before. Also try lifting some of the objects that you have several of. Can your child's electromagnet lift more than it could before? Have her record the results in her science notebook.

WHAT'S MORE

Does the kind of wire you use make a difference? Try a variety of wires. Use a sharp knife to slice open an old piece of electrical appliance cord (zip cord) for your child and have her pull out the strands of copper wire. She can experiment to see if the winding of a single strand or multiple strands already wound together makes a difference. Record and compare your results.

Does the kind of nail used make a difference? Try galvanized and non-galvanized nails. Try nails of varying lengths. Record and compare your results.

Does the size or kind of battery used make a difference? Try various sizes and makes of battery (voltage is usually marked right on the side of a battery). Don't however, use anything larger than standard toy and flashlight batteries; stay away from the family car battery! Record and compare your results.

PLUG INTO EARTH SCIENCE

Look into Pacific Interactive's software title *Bill Nye the Science Guy: Stop the Rock!* (ages 9 and up). Your child will perform experiments in order to save our planet from an off-course comet. This title, and other science greats on today's retail shelves, turn learning into an exciting game. Another Earth Science title to check into: 7th Level's funny and learning-filled primer, *The Universe According to Virgil Reality* (ages 8 and up).

CRYSTAL BALL

When your original cup has melted back to water, note the time and discuss how close each of you came to guessing right. Scientists always make predictions of how their experiments might turn out; then they observe the results to see if they were on the mark.

Step Three

Have your child follow her magnetic curiosity by getting some more wire and making even more winds. Keep recording notes in the science notebook on all that you and your child do. How strong can you make a magnet using one battery?

Try making a graph to illustrate your results. Write the length of wire wound on the nail in inches on the vertical axis and the number of objects lifted on the horizontal axis. Plotting the number of winds around the nail might be more precise, but not many people have the patience to do this!

▸ KITCHEN CHEMISTRY

Much of what goes on in everybody's kitchen depends on chemistry and chemical processes. Most people's kitchens are good places to demonstrate some basic physical and chemical changes. So is yours!

For instance, boiling water and ice cubes are all that you need to show some of the physical changes that happen when materials—in this case, water—move from one state of matter to another. You'll find all the equipment you need in your kitchen.

At a Glance

Grade/Subject: 5th/Science—Physical Science
Skills: observing properties of matter, effects of heat and cold
Materials: two transparent (clear plastic or glass) measuring cups
metal cake or roasting pan
small saucepan
stove and refrigerator freezer compartment
oven mitt or potholder
science notebook
Time: 1–2 hours, depending on freezer temperature for the basic experiments (you can spread the activity over time spent doing other things)
brief follow-up observations a few days later

Getting Ready

Since this activity involves doing a few simple things over a period of an hour or two, choose a suitable time—perhaps during TV time, since the steps fit nicely into commercial breaks.

As you and your child work through the simple experiments in this activity, you'll be watching the physical changes that occur as water moves from a liquid to a solid (ice) and to a gas (water vapor). Before starting, talk together about the characteristics of each of those states of matter: solid, liquid, and gas.

Here are the basics of the three states of matter:
- A *solid* has a definite shape and volume, whether it's a fluffy cotton ball or a chunk of granite.
- A *liquid* does not have a rigid shape—it changes shape to fit its container without changing its volume (quantity).
- A *gas* has no definite shape or volume but expands to fill whatever it's in, from a balloon to the global atmosphere.

Step One

Have your kid fill one of the measuring cups exactly to the 1/2-cup mark using ordinary room-temperature tap water, and then put the cup into the freezer compartment. Note the time.

Challenge her to guesstimate how long it will take the water to freeze. Make your own estimate and both of you write down your guesses. Later you can see whose guess was closer.

At the same time, put the metal baking pan into the freezer to get cold. You'll need it later.

Step Two

Check the freezer after about 20 minutes, then keep checking until the water has solidly frozen into ice. (Don't let the freezer door stay open long or it will slow down the process.) How long did it take for the water to freeze? Have your child make a note of the time in her science notebook.

Now look together at the *amount* of water (well, ice now) in the cup. Notice that it's now at slightly more than the 1/2-cup mark, perhaps only as a bulge or crack on the frozen surface. Can your child explain or figure out that water (unlike most substances) expands when it changes from liquid to solid?

Step Three

In this step, turn the solid water (ice) back into a liquid. Take the cup from the freezer and set it on the counter. Have your child note down the time again. Discuss how long each of you thinks

WHAT'S MORE

During everyday activities around the house, look for the different states and properties of common materials. Is this a solid, a liquid, or a gas?

Notice some of the other, real-world effects caused by water expanding as it freezes—"frost heaves" in roadways; rocks, concrete steps, and sidewalks split by water as it freezes in the cracks.

For a dramatic demonstration of the power of freezing water, take an empty plastic bottle—preferably one that has a long neck—and fill it to the top with water. Put its cap on if it is a snap-on cap. If it has a screw top, just put the cap on top without screwing it on. Then put it in the freezer. When the water freezes and expands, it will push the cap up.

the water will take to turn back to a liquid. Will it take more or less time than it took to freeze? Will there be exactly 1/2 cup of water again? Note each of your predictions.

Step Four

While the first cup of water is melting back into a liquid, have your kid fill the other measuring cup exactly to the 1/2-cup mark. This time, though, use very hot tap water.

Again, make your guesstimates of how much time the water will take to freeze. Will it freeze faster or slower than the cold tap water did? Check later to see who was right, and have her note in her science notebook what happens.

Step Five

While the second cup of water is freezing, and when your original cup has melted back to water, go on to make the third stage of matter—gas. Pour the original cup of water into a small saucepan over medium heat on the stove. (Using the same cup of water reinforces the idea of changing states of matter, but if it has not finished melting yet, you can use new tap water to save time.)

As the water boils, note that it's turning into *water vapor.* But water vapor is invisible—how can you be sure it's really there? Some may be visible as steam, but there's another way you can prove it!

Being sure to use an oven mitt or potholder (steam burns!), have your child take the cold metal pan from the freezer and hold it upside down above the boiling water. After a few minutes, look into the pan. It's covered with drops of liquid water—water vapor that condensed back into liquid when it struck the cold metal.

Step Six

Talk about what you've done. You and your child have taken the same cup of water through a complete cycle of the three stages of matter—from liquid to solid, back to liquid, then to gas and back to liquid again.

RED ROVER, RED ROVER

The NASA Mars Pathfinder spacecraft will land on Mars around July 4, 1997, controlled by scientists and engineers 35 million miles away. Mars studies will heat up in your child's science classroom for years to come! See if your child's teacher knows about the "Red Rover, Red Rover" project launched in cooperation with LEGO's Dacta division, the Center for Intelligent Systems at Utah State University, and Visionary Products, Inc. Students from classrooms all over the world will build their own Mars-scapes and LEGO space rovers operated via computer software that mimics NASA's control programs. They can use the Internet to work with other classrooms and control rovers thousands of miles away! For detailed information you can pass on to your child's teacher, call LEGO Dacta at (800) 362-4308, or visit their Web site at http://www.lego.com/learn

- How good were your predictions?
- What might happen if you did the same steps with a different liquid (e.g., juice, soda, vinegar?)
- How does nature perform these same steps?

THE ACID TEST

This experimental activity dramatically demonstrates the results that acid rain can have on plant life—and it's fun to do. Your child will also learn a lot about the conditions and processes that are necessary for living things to grow and survive.

You've probably often read and heard about acid rain in the media. It's a process that takes place in the atmosphere when factories (especially those that burn coal), highways, and other places send the chemicals of sulfur and nitrogen into the air. Those chemicals then combine with chemicals already present in the air, forming sulfuric acid and nitric acid and water. That concentration of chemicals turns precipitation—not just rain, but also snow, fog, and even morning mist—into a highly acidic solution. In some lakes and streams, acid precipitation has been measured as being stronger than vinegar!

What happens when highly acidic water falls on plants and trees? You and your child can find out as you do this experiment at home.

At a Glance

Grade/Subject: 5th/Science—Life Science, Inquiry Skills
Skills: observing chemical processes, understanding ecology
Materials: 2 glass jars of the same size (such as pickle jars)
vinegar (any kind; plain or cider vinegar will be best)
tap water
trowel or small spade
2 clumps of grass and sod
notebook for keeping a record
Time: 1/2 hour to get started; observe daily for one week

WHAT'S MORE

Investigate whether acid rain poses any problems in your own locale. Your child can use the library, make phone calls to local officials, and write or phone for information from organizations like the Environmental Protection Agency (EPA).

What other kinds of environmental issues are a problem in your city or region?

WHAT'S MORE

Acid rain has been particularly devastating in parts of eastern and northern Europe, destroying entire lakes and the fish and other life in them. Help your child to look up articles and illustrations about acid rain in back issues of periodicals in the library. This kind of research develops library skills and has applications in other curriculum areas, such as social studies.

A GOOD RELATIONSHIP

Parents should motivate their children. They should also talk with their teachers and be the one to express what's happening at home. It's crucial to be a good role model. I always tell my children, "When I was a kid . . . ," and they say, "Oh, really?" They appreciate a parent's involvement in their lives and their attention. It's important to show them what the the interesting things in life are.

Getting Ready

It's best to plan this activity according to the season, as you need access to growing grass. Also, check whether your kid has been introduced to the idea of acid rain and its harmful effects on plants and animals. If not, talk with him about it. Ask him what he thinks pouring acid (such as vinegar) on a plant will do to it.

Step One

Have your child prepare the two glass jars by washing them and then labeling one "Water" and the other "Vinegar."

Step Two

Together, dig up two clumps of sod and grass from your yard or from an empty lot. Put one clump in each of the glass jars. Have your kid add 1/2 cup of water to the "Water" jar, and 1/2 cup of vinegar to the "Vinegar" jar. Pour the liquids directly over the grass clump.

Step Three

Each morning for the next week, observe together what's happening to the grass in each jar. As you begin to see changes, have him describe what he sees and record the changes in the notebook. If the jars dry out, add the same amount of plain water to both.

Step Four

Continue the experiment until the grass in the "Vinegar" jar is visibly affected, illustrating the effects of acid rain on plant life. This will probably take no more than 4 to 6 days. Record the results.

Soil Chef

What's underfoot when you walk outside in the park or into your yard or garden? Well . . . just plain dirt, right? Or soil, or earth, or whatever you want to call it. (Most science textbooks call it *soil.*)

But there's no "just plain . . ." about that substance under your feet. Soil is a fascinatingly complex mixture of different kinds of organic and nonorganic material. In everyday language, that's living (or once-living) and nonliving material.

Nature takes years and years to create the ingredients of soil and then mix them together. And those components vary a lot from place to place. Still, with a few simple ingredients—and this easy recipe—you and your kid can cook up a fair approximation of real soil. You can test your soil out by actually sprouting seeds in it.

At a Glance

Grade/Subject: 5th/Science—Earth and Space
Skills: understanding the properties and formation of soil
Materials: small clay flower pot (like those used for seedlings)
spoon
hammer
small pieces of soft rock (like sandstone or limestone)
crumbled particles of clay (a broken pot will do)
peat moss
crumbled dry leaves
plant fertilizer
dried fish food (check out pet supplies)
dead insects (collect 'em)
bean seeds or seeds saved when you eat red or green bell peppers
science notebook
Time: initially, 1/2–3/4 hour after materials are assembled; brief daily observations for 7–10 days

Getting Ready

To avoid frustrating delays in working on this experiment, help your kid to assemble all the "ingredients" beforehand. Some of them, such as the dead insects, are just disgusting enough to intrigue kids of this age. You can probably supply the flower pot and hammer (needed to crush the rocks and clay). If necessary, make a shopping trip to a pet or gardening supplier (check out pet and gardening departments in big supermarkets or discount stores).

Step One

Cooperate in rubbing together the pieces of soft rock to make a fine powder. Do the same with the bits of clay. If necessary, use the hammer to crumble them. Make at least 1/2 cup of rock-clay powder. Cover the hole in the bottom of the flower pot (a small piece of paper towel will do) and pour the powdered rock in.

Step Two

Now add a small amount of the other ingredients—a couple of teaspoons of the crumbled bits of the peat moss and leaves, a

WHAT'S MORE

Though the basic process of soil-building is the same, the actual components vary greatly from place to place. Your own native soil may be heavy on particles of clay or rich with lots of decayed leaves. You and your child can do an informal soil test by taking a handful of soil, rubbing it between your fingers, noting the color, sniffing it, and, if possible, looking at it under a magnifying glass. All the observations should be written up in the science notebook.

Get curious about your local soil. Do an analysis with a soil test kit, which you can get at a garden store or from a county extension agent.

WHAT'S MORE

People around the world use natural building materials like adobe blocks. Read about adobe in an encyclopedia or other resource. Try making your own by mixing soil or clay with chopped up straw, hay, or similar material. Add water to make a mixture that is gooey, but not runny. Put the mixture in an ice-cube tray and bake it in a warm, sunny window or outside until your little adobe bricks are good and dry.

pinch of fish food, and a few dead, dried-up insects. As you do, discuss which ingredients are organic (once-living things) and which are nonorganic.

Add a pinch or few drops of plant food or fertilizer.

Stir the soil mixture until it is blended. Add a few drops of water, if needed, to make it easier to stir.

Step Three

Now help your kid plant a couple of bean seeds or a few pepper seeds in your soil mixture. Plant them near the surface. (We recommend those seeds because they sprout quickly. If you have other kinds of garden seeds with quick sprouting times, they'll work too.)

Add enough water for your soil to be thoroughly damp. Put the flower pot in a warm place.

Step Four

After a few days, have your kid check the flower pot and add water if your soil seems to be getting dry. By the end of the week, or perhaps a little longer, you will both see how successful your recipe for making soil was.

Learning Adventures—6th Grade Science

FLYING HAMSTERS

The Society for Amateur Scientists (at http://www.thesphere.com/SAS) helps people take part in all kinds of science adventures. SAS's Dr. Paul MacCready believes students should learn science by tackling exciting problems that capture their imagination and require original research to solve. Example: He worked with inner-city Los Angeles kids to design, build, and fly the world's first *hamster-powered aircraft*!

BUILD A BETTER MAGNET

Simple electromagnets have several components: a battery, a central core, and a coil of wire wrapped around the core. Each of these parts can be altered in a number of ways and maybe the alterations will increase the strength of your electromagnet. Investigating the changes your child can make in the strength of the electromagnetic force by manipulating these elements is a challenging and fascinating activity.

At a Glance

Grade/Subject: 6th/Science—Physical Science
Skills: multiple lines of investigation
Materials: electromagnet (see instructions on how to make one in the 5th grade science activity "Give Yourself a Lift")
2 9-volt batteries (or other low voltage hobby batteries)
variety of short wires, strips of thin metal, and nails
fat soda straw—wide enough to accommodate a nail inside it
battery connectors (these are small alligator clips from a hobby store or catalog) or tape (masking or surgical)
plastic model cement
materials for a second electromagnet (optional; they are listed in "Give Yourself a Lift," along with assembly directions)
science notebook

Time: 1–1 1⁄2 hours

WHAT'S MORE

Magnetism is one of many fascinating science subjects you can read about in library books or experience firsthand at a science museum. Go ahead and explore!

Getting Ready

Spread out your materials on a table. If your child doesn't already have an electromagnet, have him assemble one before you begin.

Step One

The first question you can explore is, "Does the amount of wire coiled around the core nail in your electromagnet make a difference in the power of the electromagnet?" Write this question in the notebook and list the materials your child will use to find the answer.

Try your present electromagnet on a paper clip. Then see how many clips it can lift all at once. Have your child cut a piece of wire that is at least twice as long as the one now coiled on the core. Replace the old coil with your new longer one. It should be coiled as tightly as possible and it's okay to have it wrap back over itself. Try it out on the same number of paper clips. Can the larger coil pick up more?

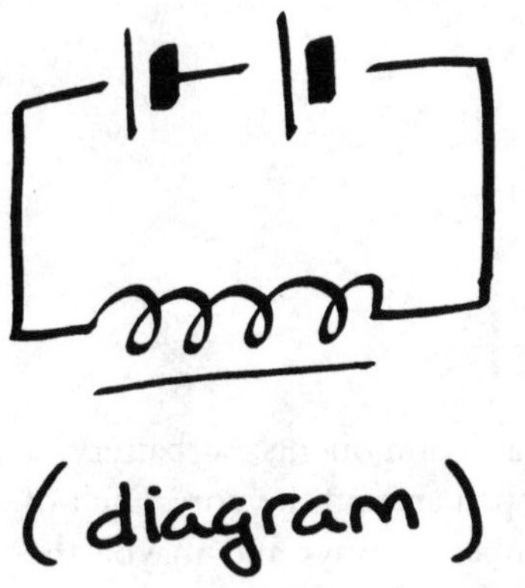

Step Two

Another question to investigate is whether adding more batteries increases power. There are two principle ways to add elements to a simple electrical circuit. One of these is by connecting them in a *series*. Flashlight batteries are linked this way. The positive end of one battery is connected to the negative end of another and the working element (the bulb) is placed in the circuit.

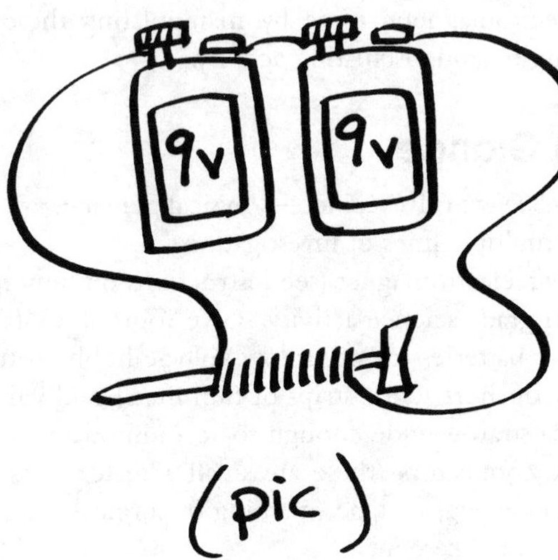

The second way of wiring elements in a simple circuit is called *parallel*. In this kind of a circuit the batteries are connected positive to positive and negative to negative, and the working element is inserted (in our case the electromagnet) in the circuit. Which of the two methods creates a stronger magnetic force?

Use your notebook to write up your plan for testing out each of these methods. Then conduct your tests and write up the results, including any sketches or diagrams you feel will be helpful in making your experimental record clear.

Step Three

Another element that might affect the strength of your electromagnet is the characteristic of the core that the wire is wrapped around. Your child can prepare a page in his notebook for planning and reporting this experiment.

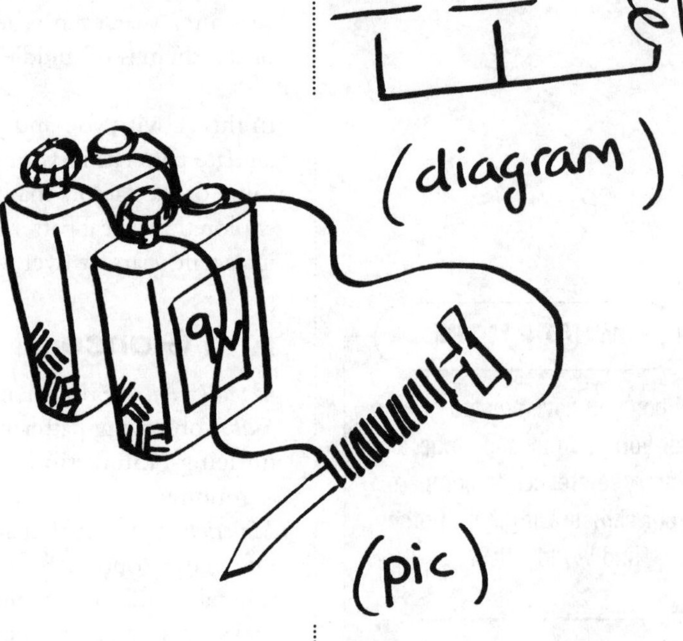

Since wrapping and unwrapping wire around different rods of metal can be extremely tedious, your child can speed up the process of experimenting with this variable by making a coil around a tube that different nails and lengths of metal can be inserted into. (You wondered how that straw would come in handy?) Unwrap your most successful electromagnet and wrap its wire (with just as many wraps) around a straw wide enough for the nail to slide into. You can secure it by spreading some model cement over the wires. This gives you a hollow shaft into which you can slide different cores.

Try a variety of inserts and record what happens with each new core in your notebook. Here are some possible cores to try:

- Toothpick
- Piece of copper wire
- Different sized nails
- Picture hanging wire
- Anything else you and your child can think of

What works the best? What are the characteristics of the material that worked best? Make a chart showing the different materials and their strengths and weaknesses.

WHAT'S MORE

Have your child build a second separate electromagnet identical to the one that you already have. What happens when you bring them together side by side or front to back? Can they work together to pick something up? What happens when they oppose one another?

Invent your own combinations of electromagnets and batteries. Use the circuit diagram symbols to make plans and then construct them.

CHECKING THE CLIMATE

A country as large as the United States falls into many different *climate regions*—places where the general patterns are the same year after year even when day-to-day weather is changing. One of the themes of middle grade science is climate and its causes.

In this activity, you and your child can track and chart long-term climate patterns in your locale. At the same time, you can look at some of the factors that influence your climate. And you can also explore historical patterns to see whether the climate has changed in recent years or over a longer period.

WHAT'S MORE

When you have created graphs for your own location, check library references to compare your climate with that of other U.S. and world cities.

Determining the average temperature and precipitation for the month provides good practice in figuring averages.

Write a poem or draw a poster about your local climate.

If you live near an ocean, check the tides reported in daily weather reports and notice how they correlate with the phases and position of the moon.

At a Glance

Grade/Subject: 6th/Science—Inquiry Skills, Earth and Space
Skills: observing patterns and changes in climate and their causes; noticing interactions between geology, meteorology, and astronomy
Materials: outdoor thermometer
rain gauge (optional)
tide tables (if you live near the ocean)
newspaper weather reports
notebook and pencil
graph paper
Time: 10–15 minutes in the morning and evening, twice a week, for several months (To get a full picture of your local climate, keep this activity up for a full year.)

Getting Ready

Before you start, have your child look in her science or geography book to discover in what general climate region you live—for instance, humid continental, marine, Mediterranean, or desert. Also before starting, check a map to see your latitude—distance from the Equator in degrees North or South. Check your altitude too. Those two factors play a big role in climate.

Unlike weather watching, studying climate is a long-term activity. To get a picture of your climate, you and your child should observe the weather over an extended period. Set up a corner where you can keep your records over the course of several months. If possible, make it near a window where you can read the outdoor temperature.

Step One

Make your own weather observations—temperature and amount of precipitation—morning and evening, at least twice a week. Compare your findings with those given in local weather reports in the newspaper. As their observations are made more frequently (and with high-tech equipment), your results may differ somewhat. Write down both figures.

Along with factual data on temperature and precipitation, have your child write a short description of the weather on each day you observe. If there's been a long-term trend—say, a week of gloomy days or a spell of hot, muggy weather—include that too. Climate is the big picture, not the details.

Step Two

At the end of the month, figure an average for temperature and for amount of precipitation. Compare it with reports in the newspaper, and record their average figures along with yours.

With your kid, come up with your own general description of the weather patterns for the past month. Was the weather consistent? Very changeable? A mix of different patterns? All those factors are part of climate.

Step Three

Along with your day-to-day observations, the two of you can investigate other influences on the local climate. These vary from place to place, of course. Altitude and latitude are factors that don't change. Others, such as prevailing winds, are affected by the local landscape and geology.

Here are some factors to consider:

- Are you near an ocean or large lake?
- Are you at the foot of a mountain range or at the edge of the desert?
- If you're on the water, are you on the western or eastern shore?

IT'S IDEAL

Educational supply stores are great resources for home learning books, kits, materials, and ideas. One company you'll probably find represented is the Ideal School Supply Company (call 1-800-323-5131 for a catalog). Check out their telescopes, microscopes, weather board, science measuring sets, and "Science Pockets" (complete science units in a small book).

CONFIDENCE AND CONVICTION

Score@Kaplan's major impact on kids is the difference in self-confidence that you can very visibly observe. Kids come into the program thinking they're horrible in something, they can't do well in it in school—and it's great to watch them develop confidence and conviction in a subject. They see that they can do the schoolwork and they might even be really good at it. Just having that self-confidence can carry into all areas of a child's life. Any time parents can make a change like that in a child, it's the most productive thing they can do!

TAKE A SPIN

Not only does Earth turn beneath the stars on a daily basis, we move in two other ways as well. Our planet is tilted, and as we circle the sun, the tilt changes our position so that the stars appear to take a seasonal as well as daily trip. There is also a very slow but steady wobble in the tilt of our planet. This wobble brings us all the way around in a small circle in relation to the sky once every 25,000 years (+ or – a few).

Step Four

As you accumulate data, have your kid construct two graphs that show monthly averages for temperature (bar graph) and precipitation (line graph) for the whole year or at least for the months that you have made observations. The sample graph on the preceding page, which shows the patterns from Tokyo, combines those two kinds of data on one graph. Notice how this graph gives an instant picture of a place's climate, showing which months are warm and wet or cold and dry.

Step Five

For a still bigger picture of climate in your locality, check the local library, newspaper, or historical society to find out what climate patterns were like 20 or 50 or 100 years ago. Interest your child in reading about important events in the past, such as hurricanes, floods, or blizzards. Discuss what changes you see—or don't see—in the local climate.

Follow Your Star

Whether or not you pay attention, the stars are up there every night just twinkling away. If, however, you watch the stars from dusk to dawn or look at them carefully each evening over a period of time, they appear to wheel through the sky.

Actually, we're the ones doing the moving. We spin beneath the stars as our planet makes its daily rotation around its axis and its annual trip around the sun. (Our wheeling continues during the daylight hours although the brightness of our star, the sun, makes seeing beyond its light to the stars impossible.) Observing the stars tells us a great deal. You and your child can use them to chart part of our cosmic trip.

At a Glance

Grade/Subject: 6th/Science—Earth and Space, Inquiry Skills
Skills: observation, record keeping
Materials: star chart (from newspapers, periodicals, or reference books that show the sky for the time of year when you will be doing this activity and/or astronomy book or chart that illustrates the principle constellations and names the brighter stars)
sheet or two of black construction paper and "liquid paper," white grease pencil, eye-liner, or erasable magic marker

science notebook or booklet for record keeping
compass (optional)
Time: 1⁄4 hour observations, once a night or every other night for two weeks (or longer, if you wish)

Getting Ready

Find a magazine or newspaper that publishes a star chart and clip it out. (You can also find star charts for your local area in library books and some general science magazines.) Have a star guide book, chart, or similar reference work available that names the constellations and some of the stars (see our Resources section).

Step One

This step is a sort of warm up. Try various trial sky sightings from windows in your home to select one that has a good view of a section of the night sky. Observation is easier with the lights in the room off; give your eyes a few minutes to adjust to the dark. On your first evening's observation, spend 1⁄4 hour looking at the sky and helping one another pick out stars, faint or bright. Look over the star chart and talk about the stars and constellations indicated on it. See if you can find any of the chart's constellations in your view of the sky.

Step Two

On the second observation, decide on a comfortable place to watch from and pick out several bright stars. Use your chart or book to identify the stars you are choosing.

Even where brightly lit cities or having only a narrow view of the sky limits how much you can see, some stars will be visible (under these conditions, however, it can take a little longer to locate and identify celestial objects). Most guides will give you some standard tricks for locating things in the sky. Once you learn them, it's quite easy. Decide on one star that you will keep track of. Find its name on a star chart and write it down. Note its direction in the night sky (to the north, south, southeast, etc.) and roughly how high in the sky it is.

Step Three

Now you are ready to pin information down at the observation site. This task requires both of you. Have your child mark where he is sitting or standing with a small X of tape. Locate the chosen star and, based on your child's directions from the X-marked spot,

GETTING YOUR BEARINGS

If you have a compass handy, use it to discover the direction your window is facing. If you don't, use the positions of sunrise (roughly east) and sunset (roughly west) to help you. When you face the setting sun, north is to your right, and south to your left.

WHAT'S MORE

Planets move along a particular curved stretch of the night sky which may or may not be visible from your observation station. If it is, and there is a planet visible in the night sky, track its movements as well as that of your star.

You and your child can track more than one star, one for each of you. Do they appear to move at the same rate and in the same direction?

What about Web stars? Surf for online stargazing resources.

BY HAND

Most star guides will give you rough-and-ready ways to determine a star's or planet's position in the sky. They usually use the width of your fist held at arm's length as a way to measure relative distances. You can use this fist-at-arms-length guide inside as well, although since the movements you are recording will be smaller, you may want to use finger widths as your standard unit of measurement instead of fists.

WHAT'S MORE

If there is a science center or museum near you, find out if they have a planetarium and arrange a visit. Check our Resource section for the Association of Science and Technology Centers listing—they'll help you locate the closest science center and planetarium.

make a small mark on the window with a grease pencil, very small piece of tape, or easy-to-remove marker to indicate the location relative to your child's observation post. Have him note the exact time and write it down. Find two static landmarks, like a rooftop, satellite dish, distinct treetop, or chimney and make a mark for each on the window.

From his X-marked spot, have your child draw a large diagram of the window showing the star's position and the landmarks. Mark the location for the first observation and note the time next to it.

Step Four

Set up a regular schedule of observations. The two of you could do this every night or every other night for two weeks or longer, if you wish. Keep a careful record of the star's position each night at exactly the same time. Don't worry if weather intervenes; just note the missing nights somewhere on your diagram.

Help your child transfer the information about your star and use it to make a chart of your star's progress through the night sky. Use a large piece of black construction paper and dots of white to trace out the star's movement (you could also use little star stickers from a stationary store). He can use a white grease pencil, crayons, or pieces of colored paper to indicate the horizon and the landmarks you used. While the two of you are doing this, you can ask your child for ideas about:

- What he thinks is making the star appear to move
- Where he predicts it will move next
- Where it will be at this time in another two weeks
- Whether it will disappear below the horizon, and, if so, when
- Or whether it is one of the stars that is visible all year long

Step Five

The brightest stars have been observed for many hundreds of years and have colorful stories and beautiful and intriguing names (often Arabic—you and your child could find out why). During the period when you carry on the observations, your child can research his star and write down its story to accompany the observation diagram and star chart. He can also note its magnitude, color, what scientists know about it, and its part (if any) in a constellation.

▶ Grow Your Own Rock

Crystals are everywhere. Salt, sugar, diamonds, the silica sands of lake beaches, and the flakes of snow drifting down from the winter sky are all examples of crystals. They are elements and compounds that have had the opportunity to grow into their crystal forms.

At a Glance

Grade/Subject: 6th/Science—Physical Science, Inquiry Skills
Skills: investigation and observation
Materials: quart of water, more or less, depending on the size of your jar (tap water will do, but distilled water is better)
pencil, tongue depressor, or craft stick
1/2 quart or larger jar, or other glass or clear container with lid
cotton twine (thin), small stainless steel washer or nut
about 2 cups of sugar
large mixing bowl
science notebook
Time: 1 hour to set up; about a week to grow sugar crystals

Getting Ready

Assemble your materials in the kitchen. Have your child fill the jar with water and then pour it into the pot; set it on the stove to boil. She should then carefully fill the jar with very hot tap water and set it aside. Since you're going to pour almost boiling water into it soon, this pre-warming will prevent the sudden heat from cracking it.

Cut a length of string slightly longer than the jar is tall and tie the washer or nut to one end. Lay the pencil (or whatever you chose) across the mouth of the jar and drop the washer in. Pull it back up so that it hangs just above the bottom of the jar and then tie it to the pencil to keep that length.

WHAT'S MORE

Use the technique described in this activity to see if you can grow large crystals from table salt or Epsom salts. Many of the inorganic compounds known as salts can be used to grow beautiful crystals of different shapes and colors. Alum and Rochelle Salt are two examples. If your child is interested in doing more, ask your librarian to help you find books that will explain this subject in greater depth and help you with crystal growing experiments of greater complexity.

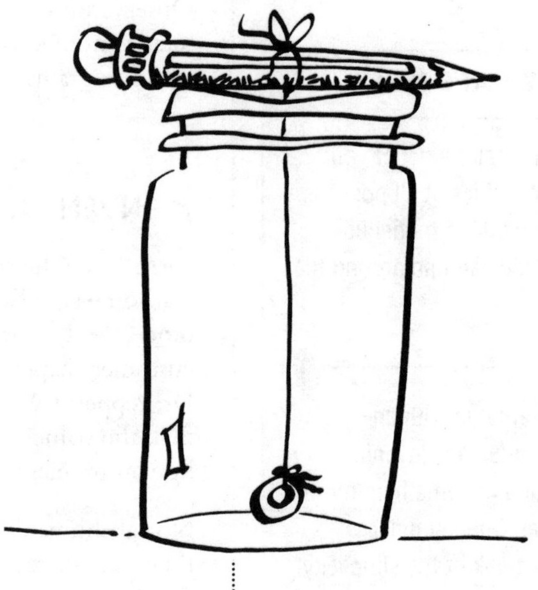

WHAT'S MORE

Use a strong magnifying glass or microscope to examine salt, Epsom salts, and sandbox or beach sand. If you have a potted plant, scoop out a tablespoon of dirt and mix it with water. Pour off the muddy water and wash the gritty remains again. Then observe them under magnification. Can you see any crystals?

Step One

Put the sugar in the bowl. When the water comes to a boil, slowly pour it over the sugar while your child stirs the water and sugar together. If all the sugar quickly dissolves, add some more sugar. You need to make a supersaturated solution—one that has absorbed so much of the dissolved ingredient at this temperature that it won't take any more. When no more sugar dissolves, slowly pour your syrupy mixture into the jar with the string.

Step Two

Put the jar in a safe place where it can remain very stable, without being bumped into or rattled around. Observe it at least twice a day for several days to watch the crystals begin to form. In her notebook, have your child note what she sees each time by entering the date and describing the progress of the crystal growth.

- Note the shapes that you see.
- As the crystal or crystals grow, do they change shape?
- What color is your crystal?

Step Three

When you and your child grow crystal from sugar, you make an old-fashioned treat called Rock Candy. Taste your crystal. Observations based on taste should also be recorded in the science notebook. Compare the taste of your crystal with the taste of a few grains of sugar. Any difference?

WHAT'S MORE

Make a small model of your invention. If it's at all possible, make a working model using things you can find around the house.

If you came up with an elaborate fantasy invention, try your hand at something more practical. Often simpler is better—think of the simplicity of the rubber kitchen jar gripper or the mail slot!

Invent a Dream Machine

Farm boy Chester Greenwood had cold ears. Engineer Chester Carlson wanted a quicker and cheaper way to make copies in a law office. And pharmacist Chester Alderton wanted to make his customers happy. The results? Earmuffs, the Xerox™ machine, and Dr. Pepper™. What did these three people have in common (other than the name *Chester*)? Each needed an invention to solve a very human problem, and each found ways to satisfy that need.

Not all human inventions can be traced to a single person, but they all share a common trait. Inventions are the use or development of technology to solve a human problem. In this activity, you and your child are asked to take a not-so-serious look for a solution to a problem that you identify together.

At a Glance

Grade/Subject: 6th/Science—Technology
Skills: explore the process of developing technological solutions to a problem
Materials: pencil or pen and note paper
colored pencils or markers and drawing paper
books on inventions or an encyclopedia (optional)
watch
Time: 1–2 hours

Getting Ready

Inventions can spring from big *what if* dreams (how many—from Leonardo to the Wright brothers—have turned dreams of flying into inventions), or from a simple human desire to make things a little better (Chester Greenwood just wanted warm ears).

Step One

Discuss with your child some of the things that your family does around the house (cooking, cleaning, dressing, eating, studying, playing, for example). Talk about improvements or assistance that any of you might welcome for any of those activities. Pick one activity that you imagine could benefit from an invention.

Step Two

Once you've identified a task or aspect of living that could be improved by a little invention, give yourselves permission to let loose in a wild brainstorming session. Take turns thinking up the wildest possible solutions to your problem. Each of you should take ten minutes to think out loud while the other writes down all the ideas. The only rule to follow is that *nothing* is too weird or too improbable, *everything* is possible, and *all* thoughts are worthwhile. (You could invite other family members to offer ideas too.)

Step Three

In the course of your brainstorming, you and your child might come up with a very practical idea, or your ideas may just be fantastical ones.

You will probably come up with something a little on the wilder side, and that's fine. Let's move it a step further along. Take one idea for one problem-solving device and talk it through together.

A WILD WAY TO RISE

One parent who is a Registered Nurse worked on a rotating shift that required getting up at 5:30 twice a week. It wasn't much fun, but everyone got a lift from the highly original device her family drew up. They planned a large and complicated wake-up machine that worked like this: A shower is set up at the foot of the nurse's bed. When her alarm clock rings and she pushes down on it to shut it off; that squeezes a bellows under the clock. This blows a puff of air that extinguishes a candle that had been supporting a small hot air balloon. The balloon descended and hit a pin. The explosion shocks the family cat which leaps up knocking books off a shelf that trips a lever that releases a giant spring under the nurse's bed activating the shower faucets with strings and pulleys. The spring tips the bed up sliding the nurse into a warm shower. This ridiculous device didn't really work (the cat was unreliable), but the laugh made things lighter on dark mornings.

WHAT'S MORE

Research the history of some inventions that have made a difference in your life, like adhesive bandages, the ice cream cone, or the zipper. What got people started thinking about these inventions? How did they go about realizing their goals?

Have your child pick a favorite piece of technology and do research on its development. Who invented it? What kind of a person was he or she? Is it just as successful today as it was when it was invented? You could suggest looking into the origination of the paper bag, the stop light, or chewing gum.

EVERYDAY FUN

We do a lot of cooking together with our kids. We measure food coloring and other ingredients together. Parents need to make education practical for kids, and if learning is part of the everyday, it can be fun because kids like participating in real life.

- What kinds of materials will it need?
- What energy sources will it use?
- How big will it be?
- Could you put it together in your house?

Step Four

After the two of you have talked through your invention idea, have your child write it up. The write-up should describe what it is and how it works, step by step. Keep discussing ideas for the invention and make as many changes as you want as you go along.

As a part of the write-up, your child should make a drawing of the invention. Do the drawing in two stages:

- First, make sketches of the overall device and its different components on different pieces of paper. Lay them out, look them over, and make any changes you want.

- Then make a larger complete drawing. It should show all the steps, have close-ups of complicated components, and have a written description of how it works in one corner or at the bottom.

Step Five

Proudly hang your drawing on the wall, along with a neat copy of the write-up. Contact your patent lawyer and wait for fame and fortune!

(If you happen to come up with something truly practical, get a book on how to develop and sell inventions from the library, get to work, and let us know how it worked out!)

Light Magic

When your child was younger, she discovered that mixing red and yellow finger-paint made orange, but mixing yellow and blue paints would make green. Ask your child whether the same thing will happen if you mix red and yellow lights, like lights on a stage. The answer is *no*, and this activity shows why.

Because white light is actually a mixture of all the colors, experiments with mixing lights can be magical and mystifying. The three primary colors of white light (unlike those of paint) are red, green, and blue. Transparent filters, like the cellophane in this activity, let one or more colors of light pass through but absorb the others.

At a Glance

Grade/Subject: 6th/Science—Physical Science, Inquiry Skills
Skills: analyzing properties of light and color, carrying out investigations
Materials: 3 flashlights
rubber bands
green, blue, and red cellophane or gels
white paper (or a white-walled room)
science notebook
Time: about 45 minutes to 1 hour (you may want to repeat the activity several more times with different combinations of colors).

Getting Ready

Fold several thicknesses of blue cellophane into a square and use a rubber band to fasten it over the end of one flashlight. Have your child do the same to two other flashlights using red and green cellophane squares.

Step One

Darken the room. Shine the blue flashlight on a white paper or a white wall. Have your child shine the green flashlight so its light overlaps the blue. Discuss what color you see where they overlap (cyan blue) and why.

Step Two

Keeping the blue and green flashlights directed toward the white paper or wall, ask your child to turn on the red flashlight to overlap the other two circles. Can she explain what happens where all three lights overlap (white light)? Notice that the new colors—yellow, cyan blue, magenta—are lighter than the original lights. That's because as you add more colors together, you get closer to white light, which contains all the colors.

Step Three

Take turns moving each flashlight closer to and farther from the paper. Discuss how the colors change and why.

WHAT'S MORE

Sunglasses are another kind of light filter that absorbs colored light passing through it. Have your child look at an object through different shades of sunglasses to discover how the color of the glasses changes the color of objects seen through the lenses.

Using transparent colored paper, cut out and paste shapes to make stained glass panels to tape over panes of a window.

Practice with the colored-light flashlights to see how stage designers can use lighting to change mood and atmosphere. How do different light combinations change the appearance of people and objects on the stage?

HOW AM I DOING?

We constantly brainstorm at home about how important the future is for our children, and it's all tied in with how well they're doing. We constantly mention their progress, and they like to hear how much they're accomplishing.

Step Four

Ask your child to write down or make a drawing in her science notebook of what she observed about mixing colors of light in this activity.

Moon Watching

Our nearest neighbor in space, the moon, is one of the easiest heavenly bodies to observe from Earth. People have, in fact, been moon watching for centuries. Since it is the only other place in the solar system to which humans have actually traveled, the moon has a special fascination.

The moon also undergoes regular, easy-to-see changes. Observing and interpreting those changes is the focus of this activity.

At a Glance

Grade/Subject: 6th/Science—Earth and Space, Inquiry Skills
Skills: observing and understanding relationships between Earth, the moon, and the sun
Materials: calendar showing moon phases (many show new moon, first quarter, full moon, last quarter, either in words or with icons)
notebook, pen, and soft pencil for sketching
binoculars or telescope (optional)
Time: 10 minutes a night, about twice a week (every 3–4 days) for a full moon cycle (30 days)

Getting Ready

You may want to time your observation period to match with a phase of the moon's own cycle. Check a calendar to see when the moon will be new, a logical starting place. Or you can start at the beginning of any other phase. Pick a convenient time for you and your kid.

As there are about six to seven days in each phase (new, first quarter, full, last quarter), plan to observe the moon at least twice in each phase, perhaps once at the beginning of the phase and once at 3 to 4 days later.

If the sky is overcast, try again the next night. Binoculars or a telescope (although they aren't necessary for this activity) will add greatly to the detail of what you can see on the moon's surface.

WHAT'S MORE

A visit to a planetarium will excite a lot of interest in the moon, stars, and night sky. Try to catch a special moon-watching show!

Many colleges and universities have large telescopes for their astronomy courses and research. Call the schools near you to see if they offer evening viewing times for the general public—many do!

Step One

To get a true picture of the moon's changes and movements, make your observations at the same time each night. Each time, have your child record in the notebook what you both observe. Try to answer these questions:

- What is the moon's position in the sky?
- What does it look like? How big does it appear?
- What shape is it? How is its shape different from how it was three or four days ago?
- What color is it?
- How is the last quarter different from the first quarter?

Step Two

As you observe the different phases and positions of the moon in the sky, discuss with your kid just what you're seeing and what it means about the relative positions of Earth, the sun, and the moon. Making sketches of the three bodies will be helpful.

For example, if you're watching the moon just at sunset, what does its illuminated part tell you about the position of the sun? Can you see a faint outline of the rest of the sphere, even when the moon is just a quarter full?

Step Three

When the moon is full or nearly full, have your kid sketch the patterns of light and dark areas that you see. For a better picture, start your sketches just before the moon is full. Then check the details, or revise your drawing, during the next two observations.

Step Four

Once you and your kid have observed a full cycle of the moon, compare your sketches with an actual map of major features on the moon. (You can find such a map in most library books on the night sky, encyclopedias, or in a Physical Geology textbook.)

With the map, try to find the names of the dark lava plains, called *maria* or "seas" (from Latin; the singular is *mare*) and some of the larger craters. Label them on your own drawings.

WHAT'S MORE

Words show how important the moon has been to humans over the centuries. Have your child use the dictionary to look up the derivations of words like these: *Monday, semester, lunatic.*

Any eclipse—lunar or solar—is an exciting demonstration of the relative positions of the sun, the moon, and Earth. Try to find out when the next partial or total eclipse is due and watch it together.

The dark patterns that make up "the Man in the Moon" are actually the dark lunar "seas." Visit the library or go online to get more information about the moon.

SCIENCE ON A VACATION

Imagination and good planning can be more valuable than lots of money in making a nature-oriented vacation trip something your family will all remember and learn from. If you want to be outdoors, look into nearby state or national parks with campgrounds, and check into park ranger or park board programs that emphasize science and nature. Depending on your locality, opportunities will range from short walking tours along a local river to extensive hands-on programs for both kids and adults. On your own, you don't have to wait for a long vacation—spend a Sunday afternoon picnicking in a local forest preserve. Take short trips to nearby zoos or natural wonders such as caves, waterfalls, fossil beds, and rock formations.

For full-fledged vacations, investigate working farms and ranches that welcome guests in exchange for help or small fees. Investigate the moderately priced family-oriented vacations run by groups such as the National Wildlife Federation. For families where money isn't an issue, there are many international "ecotours" and "adventure/exploration" treks; find out more through a travel agent.

Step Five

Encourage your kid's continuing interest in sky watching and moon watching. Look to see the moon faintly in the daytime, too. Have her add some observations of the daytime moon to her notes.

▶ Sidewalk Safari

It's not just plants or animals or endangered species that live in an ecosystem—a community of organisms that interact with each other and the environment. Since you and your family are living things too, you and your kid live in an ecosystem of your own.

Drawing on what your child has learned in science, you can set off together on an expedition to explore your ecosystem. Here's how to organize your sidewalk safari.

At a Glance

Grade/Subject: 6th/Science—Life Science
Skills: observing the details of an ecosystem and the interactions of organisms within it
Materials: notebook and pencils
sketch pad or camera
pocket guides to plants, trees, animals (from the library)
map of your town (optional)
pocket loupe or magnifying glass (optional)
walking shoes!
Time: 1–2 hours once a week for about a month
(To have daylight, plan winter safaris for a weekend day; in other seasons, you may be able to find 1–2 hours of exploration time after work and school are over for the day.)

Getting Ready

To get ready for a safari in your neighborhood, you need only equipment to help you and your kid identify the other living things that make up your local ecosystem. Your basic equipment is your own eyes and ears (and feet).

Small pocket field guides to plants, trees, and animals are fun to own, but you can also borrow them from your library. A pocket loupe or magnifying glass lets you get a close-up view of small flowers or insects.

Step One

Decide together on the area of your neighborhood to explore—that is, set up the boundaries of your ecosystem. Limit it to an area small enough to explore on foot, but large enough to provide good variety for several weeks of exploration. Probably the minimum area is at least six blocks square. If you live in a city or built-up area, try to include some open spaces such as parks, gardens, or empty lots.

Mark the area on a local map or draw your own map. Post it on a wall where you and your child can keep track of your travels.

Step Two

Plan the stages of your safari. For example, if you plan to do this activity over a period of about a month, with weekly expeditions, plan four different walking tours that will take you to all parts of your ecosystem.

Step Three

As you start off together on your first safari, develop a pattern for observing the natural parts of your neighborhood ecosystem. Put your kid in charge of the notebook, allowing several pages each for categories such as Trees, Flowering Plants, Green Plants, Fungi, Birds and Animals, and Landforms (such as hills, ponds, and streams).

Make your observations together, pointing things out to one another and deciding what you are seeing and what they're called. (This is where the pocket field guides come in handy.) Note where and when you see each plant or animal. For example, "Gray squirrel in pine tree, in front of Methodist Church/Saturday, Oct. 23, 2 p.m." Add any notes or details you wish to describe what you see.

Step Four

If you don't know what something is, write down as detailed a description as possible. If you've brought a camera or sketch pad, make a visual record of what the mystery organism looks like. Your child can practice some scientific research skills by looking it up later.

WHAT'S MORE

When you've finished exploring and recording the elements of your ecosystem, suggest to your child that he draw an illustrated map entitled *Our Ecosystem.* He should include on it the location of some of your ecosystem's outstanding or memorable components.

Use your sketches and photographs to put together a poster or scrapbook illustrating what your neighborhood ecosystem is like.

Look in your local newspaper for any articles or news items regarding things that might affect your ecosystem.

Are there elements of your local ecosystem that are endangered? For instance, find out whether there are any local groups working to clean up the riverbank or protect a park area.

Step Five

When you get home from each safari through your neighborhood, look back over the notebook record of what you saw. Discuss how the birds, insects, animals, and even reptiles and amphibians you saw relate to the ecosystem you share:

- Where do they live?
- What do they eat?
- How do they accommodate to things like people, buildings, and cars?

Discuss how the plants and the creatures within the ecosystem interact—with each other and with humans. With your kid, become aware of how the natural surroundings affect you.

- Does a tree shade your house? drop leaves on the yard or sidewalk?
- Are birds eating pesky insects that might otherwise bother you?
- How about what insects themselves are doing for or against you?
- Are the birds themselves sometimes a nuisance?

Discuss, in turn, how human actions (including those of your family) affect the plants and creatures in this ecosystem.

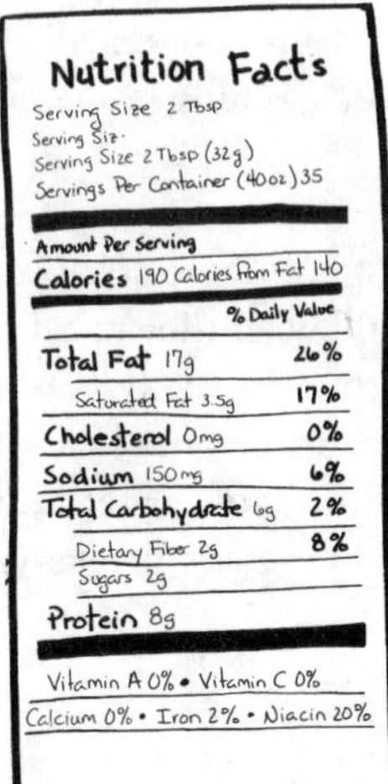

▶ Supermarket Sleuth

Today's food packages and canned goods now tell us more than ever about what's really inside the package, what's been added, and what's been left out. But all this information does no good unless people read and understand the new labels.

How about forming an investigative partnership with your kid? Together, you can look into this wealth of nutritional information whenever you shop. Allow a little extra shopping time for this cooperative sleuthing so that you can read, compare, and discuss what's in products you consider buying. It's worth it—not just for your health, but maybe for your pocketbook.

At a Glance

Grade/Subject: 6th/Science—Health
Skills: reading food labels thoroughly, understanding nutrition
Materials: shopping list
science notebook
calculator
Time: Your regular shopping time, plus 10 to 20 minutes for reading, calculations, and discussions (This can be a continuing activity whenever you take the time during a regular shopping trip.)

Getting Ready

With your kid, look over the labels on some food boxes and cans already on your kitchen shelves. Decide on a few key ingredients that you will investigate in the supermarket: the amounts of fat, sodium, Vitamin C, calories, or calcium in different products.

Discuss whether you will look for relatively small percentages of things people want to avoid (for most people, fat and sodium; for some, calories) or fairly large percentages of things that are good for you (such as Vitamin C or calcium).

Step One

Make a shopping list and choose three or four items on it to do research for their nutritional content.

Help your child prepare a page or two for each item in his science notebook. You'll need several columns for comparative purposes on each page. One column is the size of serving from each can or box; the others are for the nutrients you've decided to look for.

Step Two

Start with one item on your shopping list, and look at the choices available on the supermarket shelf. For example, you might start by working with your child to compare different brands of canned and packaged chicken soup.

As one of you reads aloud the information on each label, the other should list its information on a notebook page.

Discuss the ingredients that are listed by quantity (grams or milligrams) and the calories. Look over the comparative quantities of fat and sodium.

NET MORE INFO

Many of the Food and Drug Administration's rules regarding food labeling went into effect in 1994 for most foods. On the Internet, visit the FDA's site at http://www.fda.gov/. Look up "food labeling" and check out the great health information under "Using the Food Label"—how to prevent heart disease, lose weight, and more!

WHAT'S MORE

Reading food labels carefully can benefit the whole family. If there are several kids in your family, you might put each of them in charge of researching new foods in different categories: breakfast cereals, snacks, juice drinks, etc. They should research the labels and bring their findings to a family roundtable about trying new brands.

WHAT'S MORE

Provide mental math practice. For example, the label may say that one serving—about a cup—of soup contains 70 calories and that the can holds about 2 1/2 servings. How many calories would you get if you ate the whole can of soup? Of the 70 calories in a serving, 20 calories are from fat. What percentage is that?

Supermarket sleuthing can extend to value as well as nutrition. Bring along a small calculator so that your kid can figure out the comparative prices per ounce or per pound or per piece for competing products.

Talk about how you might rank the different soups according to fat content, noting any differences in the size of servings. Discuss why differences in the size of serving will throw off your calculations. How could you adjust the numbers in order to really compare the two soups? For instance, use a calculator to figure out the ratio of calories to serving size in each product. (The math content in Section II of this book has a quick review of ratios, if you need it.)

Step Three

Will you buy one brand of soup instead of another on the basis of this nutritional information? Decide with your child how significant the differences are.

- Is low fat important to your family? Why?
- What difference does sodium make?
- How about calories?
- Are you concerned about vitamin content? Which vitamins?

Step Four

Use this activity to arouse your family's awareness of the information found in nutritional labeling. From time to time, bring up the label issue as you serve a packaged soup or product.

When your child is helping out in the kitchen, ask him to analyze the labels on cans or boxes. Talk together about how basically "healthy" your various food choices are. What reasons can be given for various products' claims of promoting good health?

How Can Our Family "Make the Grade"?

What Should I Do About . . .?

HOMEWORK

Ah, homework—most of us dreaded doing it, and most of us wind up making sure that our children get it done! It's useful to keep in mind the two important functions that homework serves in education.

What we know of the process of long-term learning shows us that information needs to be processed several times for it to become a part of anyone's store of knowledge. Hearing something in the classroom is a first time and, if students don't think about it or use it a second or third time soon after, that first time becomes the *last* time. Homework is an opportunity to make a new piece of learning stick. Homework also helps to make teaching more efficient. When your child makes the effort to be prepared for a class, she and her teacher can then use their time together to expand on the knowledge, share insights, and move into new areas of learning.

How can I be sure my child does her homework?

If only parents could just wave a homework wand! Without it, here are some guidelines that may help homework time be less stressful.

Establish a routine and help your child stick with it. This is likely to require some time from you at the beginning, but it's well worth the effort. Let your child know that you expect that she will do her homework in the same way you expect that she'll eat dinner, participate in sports, or go to bed at a certain hour. Even if you hear the cry, "But I don't have any," sit and spend some time talking about what she did that day at school. (Maybe your child's teacher requires students to keep an assignment notebook—wouldn't that be great!) Encourage her to write in a journal, do a little online research on nights when there isn't a real assignment to do, or do one of the Learning Adventure activities in this book. Your attention and involvement will help your child see that it is part of her day to think about school things at home.

Practice some time management with your child. Look at her other time commitments (sports, music lessons, that favorite and acceptable TV program, other family routines) and help her set out a schedule that she can maintain reasonably. A set time every day is the easiest to remember but may not always be feasible. The point is to have the homework schedule make life easier not harder. Be sure to work in the extra time required for doing long-term research papers and special projects.

Create a study area. Make sure that it has few to no distractions and good lighting (stay outside earshot of the TV if you can manage it). Going to a space that encourages your child to focus on work is an important part of the routine too. It might be where the computer is (as long as she has room to set out her books or papers and write) or it might be the table after supper is cleared. Keep homework items in a bag or box so they can be easily laid out and then picked up each night.

Make time in your own schedule. Those few moments you spend taking an interest in what your kid is doing, reviewing her progress, or giving a little help where needed make a big difference. (But do resist the temptation to actually do the work for her!) Keeping in touch prevents your child from thinking she is banished to do her homework in solitary confinement. Some work should certainly be done alone but a lot of problem solving and creative thinking can be done through dialogue. If you care about what she is doing, she'll care more too.

My child's math is way over my head. How can I be helpful?

This isn't an uncommon problem for parents. Some basic school content will always be the same, but emphasis, styles of teaching, and (particularly in the case of science and some areas of mathematics) new discoveries and teaching techniques mean changes in the standard curriculum. There are several things you can do.

- First, remember that you don't have to replace the teacher. What you can most easily provide is a comfortable and supportive environment for your child's homework. This may mean putting a firm hand on the television power switch. It may mean setting aside a space where your child can work quietly and without disturbance. At all times, respect your child's ability and express confidence in him. Reassure him that you will help in whatever way you can.

- Second, if the problems are with understanding specific material or just a general failure to be able to get and follow directions, consult with your child's teacher. Some children find it difficult to ask for help or information in the classroom. Work with the teacher to make it possible for your child to ask.

- Third, use the Learning Adventure activities in this book to turn potentially difficult subject matter into something both fun and understandable.

- Fourth, some communities sponsor call-in homework phone assistance. Others have programs to connect students with mentors or tutors. After-school programs like Score@Kaplan provide subject matter remediation and enrichment for the community. Check with your school's principal and with other parents to find out what is available.

- Fifth, ask your child's teacher for suggestions about books, magazines, and other resources that you can use to stimulate an interest in the subject. Try the Resources section in this book for further ideas.

How much help should I give my child with grammar and spelling in his written work?

In this situation, you need to walk a fine line between answering your kid's questions and actually taking over what ought to be his practicing of the editing and proofreading steps of the writing process. Encourage him to do as much as he can on his own. Even when you answer a question, try to cast yourself as the last resort. For instance, the first response to, "Mom, how do you spell . . . ?" probably should be, "Have you tried finding it in the dictionary?" or it could be asking him about a spelling guideline. After that, you can give some guidance in finding the word and, finally, help with the actual spelling.

If you're not certain about grammar and usage questions, admit your uncertainty. See if you can look up the rule or explanation together. Turn your rusty skills into a positive opportunity for you both to learn something.

What can I do when my child doesn't do his homework?

While this is a familiar problem, it has many answers—depending mainly on what problems or issues stand between your child and his homework. If he doesn't have a place to work, if his time is taken up with family chores, or if he has a TV in his room, those problems need to be solved first.

If there are no outside reasons or interference, it may be just a question of his developing self-discipline. There should be a definite time set aside for doing whatever homework has been assigned: no TV, no phone calls. Make it clear that the faster the homework gets done, the sooner he can be on the phone or doing something else.

If there's a serious problem, he may try to convince you that he just doesn't have any homework. In most schools today, having no homework is unlikely. Try to find out the truth—from other parents or, if necessary, from the teacher. Then you'll have to impose discipline from the outside.

TECHNOLOGY

Technology is a confusing and difficult area for both parents and educators. Although schools grew in size and complexity from the eighteenth century to the early twentieth century, the basic technology of education—blackboards, books, paper, and simple writing instruments—remained almost the same from decade to decade for almost 250 years.

Suddenly, following the Second World War, school equipment began changing, and they have been changing ever since. Technology like tape recorders, slide projectors, television, photocopiers, and film loop equipment became an increasingly regular part of school apparatus. But these additions were minor compared to the upheaval caused by computers. Today's information technology is so powerful, so full of promise, and so certain to alter how we work, play, and learn that schools and parents alike have to struggle to comprehend its implications.

Two problems stand out for parents and schools. One is trying to understand a technology that is still developing and whose implications for us are still unclear. The other is the enormous expense of this technology. Families and schools face hard economic and educational decisions as computer consumers and users.

How do I decide which computer to buy for my family?

Your decision will involve a combination of research and self-assessment; and unfortunately the answer may not be cut-and-dried for you. But here are the things to consider:

- Who will be using the computer?

- What programs will you want to use now? in the future?

If both you and your children will use the computer, you should consider checking into what your child's school has for hardware and software; kids tend to be pretty flexible when it comes to jumping from one program to another, but continuity is good if you can arrange it. (Many programs today can run on either a Windows™ or Macintosh™ computer, so compatibility issues are less important than they used to be.) Depending on what you plan to do with the computer (word processing, telecommunicating), you may need to consider buying add-ons like a printer and a modem. As you consider what computer model to select, try to think ahead to what your computing needs will be a year or so from now. As with any electronic device, today's model may be outdated tomorrow; but if it meets your budget now and can meet your work plans for a couple years, then it is probably the right choice for your family.

How do I pick educational software that is good and that my kids will use?

It's sort of like picking out toys or books or clothes for children—some guesswork, some research, some sense of your child's likes and dislikes, and some luck. And after all that, they may still grow out of it in a year too . . . . Given the number of new software titles that appear on store shelves every month, it is a bit daunting to go into a store or open a catalog and know what it buy. In general, your home software library should include a variety of programs (as your budget allows) in several main categories:

- Tools like a word processor (there are some very simple ones for even the youngest kids) and database or spreadsheet programs for older kids
- Creative programs like art, music, and card-making programs
- Academic programs that provide instruction and practice in areas like spelling or math
- Games that result in learning something like words, geography, or historical events (if you look around, you can find many that kids are motivated to play, but aren't the shoot-'em-up kind)
- Simulation programs and other thinking-skill activity products (they involve kids in decision making, problem solving, and anticipating outcomes)

Here are several solid ways to help you make your purchasing decision.

Find out what your kids are using at school. There may be a title that your child particularly enjoys or that the teachers think is great. This is a good opportunity to strengthen the home-school connection.

Talk to other parents. Someone may have done some research that can benefit you. Fellow parents can give you first-hand reports of what their kids are doing with products they have or why they like them. Recommendations from them about what not to buy can be helpful, too.

Subscribe to one of the many family-oriented periodicals with software reviews. New ones come on the newsstands every month (Another choice to make!), and there are a bunch that specialize in home computing software. Reviews and articles are likely to talk about a range of issues like titles that are good for 5-year-olds but are also enjoyed by 2nd graders and safety tips for letting your kids use your home computer.

Make note of brand names that are usually good. When your kids have a really good time with a particular title, see what else the company makes.

Keep your eyes open for reviews. Software and multimedia reviews appear in lots of places: weekly news magazines, your daily newspaper, flyers that you pick up in a store, on the Internet, and on other online services.

What should I know about the World Wide Web?

To understand the World Wide Web (WWW), we need to start with the Internet, which is an immense linkage of computer networks all over the world. When it started in the 1950s, the Internet was used primarily by the government and universities to conduct and communicate research projects. It displayed only text (words, numbers, symbols) on screen, and users had to type in commands to do anything. Since then, the Internet network of computers has expanded to include thousands of new users—business people, educators, and families like yours—and in ways that are extremely more friendly and easy to use.

Another major development in the Internet is the way in which you can see and use information on screen. You use one portion of the Internet—called the World Wide Web—by clicking on pictures and images rather than typing in words. Probably because of this ease of use, it is said to be the fastest growing part of the Internet. There were an estimated 30 million users of the Net in 1996, and that figure may double at an annual rate!

Now, thanks to programs called Web browsers (perhaps you've heard of Netscape™ or Internet Explorer™), you see screens that look like the colorful pages of a magazine, but besides text and images these pages also offer sounds and sometimes even video clips. Some of the graphics and text on these pages are highlighted. By clicking on highlighted items, you can jump to other places (sites) in the Web. (Think about the intricate arrangement of a spider's web, and the name World Wide Web makes sense.) The first page of any Web site is called its home page—sort of like the contents page of a magazine. The home page usually contains a table of contents for the rest of the site.

Should I let my child have access to the Internet considering some of its bad press?

With some guidance, your child can use the Internet as a very beneficial tool. Our children live in a dynamic, video-oriented age; their daily worlds are filled with videotapes, music videos, cartoons, TV shows, and advertisements. The Internet can merge this video culture with traditional academic learning. Furthermore, it adds interactivity, which is not available in the passive surround of video and TV. To use the Internet, children have to get involved rather than just sit and watch. And their involvement can take place in the form of writing, critical thinking, math, conversation, or research—all with a level of excitement that you seldom see in other learning situations. In the same way that you monitor what TV shows your child watches (or where she goes or what she eats), you can set up guidelines for how and when your child uses your online service. Check into one of the many new software programs that allow you to restrict access to certain areas of the Internet.

What should I do about how much TV my child watches?

We can't ignore television. We all grew up with it and lived to tell the tale. But the degree to which TV can dominate the development of many children is much greater now than it was when there were fewer programs, channels, and TV sets in a home—and more scruples about what finds its way onto the screen. Sure, TV can be addictive and too many parents use it as a pacifier or baby-sitter, but it is also a powerful tool that can be turned to the advantage of valuable learning. Your challenge, as a parent, is to reduce the role of the television to one of educational support, supplemented with a small dash of recreation. Do not put a TV set in your child's room. Find some programs that are educational—whether drama, science, history, the arts, or whatever. Watch WITH your child as often as possible and talk together about what you see. If you're not monitoring family TV viewing, your child may be spending too much time with TV. Show that you care about what and how your children learn by setting some serious goals (and examples), and follow through with them.

Should I regulate which TV shows or videos my child watches?

Yes, when possible—in much the same way that you make choices for her about what to eat, what books to read, and what language to use. Young children usually need clear guidance in the choices available to them and there are many lists available in print and online that provide guidelines for age-appropriate viewing. As they progress through elementary school, children can begin to make some of their own decisions well IF you talk with them about what they are watching, what they think of it, and what alternative things might be as engaging for them as watching TV.

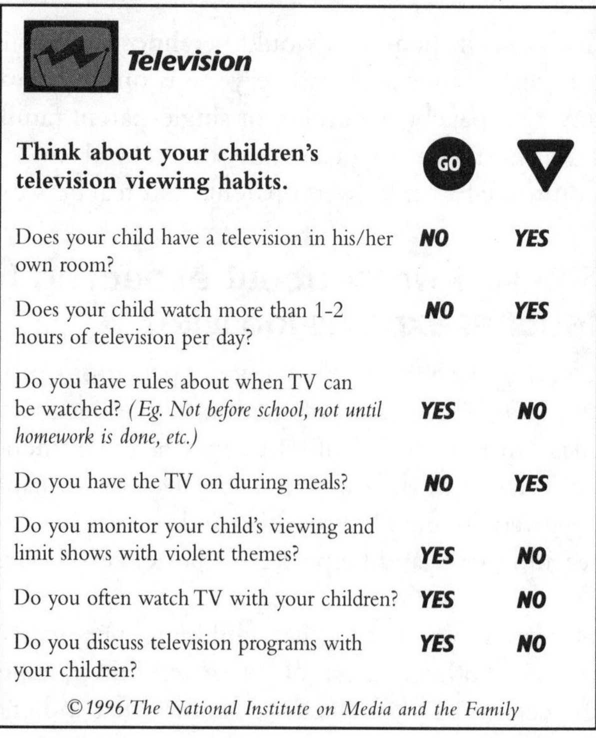

Television

Think about your children's television viewing habits.	GO	▼
Does your child have a television in his/her own room?	***NO***	***YES***
Does your child watch more than 1-2 hours of television per day?	***NO***	***YES***
Do you have rules about when TV can be watched? *(Eg. Not before school, not until homework is done, etc.)*	***YES***	***NO***
Do you have the TV on during meals?	***NO***	***YES***
Do you monitor your child's viewing and limit shows with violent themes?	***YES***	***NO***
Do you often watch TV with your children?	***YES***	***NO***
Do you discuss television programs with your children?	***YES***	***NO***

©1996 The National Institute on Media and the Family

Here are some helpful ways to start such discussions. Ask for your child's ideas on:

- How to choose between two programs (If you could watch only *Nick News* or *Goosebumps*, but not both, which would you pick? Why?)

- How to distinguish between reality and fantasy programs (What did you think when the man jumped out of the window and didn't get hurt? What do you think would happen if someone you know tried it?)

- How commercials influence our behavior
  (Why do you want that toy, cereal, soda . . . ? Where did you hear about it? How do you know whether it is good or not or whether you would actually like it or not?)

- How to set a schedule for viewing
  (Let's pick some shows together for you to watch during your TV hour today. Let's figure out some fun things for you to do when TV time is over.)

The Parent-School Partnership

Forty years ago it would not have been unlikely for your 8th grade teacher to look you in the eye (in the way that only 8th grade teachers could) and say, "I remember when your father used to have the same trouble with square roots."

Today, such memories would be almost impossible. Teachers and students have become part of a highly mobile society. Everyone is on the move. Everyone is also working longer and longer, and two-paycheck families or single-parent families are common. Increased mobility and busier families mean extra strains on school and parent relationships, and this makes good communication between parents and teachers extremely important.

Should I worry about expecting too much of my child or when a teacher expects too little?

Children respond to their own expectations of what they can and cannot learn. If they believe they are able to learn something, whether solving equations or riding a bicycle, they usually make real headway. But when they lack confidence, learning eludes them. Children grow in self-confidence as they experience success in learning, just as they lose confidence in the face of repeated failure. Thus teachers and parents need to provide them with challenging but attainable learning tasks and help them experience success.

Research has shown that children's personal expectations are closely linked to what they perceive others think of them. Children, especially many girls, are quick to pick up the expectations of success or failure that others have for them. The positive and negative expectations shown by parents, counselors, principals, and peers affect students' expectations and hence their learning behavior.

In addition, we know that parents and teachers who expect a child to succeed tend to more effectively support that child's learning. If you suspect that your child's teacher has low expectations for her, address the problem head on before it becomes a self-fulfilling prophesy. And you and your child's teacher need to bolster your child's enthusiasm for learning—even in a school and youth culture that may not think being smart and working hard is "cool."

How can I make the most of parent-teacher conferences?

Preparation is the key to a good conference. Most teachers will have gathered up marks, thoughts, and examples of your child's work to bring to your conference. If you plan out beforehand what you want to ask about, you'll be able to get the most out of your meeting:

- Ask your child if there is anything she wants you to talk over with her teacher.
- Think about what you want to cover and make a list of questions; then order them to put the most important questions first.
- Check your list frequently during the conference so that if you and the teacher get sidetracked you can be sure to cover what is most important.
- Jot notes during the conference and then take a moment afterwards to fill in the notes enough so that you can follow up on comments and suggestions over the year.
- If there are problems, whether it's homework, classroom behavior, or social issues, ask for specific ways to help your child.
- After the conference, check back in with the teacher on a regular basis.

What can I do to support my child's teacher?

For starters, just keep in mind that teachers are people. We all tote around baggage left over from our own childhood as well as our present anxieties about our children. If feelings take over our relationship with a teacher, it's very hard to communicate anything.

It can be helpful to remember that teaching is an extremely demanding occupation and, considering the expectations we have of the profession, not a very well paid one (compare the starting salaries for the department of sanitation or public transport workers to those for teachers in your community). Classroom teachers are answerable to principals, superintendents, school boards, a large number of ever-changing parents, and their own desires to do the best they can for their students. In most schools, they work steadily, with few breaks and little opportunity to interact with other adults, and then they take work home with them in the evening.

So begin all interactions with a measure of patience. This doesn't mean you should not be firm and persistent, but you'll get off to a more productive start if you assume that you and your child's teacher have the same goal—to do what is best for your child.

Should I speak up if I disagree with how my child is being taught math, science, art . . . ?

Please do. Education is best conducted as a partnership between parents and schools. We rely on teachers to be skilled at running their classrooms and competent in their fields. That's a fair expectation. Teaching is a profession and most teachers, in addition to their regular work in school, take refresher courses, workshops, and pursue advanced degrees. Education, like other fields, changes, and new ways of presenting material, organizing classrooms, and evaluating students appear regularly. Sometimes these new ways of doing things baffle parents, particularly when they suddenly appear during a homework session at the kitchen table.

Teachers are usually eager to share what they have learned and what they are doing, so if you have questions about what kids are doing in the classroom, teachers are generally glad to meet with you and explain it. In the rare instance when a teacher is not performing up to the standards of the school system, it is important for you and other parents to speak up and work with the school administration to solve the problem.

Should I spend time finding out the details of our school's curriculum?

Absolutely. School conferences and open houses are times when you can ask questions about the specifics of classroom instruction as well as about the curriculum in general. If there isn't time to cover everything, ask your child's teacher for recommended books and periodicals. If enough parents are interested, a school may be willing to arrange an evening devoted to presenting information about curriculum specifics. If individual parents or parents working through a PTA or other parent-school organization offer to set up and arrange the meeting, they will probably be even more willing.

My child's teacher doesn't seem to like my child; what can I do?

Talk with your child's teacher. In almost all cases, and particularly with younger children, apparent slights or injured feelings are the result of misunderstandings. Most teachers have had years of experience with many children and families. They are happy to sift through the problems of communication to find ways to support your child and make him comfortable. In the rare case where a teacher has for some reason taken a dislike to your child, also begin by talking with the teacher. But don't be confrontational. The teacher who dislikes a child and acts upon it is behaving in an unprofessional way, even if unintentional. A gentle nudge may alert the teacher to an awareness of her actions, thereby prompting her to do whatever is necessary to correct the situation. If your effort is not successful, consult the principal, and then if necessary, talk with other parents.

Teachers here are big on "cooperative learning," but my child works best alone. What should I do?

It's a good idea at a parent-teacher conference to bring up any question like this that's troubling you and your child. It's true, there's a lot of emphasis today on cooperative projects that bring together students of varying abilities and skills. And it's also true that some kids—like yours—may be more comfortable with other approaches.

But before dismissing the idea of cooperative learning, take a look at what it's all about. One of the ideas behind cooperative learning is that it's good preparation for the real world, where interpersonal skills and teamwork are often required.

Genuine cooperative learning differs from traditional group projects, though, in the way it involves every member, not just the smartest kid or the strongest leader. The aim in cooperative learning is to develop youngsters' capacity for working as a real team. Most importantly, each member of the group is responsible for a specific part of the overall project or goal. Those goals and ideals mean that cooperative learning may actually be a good experience for a kid like yours, who already knows how to work by herself (an equally valuable gift). At the same time, do bring this issue up at a conference. The teacher who is guiding the cooperative learning activity needs to keep such individual differences in mind when structuring the group and to keep watching for how each child participates and benefits.

School Services

It's part of every school's mandate to meet children's physical, social, and intellectual needs. Toward that end, school buildings are being modified for access by students of all mobility levels and are becoming increasingly equipped for a wider range of educational needs and activities. As budgets allow, school staff lists include both the core teachers and the specialists needed to meet students' group and individual needs.

What is Attention Deficit Disorder (ADD)?

Everyone can remember a few kids from their school years who never stayed in their seats, talked out of turn, threw spitballs, or turned in sloppy papers. And the teacher may have ignored them or sent them on an occasional trip to the principal's office. So what's all this recent fuss about kids who are hyperactive or have an attention problem? How is "hacking around a little" now considered a *special need?*

Well, we have a little more information to work with now. It is reported that approximately 3–5% of all American children—up to 3.5 million—have Attention Deficit Disorder. ADD is a neurological disability (that is, it has to do with the brain). Some researchers believe that ADD is due to altered brain biochemistry. Research has shown that the rate at which the brain uses glucose, its main energy source, is lower in persons with ADD—especially in the portions of the brain that are responsible for paying attention, handwriting, motor control, and inhibition responses.

Since the symptoms of ADD—among them being fidgety, talkative, bossy, and inattentive—are behaviors seen in most children at some point in their lives, the diagnosis and labeling of a child with ADD is often the subject of debate. Some kids who seem jumpy or act out now may simply grow out of it; others may need intervention to learn how to have more control. It is vitally important to put together a complete picture of a child's development and draw from many sources of information before rendering a diagnosis.

School is often where the characteristics of ADD may be more easily recorded, since the school setting requires the very skills that are difficult for kids with ADD—sustained attention to a task, waiting turns, and staying seated.

A child suspected of having ADD should receive a comprehensive evaluation, including medical, psychological, educational, and behavioral components.

Can I ask to meet separately with the special teachers who see my child?

This depends entirely on your local school system's policies and resources. Widespread reluctance to adequately fund education at both the local and national level means that the specialist teachers are frequently overburdened. Many are willing to work with parents, but they feel that their limited time is best spent with the children. If you have a special need, begin first with your child's regular teacher. She or he is in the best position to help get you the information you need. If this is not successful, consult with your school's principal.

How Do I Know if My Child Has a Learning Disability?

A big indicator is when you, as a parent, sense something is amiss. You may notice that your child, who generally seems smart, has no major physical problems, and does very well in some things, just can't cut it in some other basic areas. Your suspicions may be reinforced at parent-teacher conference time when you hear things like: "He's a good kid and does very well in math, but he doesn't apply himself, especially when it has to do with reading or following directions. He should be doing a lot better."

Putting a finger on a learning disability is tricky because there are as many combinations of problems as there are children who have them. But some familiar patterns can be identified. Basically, kids with a learning disability have trouble learning some things, but not all things. They may

- Consume reading material like crazy, but not deal well with even simple social situations; or have great difficulty reading and act out to avoid having to read

- Be completely aware of current events and enjoy talking about them, but be completely frustrated by any attempt to put pen to paper

- Do academic subjects well but not be able to ever follow directions (especially oral ones) or do something that requires physical coordination

Success in school (and in life, for that matter) has to do with making sense of what we see and hear. Think of the brain as a big filing cabinet. If all the information is in neat files and in alphabetical order so we can get to it easily, then reading, writing, computing, and talking is generally pretty problem-free. For kids with LD concerns, however, the information is there, but not neatly piled and alphabetized; it takes longer for these kids to figure some things out. One of the goals in providing them with special education services is to help them develop better information-processing skills.

The severity of an LD problem may seem to rise and fall over the years. That's usually because different classroom environments can either amplify what's hard for a child or support what he can do well. People don't generally grow out of a learning disability but rather learn to compensate for a weakness by focusing on the things they are very good at. (Lots of kids with learning disabilities even use their smarts to sidestep doing what's hard for them!)

It's definitely possible to be a student with a learning disability and still be successful. Consider just a few famous examples: Winston Churchill, Albert Einstein, Beethoven, John F. Kennedy, Walt Disney, Whoopi Goldberg—there are lots more. With perseverance, they made it—and so can your kid.

School Programs and Choices

It was simpler back then, wasn't it? Kids went to school and parents basically knew what was going on. Things were solid. It felt right. Now you overhear your kids' conversations, get flyers at home, read newspaper articles that talk about alternative classes and magnet schools. You can even choose to attend a school out of your neighborhood!

The school wants to put my daughter into the next higher grade. Is that a good idea?

Moving to a new community or changing schools can present this problem at least as often as having an especially bright child. Regardless of the reason, there are several factors to consider. One important one is your child's social and physical maturity—will it be obvious that she's younger? Might she be teased or bullied as a "baby" by her older and bigger classmates? Will she feel socially different or unprepared? Such problems could outweigh the benefits and cause lasting problems with social relationships.

On the other hand, if she's grown-up enough to fit in and deal with slightly older kids, it could be a good opportunity to challenge her intelligence and avoid her being bored by materials and skill lessons she may have already mastered or learned in her old school.

What happens if my child works too far ahead of her class in some subjects? Will she be bored?

This can be a problem, particularly in classrooms that adhere closely to a standardized curriculum. When students have already accomplished the classroom goals, they are placed in a difficult position. Going over what they already know is boring and they may either suffer in silence or get into trouble. Neither of these is a desirable alternative.

This doesn't mean that you should hold back on your child's academic development or that you shouldn't make an effort to extend her education. The best solution is to consult with your child's teacher. Together you can plan learning paths that supplement and extend the standard curriculum without overlapping what the whole class is doing together. Your child can forge ahead at her own pace, explore new material, and continue to be challenged. In the "What's More" sidebars with the Learning Adventure activities in this book, you will find sets of supplemental activities. These extend the skills practice or knowledge base of the activities and are an example of how a single learning activity can encompass a greater depth of learning.

Should I worry that there is less and less physical education in my daughter's school?

Yes, it should be a concern to all parents for two reasons. The most important is the physical well being of your child. Modern children lead increasingly sedentary lives and this is probably related to the alarming increase in obesity throughout our country. C. Everett Koop, the former U.S. Surgeon General, and other health experts identify obesity as a major health problem and a contributing factor in a number of disease conditions ranging from diabetes to cancer. Removing any opportunity for movement and exercise should be protested by concerned parents. Try to enlist your local public health figures in efforts to maintain physical education programs.

The second (and more academic) reason is that children learn better when study time is broken up by the opportunity to move around and change environments. Japanese schools, often cited as models of intense academic pursuit by some educators, do have longer days and longer school years, but they also build in many more breaks for exercise, relaxation, and organized sports. All work (and sitting at a desk all day) does indeed make Jack a dull boy.

What is this America 2000 plan that people talk about?

The Goals 2000: Educate America Act was signed into law on March 31, 1994. This act serves as an outline for redefining United States school systems in an attempt to ensure that all students are prepared for life in the twenty-first century. It targets areas that need to change, particularly in light of the developments in information processing and global connectivity. It talks about changing roles/expectations of teachers, functions of schools, and attitudes/behaviors of students. Here are the eight national goals. The actual document is over 200 pages long, so just highlights are included here:

1. **School Readiness:** By the year 2000, all children in America will start school ready to learn.
2. **School Completion:** By the year 2000, the high school graduation rate will increase to at least 90 percent.
3. **Student Achievement and Citizenship:** By the year 2000, all students will leave grades 4, 8, and 12 having demonstrated competency over challenging subject matter including English, mathematics, science, foreign languages, civics and government, economics, the arts, history, and geography, and every school in America will ensure that all students learn to use their minds well, so they may be prepared for responsible citizenship, further learning, and productive employment in our Nations' modern economy.
4. **Teacher Education and Professional Development:** By the year 2000, the Nation's teaching force will have access to programs for the continued improvement of their professional skills and the opportunity to acquire the knowledge and skills needed to instruct and prepare all American students for the next century.
5. **Mathematics and Science:** By the year 2000, United States students will be first in the world in mathematics and science achievement.
6. **Adult Literacy and Lifelong Learning:** By the year 2000, every adult American will be literate and will possess the knowledge and skills necessary to compete in a global economy and exercise the rights and responsibilities of citizenship.
7. **Safe, Disciplined, and Alcohol- and Drug-Free Schools:** By the year 2000, every school in the United States will be free of drugs, violence, and the unauthorized presence of firearms and alcohol and will offer a disciplined environment conducive to learning.
8. **Parental Participation:** By the year 2000, every school will promote partnerships that will increase parental involvement and participation in promoting the social, emotional, and academic growth of children.

In the first two years of the plan, 46 states wrote school improvement plans and were granted Goals 2000 funds. Some states and communities are creating new schools—called *charter schools*—while others are revitalizing existing ones. Community participation in schools is a vital part of local reform efforts. If you are a parent who wants to make an impact in your school system, Goals 2000 may offer an opportunity for you. Check with your local school board to see what is happening in your community.

THE SOCIAL SIDE OF SCHOOL

School is a social setting and, like it or not, social issues play a large part in the success of the learning environment. It is a major challenge for us as parents to be aware of the moods and feelings of our children, and it's one of the challenges that gets more difficult as they mature. Sorting out the normal grumps and bumps from the unusual mood swings that signal a problem isn't easy, but it is important to keep checking. Most children, and probably yours, have days when they are reluctant to go to school, but have these suddenly increased? Has normal play outside of school diminished? Has your child's performance in school inexplicably dropped off? This is an area where communication between you and your child's teacher will make a tremendous difference.

What should I do when my child is teased?

Differences in size or weight—even wearing glasses—can sometimes be cause for suffering among school children. Whatever the problem, your child needs you to be accepting of his feelings and to give him emotional support. At the same time, let him know that he is a strong and capable person. Bullying and teasing behavior comes from children who are bullied and teased themselves and, although they are the perpetrators rather than the victims, these children are also hurt by situations in which they act out unchecked. This information may not seem immediately helpful to your child, but it is useful to have.

The point is not to minimize the emotional hurt your child receives, but to demystify the menace by putting it into perspective. Make contact with your child's teacher right away. A note or phone call will serve as an alert, and make an appointment to meet as soon as possible. Children can sometimes be cruel, but they can also be very supportive, and a good teacher who catches potentially hurtful situations in the early stages can turn them around. If you notice or hear of things going on before the school does, don't hesitate to speak up.

Should I worry that my kid, an only child, tends to be a loner?

Some of the world's most interesting and creative people have been loners. A lot depends on your definition of "loner." Is your kid simply self-reliant and self-sufficient, and good at being alone and entertaining herself? Many only children develop such valuable traits.

Since there are no other kids in your family, an only child may sometimes feel very much at home among adults. You can help her be more sociable with people her own age simply by facilitating visits to other kids' houses and having friends over. You also can encourage her to take part in activities where she'll be with kids with similar interests.

On the other hand, some kids—and not just only children—seem to be loners to an extreme degree. If your kid is truly withdrawn and seriously moody or hostile, the situation probably demands stronger interest and intervention, and possibly some outside counseling.

Time Outside of School

It has always been true that children receive a good share of their education outside of the schools. In fact, kids are always learning (aren't we all!) so it matters what they are learning during the majority of their time, which is spent away from school.

The quality and quantity of outside educational experiences is directly proportional to parental involvement. The more you put into it (whew, being a parent is tiring), the more they get out of it. Whether it's locating enrichment programs, supporting youth programs, doing a little teaching yourself, or just offering your support for your child's quest for knowledge, you make a tremendous difference.

I don't have much time or money to provide my child with after-school activities. Help!

You're not alone. Many parents have discovered that our schools have less and less to offer in the way of extracurricular activities. Even though they have less and less time, parents are having to do more and more. The Learning Adventure activities in this book have been designed for after-school fun with little or no cost to parents—so there's one place to start!

Other help is available. Established after-school or extended day programs, both commercial and community supported, are becoming more common. Shopping around isn't always possible, but if it is, look for programs that have a specific focus. Programs built around activity—whether it's sports, supplemental education, ethnic identity, the arts, or crafts—tend to be more stimulating and thoughtfully run, than those that are just places for kids to stay. But after-school centers simply designed for kids with nowhere else to go can include aspects of all such activities. And you can encourage these centers to offer more by making suggestions, helping think of places to visit, and the like.

Sometimes just beginning to look for opportunities for your child will help. As you look for programs and activities, people will suggest other resources and, more importantly, you will encounter other parents engaged in the same search. Connecting with other busy parents means you can share resources and information and pool your energy. Connecting can be as simple as talking about your search with other parents at the playground, church, or at a PTA meeting. A note on the local library bulletin board or a message in the school newsletter may be enough to organize other parents around a particular activity.

Is enrolling my child after school to learn our ethnic culture and language asking too much of her?

Being proud of one's heritage is an important component of every person's self esteem. Programs that support this are excellent supplements to regular schooling. Indeed, given the frequent cutbacks in school arts programs, these can be an important resource for your child's intellectual growth. The experience may even help her do well at school. Whether or not committing her time to such a program serves your child well depends entirely on your assessment of her abilities and needs.

Learning a second language is extremely valuable. Many of us forget how immigrants to North America, including those who've made major contributions on this continent, became bilingual and, not infrequently, trilingual. Having a second language and being intimate with another culture gives your child an educational advantage, particularly if it's also a source of pride.

What kinds of reference books should I get my child?

A quick answer: small ones! Thick atlases, massive encyclopedia sets, and other large reference books look impressive, but the old idea of encompassing all of human knowledge in an expensive shelf of books has gone out the window. Our body of knowledge continues to undergo rapid change (just look at the cartographic scramble when the Soviet Union came apart or the overnight shifts in thinking in the medical and biological sciences). Large atlases, encyclopedias, and other reference books themselves have changed and most of them are available at the library, in software, or online; many are capable of being rapidly and inexpensively updated on a regular basis.

Dictionaries, almanacs, field guides, and smaller reference books are a different story. These contain information that is more useful on a day-to-day basis and they are inexpensive, portable, and worth buying. Besides, even if you have a computer-based encyclopedia program, you'll need something if the power goes off!

What books for kids does it make sense to buy?

Sometimes it seems like books for children are a little like their shoes, too expensive and too quickly outgrown. Most of us, however, have a cherished old book or two tucked away in the bottom of a box or bookcase. Good books are treasured—read and reread and worth the investment. That doesn't mean you have to buy every book that comes along. Use the school and public libraries to discover the particular books that will strike your child as wonderful. Read reviews of literature for children in newspapers and magazines. Check out lots of library books and encourage your child to participate in the selection. Not every one will be a hit; but over time, you will find books, authors, and subject matter that both suit and fascinate your child. This can be your guide to the occasional purchase.

If money is tight, think twice about spending money on fad toys. Toy makers and sellers spend vast sums on market research that, at its heart, only creates new ways to exploit children's gullibility and parental guilt. Stroll past any yard sale and add up the amazing amount of money that was spent on yesterday's gotta-have-it toy. And while you're there, check through the children's books—you may find some buys.

Birthdays and holidays are prime occasions for book buying. A gift list of books can add to your home library. Grandparents and relatives often ask for gift suggestions. If they don't, drop them a note with ideas before the holidays or birthdays roll around. This helps them with their gift buying and (sometimes) means you won't be getting that toy that you really don't want in the house! If you have a ready list of books, sharing it with others makes life easier.

How can I find good children's literature?

Check the Sunday papers around the winter holiday times. There are often articles or supplements that provide listings and reviews of what's new and recommended in children's literature. Cut these out and save them for future reference.

When you're in a library, wander around in the periodical section looking for articles on children's books in magazines for parents. Most libraries have bookmarks, pamphlets, or information from the American Library Association on their annual award-winning books (ask for the Caldecott, Newberry, and Coretta Scott King awards). Periodicals as different as *Mothering* and *The Scientific American* have book review sections that occasionally feature children's fiction and nonfiction books.

Subscribe to, or borrow from the library, children's story and special interest magazines. Authors and illustrators usually do short pieces or excerpts from books for these periodicals. The magazines also make great bedtime reading for younger children, and you will find many authors whose style or subject matter appeals to your child. You can then go to the library together to search out this author's books.

How can I add to the educational resources in my home?

Start by being selfish. Think about what you would like to learn and go for it. Even though we are constantly reminded by our children that they mimic us ("Where did you hear that, Sally?" "Dad said it when he dropped the microwave."), we forget that our children are modeling themselves on our good habits as well. Your enthusiasm for learning will be contagious.

First, recycle your own trash for craft and Learning Adventure activities—everything from egg cartons and milk jugs to shoe boxes and junk mail can be used for school and home educational projects.

Second, be a trash picker. You don't have to push a shopping cart down the street, but be alert to the value of other people's castoffs. We know a parent who scans the neighborhood on trash day. When a neighbor of his who coached a hockey team threw out an old goal net, our trash picker turned part of it into a climbing net hung from a tree branch and part of it became a fantasy spider web for a child's school project on creepy crawlies. Somebody installing lots of carpet? Those long cardboard tubes can turn into alpenhorns, flag poles, and tunnels for rolling balls (and don't forget your hamster's love of tubes!). Some towns have a transfer station (today's incarnation of the town dump) where castoffs are set aside to look for new owners.

Be an advanced trash picker. A manufacturer of file folders and envelopes produces enormous amounts of cut ends and defects. These go straight to the shredder unless an alert parent or teacher gets there first, and the company is more than happy to get the good will that comes from giving away a treasure in paper. Offices are treasure-troves of discarded memo and computer paper, envelopes, folders, and catalogs. The same is true for any small manufacturing concern that produces useful (to someone) waste material. Small electronic parts, metal stampings, and bits of brightly colored plastic, pieces of wood are all much better off as parts of collages, dioramas, and science or construction projects than they are as landfill.

How can I keep my kid's education going during summer vacation?

Of course, you'll obviously find lots of great ideas in the Learning Adventure activities in this book! Once school is out, you can involve the whole family in some of them. Take time also to play board games such as Scrabble™ or Monopoly™ as a family. Monopoly, for example, is a subtle way of being sure your kid practices math skills as the banker or the rent-collecting proprietor of Atlantic Avenue and the Water Works. Scrabble challenges everyone's word knowledge.

When summer's here, you'll want to look at the outdoor resources in your community. Some city park systems or schools have summer programs that focus on nature study and the outdoors, augmenting your kid's science knowledge. Nature experiences are usually a part of camp life too. Summer projects can offer practice in both math and science. Carpentry projects, for instance, require careful measuring. Building a rabbit cage, remodeling projects, or redecorating involve measuring, figuring square footage, estimating costs, and other math challenges. To keep up your kid's interest in language arts, turn to your local library. It may have a summer reading program or, for younger children, story and reading hours. Look for free or low-cost summer theaters, which often present Shakespeare and other theater classics. Even without special programs, your kid can learn to revel in the summer joys of reading at the beach or in a hammock.

What Resources Should I Use?

Here's our nonexhaustive list of resources in print, on disc, and online. They cover various areas, including math, science, language arts, and parenting issues. A good starting place!

PARENTING

Books and Newsletters

All Kinds of Minds, by Mel Levine (Educators Publishing Service, Cambridge, 1993). A sympathetic, light-hearted, and extremely intelligent presentation of learning abilities, learning disorders, and other learning issues.

Beyond the Classroom: Why School Reform Has Failed and What Parents Need to Do, by Laurence Steinberg (New York: Simon & Schuster, 1996). Discusses authoritative parenting and the home environment, the power of peers, ethnicity, and more.

Child Safety on the Internet, by the Staff of Classroom Connect with Vince Distefano (Lancaster PA: Classroom Connect, Prentice Hall, 1997). A guide to protecting children from accessing inappropriate material on the Internet; includes "Kid Safe" net sites.

Education on the Internet: A Hands-On Book of Ideas, Resources, Projects, and Advice, by Jill H. Ellsworth (New York: Macmillan Publishing USA, 1996). A great way for parents to tune in to good material on the Net.

Helping Your Child Succeed in School: A Guide for Parents of 4 to 14 Year Olds, by Michael H. Popkin, et al. (Atlanta: Active Parenting Publishers, 1995). Fun, supportive, and creative ways to help your children learn, including working with the school system.

Parents' Choice
P.O. Box 185
Newton, MA 02168
(617) 965-5913
Quarterly newsletter that reviews books, toys, audiotapes, videotapes, catalogs, and more.

Playing Smart: A Parent's Guide to Enriching, Offbeat Learning Activities for Ages 4–14, by Susan K. Perry (Minneapolis: Free Spirit Publishing, 1990). Hundreds of ideas for educating and entertaining kids while cultivating their creativity.

Positive Coaching: Building Character and Self-Esteem through Sports, by Jim Thompson (Portola Valley CA: Warde Publishers). Designed to be a helpful philosophical aid for any adult who works with kids. Features 50 motivational stories that can be used to develop strong communication.

The Problem Solver: Activities for Learning Problem-Solving Strategies, by Shirley Hoogeboom and Judy Goodnow (Mountainview, CA: Creative Publications, 1987).

Quantum Learning, by Bobbi DePorter with Mike Hernacki (New York: Dell Publishing, 1992). Written for students, teachers, and parents, *Quantum Learning* helps students of all ages develop a personal learning style and a positive attitude toward learning new skills.

Super Fun for One: 366 Solo Activities for Kids, by Patricia Gordon and Reed C. Snow (Kansas City, Missouri: Andrews and McMeel, 1996). Activities that require minimal materials and preparation time, organized in segments of 5, 15, 30, or 60 minutes.

The Parents' Answer Book, by Gerald Deskin and Greg Steckler (Minneapolis: Fairview Press, 1995). User-friendly, comprehensive resource for child and adolescent development questions.

Why It's Great to Be a Girl: 50 Eye-Opening Things You Can Tell Your Daughter to Increase her Pride in Being Female, by Jacqueline Shannon (New York: Warner Books, 1994). The title says it all.

Catalogs

Active Parenting Publishers
810 Franklin Court, Suite B
Marietta, GA 30067
(800) 825-0060
Books, videos, games, and programs for workshops to help parents build academic success and overall parenting skills.

Fairview Press
2450 Riverside Avenue South
Minneapolis, MN 55454
(800) 544-8207
http://www.press.fairview.org
Fairview Press publishes books on family activity guides and a variety of family- and community-related issues.

Free Spirit Publishing
400 First Avenue North, Suite 616
Minneapolis, MN 55401-1724
(800) 735-7323
Books, posters, and a wide variety of products to build children's and teen's self-esteem, assist with homework, and help confront difficult topics.

National PTA Catalog
135 S. LaSalle St., Dept. 1860
Chicago, IL 60674-1860
http://www.pta.org
Resources for educators and parents on family involvement, child safety, and local PTA activities.

Simon & Schuster, Children's Publishing Division
1230 Avenue of the Americas
New York, NY 10020
(800) 223-2336

Internet Sites

Association of Science-Technology Centers
http://www.astc.org/astc/astchome.htm
ASTC is a nonprofit organization of science centers and related institutions, including zoos, nature centers, aquaria, planetariums and space theaters, and natural history and children's museums. ASTC's membership includes nearly 400 science museums in 40 countries.

The Children's Literature Web Guide
http://www.ucalgary.ca/~dkbrown/index.html
Lists of juvenile bestsellers and great links.

Classroom Connect on the Net
http://www.classroom.net
Classroom Connect's Web site helps educators and students to locate and use the best K–12 educational resources the Internet has to offer. Includes its own search engine and a resource section.

Computer Curriculum Corporation
http://www.cccnet.com
A leading publisher of comprehensive curriculum-based educational software.

EdWeb Home Page
http://k12.cnidr.org:90/
Find online educational resources around the world, learn about trends in education policy and information infrastructure development, and examine success stories of computers in the classroom.

ERIC—Educational Resources Information Center
http://www.ericir.syr.edu
A vast clearinghouse of educational issues and links, plus a search engine.

Family Planet
http://family.starwave.com
An online magazine about education, legislation, health, and child-rearing issues, with advice and reviews of kids' products.

Global SchoolNet Foundation
http://www.gsn.org
Resources and links pertinent to integrating the Internet into K–12 classrooms

International Registry of K–12 Schools on the Web
http://web66.coled.umn.edu/schools.html
Links to school Web pages throughout the world.

National Center for Fathering
http://www.fathers.com
Resources for dads, including articles from *Today's Father* magazine, parenting tips, and humor.

Parent Soup
http://www.parentsoup.com
Online information on parenting and homework help.

Parenting Q&A
http://www.parenting-qa.com
A searchable database of parenting issues, with answers from experts in child development and behavior.

ParentsPlace.com
http://www.parentsplace.com/
A grab bag of information on parenting.

ParentTime
http://www.parenttime.com
Chat and info on parenting, personalized for your child's age and interests.

Publications for Parents
http://www.ed.gov/pubs/parents.html
An online service of the U.S. government, this site includes a vast variety of publications.

LANGUAGE ARTS

Books and Magazines

Creative Kids
Joel McIntosh
(800) 998-2208
Art, stories, poems, columns, and calendars, this magazine helps encourage young creators.

Cricket
Carus Publishing Company
(800) 827-0227
Great stories, poems, art, and activities for kids 9-14.

New Moon: The Magazine for Girls and Their Dreams
P.O. Box 3587, Duluth, MN 55803
(800) 381-4743
Written by and for girls, this magazine contains creative writing and artwork from girls worldwide.

Totally Private and Personal: Journaling Ideas for Girls and Young Women, by Jessica Wilber (Minneapolis: Free Spirit Publishing., 1996). A 14-year-old writer gives an inside look at how keeping a journal can help young writers explore feelings and sort out issues pertinent to preteens and teens.

The Young Person's Guide to Becoming a Writer, by Janet E. Grant (Minneapolis: Free Spirit Publishing, 1996). Tips for young writers on developing a personal writing style and getting work published.

Catalogs

Educational Software Catalog
Sanctuary Woods
2228 S. El Camino Real #223
San Mateo, CA 94403
(800) 943-3664
http://www.sanctuary.com
A catalog of educational and entertaining language arts, social studies, math, science, and ESL software for kids of all ages.

Great Source Education Group
A Houghton Mifflin Company
181 Ballardvale Street
Wilmington, MA 01887
(800) 289-4490
http://www.greatsource.com
Intended for in-school use, but handy for home-based learning as well, this catalog includes language arts and mathematics, for students grades K–12.

Ideal School Supply Company
(800) 323-5131
Basic Facts Bingo, and lots of other games and resources for reading, spelling, language arts, reading readiness, and science.

Simon & Schuster, Children's Publishing Division
1230 Avenue of the Americas
New York, NY 10020
(800) 223-2336
Great language arts, math, and science resources.

Software

Alien Tales
Broderbund
(800) 521-6263
Mac and Windows CD
Zap extraterrestrials while you read passages from 30 classic books, answer questions, and solve puzzles.

How Do You Spell Adventure?
Sanctuary Woods
(800) 943-3664
Mac and Windows CD
Spelling and Vocabulary lessons taught through a game based on *Ripley's Believe It . . . or Not!*

Microsoft Creative Writer 2
Microsoft
800) 426-9400
Windows 95 CD
Ready-made layouts for journals, book reports, and newsletters, plus a feature that turns creations into Web pages.

Student Writing and Research Center
The Learning Company
(800) 852-2255
Windows CD
Everything you need to create reports or research papers: a full-featured word processor, plus Compton's Concise Encyclopedia.

Ultimate Writing and Creativity Center
The Learning Company
(800) 852-2255
Mac and Windows CD
A word processing program that teaches kids to write; includes online help for every step of the writing process, plus dictionary, thesaurus, and multimedia presentation theater.

Word Munchers Deluxe
MECC/Softkey,
(800) 227-5609
Mac/Windows 95/Windows 3.1
Over 6,000 words in five difficulty levels (approximately for grades 1–5) are presented in a multiple-choice game with 3-D graphics.

Write, Camera, Action
Broderbund
(800) 521-6263
Windows and Windows 95 CD
A creative writing program that lets kids write, edit, and promote their own movie.

Internet Sites

The Book Nook
http://schoolnet2.carleton.ca/english/arts/lit/booknook/index.html
Reviews of children's books, written by kids.

Children's Literature Web Guide
http://www.ucalgary.ca/~dkbrown/index.html
This site, designed for parents and teachers, archives children's literature on the Web.

CyberKids
http://www.mtlake.com/cyberkids/
A quarterly online 'zine by and for kids ages 7–16.

Kid's Crambo
http://www.primenet.com/~hodges/kids_crambo.html
Kids can make up their own rhymes and wacky word definitions at this fun site.

KidZone
http://www.mckinley.com
Magellan's kids' site has lots and lots of great book-related links—explore!

The *New Moon* Home Page
http://cp.duluth.mn.us:80/~newmoon/
The site of *New Moon* magazine, a 'zine by and for girls who like to write and read stories.

OK Pen Pals
http://web2.starwave.com/outside/online/kids/penpals/pal.html
A safe way for kids to find Web pen pals to exchange E-mail.

Yahooligans!
http://www.yahooligans.com
Yahoo's kids' directory, with lots of reading and language arts links.

MATH

Books

Eyewitness Books: Money, by Joe Crib (New York, NY: Knopf, 1990). Great info about the history of money.

Mathemagic, by Raymond Blum (New York: Sterling Publishing Co., 1992). Magic tricks using calculators, playing cards, and more make math fun.

Math Wizardry for Kids, by Margaret Kenda and Phyllis S. Williams (Happauge, NY: Barrons Educational Series, Inc., 1995). Puzzles, games, and projects for kids ages 8–12.

Mega-Math (Greensboro, NC: Carson-Dellosa). Reproducible pages on basic operations, fractions, measurements, decimals, geometry, and more.

Problem Solving and Measurement (Greensboro, NC: Carson-Dellosa). Examines length, capacity, mass, temperature, and time through use and creation of tables, graphs, and patterns.

Catalogs

Creative Publications
5623 W. 115th Street
Worth, IL 60482-9931
(800) 357-MATH
Books, manipulatives, and teacher resources to help teach everything from counting to algebra.

Educational Software Catalog
Sanctuary Woods
2228 S. El Camino Real #223
San Mateo, CA 94403
(800) 943-3664
http://www.sanctuary.com
A catalog of educational language arts, social studies, math, science, and ESL software for kids of all ages.

Educational Toys and Games Catalog
American Educational Products Inc.
401 Hickory Street, P.O. Box 2121
Fort Collins, CO 80522
This supplier of educational toys and games for schools offers math and science products for parents and children to use at home.

Great Source Education Group
A Houghton Mifflin Company
181 Ballardvale Street
Wilmington, MA 01887
(800) 289-4490
http://www.greatsource.com
Intended for in-school use but useful for home-based learning as well, this catalog includes language arts and mathematics materials—workouts, games, and study plans—for students grades K–12.

Holey Cards
3817 No. Pulaski
Chicago, Il 60641
(312) 588-5761
Kids have two minutes to get math facts questions right. Use the cards over and over again until the two-minute goal is reached. Multiplication, subtraction, and addition cards available.

MPH Catalog
P.O. Box 1125
Fairfield, CT 06432
Deck of 52 cards, all marked differently from 1 to 25. Fun card games for learning addition, subtraction, division, and multiplication.

Simon & Schuster, Children's Publishing Division
1230 Avenue of the Americas
New York, NY 10020
(800) 223-2336

Software

Geometry Blaster
Davidson & Associates
(800) 545-7677
Mac, Windows, and Windows 95 CD
Save Zoid's homeland from turning from 3-D to 2-D, and learn geometry in the process.

Math Heads
Theatrix
(800) 955-8749
Mac and Windows CD
Kids act as contestants and create videos in games about fractions, decimals, percentages, and pre-algebra, hosted by silly characters.

Mighty Math Number Heroes
Edmark
(800) 691-2985
Mac and Windows CD
Funky and fun: Fraction Man and GeoBot teach complex mathematical concepts.

The Fennels Figure Math
McGraw-Hill Home Interactive
(800) 937-4663
Windows CD
The Fennels are hosting a house full of guests (from throughout history) and need help feeding them. Learn how to convert weights, use a thermometer, read a map, and more.

Internet Sites

Dr. Math
http://forum.swarthmore.edu/dr.math/dr-math.html
Swarthmore College math students act as "math doctors" and answer students' math questions from all over the world. E-mailed questions and answers are gathered into an archive, organized by grade level and topic. Includes search function.

Mathematics Resource Page
http://www.deakin.edu.au
Math links for teachers and students.

MathMagic
http://forum.swarthmore.edu/mathmagic
MathMagic provides strong motivation for students to use computer technology while increasing problem-solving and communications skills. MathMagic posts challenges in each of four grade categories to trigger each registered team to pair up with another team and engage in a problem-solving dialogue.

SAMI: Science and Math Initiatives
http://www.learner.org/k12/sami
A clearinghouse of information for science and math teachers, but appropriate for home learning as well.

The Math Forum
http://forum.swarthmore.edu
This site covers simple and advanced mathematics, offering help to both students and teachers.

SCIENCE

Books and Magazines

Amazing Poisonous Animals, by Alexandra Parsons (Knopf, 1990). Looks at the world of poisonous animals, including close-up photos.

Amazing Frogs and Toads, by Barry Clarke (Knopf, 1990). Examines frogs and toads of all kinds; with full-color photographs.

Build with Beakman: Bacteria Farm (Andrews and McMeel, 1996). Fun with fungi is the focus of this book and kit (including petri dishes and other supplies). Beakman, of television's *Beakman's World*, is the host.

Experimenting with Inventions, by Robert Gardner (New York: Franklin Watts, 1990).

Girls and Young Women Inventing: 20 True Stories About Inventors Plus How You Can Be One Yourself, by Frances A. Karnes and Suzanne M. Bean (Minneapolis: Free Spirit Publishing, 1995). Inspiration for girls who love science and inventing.

National Geographic WORLD
National Geographic Society
(800) 647-5463
A monthly magazine containing lush photos from *National Geographic*, plus projects and facts.

Night Sky, by Carole Stott (London: Dorling Kindersley, 1993). This *Eyewitness Explorer* book is a pocket-sized field guide packed with projects and information on how to identify the constellations.

Ranger Rick
National Wildlife Federation
(703) 790-4283
Beautiful photos plus stories about the natural world, for kids 6–12.

Science Wizardry for Kids, by Margaret Kenda and Phyllis S. Williams (Happauge, NY: Barron's Educational Series, Inc., 1995). Magic tricks, projects, and experiments for kids age 8–12 make science fun.

Seeing Stars: A Book and Poster About the Constellations, by Barbara Seiger (Los Angeles: Price Stern Sloan, 1993). Facts and stories about the 35 most familiar constellations. Also includes full-color poster of the constellations, plus 400 glow-in-the-dark stickers to add to it.

Zero to Einstein in 60, by B. K. Hixson (Salt Lake City: The Wild Goose Company, 1989). Billed as "60 experiments guaranteed to cure science nincompoopitis," this fun book contains experiments for teachers and parents of children 8 and up.

Catalogs

Carolina Biological Supply Company
2700 York Road
Burlington, NC 27215-3398
(800) 334-5551
http://www.carosci.com/index.html
Great general science resource as well as selling manipulatives in quantities as small as twelve.

Dacta
The Educational Division of the LEGO Group
555 Taylor Road
Enfield, CT 06083-1600
(800) 527-8339
http://www.lego.com/learn
K–12 Science, technology, and math kits for constructing simple machines, gears, levers, and much more, out of LEGOs (not available in stores!).

Educational Software Catalog
Sanctuary Woods
2228 S. El Camino Real #223
San Mateo, CA 94403
(800) 943-3664
http://www.sanctuary.com
A catalog of educational and entertaining language arts, social studies, math, science, and ESL software for kids of all ages.

Educational Toys and Games Catalog
American Educational Products Inc.
401 Hickory Street, P.O. Box 2121
Fort Collins, CO 80522
(800) 466-8767
This supplier of educational toys and games for schools now offers math and science products for parents and children to use at home.

MindWare
2720 Patton Road
Roseville, MN 55113
(800) 999-0398
A catalog that contains puzzles, games, and books intended to "tap the other 90 percent of your brain," MindWare products help kids and parents develop math, science, and reasoning skills.

Simon & Schuster, Children's Publishing Division
1230 Avenue of the Americas
New York, NY 10020
(800) 223-2336

The Wild Goose Co.
375 Whitney Avenue
Salt Lake City, UT 84115
(800) 373-1498
Newton's Apple kit series and other award-winning kits, books, and science equipment and accessories for teachers and students for wacky and fun science experiments, plus posters, T-shirts, and other items.

Software

Big Science Comics
Theatrix Interactive
(800) 955-8749
Mac and Windows CD
Fun virtual experiments that cover topics such as harmonic motion, friction, force, and mass.

Bill Nye the Science Guy: Stop That Rock
Pacific Interactive/Disney Interactive
(800) 900-9234
Mac and Windows CD
Answer seven science riddles and divert an asteroid's deadly course. Hosted by Bill Nye, the disc features lots of scientific facts and virtual experiments.

Explore Yellowstone
MECC
(800) 227-5609
Mac and Windows CD
Hands-on activities help kids explore the national park and solve scientific problems in the process.

Eyewitness Virtual Reality: Dinosaur Hunter
DK Multimedia
(800) 356-6575
Mac and Windows CD
Video, animation, 3-D models, and a dinosaur excavation site let budding paleontologists dig for dinosaurs and bring their finds to life.

GeoSafari Multimedia
Educational Insights Interactive
(800) 381-0381
Mac and Windows CD
Multiple choice games teach kids science, history, and geography.

The Way Things Work 2.0
DK Multimedia
(800) 356-6575
Mac and Windows CD
Based on the bestselling book, this multimedia disc of inventions and inventors includes an online link to *mammoth.net*, a site for young inventors.

What's the Secret? Vol. 2
3M Learning Software
(800) 219-9022
Kids learn about such diverse topics as brains, flight, and the Arctic in a disc based on PBS' *Newton's Apple*.

Internet Sites

Ask An Expert
http://njnie.dl.stevens-tech.edu/curriculum/aska.html
Send your science, technology, or math questions to these experts!

KidZone
http://www.mckinley.com
Magellan's kids' site has lots and lots of great science links to explore

Liberty Science Center
http://www.lsc.org/
Homepage of this cool science museum.

MayaQuest 98
http://www.mecc.com/Maya/More/html
Learn more about the ancient Maya civilization with a group of explorers in Central America.

NASA Homepage
http://www.nasa.gov/
Exciting photos and lots of great space links.

National Institute for Science Education's Why Files
http://www. whyfiles.news.wisc.edu
Explains the "science behind the news" for children, teachers, and parents.

Nye Labs Online
http://nyelabs.kcts.org/
Public Television's Science Guy Bill Nye's homepage, with online experiments and a "Demo of the Day."

OER—Online Educational Resources
http://quest.arc.nasa.gov/OER/EDRC22.html
Collection of links to science-related educational sites, including: the "Star Child" page of K–12 astrophysics images/text; NASA K–12 Internet Project Home Page; "Virtually Hawaii" K–12 remote sensing data project; and ASU/NASA K–12 Mars program, among others.

Possibilities in Science
http://kendaco.telebyte.com:80/billband/possibilities.html
Virtual field trips, structured online learning, and resources for parents and teachers.

Science Hobbyist
www.eskimo.com/~billb/
Cool science, weird science, amateur science: a fun page with experiments and lots of links.

Sierra Club Kids
http://www.edginternet.com/angeles/sckids.html
Environment, conservation, life sciences, astronomy and more from one Sierra Club chapter, plus information on camping and outdoor sports.

Yahooligans!
http://www.yahooligans.com
Yahoo's kids' directory.

The Yuckiest Site on the Internet
http://www.nj.com/yucky/index.html
Yuck! All about cockroaches, courtesy of New Jersey's Liberty Science Center.

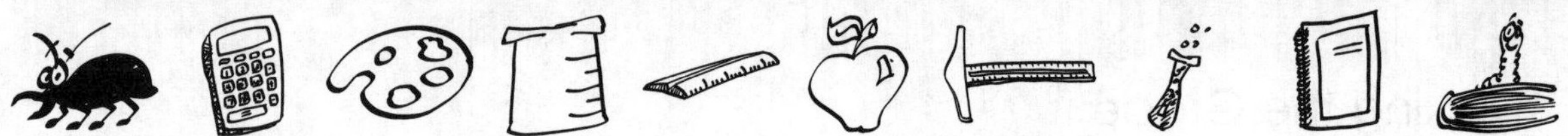

The Home Learning Quizzes

Your child learns in a unique way. In fact, all children vary greatly in learning style, level of maturity, individual personality, and how they learn on any given day. This is why single standardized tests administered across a grade level are not always accurate indicators of what academic skills your child has mastered. What these tests can indicate are possible problem areas or concepts that your child may need further practice to understand and material your child has not yet been introduced to in school.

YOUR CHILD'S QUIZZES

As a bonus, we've added our pull-out *Making the Grade* Kids' Home Learning Quizzes (the last eight pages of this section) to help you and your child locate possible problem areas or gaps in learning in language arts, math, and science. The questions cover material that your child *might* have encountered in 5th and 6th grade. Each quiz starts with 5th grade work and progresses to 6th grade items (an equal number from each grade level).

After your child quizzes herself, use the grade- and subject-specific Learning Adventure activities in *Making the Grade* to help her practice and hone skills in particular subjects. The quizzes are not meant to serve as definitive tests of your child's intelligence or an indication of subject mastery; they serve only as a supplement to the Learning Adventure activities to help you and your child spend more time on specific activities that correspond to problem areas or brand new material. Keep the home learning focus on having fun and "serving the learning in welcome helpings"; never pressure your child to "score high" or "learn on command."

YOUR QUIZ

The first eight pages of this section are for parents only. They contain your *Making the Grade* Parents' Home Learning Quiz, explanations for the quiz, and the answer key for the kids' quizzes. Taking the parents' quiz will help you identify possible gaps in your own knowledge and awareness of your child's growth and educational development. Like the subject-specific quizzes for your child, the parents' assessment is not an all-encompassing evaluation of your parenting or home education skills; just take the assessment to acquaint yourself with the latest educational and development issues. As with the kids' quizzes, there is no emphasis on how you score. Approach it as another level on which to discover something new or reinforce previous learnings.

USING THE QUIZZES

Your Parents' Home Learning Quiz is self-explanatory. Take it on your own, at your convenience. It's a little more complicated with the Kids' Home Learning Quizzes, but you can be sure that there is no *right* way for your child to take them. Take all the quizzes in a row, or take one quiz one day and save the others for different occasions. Your child can quiz himself—like taking a fun activity break with *BrainQuest*™—or you and your child can take the quizzes together for an exercise in finding out how much you both know about 5th and 6th grade subjects. Photocopy his pull-out quiz pages and time each section. Compare notes and answers when you finish.

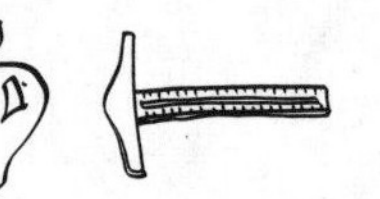

Have your child use a pencil to fill in the answer ovals and make scratch-note calculations; provide an eraser to change answers. Also discuss the purpose of the last two answer ovals. One oval (e) will indicate to both of you that a question covers skills your child hasn't learned in school yet; your child can mark this oval without selecting an answer (there's no point taking time to guess). The last oval (f) signals that a certain question covers previously learned material that is still difficult for your child; this can be marked along with one of the answer choices to the question.

Here are some specific ideas for sitting down with your child after taking the quizzes:

- Praise your child's correct answers on the quizzes, and have him show you how he made his calculations or worked through the steps that led to the correct answer.
- If your child chose an incorrect answer and didn't indicate that the material was difficult, go through the answer with him and try to clear up any confusion with the skills covered. An appropriate Learning Adventure activity can clarify skills and reinforce learning.
- If your child scored correctly and indicated difficulty with the material, celebrate the correct answer and bolster your child's confidence! Perhaps your child is ready to tackle new material in a particular subject matter; use a Learning Adventure activity to introduce the new skills in an informal, enjoyable way.
- If your child indicates that a question covers new material not yet taught in school, you have the future option of introducing the new skills through a Learning Adventure activity—if and when your child is ready and open to the new material.
- You might want to review the quizzes with your child's teacher to verify the responses, learn when new skills will be covered, and work together to develop a plan of action to bolster weaknesses and fill in learning gaps.

Using the Activities

Work with your child on the Learning Adventure activities in this book. Pace the flow of activities from day to day, week to week. Never push the learning, but develop a natural pacing that meets your schedule and reinforces your belief in fostering learning at home. As you do an activity with your child, observe her progress. On-the-spot observations of a specific activity will tell you more about what's really going on than the quizzes. And you will be giving your child the attention, support, and encouragement that enhances any learning activity.

Build a picture of your child's learning style. Everyone learns in a unique way. Determine your child's learning style(s) by noting what goes on as she works on an activity. Does she learn more easily by reading the material or by listening to you as you direct the activity? Does she become more enthusiastic when drawing and performing other hands-on activities? Noting these subtleties can help you better suit the activities to your child's strengths, as well as work on her weaker learning styles.

Assess what your child knows. Evaluation does not depend on tests alone. Observe your child working on an activity and assess how well he understands and handles information. Are there basic concepts that he needs to work on? In a math activity, does your child grasp the main idea but have trouble with the process, the basic math calculations? Does he write creatively but have trouble with quotation marks and punctuation? It's not necessary to grade the work or point out the deficiencies; just use these notes to select the activities, resources, and ways of supporting your child that will build competence and confidence.

Learning Tips for Home

The *Making the Grade* Parents' Home Learning Quiz concludes with evaluations and suggestions to help you become even more knowledgeable and aware of your child's education and development. In addition, we offer three simple guidelines—Be Alert,

Be Patient, and Be Positive—to establish a successful learning environment in your home.

Be Alert. There was once a master of the martial art t'ai chi who was so adept, a sparrow landing on his upraised arm was unable to fly off. The art of this master was neither speed nor strength, it was awareness. He was so alert that as soon as the sparrow crouched to take flight, he sense it and lowered his arm just enough to interrupt the sparrow's upward spring. The goal of education is, of course, just the opposite. We want to encourage the upward spring of our young sparrows.

The technique, however, is the same. Being alert at the end of a long day is easier than you think. Being alert is really only enhanced relaxation. Just remind yourself, once in a while, to relax and be open to your child.

Watch for subtle cues. Children communicate with their bodies. Closely watch your child at work. Is she slouched over or poised and energetic, calm or fidgety, morose or happy? Is she easily distracted or attentive? Facial expressions and tone of voice are also key clues.

Allow for emotional needs. Some children tell their parents what is going well and what isn't, but many won't. Sometimes your child's issues surface at home in ways that have nothing to do with your home life. Tensions surrounding your child's friends and school often surface indirectly at home. Emotions will probably spring to the surface during some of the activities.

Tears may erupt over a broken pencil tip, or a sulk develop over a misunderstood word in a reading assignment. These reactions may often be much stronger than the situation warrants. Don't let these moments defeat either of you. Children generally feel safer about showing their feelings to their parents than they do to their teachers. They feel safer at home, and it's good that they do, but it sometimes makes your job a little harder. The trick, and it works most of the time, is to accept the feelings, acknowledge the hurt, and weather the emotional release. And *weather* is the key word. The storm passes, the sun comes out, and then, in most cases, you'll be able to move on. For the times when this doesn't work, heed the advice of the Kenny Rogers song, "know when to hold 'em and know when to fold 'em." There will always be another time to try a Learning Adventure activity.

Note lack of interest. Your child may show signs of boredom, whether physical or verbal. These are important to watch for, but they can be ambiguous. Boredom can mean a task is too hard; it can be your child's way of reacting to an activity that asks too much. But boredom can also mean that an activity is too easy. Figure out what your child is really communicating; don't react to the sometimes irritating signs of boredom itself.

Note signs of interest. One child's enthusiasm may be communicated with an exuberant, "Look at these earthworms!" Another may react with increased concentration and silence as she focuses on a task that excites her. Indications of interest are just as important as signs of boredom in helping you determine where to go next, whether or not to repeat an activity or move on to harder skills, etc.

Be Patient. We all feel the pressure to achieve. It's there and it's real, but it doesn't belong in home learning situations. Communicating this pressure to children while they're engaged in academic work usually doesn't do much for the learning process. This doesn't mean that hard work and the desire to successfully learn something aren't important. They certainly are. However, external tensions, particularly those brought in from the adult world, can interfere with learning. The more you can relax and be your child's guide and supporter, the more successful you both will be.

Adjust to your child. Take your time doing the activities and pace yourself to allow your child to take his time. Each of us has his own style and pace for learning. Adjust the rate to which you start new activities to your child's natural pace. Remember that there are day-to-day events such as head colds, late evenings the night before, or the anticipation of birthday parties that affect your child's concentration and energy. Longer-range maturational changes also alter behavior and ability. Read (or browse through again) the essay on development in Section I.

Focus on individual learning tasks. Enjoy each moment of learning with your child and don't worry about what is next or where it's all headed. The Learning Adventure activities are meant to function as building blocks. Each activity should give your child a taste of success—which you can both celebrate!

Be patient with yourself. No teacher or parent gets it right every time. Learn from any mistake, and don't let it derail you. You care enough to spend time on your child's education, so give yourself a pat on the back—and then figure out what to do differently next time.

Be Positive. Each step in learning is important and deserves praise. The old "ruler on the knuckles" technique produced children who couldn't wait to get out of school. Help your child get the most out of staying in school and develop a lifetime love of learning.

Positive doesn't always equal fun. Some things are just plain old hard work. For some children, mastering the frustratingly inconsistent spelling of English is a chore. Others find it difficult to calculate sets of math facts such as the times tables. Effortless spelling and ease of computation will come, but the process is sometimes hard going. You can acknowledge this truth and yet regard the work in a positive light. The rewards are real. As different skills are mastered successfully, hard work and practice will pay off.

Use praise that works for both of you. Although children need positive reinforcement, they are able to see through transparent praise. Kids are the best spotters of what is phony. Specific praise for achievements, on the other hand, always works. Statements like, "You did that math problem very well" and "That graph explains things so that I can understand" are more useful than a general pat on the head because they tell your child that you have paid attention to what she has done. If things aren't going well, that problem also needs to be acknowledged and, just like the praise, put in concrete terms. Focus on the positive (even in the problem) and draw upon that to tackle what might not be going well.

SIMON SAYS

Here are some recommended books for 5th and 6th graders to help your child "Make the Grade":

MATH

Math Mini-Mysteries by Sandra Markle
Measuring Up: Experiments, Puzzles, and Games Exploring Measuring by Sandra Markle
Number Art: Thirteen 1 2 3s from Around the World by Leonard Everett Fisher

SCIENCE

Bats, Bugs, and Biodiversity: Adventures in the Amazonian Rain Forest by Susan E. Goodman
Science to the Rescue by Sandra Markle
The Kids' Earth Handbook by Sandra Markle
Dolphin Man: Exploring the World of Dolphins by Laurence Pringle

WRITING

Robert Louis Stevenson: Teller of Tales by Beverly Gherman
Where the Flame Trees Bloom by Alma Flor Ada
Taking Hold: My Journey Into Blindness by Sally Hobart Alexander
Great Lives: American Literature by Doris Faber

READING

Tom, Babette and Simon: Three Tales of Transformation by Avi
Brooklyn Doesn't Rhyme by Joan W. Blos
Bigger by Patricia Calvert

These books can be found at your local bookstore or from Simon & Schuster Children's Publishing Division at (800) 223-2336. For a catalog of titles write: Simon and Schuster, Children's Marketing, 1230 Avenue of the Americas, New York, NY 10020.

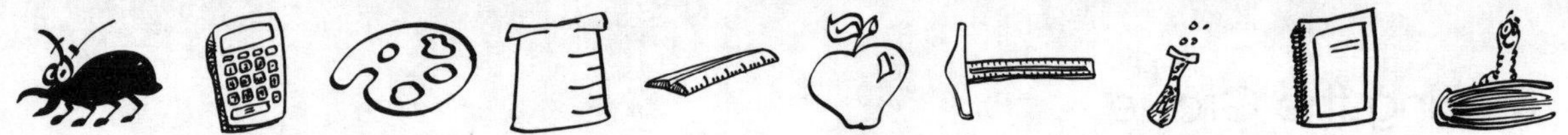

Parents' Home Learning Quiz

How much do you know right now about your child's growth and educational development? Test your knowledge and awareness.

Directions: Mark Y (yes) or N (no) for each statement below, as it applies to you.

Ⓨ Ⓝ **(a)** I praise my child—even for small achievements.

Ⓨ Ⓝ **(b)** Doing well on weekly assignments is fine, but I think my child's test scores and grades are what really count.

Ⓨ Ⓝ **(c)** I talk to my child about school at least twice a week.

Ⓨ Ⓝ **(d)** I meet my child's teacher(s) fewer than three times a year.

Ⓨ Ⓝ **(e)** I do not feel adequately prepared to help my child with homework.

Ⓨ Ⓝ **(f)** I attend my child's school-related programs most of the time.

Ⓨ Ⓝ **(g)** My child watches more than three hours of television per day.

Ⓨ Ⓝ **(h)** If I learned that my child had stolen something from someone, I would first want to know why and then discuss a plan for repayment.

Ⓨ Ⓝ **(i)** If I learned that my child was doing poorly in a particular subject at school, I'd handle the problem myself rather than go through school channels.

Ⓨ Ⓝ **(j)** I believe that my child's problems at school can be readily detected at home.

Ⓨ Ⓝ **(k)** I can easily describe my child's performance in school.

Ⓨ Ⓝ **(l)** I sometimes feel guilty about not providing more enriching experiences for my child.

Ⓨ Ⓝ **(m)** There have been incidents involving violence, harassment, or drug use at my child's school.

Ⓨ Ⓝ **(n)** I am a single parent.

       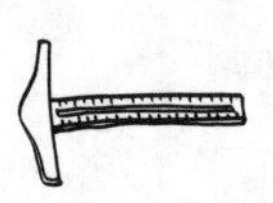   

Explanations: Parents' Home Learning Quiz

That was relatively painless! Here's an explanation of the yes and no responses for each statement:

(a) *I praise my child—even for small achievements.* If you chose *yes,* good for you! Even acknowledging small hurdles and achievements helps your child maintain a positive attitude about learning. Try coming up with creative, fun expressions of pride and celebration instead of giving him gifts or monetary rewards. A special meal you plan and cook together, an outing, going to the movies, playing one-on-one sports, or just hanging out together are rewards your child will appreciate. Spending some private time together works well, especially in families with several children.

(b) *Doing well on weekly assignments is fine, but I think my child's test scores and grades are what really count.* If you said *yes* to this statement, you're half right (the first part is positive). If your child practices solid learning skills and study habits, the good scores and grades will come in due course, and she will develop excellent skills for a lifetime of learning. Use test scores and grades as feedback to help your family focus on successes and problem areas, but also give your child praise for plugging away on those weekly assignments. Emphasizing the whole learning process is the right message to send to your child.

(c) *I talk to my child about school at least twice a week.* Great, if this applies to you! It's important that parents make their interest in education clear to their children. This is especially necessary given a recent survey by Dr. Laurence Steinberg, co-author of *Beyond the Classroom: Why School Reform Has Failed and What Parents Need to Do* (Simon & Schuster, 1996), which found that 72 percent of students aged ten to thirteen said they would prefer to talk more often to their parents about their homework, while only 40 percent of parents believe they are not attentive enough to their children's education. This discrepancy suggests that children would open up more about school-related issues or difficulties if they were given the opportunity to do so by their parents.

(d) *I meet my child's teacher(s) fewer than three times a year.* Meeting with your child's teachers has more educational value than you may be aware of. By offering insights about your child's home life and social habits, you help the teacher gain a fuller understanding of your child. You are also conveying to the teacher your interest in your child's education, and your willingness to collaborate to further his learning progress.

(e) *I do not feel adequately prepared to help my child with homework.* Even if you said *yes* to this, there are many ways to support your child's education, and all of them require only your energy and enthusiasm for learning. If you have a little time and willingness, you can use your feelings of inadequacy as motivation to learn with your child and test your skills together. In doing so, you'll be teaching your child an important lesson: Don't hesitate to undertake something that you might not do well. As a fellow student, you'll also be more sympathetic to your child's struggles, and he will appreciate the interest and attention. If time and other responsibilities do not allow for these sessions, you can still work on the activities together, offer support, and keep in touch with his teacher.

(f) *I attend my child's school-related programs most of the time.* If you answered *yes* to this, good! Parents who attend school functions—extracurricular activities, teacher conferences, and "back to school" nights—are indicating that school is important to them and that, by extension, it should be equally important to their children. When parents don't get involved in some capacity with their child's activities, intended or not, they're sending a strong message that they're not interested. Make the time; your effort will not go unnoticed by your child.

(g) *My child watches more than three hours of television per day.* Educators generally agree that watching too much television can affect a child's emotional makeup. Without supervision, children will be disturbed by particular types of programs or news pieces, depending on their maturity level. TV is also a passive activity. Monitor your child's viewing habits. Watch TV with your child and carefully screen programs. Some TV shows have sound information and entertainment content, but try to offer more active ways to spend free time with the family (like after-school or community-based programs).

(h) *If I learned that my child had stolen something from someone, I would first want to know why and then discuss* *a plan for repayment.* That's the way to go. By encouraging your child to come up with his own plan for restitution (for example, saving money through odd jobs and allowance to pay off what he stole), you're also making him face the consequences of his actions. This will go a long way toward helping him become more autonomous while taking responsibility for the theft. Your child's stealing might be a warning sign. It could be that this is merely the first time your child has been caught; repeated offenses could be indications of a larger problem, like drug abuse or extreme peer pressure. On the other hand, your child may be trying to get your attention or test your limits and see how much he can get away with. Monitor your child for a while, just to be sure. Don't feel as though you've done something to cause this behavior or that you've failed as a parent. Children naturally test rules. Provide direction and be a positive disciplinary force. Other reactions:

Punitive punishment Any action that emphasizes your anger rather than the issues at hand teaches children to behave by intimidation rather than by education. Help your child develop a sense of responsibility and autonomy, and obedient behavior should follow.

Light reprimand Parents who treat this matter lightly run the risk of conveying to their children that their behavior is not entirely inappropriate. When parents fail to discipline their children in proportion to the seriousness of an offense, kids may fail to develop a sense of value and responsibility. Instead of standing by idly, help your child see the larger picture and take responsibility for his behavior.

(i) *If I learned that my child was doing poorly in a particular subject at school, I'd handle the problem myself rather than go through school channels.* The problem with trying to tackle these difficulties at home is most children are taught subjects differently from how their parents learned, and this can make helping out more difficult. When a child doesn't understand a concept *or* a parent's explanation of it, no amount of increased study time is going to help. Try meeting with teachers and counselors and discussing ways in which the school can help. You do your child the service of getting involved in her education, and you do teachers and counselors a service by conveying you have faith in their abilities. Set up an appointment with a teacher or counselor. Discuss how they can better serve your child, and offer your assistance. Exploring other strategies . . .

Punishment You could punish your child for his lack of diligence, but that makes parents believe that their child's performance will improve. In reality, punishment may help a child understand how important schoolwork is to his parents, but it will not help the child understand the material itself. Instead of alienating the child through punishment, parents should try to affect the learning process itself by getting involved, speaking and collaborating with teachers to isolate problem areas, and supporting their child's efforts.

Doing nothing You've never heard of your child having such problems before, so you let the kid tackle it on her own. Be careful! There are any number of reasons your child's performance decreased: learning problems, increased social calendars, needing reading glasses, drug abuse, or emotional trauma (to name a few). Observe your child for indications of change, and arrange to speak with teachers.

(j) *I believe that my child's problems at school can be readily detected at home.* Parenthood is probably the most difficult job—you deal with every aspect of your child, including emotions that are either revealed or hidden. You can't expect yourself to know everything your child is feeling, thinking, and experiencing. What you can do is observe your child and pick up on warning signs. Look for changes, and discuss them openly and calmly. Your child may not know how to approach you with difficulties she may be experiencing, so reassure her of your love and support. Emphasize that if she has done something wrong or been hurt or confused, you want to know about it regardless of how it will make you feel.

(k) *I can easily describe my child's performance in school.* Good job if you said *yes* to this one! The concern that enough parents don't demonstrate an interest in their child's performance in school is warranted. According to a study published by Dr. Laurence Steinberg, co-author of *Beyond the Classroom: Why School Reform Has Failed and What Parents Need to Do* (Simon & Schuster, 1996), nearly one-third of students believe their parents have no idea how they're doing in school, one-sixth don't think their parents care whether they earn good grades, and more than half say they could bring home grades of C or worse without upsetting their parents. Regardless of whether these findings pertain to you and your child, the fact that so many students believe them means that both parents and children need to break some communication barriers.

(l) *I sometimes feel guilty about not providing more enriching experiences for my child.* Parents often feel guilty when they can't spend enough money on their children's needs or do all the things they'd like with their children. Instead of pressuring yourself, investigate the variety of quality, inexpensive opportunities offered in your community, namely after-school and community-based programs in art, music, dance, and sports. By encouraging your child to participate in these activities, you can engage him in worthwhile experiences without expending energy or money that you don't have. Consider letting your child know that your family must prioritize purchases; by comfortably discussing your financial situation, you stand a better chance of raising a child who is more conscious of and responsible about money matters.

(m) *There have been incidents involving violence, harassment, or drug use at my child's school.* It's sad if you had to answer *yes* to this statement. There's really no way to shield your child from being aware of these incidents, but you can stop your child from experiencing them directly by stunting their innocent curiosity with cold hard *facts.* If you need to get informed yourself, check out the resources listed in the back of *Making the Grade* or check out your local library. Don't wait for schools to teach your child about these issues. Schools may address them, but schools are not administrators of social service—they are administrators of curriculum-based education. A parent is the only reliable resource a child has on these and other developmental issues. Please make yourself available!

(n) *I am a single parent.* Single parenthood can be hectic, and many parents find they must budget time wisely just to complete day-to-day responsibilities. Under these circumstances, you may not be able to spend as much time with your child as you would like. But even two-parent families experience time crunches and hectic lifestyles. Whether you're a single parent or not, allow your child to handle some of the responsibilities, preferably those that could be finished faster with two individuals. This way, you and your child can talk and bond while you work. Hopefully, handing over some of the responsibilities will also free up some time that you can spend with your child in more entertaining and educational activities. Try preparing in advance so you can attend meetings with your child's teachers and school programs in which your child is participating. And don't feel guilty for putting your child to work; by letting your child help you out, you're actually teaching good values and responsibility. Success at school and success at home—that's what "making the grade" is all about!

For Parents Only: Answers to the Kids' Home Learning Quizzes

Language Arts

1. (b)
2. (d)
3. (d)
4. (d)
5. (a)
6. (b)
7. (d)
8. (d)
9. (c)
10. (a)
11. (d)
12. (c)
13. (d)
14. (c)
15. (c)
16. (a)
17. (c)
18. (d)

Math

1. (b)
2. (a)
3. (c)
4. (c)
5. (a)
6. (c)
7. (a)
8. (d)
9. (a)
10. (c)
11. (b)
12. (d)
13. (a)
14. (c)
15. (b)
16. (d)
17. (c)
18. (a)
19. (b)
20. (a)
21. (c)
22. (d)
23. (a)

Science

1. (c)
2. (a)
3. (b)
4. (d)
5. (d)
6. (c)
7. (b)
8. (a)
9. (c)
10. (d)
11. (b)
12. (d)
13. (c)

Kids' Home Learning Quizzes

Language Arts See how many questions you can get right! Follow the directions for each question. Read everything carefully before filling in one answer bubble. Fill in the (e) bubble if you haven't been taught something in the question. Fill in the (f) if you've learned this already in school, but it's still hard for you.

Questions 1–3: Select the sentence with correct capitalization and punctuation.

1. (a) Surveying his bedroom Brady said: "I want to move my furniture around."
   (b) Leaning against the bureau, Naomi suggested, "Let's move your bed over by the window."
   (c) After moving the bed Brady set his nightstand next to it; and Naomi pushed the desk into a corner.
   (d) Brady stood back and exclaimed "Wow? There's so much more room now!"

(e) We haven't studied this in school yet.
(f) We've studied this, but it's still hard for me.

ⓐ ⓑ ⓒ ⓓ ⓔ ⓕ

2. (a) "Why is this plant so healthy while the one in my room is dying," Dina wondered?
   (b) Indeed, the Fern was growing larger everyday but the Philodendron was wilting.
   (c) Dina's Mom suggested, "Maybe, we ought to water the Philodendron."
   (d) Dina poured some water into the plant's soil, and her mom said, "Don't worry, it'll be just fine."

(e) We haven't studied this in school yet.
(f) We've studied this, but it's still hard for me.

ⓐ ⓑ ⓒ ⓓ ⓔ ⓕ

3. (a) Did you know that rock singer, Bruce Springsteen, was born in new Jersey!
   (b) He began his career in the late 1960's playing at small east coast clubs.
   (c) Springsteen combines traditional rock melodies, with reflective lyrics on working class life.
   (d) His nickname is "The Boss," and his most popular albums are *Born to Run* and *Born in the U.S.A*.

(e) We haven't studied this in school yet.
(f) We've studied this, but it's still hard for me.

Questions 4–7: Select the answer that best completes the sentence.

4. At the talent show yesterday, Mel ______ a song from *Rent*.
   (a) sung
   (b) has sang
   (c) having sung
   (d) sang

(e) We haven't studied this in school yet.
(f) We've studied this, but it's still hard for me.

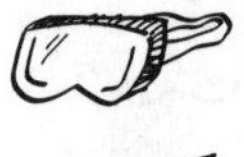

5. Leena's hair is ______ than Marty's.
   (a) longer
   (b) more long
   (c) longest
   (d) more longer

(e) We haven't studied this in school yet.
(f) We've studied this, but it's still hard for me.

6. Shawn ______ seen the Grand Canyon before.
   (a) hadn't never
   (b) had never
   (c) hadn't not ever
   (d) never

(e) We haven't studied this in school yet.
(f) We've studied this, but it's still hard for me.

7. ______ played basketball together.
   (a) Her and me
   (b) I and her
   (c) Me and she
   (d) She and I
(e) We haven't studied this in school yet.
(f) We've studied this, but it's still hard for me.

ⓐ ⓑ ⓒ ⓓ ⓔ ⓕ

Questions 8–11: Read the following sentences, and select the response that combines them most effectively into one sentence without changing their meanings.

8. Agra is the site of the Taj Mahal.
   Agra is a city in India.
   (a) Agra is the site of the Taj Mahal a city in India.
   (b) A city in India is Agra, the site of the Taj Mahal.
   (c) Agra is the site of the Taj Mahal and a city in India.
   (d) Agra, a city in India, is the site of the Taj Mahal.
(e) We haven't studied this in school yet.
(f) We've studied this, but it's still hard for me.

ⓐ ⓑ ⓒ ⓓ ⓔ ⓕ

9. Rama is a Hindu god.
   He is the hero of the epic poem, *Ramayana*.
   (a) Rama is a Hindu god, and he is the hero of the epic poem, *Ramayana*.
   (b) A Hindu god, Rama, the hero of the epic poem, *Ramayana*.
   (c) Rama, a Hindu god, is the hero of the epic poem, *Ramayana*.
   (d) Rama is the hero of the epic poem, *Ramayana,* a Hindu god.
(e) We haven't studied this in school yet.
(f) We've studied this, but it's still hard for me.

ⓐ ⓑ ⓒ ⓓ ⓔ ⓕ

10. Sonya mowed the lawn this afternoon.
    Sonya pulled weeds this afternoon.
    (a) Sonya mowed the lawn and pulled weeds this afternoon.
    (b) Sonya mowed the lawn and this afternoon pulled weeds too.
    (c) Sonya mowed the lawn, and she pulled weeds this afternoon.
    (d) This afternoon, Sonya mowed the lawn and Sonya pulled weeds too.
(e) We haven't studied this in school yet.
(f) We've studied this, but it's still hard for me.

ⓐ ⓑ ⓒ ⓓ ⓔ ⓕ

11. Layla bought a model airplane for her brother, Leon.
    The airplane came with a remote control device.
    (a) Layla bought a model airplane that came with a remote control device for her brother, Leon.
    (b) A model airplane coming with a remote control device was bought by Layla for her brother, Leon.
    (c) A model airplane Layla bought for her brother, Leon, came with a remote control device.
    (d) Layla bought a model airplane for her brother, Leon, and it came with a remote control device.
(e) We haven't studied this in school yet.
(f) We've studied this, but it's still hard for me.

ⓐ ⓑ ⓒ ⓓ ⓔ ⓕ

Questions 12–13: Read each paragraph, and select the best response to the question.

12. What is the best topic sentence for the following paragraph?

______ Many economists, astronomers, and other scientists have published theories on dinosaur extinction, but no one truly knows what happened. Dinosaurs never coexisted with humans, who began to evolve only about six million years ago. Today, crocodiles and birds are the closest living relatives of dinosaurs.

   (a) The pterodactyl is one type of dinosaur.
   (b) Most dinosaurs were large creatures, but some were as small as lizards.
   (c) Dinosaurs became extinct approximately 65 million years ago.
   (d) The almost complete skeleton of a dinosaur was found in the Andes Mountains in 1969.
(e) We haven't studied this in school yet.
(f) We've studied this, but it's still hard for me.

ⓐ ⓑ ⓒ ⓓ ⓔ ⓕ

13. Which answer is the best summary of the following paragraph?

In 1951, J. D. Salinger published the widely popular and controversial novel, *The Catcher in the Rye.* The story describes a young man, Holden Caulfield, who struggles to maintain his integrity in a hypocritical adult world. Ever since the book's publication, Salinger has been criticized by those who believe the subject matter is too mature for an adolescent audience. The criticism has forced Salinger to lead a reclusive life.

(a) The publication and subsequent criticism of *The Catcher in the Rye* forced Salinger to lead a reclusive life.
(b) Controversial books have mature themes.
(c) Parents, not authors, know what is best for adolescents.
(d) Books with mature subject matter are inappropriate for an adolescent audience.
(e) We haven't studied this in school yet.
(f) We've studied this, but it's still hard for me.

Questions 14–18: Read each question carefully, and using the following timeline, select the best answer.

Timeline

1917 John Fitzgerald Kennedy is born in Brookline, Massachusetts, to successful financier Joseph Kennedy.

1946 JFK is elected to the House of Representatives.

1952 JFK is elected to the Senate, representing Massachusetts.

1953 JFK marries socialite Jacqueline Bouvier.

1960 JFK defeats Richard Nixon in the presidential election and becomes the youngest president of the United States.

1961 JFK establishes the Peace Corps, an organization that sends trained volunteers to work in developing countries that need help in teaching, agriculture, and health.

1963 JFK is assassinated by Lee Harvey Oswald during a visit to Dallas, Texas.

14. In what year was JFK elected to the Senate?
(a) 1917
(b) 1946
(c) 1952
(d) 1953
(e) We haven't studied this in school yet.
(f) We've studied this, but it's still hard for me.

15. In what year was the Peace Corps established?
(a) 1952
(b) 1953
(c) 1961
(d) 1963
(e) We haven't studied this in school yet.
(f) We've studied this, but it's still hard for me.

16. Whom did JFK defeat in the 1960 presidential election?
(a) Richard Nixon
(b) George Bush
(c) Bill Clinton
(d) Jacqueline Bouvier
(e) We haven't studied this in school yet.
(f) We've studied this, but it's still hard for me.

17. About how old was JFK when he married?
(a) 46
(b) 53
(c) 36
(d) 30
(e) We haven't studied this in school yet.
(f) We've studied this, but it's still hard for me.

18. To which of the following seats was JFK never elected?
(a) Senate
(b) Presidency
(c) House of Representatives
(d) Governor
(e) We haven't studied this in school yet.
(f) We've studied this, but it's still hard for me.

You're done! Now look up the answers and see how many questions you got right.

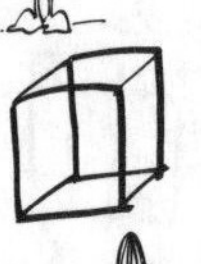

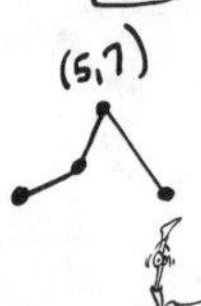

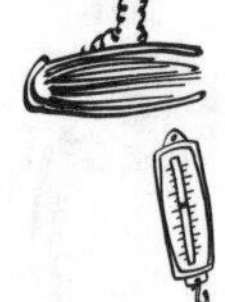

Making the Grade

Math See how many questions you can get right! Keep some scratch paper handy if you need extra space to work out the problems. Read everything carefully and "do the math" before filling in one answer bubble. Fill in the (e) bubble if you haven't been taught something in the question. Fill in the (f) if you've learned this already in school, but it's still hard for you.

1. Jennell gets $5 a week for her allowance. She wants to buy a Bush compact disc, valued at $15.98, and a pair of headphones that cost $8.95. She has to pay an extra $1.50 in sales tax. If she saves up all her money for six weeks, how much money will she have left over after her purchases?

   (a) $4.67
   (b) $3.57

   (c) $3.67
   (d) $4.57

(e) We haven't studied this in school yet.
(f) We've studied this, but it's still hard for me.

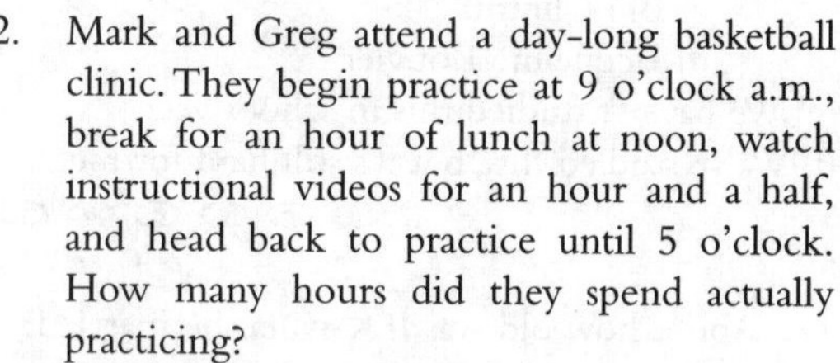

2. Mark and Greg attend a day-long basketball clinic. They begin practice at 9 o'clock a.m., break for an hour of lunch at noon, watch instructional videos for an hour and a half, and head back to practice until 5 o'clock. How many hours did they spend actually practicing?

   (a) 6.5
   (b) 4.5
   (c) 5.5
   (d) 3

(e) We haven't studied this in school yet.
(f) We've studied this, but it's still hard for me.

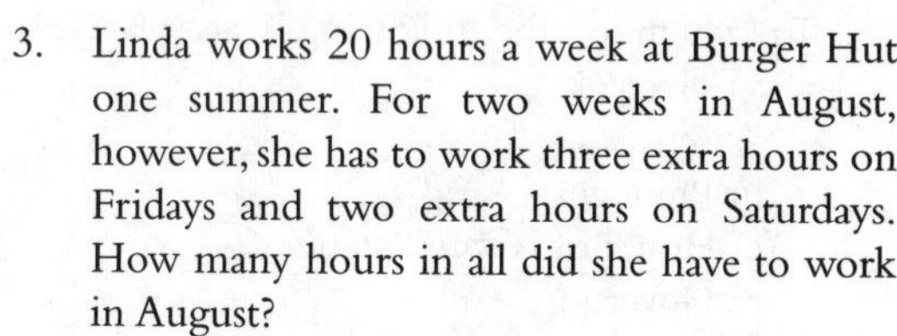

3. Linda works 20 hours a week at Burger Hut one summer. For two weeks in August, however, she has to work three extra hours on Fridays and two extra hours on Saturdays. How many hours in all did she have to work in August?

   (a) 85
   (b) 30
   (c) 90
   (d) 50

(e) We haven't studied this in school yet.
(f) We've studied this, but it's still hard for me.

4. What is the surface area of the following shape?

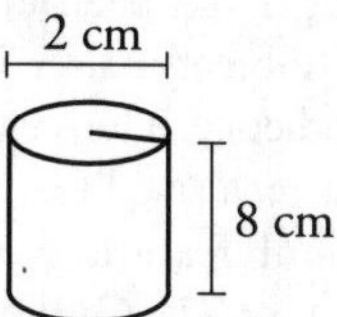

   (a) 16π cm²
   (b) 20π cm²
   (c) 40π cm²
   (d) 10π cm²

(e) We haven't studied this in school yet.
(f) We've studied this, but it's still hard for me.

5. What is the area of the following shape?

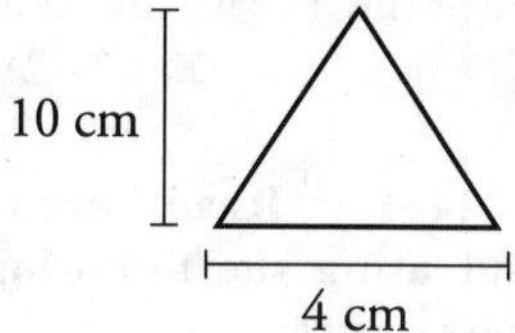

   (a) 20 cm²
   (b) 13 cm²
   (c) 80 cm²
   (d) 40 cm²

(e) We haven't studied this in school yet.
(f) We've studied this, but it's still hard for me.

6. What is the volume of the following shape?

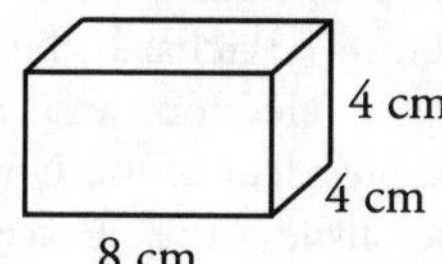

   (a) 16 cm³
   (b) 36 cm³
   (c) 128 cm³
   (d) 24 cm³

(e) We haven't studied this in school yet.
(f) We've studied this, but it's still hard for me.

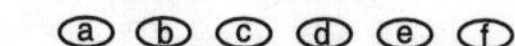

7. What is the volume of the following shape?

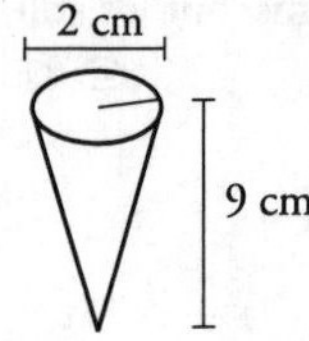

(a) 12π cm³
(b) 6π cm³
(c) 9π cm³
(d) 18π cm³
(e) We haven't studied this in school yet.
(f) We've studied this, but it's still hard for me.

8. What is the volume of the following shape?

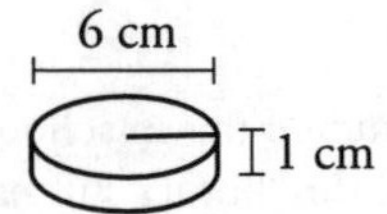

(a) 12 cm³
(b) 6 cm³
(c) 3 cm³
(d) 9 cm³
(e) We haven't studied this in school yet.
(f) We've studied this, but it's still hard for me.

9. 2/3 + 2/3 =
(a) 1 1/3
(b) 4/6
(c) $(2/3)^2$
(d) 4/9
(e) We haven't studied this in school yet.
(f) We've studied this, but it's still hard for me.

10. −11 + (−32) =
(a) 43
(b) 21
(c) −43
(d) −21
(e) We haven't studied this in school yet.
(f) We've studied this, but it's still hard for me.

ⓐ ⓑ ⓒ ⓓ ⓔ ⓕ

11. −16 × 18 =
(a) −188
(b) −288
(c) 188
(d) 288
(e) We haven't studied this in school yet.
(f) We've studied this, but it's still hard for me.

12. An obtuse angle is one that ______.
(a) equals 45 degrees
(b) measures less than 90°
(c) equals 90°
(d) measure more than 90°
(e) We haven't studied this in school yet.
(f) We've studied this, but it's still hard for me.

13. Two lines are congruent if they ______.
(a) have the same length
(b) form an acute angle
(c) are bisected
(d) form an obtuse angle
(e) We haven't studied this in school yet.
(f) We've studied this, but it's still hard for me.

14. 1/4 + 3/8 =
(a) 1 1/2
(b) 1/2
(c) 5/8
(d) 3/4
(e) We haven't studied this in school yet.
(f) We've studied this, but it's still hard for me.

15. What is the lowest common denominator of 2/9 and 1/3?
(a) 3
(b) 9
(c) 12
(d) 27
(e) We haven't studied this in school yet.
(f) We've studied this, but it's still hard for me.

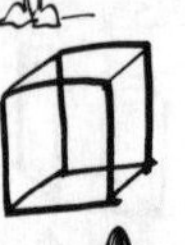

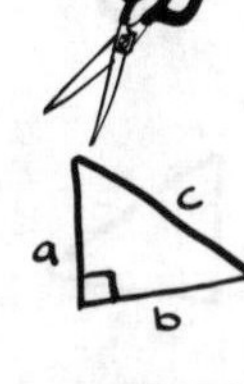
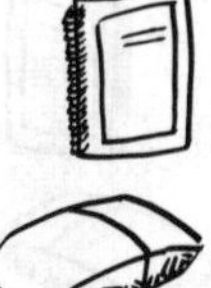

16. 5/8 × 2/3 =
    (a) 7/24
    (b) 1 1/4
    (c) 15/16
    (d) 5/12
(e) We haven't studied this in school yet.
(f) We've studied this, but it's still hard for me.

17. 1 4/5 × 2 7/9 =
    (a) 25 2/3
    (b) 2 28/45
    (c) 5
    (d) 81/125
(e) We haven't studied this in school yet.
(f) We've studied this, but it's still hard for me.

18. 6/7 ÷ 2/3 =
    (a) 1 2/7
    (b) 8/21
    (c) 7/9
    (d) 4/7
(e) We haven't studied this in school yet.
(f) We've studied this, but it's still hard for me.

ⓐ ⓑ ⓒ ⓓ ⓔ ⓕ

19. 1 1/2 ÷ 1 3/8 =
    (a) 16 1/2
    (b) 1 1/11
    (c) 1 9/16
    (d) 1 1/3
(e) We haven't studied this in school yet.
(f) We've studied this, but it's still hard for me.

ⓐ ⓑ ⓒ ⓓ ⓔ ⓕ

20. Therese has a paper route; her sister, Dominique, mows lawns in the neighborhood; and their younger brother, Phillipe, dusts and vacuums the house every weekend. Dominique's neighbors pay her three-fifths the amount that Therese makes for delivering newspapers, and their parents pay Phillipe one-third of what Dominique makes. If Therese earns $183 every month, how much does Phillippe make every month?
    (a) $36.60
    (b) $24.80
    (c) $109.80
    (d) $61
(e) We haven't studied this in school yet.
(f) We've studied this, but it's still hard for me.

ⓐ ⓑ ⓒ ⓓ ⓔ ⓕ

21. 7.52)14.8896 =
    (a) .0198
    (b) .198
    (c) 1.98
    (d) 19.8
(e) We haven't studied this in school yet.
(f) We've studied this, but it's still hard for me.

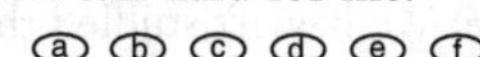

22. If $7x–4 = 10$, then $x =$
    (a) 2/5
    (b) 1
    (c) 7/6
    (d) 2
(e) We haven't studied this in school yet.
(f) We've studied this, but it's still hard for me.

23. In the equation $y = x + 9x÷4 - 13$, if $x =4$ then y must equal to
    (a) 0
    (b) 6 3/4
    (c) 13
    (d) 7 1/4
(e) We haven't studied this in school yet.
(f) We've studied this, but it's still hard for me.

You're done! Now look up the answers and see how many questions you got right.

Science See how many questions you can get right! Follow the directions for each question. Read everything carefully before filling in one answer bubble. Fill in the (e) bubble if you haven't been taught something in the question. Fill in the (f) bubble if you've learned this already in school, but it's still pretty hard for you.

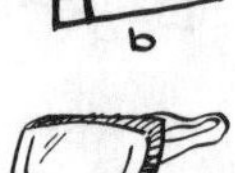

1. All animals share basic functions. Which of the following is not one of them?
   (a) eating
   (b) breathing
   (c) growing up
   (d) eliminating waste.
(e) We haven't studied this in school yet.
(f) We've studied this, but it's still hard for me.

ⓐ ⓑ ⓒ ⓓ ⓔ ⓕ

2. An invertebrate is an animal that does not have a
   (a) backbone
   (b) skeleton
   (c) circulatory system
   (d) heart with ventricular chambers
(e) We haven't studied this in school yet.
(f) We've studied this, but it's still hard for me.

3. Plants and animals share some habits. Which of the following is not one of them?
   (a) Some members of both groups can survive in dry climates, like a desert.
   (b) Some members of both groups use the sun's energy to make food, a process known as photosynthesis.
   (c) Some members of both groups can survive under water.
   (d) Some members of both groups eat insects.
(e) We haven't studied this in school yet.
(f) We've studied this, but it's still hard for me.

4. Which of the following occurs when two organisms share a symbiotic relationship?
   (a) Both organisms are harmed because of the association.
   (b) One organism lives or gets nourishment at the expense of the other.
   (c) One organism lives off the other, which is not harmed as a result.
   (d) Both organisms benefit from the association.
(e) We haven't studied this in school yet.
(f) We've studied this, but it's still hard for me.

5. Which of the following statements is true?
   (a) Predators hunt and kill other animals for food.
   (b) In the long run, predators can help the prey species by controlling prey populations.
   (c) Cheetahs are predators.
   (d) all of the above
(e) We haven't studied this in school yet.
(f) We've studied this, but it's still hard for me.

6. Asexual reproduction occurs
   (a) when elements from different individuals combine to produce new individuals.
   (b) only in multicellular creatures.
   (c) when one individual cell produces an exact copy of itself.
   (d) only in unicellular creatures.
(e) We haven't studied this in school yet.
(f) We've studied this, but it's still hard for me.

7. When a light bulb gets hot, which energies are transferred?
   (a) Chemical energy is transferred to kinetic energy.
   (b) Electrical energy is transferred to heat energy.
   (c) Mechanical energy is transferred to electrical energy.
   (d) Kinetic energy is transferred to mechanical energy.
(e) We haven't studied this in school yet.
(f) We've studied this, but it's still hard for me.

ⓐ ⓑ ⓒ ⓓ ⓔ ⓕ

8. Earthquakes are caused by ______.
   (a) the pressure, cracking, and sliding of Earth's plates.
   (b) slight changes in the earth's orbit around the sun.
   (c) the same forces that make tornadoes and hurricanes.
   (d) an increase in global warming.
   (e) We haven't studied this in school yet.
   (f) We've studied this, but it's still hard for me.

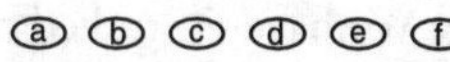

9. What kind of rock is formed by the accumulation of sand, silt, and clay from the earth's rivers and seas?
   (a) igneous
   (b) metamorphic
   (c) sedimentary
   (d) continental
   (e) We haven't studied this in school yet.
   (f) We've studied this, but it's still hard for me.

10. Which first-aid technique would you administer first to someone who was choking?
   (a) cardiopulmonary resuscitation
   (b) mouth-to-mouth resuscitation
   (c) Electro-Convulsive Therapy (ECT)
   (d) the Heimlich Maneuver
   (e) We haven't studied this in school yet.
   (f) We've studied this, but it's still hard for me.

ⓐ ⓑ ⓒ ⓓ ⓔ ⓕ

Questions 11-13: Refer to the chart below to answer these questions.

Animal	Size	Description
Baboon	to 3.5 feet	long dog-like muzzel, large teeth, spends most of their time on the ground
Orangutan	to 5.5 feet	feeds primarily on fruit, often lives in trees, covered with red-brown hair
Chimpanzee	to 4.5 feet	climbs well but lives mostly on ground. Closest ape to human, shares 99% of same genes
Gorilla	to 6.5 feet	attacks only in self-defense breast beating indicates nervous excitement

11. Which animal spends most of its time in trees?
   (a) baboon
   (b) orangutan
   (c) chimpanzee
   (d) gorilla
   (e) We haven't studied this in school yet.
   (f) We've studied this, but it's still hard for me.

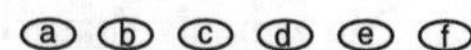

12. Which animal can grow the tallest?
   (a) baboon
   (b) orangutan
   (c) chimpanzee
   (d) gorilla
   (e) We haven't studied this in school yet.
   (f) We've studied this, but it's still hard for me.

13. Which animal is closest to human?
   (a) baboon
   (b) orangutan
   (c) chimpanzee
   (d) gorilla
   (e) We haven't studied this in school yet.
   (f) We've studied this, but it's still hard for me.

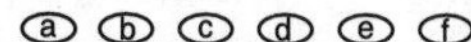

You're done! Now look up the answers and see how many questions you got right.